COWARDLY
LIONS

COWARDLY LIONS

Missed Opportunities to Prevent Deadly Conflict and State Collapse

I. William Zartman

LYNNE
RIENNER
PUBLISHERS

BOULDER
LONDON

Published in the United States of America in 2005 by
Lynne Rienner Publishers, Inc.
1800 30th Street, Boulder, Colorado 80301
www.rienner.com

and in the United Kingdom by
Lynne Rienner Publishers, Inc.
3 Henrietta Street, Covent Garden, London WC2E 8LU

Library of Congress Cataloging-in-Publication Data
Zartman, I. William.
   Cowardly lions : missed opportunities to prevent deadly conflict and state collapse
/ I. William Zartman.
      p.   cm.
   Includes bibliographical references and index.
   ISBN 1-58826-357-6 (hc : alk. paper)
   ISBN 1-58826-382-7 (pbk. : alk. paper)
   1. Diplomatic negotiations in international disputes—Case studies.
2. Mediation, International—Case studies.   3. Conflict management—Case studies.
4. Political stability—Case studies.   I. Title.
JZ6045.Z37   2005
327.1'7—dc22   2005010885

British Cataloguing in Publication Data
A Cataloguing in Publication record for this book
is available from the British Library.

Printed and bound in the United States of America

The paper used in this publication meets the requirements
(∞) of the American National Standard for Permanence of
Paper for Printed Library Materials Z39.48-1992.

5   4   3   2   1

To President Carter

*Courageous peacemaker among
unsavory characters and epidemic destruction*

———

*Blessed are the peacemakers,
for they will be called sons of God—Matthew 5:9*

Contents

Acknowledgments

I am grateful to the Carnegie Commission for the Prevention of Deadly Conflict and to the Woodrow Wilson International Center for Scholars for support for this project, to my many students in conflict management for their association in the pursuit of this intellectual and policy-relevant interest, to Theresa Taylor Simmons for her careful management of many manuscripts, to Dijana Duric and—as always—to Linda Carlson for elusive minutiae, and to Lynne Rienner for her support in many publishing ventures.

—*I. William Zartman*

1
Opportunities

IN A WORLD SCARRED BY STATE COLLAPSE AND DEADLY CONFLICT, EXTERNAL actors can no longer sit by and watch, mesmerized by the blood on their television screens. Nor can they hide behind the fear of their own casualties or of long-term involvement as an excuse for inaction. External engagement is required when it is necessary to protect populations from their rulers and from each other. Such protective engagement is justified for its own sake, for humanitarian reasons, and for preventive security purposes, because these conflicts will continue to destabilize their regions and impose costlier involvement later on. Intervention in other peoples' affairs pits an actual abuse, the misuse of sovereignty as a cover for a state's neglect and repression of its citizens, against a potential one, the danger of dominating a weaker state through interference in its internal affairs. Between the two, the real abuse is paramount over the hypothetical one and requires a careful and appropriate response.

The terrible fact is that in major cases of state collapse in the post–Cold War era and its antecedents, specific actions identified and discussed at the time could have been taken that would have gone far to prevent the enormously costly catastrophes that eventually occurred. These actions were not exceptional measures in foreign relations: they were all moves that had been made elsewhere at other times or even moves begun earlier or used later in the same conflict, but incompletely or belatedly. The optimal agent in these preventive actions varies: often it was the United States, the remaining world superpower, acting alone or with other great powers in the UN Security Council; but sometimes it was neighboring states in the conflict region or even a nongovernmental organization (NGO). The reason why no action was taken also varies, ranging from loss of nerve to preoccupation with other crises elsewhere. As a result, up to millions of lives and productivity dollars were lost in each case; new and worse situations were created, making reconciliation and reconstruction even more difficult; distracting conflict was introduced into great power relations; and local and international efforts of enormous and prolonged magnitude were required to reinstitute legitimate authority in a restored state. Following state collapse, the situation became a major problem for international actors who had not deemed it worthy of their interest beforehand.

This is a book about the international politics of domestic conflict, examining moments in the recent past when an arguably better response from interested third parties could have changed the course of events and reduced the chances of deadly conflict and state collapse. It seeks to stimulate debate about the clash between the inhibitions of sovereignty and narrow interest and the impulses of global responsibilities and human concern. On one side stand protective notions of sovereignty against foreign interference in domestic mayhem and restrictive notions of interests as being only vital or inexistent. On the other side move ideas of sovereignty as responsibility, concern for human life, and enlightened interest in the restoration of domestic and international order. These concerns about responsibility and order meet most sharply when domestic actors cannot hold their conflicts down and their state together and need help to restore internal order so that domestic welfare and international order can be protected. The instances analyzed here provide data for the debate. Some are clear, strong, and well-known; others may be more debatable. Together, they provide a compelling setting for a reexamination of current doctrines of roles and responsibility.

This study has two purposes, analytical and hortatory. It seeks to evaluate decisionmaking alternatives focused on conflict management and reduction, examining why they could and should have been taken and why they were not. And it seeks to make an argument—a case—for greater responses in the direction of conflict reduction, by showing that in all or at least some cases there was a real opportunity, for which some knowledgeable voices argued, that was missed. Some may say that this is to apply today's wisdom to yesterday's events, but that is not so and need not be so. It is not so because all of the actions proposed were part of the arsenal of diplomatic measures at the time and for a long time. It need not be so because the adoption of these measures would have hastened the day when one practice among many would become mainstream behavior. But then analysis is always hortatory, serving as the basis for action, and exhortation should always be analytical, based on sound examination and reasoning.

The Past Conditional

Counterfactual analysis is a minefield.[1] Launching lightly into armchair quarterbacking is disrespectful to serious actors in the field, and superficial glances of hindsight serve no useful purpose. Backward-looking debate often remains on the level of a confrontation between peremptory assertions that obvious alternatives were available and authoritative defenses that all options were considered. In general, history is authoritative: only what did happen could happen. There are always reasons—real even if not good—why alternative actions did not take place. Moreover, counterfactual propositions carry no guarantee of results, and even real events subsequent to the moment of action can no longer serve as a guide to the altered path of history. If one ingredient in the scenario is changed, one must assume that all other elements—or at least some other elements—are open to change as well. Playing with history, it can be claimed, is merely creating fiction, from which few lessons can be learned. George Ball expressed the practitioners' ambivalence about second-guessing in his testimony to Congress on the 1974 Turkish invasion of Cyprus: "While I think it is always unfair for someone outside the Government to criticize on the basis of press reports or whatever other intelligence he may have, I do feel that an opportunity was missed."[2] The other side of the issue was a statement attributed to the historian Sir Lewis Namier, "The enduring achievement of historical study is a historical sense—and intuitive understanding—of how things do not work."

Yet every action results from a choice among alternatives, so that the course of history is made up of an unending chain of choices. Any decision can be examined in the context of its alternatives, for it was in that context that it was made. To do so means placing oneself again in that momentary context, with as full an understanding of it as possible.[3] That understanding involves a careful weighing of the options and also of the reasons why the given choice was made, before an argument can be made for an alternative choice. Many associated questions need to be examined as well—the agent who is to carry out the policy, the means required and available, the way in which the policy would be carried out, the desired and expected outcomes, the implications and consequences of the action, including its success and its failure. These various questions can be subsumed under two headings: What would have been required for the alternative decision to have been taken? What indicates that that alternative decision would have produced an alternative result?

Thus evaluations of alternative actions presented as missed opportunities must make the case not only for the feasibility of the action in the specific circumstances but also for its ability to produce better outcomes than those obtained in reality.[4] This argument can be made case by case, inductively, or in a systematic, deductive way.[5] The first is difficult enough; very little has been done toward the second. An ad hoc case needs to develop a scenario that is logical and feasible at each point, given the circumstances that obtained at the time on the part of the agent and the target as well as the new circumstances created by the action as the scenario unfolds.[6] The effectiveness of the scenario has to be judged internally, within the specifics of its own action and context. It has to make a reasonable case that, at some specific decision point, "the other" decision could have been made and would have had good chances of producing an indicated outcome. And that is generally the way foreign policy decisions are made.

A deductive case rests on the basis of theoretical causality, embodied in generalized rather than specific scenarios. These are established by internal logic and tested for their record in producing the hypothesized results. The action is then judged on the basis of its fit to a specific situation, feeding back new evidence for a generalized type of action that usually produces given results. This sort of justification adds another dimension of support for an action and, as in any social analysis, enriches the debate by lifting it out of the ad hoc and turning it into knowledge. It is the way analysis can be made, to improve future ad hoc decisions.

Which type of justification for an alternative action is used is a matter of taste and susceptibility to the particular type of argument. Many practitioners are put off by deductive arguments, although they use them all the time, much as M. Jourdain spoke prose and cooks use recipes.[7] They tend to forget that deductive propositions are simplified ceteris paribus statements that have to be applied to complex nonparibus reality in order to be useful. Many analysts are dissatisfied with ad hoc or inductive arguments, forgetting that ad hoc applications are the test of their deductive propositions and must be fully developed if only to make sure that the deductive generalization fits the case.

The value of both approaches should be recognized by both camps, on pain of ignorance and failure. Propositions about the nature of opportunities enrich knowledge and action, for it is only monastic historians who are interested in the unreplicable specifics of past events. Facts about the specific opportunities test the decisionmaking challenge, for it is only monastic mathematicians and philosophers who are interested in unreal syllogisms. Thus, a useful and telling presentation on missed opportunities to prevent deadly conflict and state collapse must set itself the tough task of addressing and satisfying both camps. This study looks for opportunities in specific instances, with some deductive guidance about opportunities and responses, and then draws conclusions inductively from the case instances, to provide a richer understanding of the ways to identify and exploit opportunities, so as to be useful to policy the next time. This is an exercise not in fault-finding but in discerning lessons to guide better action.

In practice, there are plenty of early warnings to help identify opportunities. The biggest problem in the early warning debate is not whether an event is preceded by warning signals but whether warning signals are followed by an event. (A knowledgeable commentator once noted, "O we are good at predicting crises; we have predicted all ten of the last three of them!") There are many more prior indications than there are ensuing events; many warning signals simply fizzle out, and seemingly impending events work themselves out. Therefore, counterfactual analysis, like policy recommendations in the real world, must show convincing evidence at the time that the impending event or crisis will indeed occur if not acted upon and not simply dissipate at the warning level. What is needed is tornado warnings that announce tornadoes but also that do not announce low pressure areas that do not turn into tornadoes. Such distinctions do not prevail in meteorology or in politics as yet. The corridors of policymakers reverberate with cries of "Wolf!" Predictions of a coming event can never be made with assurance, but they can be made surer if it can be shown that similar events were preceded by similar signals and similar responses led to desired results. Counterfactual analysis has to be rooted not only in the causative sequence of the event but also in the comparative context of other similar events.

Finally, counterfactual policy analysis needs to examine why the policy proposed was not adopted at the time. Neglect, obliviousness, and stupidity always take their toll, but generally it can be assumed that policymakers thought they knew what they were doing and why. The reasons for one action (or inaction) rather than another deserve respect, both to evaluate the reasons and chances for an alternative decision and to learn how to make the most effective one next time. The practitioners' defensive response to proposed alternative policy actions, "It couldn't be done, and anyhow we did it," stifles debate and blocks improvement.

Cases of Conflict and Collapse

It is a mark of the post–World War II era, accentuated in the post–Cold War era, that most conflicts are internal, for the control of a state or a piece of it, and not interstate.[8] Security then concerns the condition of people within the state and of the international (global or regional) balance of forces, not the protection of one state against another. In this situation, security is the material of conflict management, not defense. In interstate wars, third-party involvement is a natural and assumed aspect of the conflict, as each warring state lines up allies for its cause in the name of self-defense, as provided for in the UN Charter (Article 51). In intrastate conflicts, in contrast, third-party involvement is caught in a vise of contradiction: legitimate involvement is biased in favor of the government, which has the right to call in help against an internal rebellion, but any other involvement is illegitimate interference in internal affairs, which is banned by the right of sovereignty. In the first, third parties intervene for their own security; in the second, they intervene for more distant concerns, either narrower (domestic humanitarian) or broader (neighborhood stability). Thus preventive intervention runs up prima facie against the inhibition of illegitimacy and in addition is not covered by the justification of a direct threat to the third party's security that operates in interstate conflicts. Preventive action of any sort needs to be justified by the clear and future danger from continuation on the present course; preventive intervention needs to be justified by the domestic humanitarian costs of the present condition or by the threat to security and stability that impending collapse and conflict pose to the regional or global community.

This book examines six cases of conflict and collapse for possible moments of preventive action by a variety of agents and presents the results in Chapters 2 through 7. The defining terms are used in a general way, leaving to other current literature the task of providing them with skin-tight identifications. *Deadly conflict* is a condition that occurs when political incompatibilities turn violent and cause heavy casualties. Although its precise threshold has sometimes occasioned almost-deadly conflict and varying statistical indications among academics, the treatment by the Carnegie Commission on Preventing Deadly Conflict has brought to light not only the humanitarian but also the security interest for external parties in prevention.[9] The cases used here suffered a load of casualties representing significant proportions of their populations and dominating the agendas of other states, international organizations, and humanitarian NGOs for years.

Although, as with definitions, this is not the place to debate theory or develop an etiology of deadly conflict, it is useful to lay out a rough idea of the process involved, if only to understand the nature of early warnings of widespread violence.[10] Even though conflict—competition between incompatible positions—is a continual fact of life, passage from politics to violence comes when peaceful change is no longer possible; when "normal politics" can no longer handle the expression of grievances from significant parts of the population; when deprivation, discrimination, or resources provide the opportunity for political entrepreneurs to harness dissatisfaction and contest the current order.[11] All of these elements can be pushed into important conceptual debates by a search for the "when" behind the "what." The focus of the present inquiry is not on generic causes and preventions but on "last-minute early warnings" when conflict is present and violence predicted.

Similarly, the causes of *state collapse* (and even the distinction between failure and collapse) are still the subject of wide-ranging attempts at conceptualization and are beyond this current scope.[12] But for the purposes of dealing with the process, the distinction needs to be made between the many challenges to its capacity and legitimacy to which a state responds with success and those that threaten its ability to perform its defining functions, that is, to deliver expected goods and services, provide a framework for legitimacy and identity, and maintain law and order.[13] In all of the cases discussed here, the state had clearly failed to fulfill its functions and was on the way to collapse. The challenge was not to debate how far it had gotten between these two "points" but to determine how to act to prevent it from going any further.

State collapse is both the cause and the result of internal or civil wars, as weak and illegitimate order permits violence and violence consumes legitimacy and order. Although no two cases of state collapse are the same and "collapse" can take on a variety of specific manifestations, the fundamental fact of the disappearance of state institutions, law, and order creates inhumanities and insecurities that affect the surrounding countries. The cases studied here all experienced the disintegration of legitimate authority in various forms, sucking external interference into the vacuum.

Out of a potential pool of some three dozen cases that filled these conditions, six—Lebanon, Liberia, Somalia, Zaire, Haiti, and Yugoslavia—have been selected. Many others at various times—for example, Rwanda, Burundi, Uganda, Chad, Ethiopia, Sierra Leone, Congo-Brazzaville, El Salvador, Guatemala, Tajikistan, Chechnya, Azerbaijan, Georgia, Macedonia, Afghanistan, Albania, Algeria, Sri Lanka, Cambodia, among others—could have been used.[14] It is doubtful that the lessons from an alternative list would have been different.

Five of the six conflicts stretched over much of the 1990s, often with an advance warning and opportunity at the end of the preceding decade; one case, Lebanon, which suffered its conflict and collapse in the late 1970s and 1980s, was chosen so as to include an example from before the end of the Cold War, although in fact East-West considerations had relatively little impact on Lebanese events. Three of the cases come from Africa, as do many of the internal conflicts and state disintegrations of the post–Cold War period, but the major conflict of the 1990s, spilling over unabated into the new millennium, comes from Europe in the collapse of the Yugoslav state and the eruption of violence within its constituent republics. The most egregious case of internal conflict (although less clearly of state collapse), Rwanda, was passed over in the selection because it has already been so frequently discussed.[15] If Haiti in the early 1990s was not typical of the Latin American conflicts, either in Central America in the 1980s or in the Andean region in the 1990s, it was at least a test of hemispheric policy on the overthrow of democratically elected regimes. Doubtless an Asian case could have been included, although the possibilities are fewer. Thus, no complicated subcategorizations have been used to select "typical" cases: those chosen have been illustrative of the problem and salient enough to stand as raw material for lessons.[16]

All six cases involve violent internal conflict within a state at different points of collapse. In some cases, an entrenched ruler at the head of a narrow support group exerted a repressive, predatory control over a part of his country, typifying a "hard, brittle" state that was very much present to the objects of his brutality but totally ineffective in performing the normal functions of a state—the egregious ruler phenomenon. Such was the cause of conflict and condition of the state in Doe's Liberia, Siad Barre's Somalia, Mobutu's Zaire, and Cedras's Haiti, with Yugoslavia's Milosevic growing into the role. In these cases, a focus of the conflict was the ruler, and the restoration of the state and the control of conflict necessarily had to pass through his removal.

At the other end of the spectrum was the state that no longer existed except as a physical location (but not even a limitation) for the occurrence of the conflict—the fully collapsed state phenomenon. Even though Somalia was the epitome of this condition after Siad Barre's downfall, Liberia was not far behind after Doe's death, despite the presence of an Interim Government of National Unity (IGNU). Lebanon reached the same condition by the middle 1980s, despite the simultaneous presence of several governments and still one legal president. In Yugoslavia, it was the federal republic that collapsed, but the component republics quickly rose to take its place, an important element in its collapse in the first place. It is important to keep the element of state collapse as well as deadly conflict in mind, since the goal of any ameliorative action must be to restore legitimate and functioning order and authority and not simply to end the killing. Without the first, the second will not last.

Moments of Opportunity

It is the identification of the missed moments of opportunity within the six cases that is one of the two major challenges and contributions of this study (the other being the types of measures to adopt). On the basis of specific criteria, thirty instances were found to provide appropriate moments for third-party action to inflect events away from deadly conflict and state collapse. The selection criteria for these instances are (1) a conceivable alternative at an identifiable decision point, following the minimal-rewrite rule; (2) a specific, timed alternative that was mentioned and discussed at the time; (3) an action that was feasible and relevant to the intended outcome; and (4) a contextual opportunity.[17]

The minimal-rewrite rule stipulates that convenient elections, assassinations, and other fortuitous changes of personnel cannot precede the action or be a condition for its occurrence. The missed opportunity has to be able to be seized by the same actors as those who had originally missed it. Obviously, something at some level has to change for an alternative action to be chosen, perhaps only in the minds of the decisionmakers, or else the analysis would be defeated by the idea that what happened was the only thing that could have happened. But the raw material with which the analysis works needs to remain the same as that actually obtaining at the time.

The prior-mention condition protects the analysis from being merely 20-20 hindsight, conceiving of alternatives that no one thought of at the time. For the most part, the alternatives examined here were present in the debate over the decision itself, although in some cases they were mentioned in broader public forums, such as op-ed pieces, newspaper editorials, or other agencies' discussions of the situation. Thus, there must have been an element of choice occurring at a narrowly defined time over a specific action. The idea that "something should have been done" is not an opportunity to do something nor an identification of what to do.

The feasible-relevant rule is common sense, in that the intended action must not just respond to a need to "do something" but must seek to "accomplish something" appropriate to the conflict and collapse. More deeply, relevancy refers to a goal, not simply of temporarily freezing the fighting but of creating a new path toward a different outcome than that indicated by the continuing conflict. There is no claim here that the alternative action would put all aright, but merely that it would start a new process of dealing with both the predominance of destruction and the absence of effective authority. Similarly, it must also fall within the means of the intervenor, a sleeper of a requirement since it is not only the limitations of the third party's resources but also the resistance of the target to particular incentives and restraints that determine feasibility.

Opportunities are favorable moments for achieving a purpose, a suitable combination of conditions for accomplishing a goal. If the goal and purpose are to reduce deadly conflict and reverse state collapse, it is the conditions of favorability that need to be defined. The opportune moment to do something is not just "whenever" but is contextually determined, in relation to the conflict. Interventions require an "entry point" or occasion that invites foreign action. Need alone does not justify the specific action; there must be some definable opening for external parties to enter, and if there is not, it must be created.[18] Opportunities or entry points can be defined by event or by context.

Events that require or justify a mediatory reaction can be either scheduled or unscheduled. In a few instances, a scheduled event such as an election requires a response that could make a major difference in the subsequent course of actions. Examples include the fraudulent count announced after the 1985 elections in Liberia, where American rejection would have triggered both internal and external reactions, or the cancellation of the November 1987 elections in Haiti, which occasioned a cut in aid but little more, or the restoration of Aristide in 1994, which was not followed by measures to restore the state as well, or the 1996 elections in Yugoslavia, where the opposition received polite notice from Washington but no help.

More frequently, unscheduled events or crises invite an external response. The 1995 shelling of Sarajevo galvanized the North Atlantic Treaty Organization (NATO) allies into intervention in Bosnia, and the 1991 advances of the Eritrean and Tigrean rebels on Addis Ababa brought in U.S. mediation.[19] But neither the 1988 massacre of dispossessed Somali tribesmen in Hargeisa, the 1991 and 1993 military and civilian riots in Kinshasa and other Zairean cities or the 1995 and 1996 pogroms of targeted ethnic groups in the Kivus of eastern Zaire, the 1991 military coup against the elected Haitian government in Port-au-Prince, nor the 1994 unconstitutional installation of a new president in Haiti brought any effective response. In an event-defined opportunity, scheduled or unscheduled, the response must be immediate, or else the opening closes and the justification looks lame.

When there is no event, scheduled or unexpected, to require a response, the opportunity is to be found more broadly in the context of the conflict. Significantly, this is the more frequent case. The established model indicates that a ripe moment for initiating mediation is composed of two perceptual elements: a "mutually hurting stalemate," out of which parties seek or are responsive to help in extricating themselves, and an equally subjective "way out," toward which the parties feel a shared willingness to move as a joint solution.[20] Such a stalemate has been seized on occasion—by the All-African Council of Churches in 1972, when the southern and northern Sudanese armies bogged down in civil war; by the United States in 1987, when the National Union for the Total Independence of Angola (UNITA)–South African and Cuban-Angolan armies checked each other at Cuito Carnevale; by Portugal in 1990, when the opposing forces in Angola fought to an impasse at Mavinga; by the Sant' Egidio community and supporters in 1990, when drought and destruction brought the Mozambican civil war to a deadlock.[21]

Ripe moments are windows of opportunity, but a ripe moment was allowed to slip away repeatedly in Lebanon in March 1978, July 1982, and March 1984 when the parties to the civil war were deadlocked and hurting but not helped out of their impasse; in Liberia in June 1990, in April 1992, or in July 1993 when the parties had fought to a temporary standstill and were brought to a cease-fire but not to effective measures for ending the conflict; in Yugoslavia in June 1990 when the republics were deadlocked over the future of the federation; in Serbia in October 1998 when the government and the Kosovar were at an impasse over the Kosovo issue; and in Somalia in March–June 1991 just after Siad Barre's fall. A mutually hurting stalemate may motivate conflicting parties to negotiation, but it is also the vehicle for third-party mediation if the parties themselves are not motivated to act on their own.[22]

But in some instances, there is only a soft stalemate that is stable and self-serving (known as the S^5 situation), with a painful but bearable effect, and the intervenors are required to create an event as the opportunity to justify their action.[23] Intervention in such cases has to be sold to the conflicting parties themselves (as well as to the intervenors' public); it is a life buoy thrown to a swimmer rather enjoying the excitement of the surf and oblivious to the approaching tidal wave that is visible only to the thrower. The image shows that an S^5 situation requires third-party intervention, even more than does a hard or hurting stalemate.[24] In these instances, the opportunity is artificial, to be constructed out of the unstable conflict or collapse before it really blows up at a less convenient time for both conflicting parties and vulnerable bystanders. "You're going to be involved willy-nilly," noted the Israeli Mideast expert Joseph Alpher of the Mideast conflict in 2001, ". . . and so it's better to take the initiative than be dragged in by some dramatic event, which, . . . is almost certainly going to be negative."[25] Opportunity in this type of situation does not exist on its own but has to be created out of a general context, with no other justification than the impending catastrophe on the distant horizon. It is a mutually hurting stalemate only in perspective, with no particular justifying moment.

Finally, there are clearer moments of opportunity when the conflict undergoes a momentary calm, opening the possibility of creating a longer-lasting, more stable outcome. It is generally evident that measures are needed to make the pause in the conflict permanent by addressing the causes of the conflict and establishing mechanisms to prevent its reoccurrence.[26] The opportunity may come from an informal lull in the conflict, from a temporary cease-fire, or even from a meeting of the parties: the point is that it offers an opening for specific measures, for it is not self-perpetuating and will fall apart at the next incident if not seized and solidified. In half the instances, third parties took advantage of a momentary lull to summon the conflicting parties to a conference to fill the political vacuum and reinstitute the state, but then failed in reality because they did not invest commensurate energy in follow-through.

But opportunities are only doors; either one enters invited, or one knocks, or one barges in. Invitations to intervene in internal conflicts and states' collapsing are not impossible to inveigle, but they are not spontaneous responses by the afflicted parties to their plight. A mediator is always regarded as a meddler to some extent, but more than ever when it comes to internal wars: by its nature, external intervention favors the weaker party, the rebellion, and it suggests that the sovereign state is not able to handle its own internal affairs. An invitation is an important part of the action of seizing opportunities to reduce conflict, which means the would-be intervenor must convince the parties that the intervention is for their own good. An invitation is unlikely to come from both sides initially, and so to sell its services the intervenor must overcome the presumption that it is favorable to the inviting side. Invitation is an interactive process, with the would-be intervenor knocking at the door of opportunity and talking its way in; in fact, in the end it may be the intervenor who is the one offering the invitation. Even when one forces the door, the diplomacy of persuasion is crucial, in which the most significant element for the conflicting parties is often the importance of their relations with the intervening country.

Invitations, the final element in opportunities, come in various forms. The United States continually reminded the parties that it could be useful to them as a way of getting their attention in the long mediation process over Namibia-Angola in 1980–1987; it was the inviting party to Camp David in 1978 and 2000 in the Middle East conflict, as France was the inviting party in December 2002 to Marcoussis in the Ivorian conflict. On the other hand, Samuel Doe in Liberia and Raoul Cedras in Haiti were persuaded to at least listen to proposals from U.S. envoys for early retirement, but Mobutu Sese Seko in Zaire and Siad Barre and Mohammed Aideed in Somalia were not.

In sum, the opportunity is defined as a moment in the conflict or collapse when the external party can get the conflicting parties' attention to constructive measures. Otherwise defined, it is a moment when external entry into the conflict or collapse is justified by either an accepted occasion for a response to an event or by the intervenor's ability to produce an attractive way out of a present or prospective difficulty. Although there is a specific element in the identification of opportunities—an event requiring a response, a stalemate impelling an exit—there is also a huge field for creativity. Opportunities can be precise moments, or they can be broader periods within which the particular moment is a matter of perception and creation.

For this analysis, the focus for action is on a third party.[27] In the end, domestic actors need to be brought back into control, but in state rebirth as in other delivery processes, midwiving is often necessary. It is true that the parties to the conflict can also seize opportunities or miss them, but a recipe for a different course of action would either have to enter their psyche, where this analysis is not equipped to venture, or enlist a third party to make the argument for change to them. That is where this analysis goes. It may be objected that it is still the third party's psyche that is being entered, one remove from the arena of conflict. But entry into conflict management through a third party is necessary to circumvent the major problem of the arena, which is the clash between the psychological demands of conflict and of its termination in the minds of the conflicting parties. Parties at conflict need help. They are too taken up with the business of conducting conflict to see the need and opportunities for a way out, unless someone helps them. Although conflicted states cannot either be saved by reconstruction or be saved from self-destruction by external action alone, external intervention of some sort becomes necessary when conflict becomes stuck in its own mire.

The potentially most powerful actor in such situations is frequently the United States, but it is not the only actor. Although it has to assume its responsibility because of its leading position in world affairs, even when other states do not, it operates best when other states assume their responsibilities too and the international community of states works in harmony. Indeed, collective action is generally the wisest course, whether the United States is involved or not, since collective action eliminates escape routes, combines sources of leverage and influence,[28] diversifies responsibility, and lessens the danger of abusing intervention. Nor are states the only actors: on occasion, NGOs may be best equipped to intervene preventively, particularly when infringement of sovereignty is involved or when official state action needs to be prepared. In the following cases, the Carter Center of Emory University is occasionally singled out and identified as the appropriate NGO, not to underscore shortcomings when opportunities were missed but to highlight the unique contributions and capabilities it can provide.[29] Even when it is a state that acts, the state may work with NGOs, each in its role and in support of each other. But action, whether taken by one actor (necessarily made up of several agencies) or by several actors, must be coordinated, and that coordination must be either institutional, through a paramount government agency or through the UN Security Council, for example, or, at the least, informal. Otherwise, collective mediation provides its own undoing.

These four criteria—minimal rewrite, prior mention, relevant feasibility, contextual opportunity—have yielded thirty instances in the six cases where arguably an opportunity was missed. As indicated, some of these were specific, whereas others were located in a broader, softer context. In a few instances, an attempt has been made to evaluate other purported moments that, on closer scrutiny, do not meet the criteria. Arguments may be made in hindsight for additional moments when there may have been an opening, but they probably do not meet the criteria, notably the condition of prior mention.

Opportunities are occasions to "do something." The types of actions to be taken will be discussed and categorized in Chapters 8 and 9 of this book, after the specific cases and instances have been examined in Chapters 2–7. These actions will be called "interventions" here, indicating an action directly involving an external party in the selection of policies or policymakers of a target state; such action may or may not be consistent with the target's will or consent, since "will" and "consent" are often difficult to establish and may in fact be the very object of the intervention.[30] Despite the military connotations of the term *intervention,* the measures analyzed are above all diplomatic actions, standard elements of diplomacy of the type conducted at other times and places and sometimes even of the same type practiced later in the same conflict when it was too late. When military forces were to be involved, they were either already present or to be produced later under less favorable circumstances, and even in these cases, it is the diplomatic activity that was wanting.[31] The spectrum of such interventions runs from dialogue meetings among civil society and political groups (in Haiti in 1996) to a muscular response to a military encounter (in Somalia in 1993), with all others lying in between. The largest number of instances, found in all six cases, involved the mediated pursuit of negotiations with broadened participation and the implementation of agreements already registered. In some instances, such diplomatic activity also required the appointment of a skillful special representative of the UN Secretary-General (SRSG), as in Liberia, Zaire, and Somalia; the condemnation of repressive government actions, as in Liberia and Somalia; or the maintenance and focusing of sanctions already voted, as in Haiti. In a few instances, notably in Yugoslavia, Lebanon, and Somalia, the situation required the international convocation of a major conference of the conflicting parties before full collapse set in. Some of the cases, specifically Liberia, Somalia, Zaire, and Haiti, required diplomatic activity to facilitate the early retirement of the egregious ruler and to provide legal conditions for his replacement; although some of these instances also involved a military role, it was to maintain order and not to participate directly in the removal. Finally, a few instances in each case concerned the earlier arrival and a larger mandate for peace-keeping and peace-enforcing forces that were to be sent later, at higher cost when the initial opportunity has passed.

If the specific types of interventions presented here are unexceptional, the spirit by which they operate may be more controversial. The approach may be called internationalist or interventionist. It holds that state collapse and deadly conflict are as much a cause for international concern and a breach of international stability as a war or a tsunami, and that sovereignty means a state responsibility to care for the welfare of one's own people and to assist other states' people to receive that care.[32] On the surface, official rhetoric on both sides of the Atlantic (and the Mediterranean) increasingly calls for international assistance in resolving others' problems and conflicts. The great powers of the North deem world security and stability their responsibility, at least in principle. Smaller, weaker countries call for international attention and assistance, and decry neglect and marginalization. In the specific, of course, action is slow in forthcoming, and that is the point of this book. Governments are reluctant to act, hiding behind sovereignty and their own interests or purported lack of them. If reluctance until it was too late was the characteristic of the 1980s and 1990s, the decisive but possibly hasty intervention in Iraq in the 2000s has highlighted all the problems of an internationalist or interventionist position. The problem is often identified as lack of political will, a label too general to be useful except in inviting further investigation. The final chapters of this book will delve further into reasons why able states were not willing to live up to their own proclaimed standards of conduct and why a broadly internationalist world outlook comes in so many shades of application.

As this study will argue repeatedly, however, opportunities to intervene in deadly conflict and state collapse are present to be exploited, not recklessly, but out of responsibility to self and others. This responsibility is held to be twofold. On one hand, from the point of view of potential intervenors, in the long run involvement is simply unavoidable. If intervention in cases of conflict and collapse is inevitable, the argument then becomes a matter of effectiveness and timing. That inevitably is based both on empirical grounds, as the record of conflict and collapse around the world shows, and on philosophical or behavioral grounds, given that great powers simply cannot accept being bystanders to the deadly breakdown of order in a shrinking, interdependent globe. Thus, although this study is written from an internationalist point of view, its argument is not based on some ideological interventionism that posits intervention as a desirable policy choice. Were it to do so, it would have to show why intervention is preferable to isolation and noninvolvement. Rather, the argument is that inevitable intervention is better practiced in certain ways at certain times rather than others. These elements will be argued in greater detail in the final chapters, but the general point of view of this inquiry should be truthfully advertised from the outset.

On the other hand, a constant theme here is that conflicting and collapsing parties need help out of their predicament. Parties become locked in the "logic of conflict" that hides the "logic of interest" and keeps them from seeing ways out.[33] This is not to say that parties do not enter conflicts for good reasons, at least in their own eyes, or that sometimes conflict is simply necessary. But it does posit a value in peaceful change, and it does recognize that conflict and collapse have a lock-in mechanism that often blocks effective attainment of the initiating goals.[34] Again, these points will be developed further in Chapters 8 and 9, but they need stating at its beginning.

In this light, the distribution of missed opportunities is significant. First, it suggests that opportunities may come in bunches, after which the chance for openings has passed, as in Zaire and Somalia. Missing the first opening may not be fatal to the prevention process, but a series of misses causes the parties to devote their entire focus and energy to the pursuit of the conflict and convinces them that no one can help develop alternatives. The parties can wear out the meddlers. Conflict can also captivate the conflictors, who find in intractable conflict and S^5 situations the excuse for turning to personal enrichment and privatized goods.[35] Second, the record also suggests that opportunities may come at intervals in the conflict or the collapsing process, each slightly different and producing a new stage of conflict and collapse, as in Lebanon, Haiti, and earlier Somalia. In this sequence, the evolving conflict repeatedly poses new challenges to the intervenors, and more than just "try, try again" is needed. Third, it also suggests that opportunities missed can destroy the solution that was salient at the time, so that good ideas can be worn out without even being tried, as in the last days of Yugoslavia. Good, even obvious, solutions do not hang around waiting to be picked up whenever; when their time has come and gone, they may no longer be available for revival.

Finally, the distribution of opportunities also suggests that there are uninhabitable spaces in the evolution of the conflict or process of collapse when simply nothing can be done. There were no opportunities to miss in Somalia after the end of the U.S.-UN intervention in 1993, in Congo/Zaire during the time of Laurent Kabila, or in Kosovo up to 1998. Ripening, positioning, and containing are the three levels of policy response available in such periods, as potential third parties await a better day when positive involvement again becomes possible. Ripening means working to sharpen one or both parties' perception that continued conflict is more costly to them than conciliatory alternatives, as the United States did in the run-up to the Dayton mediation on Bosnia in 1994–1995 but not in Liberia in 1985. Positioning means remaining minimally involved and reminding the parties that the third party is available if ever needed, as the United States did during much of the 1980s in the South Africa–Angola conflict but not in Lebanon in 1984. Containing means strengthening surrounding countries so that the cancer of collapse does not spread, as was the European strategy toward some of the former Yugoslav republics but not the European Union (EU) and U.S. strategy toward West Africa. But these secondary options are often the only choice after earlier and more direct opportunities to prevent conflict and collapse have been missed.

These implications will be examined in greater detail in the course of the analysis. Missed opportunities are not merely missed moments; they tend to be failures to gain entry into a whole phase of a conflict, after which entry is no longer or much more rarely possible, and the phase changes into something less penetrable. Opportunities are not revolving doors, where entry appears at regular intervals. They tend to constitute a period of time in the life of the conflict when preventive diplomacy is possible, after which entry becomes much more difficult. Not only opportunities but a period of opportunities was missed in Yugoslavia, Liberia, Haiti, Somalia, and Zaire (Congo), and now the countries concerned and their citizens, the regions, and also the external powers have to live with the consequences.

Instances of Decision

The thirty instances of opportunities for preventive diplomacy provide the "data" for the subsequent analysis. In all cases, the first instance identifies opportunities while the last regime was still in power and before the power vacuum occurred. In many instances, this period involved measures to deal with an egregious ruler, often in combination with a weak and beleaguered government. Thereafter, the collapse of the state was accompanied by civil war, often among the forces of rebellion themselves more than between the rebellion and the government; intervention measures focused on bringing hostilities to an end and constructing a new political contract. The emphasis is on preventive diplomacy carried out by political means, including negotiation, mediation, and consolidation, not primarily on military or other physical intervention, although in a few instances military enforcement may be involved ancillarily.

Thus, to the question, "Intervention to do what?" the general answer in the cases presented here is, "To prevent state collapse and deadly conflict." Such prevention necessarily has a negative and a positive component. It means halting and removing the immediate causes of conflict and collapse, but it also means facilitating and instituting replacements designed to move the society and polity toward stability, capacity, and accountability. State collapse is not the same as regime change, and in most cases, regime change was necessary to prevent legitimate authority, law, and order from breaking down. Nor is deadly conflict the same as political differences, and in most cases it was necessary to provide a prospect for working out legitimate differences in order for violence to be stopped. Frequently, there was someone who benefited from state collapse and was unmoved by the ongoing conflict; for them it was collapse and conflict that were the opportunity. But in all cases, there were many more potential third-party intervenors who had an interest in seeing the conflict end and the state restored, whatever the particular policy direction the state might subsequently take. Even their interests, as concerned third parties, and certainly the interests of the country and its inhabitants, would be better served by a state than by a nonstate. The United States and other external powers, notably in Europe, generally fall into this category, but so do most other states of the conflict region, for whom a partner is better than a battlefield. It is to those actors that the search for an opportunity is addressed.

The next six chapters of this book present analytical scenarios for each of these critical moments, combining a succinct portrayal of the conflict to the point of intervention, followed by an account of the action necessary to seize the opportunity. Seven different aspects of these interventions will be examined: the nature of the opportunity, the availability and credibility of (early) warnings, the type of action to be undertaken and the appropriate actor, the interest of the intervening party in getting involved, the available means of constraint and inducement, the costs and casualties involved, and the reasons why the policy was not adopted.

The presentations do not constitute detailed histories of either the factual or the counterfactual event, if only for lack of space, but simply enough of an account to portray the opportunity, its use, and its limitations. The strength of the opportunity varies. Whereas in most of the instances a rather strong argument can be made for the feasibility and potential effectiveness of appropriate action, in a few instances the opportunity's existence is less than conclusive but the instance is included nonetheless for the light it throws on the general conclusions. The analysis does not seek to test a single hypothesis or explain a theoretical outcome. Rather, it will draw insights and establish conceptual patterns from the thirty instances in order to improve an understanding of how not to miss opportunities and how to improve diplomatic interventions.

Notes

1. Tuchman, *The March of Folly;* Shields, *Preventable Disasters;* Parker, *The Politics of Miscalculation in the Middle East;* Tetlock and Belkin, *Counterfactual Thought Experiments in World Politics.*

2. U.S. House of Representatives, Committee on Foreign Affairs, *Hearings on Cyprus,* 87th Cong., 2nd sess., 19 August 1974, 38.

3. James Christoph and Bernard Brown, eds., *Cases in Comparative Politics* (Boston: Little, Brown, 1976), especially chapters 1 (Bernard Brown) and 2 (Martin Landau).

4. George and Holl, *The Warning-Response Problem and Missed Opportunities in Preventive Diplomacy,* reprinted in Jentleson, *Opportunities Missed, Opportunities Seized.*

5. Tetlock and Belkin, *Counterfactual Thought Experiments in World Politics,* 6.

6. Ibid., 18.

7. Ibid., 11.

8. Although it is usually noted that intrastate conflicts have been on the increase since the end of the Cold War, the fact is that they were predominant even before 1990, throughout the post–World War II period, as domestic forces linked to foreign allies fought for the control of the state, in both decolonization and "East-West" conflicts.

9. Lute, *Preventing Deadly Conflict.*

10. See, among many others, Coser, *The Functions of Social Conflict* and *Continuities in the Study of Social Conflict;* Bernard et al., *The Nature of Conflict;* Ted Gurr, *Why Men Rebel* (Princeton, NJ: Princeton University Press, 1970); Brown, *The International Dimensions of Internal Conflict;* Tarrow, *Power in Movement;* Lake and Rothchild, *The International Spread of Ethnic Conflict;* Pruitt and Kim, *Social Conflict.*

11. Arnson and Zartman, *Rethinking the Economics of War.*

12. Zartman, *Collapsed States;* Rosenau, "The State in an Era of Cascading Politics"; Esty et al., *State Failure Task Force Reports;* Baker and Weller, *An Analytical Model of Internal Conflict and State Collapse;* Rotberg, *When States Fail;* Clement, *Common Patterns of State Collapse.* A number of these studies do not make a clear distinction between state failure, which is a weakened performance, and state collapse, which is the disintegration of authority, law, and political order.

13. See, among many others, R. M. MacIver, *The Modern State* (Oxford: Oxford University Press, 1926); Harold Laski, *The State in Theory and Practice* (London: W. H. Allen, 1935); J. P. Nettl, "The State as a Conceptual Variable," *World Politics* 20, no. 4 (1968): 559–592; Evans, Rueschmayer, and Skocpol, *Bringing the State Back In;* Bertrand Badie and Pierre Birnbaum, *The Sociology of the State* (Chicago: University of Chicago Press, 1983).

14. On Rwanda, see Astride Suhrke and Bruce Jones, "Preventive Diplomacy in Rwanda," in Jentleson, *Opportunities Missed, Opportunities Seized;* Feil, *Preventing Genocide.* On Burundi, see René Lemarchand, *Burundi: Ethnic Conflict and Genocide* (Washington, DC: Woodrow Wilson Center Press, 1995). On Uganda, see Gilbert Khachagala, "State Collapse and Reconstruction in Uganda," in Zartman, *Collapsed States,* 33–48. On Chad, see William Foltz, "Reconstructing the State of Chad," in Zartman, *Collapsed States,* 15–32. On Sierra Leone, see Reno, *Corruption and State Politics in Sierra Leone;* William Reno, "Sierra Leone: Welfare in a Post-State Society," in Rotberg, *State Failure and State Weakness in a Time of Terror;* Jimmy Kandeh, "Criminalization of the RUF Insurgency in Sierra Leone," in Arnson and Zartman, *Rethinking the Economics of War.* On Congo-Brazzaville, see I. William Zartman and Katharina Vogeli, "Prevention Gained and Prevention Lost: Collapse, Competition and Coup in Congo," in Jentleson, *Opportunities Missed, Opportunities Seized;* Zartman, "An Apology Needs a Pledge." On Tajikistan, see Nasrin Dadmehr, "Tajikistan: Regionalism and Weakness," in Rotberg, *State Failure and State Weakness in a Time of Terror.* On Chechnya, see Gail Lapidus, "The War in Chechnya: Opportunities Missed, Lessons to Be Learned," in Jentleson, *Opportunities Missed, Opportunities Seized;* German, *Russia's Chechen War.* On Azerbaijan, see Maresca, "Lost Opportunities in Negotiating the Conflict over Nagorno Karabakh." On Afghanistan, see Rubin, *The Search for Peace in Afghanistan.* On Algeria, see Bonner, Reif, and Tessler, "Islam, Democracy and the State in Algeria." On Sri Lanka, see Rotberg, *Creating Peace in Sri Lanka.*

15. Feil, *Preventing Genocide;* Kuperman, *The Limits of Humanitarian Intervention;* Alison Des Forges, *Leave None to Tell the Story: Genocide in Rwanda* (New York: Human Rights Watch, 1999).

16. On case choice, see, among others, Sambanis, "Using Case Studies to Expand Economic Models of Civil War."

17. The minimal-rewrite rule is discussed in Tetlock and Belkin, *Counterfactual Thought Experiments in World Politics,* 23–24. The prior-mention condition is covered in Tuchman, *The March of Folly,* 5, 280. The feasible-relevant rule is discussed in Tetlock and Belkin, *Counterfactual Thought Experiments in World Politics,* 18–23, 25–26; Tuchman, *The March of Folly,* 5. Curiously, contextual opportunity is not mentioned as a condition in the literature on counterfactual analysis; it is just assumed that something can be done any time; see Tetlock and Belkin, *Counterfactual Thought Experiments in World Politics;* Jentleson, *Op-*

portunities Missed, Opportunities Seized, 17–19. This omission is consistent with the general neglect of contextual timing in the analysis of conflict management; Zartman, "Ripeness: The Hurting Stalemate and Beyond."

18. Chester A. Crocker, Fen Osler Hampson, and Pamela Aall, "Rising to the Challenge of Multiparty Mediation," in Crocker, Hampson, and Aall, *Herding Cats,* 668–674; Maundi et al., *Getting In.*

19. Holbrooke, *To End a War;* Cohen, *Intervening in Africa,* chap. 2.

20. Zartman, "The Strategy of Preventive Diplomacy in Third World Conflicts"; Zartman, *Ripe for Resolution;* Zartman, "Ripening Conflict, Ripe Moment, Formula and Mediation"; Zartman, "Ripeness: The Hurting Stalemate and Beyond."

21. Assefa, *Mediation of Civil Wars;* Crocker, *High Noon in Southern Africa;* Zartman, *Ripe for Resolution,* chap. 5; Donald Rothchild and Caroline Hartzell, "Interstate and Intrastate Negotiations in Angola," and Ibrahim Msabaha, "Negotiating an End to Mozambique's Murderous Rebellion," in Zartman, *Elusive Peace.*

22. Saadia Touval and I. William Zartman, "Mediation in the Post–Cold War Era," in Crocker, Hampson, and Aall, *Turbulent Peace.*

23. Zartman, *Elusive Peace,* 18–20, 334–335.

24. Ibid., 10. On the implications of the S^5 situation for the onset of the greed phase of conflict, see Arnson and Zartman, *Rethinking the Economics of War,* and Crocker, Hampson, and Aall, *Grasping the Nettle.*

25. Lee Hockstader, "US Role as Mideast Mediator Fades," *Washington Post,* 7 August 2001, A12.

26. On seizing the opportunity opened by a recent versus an impending escalation, see Zartman and Faure, *Escalation and Negotiation.*

27. In this, it differs from Tuchman, *The March of Folly.*

28. Cortright, *The Price of Peace.*

29. The author is a member of the Carter Center's International Negotiation Network and was President Carter's mediator in Congo-Brazzaville in 1999; see Maundi et al., *Getting In,* chap. 4.

30. See, for example, James Rosenau et al., "Intervention"; Evans and Sahnoun, *The Responsibility to Protect,* 8–9; Chester A. Crocker, "Intervention: Toward Best Practices and a Holistic View," in Crocker, Hampson, and Aall, *Turbulent Peace;* Christian Dorsch, "Maintaining World Order Through Regimes of State-Building Intervention" (Research Report, International Institute for Applied Systems Analysis, Laxenburg, 2005).

31. See Jane Holl Lute, "The Role of Force in Peacemaking," in Zartman, *Peacemaking in International Conflict.*

32. Deng et al., *Sovereignty as Responsibility;* Evans and Sahnoun, *The Responsibility to Protect.*

33. Chaim Kaufmann, "Possible and Impossible Solutions to Civil Wars," in Michael Brown, ed., *Nationalism and Ethnic Conflict* (Cambridge: MIT Press, 2001), 455.

34. Collier et al., *Breaking the Conflict Trap.*

35. Arnson and Zartman, *Rethinking the Economics of War.*

2

LEBANON,
1976–1984

THE LEBANESE SITUATION HAS OFTEN BEEN DESCRIBED AS A PROTRACTED, MULTI-dimensional conflict.[1] A mix of internal, regional, and international factors contributed to its emergence and escalation during the last chill of the Cold War. The internal dimensions of the conflict involved a number of substantive issues relating to the sharing of political power. The National Pact of 1943 distributed power along sectarian lines, with the important posts assigned to Christian Maronites, who were the majority at that time. Over the years a demographic change took place, and Muslims became the majority, demanding a reform of the system to reflect the new realities. But a third group, within the Muslim community, demanded a full transformation of the political rules and the elimination of confessionalism, that is, a non-sectarian allocation of positions. Beyond the conflict over the sectarian balance was the intraconfessional struggle for the control of the confessional communities (a struggle between the old, incumbent barons and the younger, excluded elements of the populations) and the concomitant shift in the role of the militias from banditry to the formation of ministates.[2]

Into this disruptive issue of political change were thrown the Palestinians, who came to Lebanon after the Arab-Israeli war of 1948. Because of its delicate sectarian balance, Lebanon was the principal Arab country to refuse to integrate the Palestinian refugees—some 400,000 in the mid-1970s out of 3.1 million Lebanese—and to place them instead in refugee camps around big cities. From a miserable cluster of refugees, the Palestinians, however, began to emerge as a militant force in the region after the June war of 1967, as they started to launch attacks on Israel from southern Lebanon. Their international role led them in turn to become a political force within Lebanon. After Black September 1970, when the Palestine Liberation Organization (PLO) was defeated in Jordan, the Palestinians

Missed Opportunities:
Lebanon, 1976–1984

January 1976 Militia stalemate and Arab League concern provided an occasion to broaden a Syrian initiative and reinforce the announced Constitutional Document while the civil conflict was still in the hands of civilian politicians.

November 1979 Withdrawals of external forces, weaknesses in militia leadership, and attempts at internal reform opened the potential for Arab and Lebanese efforts to restore the Lebanese polity.

July–August 1982 The new unstable situation created by the Israeli invasion of Lebanon provided the opportunity for a different Reagan initiative than the one produced, focusing on the Lebanese problem, bringing in Syria, and working on an internal peace agreement.

March 1984 Reconciliation sessions at Geneva and Lausanne offered an opportunity for Saudi Arabia and the United States, along with Syria, to add participants, incentives, and guarantees to the Lausanne agreement.

established a state within the Lebanese state with its own bureaucracy, armed forces, and social institutions.

Many regional players have attempted to gain influence over Lebanon, but the main external players in this game have been Syria and Israel. Syria's involvement in Lebanon was based on several historical and geostrategic factors. The Syrian leadership has often looked at Lebanon as part of greater Syria, since Lebanon covers the whole western and Mediterranean flank of southern Syria, controlling access to Damascus and the heart of the country. Israel has never claimed any territorial rights over Lebanon, but Palestinian raids from southern Lebanon posed a threat to northern Israel, to which it responded with cross-border raids, intensive shelling, aerial bombardment, and large-scale invasion. Israel also maintained a close relationship with some Lebanese parties, notably the Maronite Christian Phalanx militias.

Beyond these two contenders, Lebanon was a continual football in the dynamics of the Middle East peace process. When the rivalry between Syria and Egypt over the Israeli disengagement agreement in the mid-1970s and then the bitter dispute over the Camp David agreements and the Washington Peace Treaty between Israel and Egypt at the end of the decade split the Arab camp into supporters and rejectionists, Lebanon became a pawn in the struggle, a status that disrupted attempts at domestic reconciliation. When Lebanon was invaded by Israel and constrained to sign a peace treaty with it in the early 1980s, not only the government but also the prime external mediator, the United States, was delegitimized as a result. Consequently, Syria's interest and policy of tightening its control over its neighbor increased over the period.

Within a wider circle, the Lebanese conflict was also part of the politics of the Cold War and the competition between the United States, which had loosely picked up the formerly French responsibility for the country as well as a direct responsibility for neighboring Israel, and the Soviet Union, which was the patron of Baathist Syria. Once before, in 1958, the United States had assumed a direct role in assuring the independence of Lebanon through military and diplomatic intervention. Yet curiously enough, the East-West rivalry may have had less impact over Lebanon than over most other Middle East conflicts.

In this charged context, two random incidents between the Maronite Phalanx and the Palestinian militias sparked the outbreak of the civil war on 13 April 1975.[3] Over the following decade and a half, internal and external parties would produce cease-fires and proposals to handle the constitutional and the foreign issues. Although some of the cease-fires lasted a bit, they were only truces, never tied to implemented agreements on the two issues and never fully subject to cooperative efforts at resolution by inside and outside forces at the same time. On a few occasions, the truces actually held for a while, even though unimplemented, only to be overthrown by a new turn of events in the larger Arab-Israeli conflict.

The Lebanese conflict went through four phases, each with its missed opportunity to reroute the conflict. The purpose of all four interventions would have been to change the course of the conflict and head it toward resolution by focusing on the reconstruction of a viable political system out of sociopolitical change on which the state could rest, as a precondition for its assuming its role in the region. The means would be to use sustained mediation to focus the parties on internal reform and the creation of new rules for the political system, on which there was broad—if not universal—agreement in principle. The agents were available, and in fact engaged: fellow Arab states operating with U.S. pressure and assistance and providing both diplomatic muscle and peacekeeping forces. Entry was provided by varying combinations of a sense of ripeness among some or all of the parties and an occasion for initiative by the intervenors. In some cases, an effort was made, but the opportunity to carry it to fruition was lost; the internal parties and their international mediators tried for yet another conflict-managing cease-fire and then let the conflict drop, the basic issues that required a resolution remaining unattended. In other cases, elements of ripeness were present, but the opportunity to start an internal restructuring process was misused, neglected, or squandered.

The first period, covering the first two years of the war, ended with the Riyadh-Cairo agreements of October 1976. There was an earlier opportunity, however, for an Arab states' initiative, with some U.S. urging, before the army broke up, to produce a more lasting peace agreement dealing with basic issues and then implement it. Confronted with the continuing disagreements of the internal parties—they were, after all, in a civil war—the Arab states contented themselves with a cease-fire and an international (largely Syrian) Arab peacekeeping force; they left unmentioned the resolving formula for internal reform that was already on the table. Neither the domestic dimension of the conflict—the confessional issue—nor its international dimension—the Palestinian issue—was addressed, and so the Lebanese state continued on its way to collapse, left to disintegrate on the first dimension and therefore unable to handle the second.

The second period began with the Israeli incursions of 1977 and invasion of 1978; when both Syria and Israel made withdrawals over the following year, a UN peacekeeping force was installed, and the Lebanese government began to formulate internal reforms. At that point an opportunity was again present for Arab states to seize the moment for an internal settlement, but no one moved. The Arab states seemed to feel that the Lebanese problem was not worth the effort, and so they lifted no finger to help the Lebanese state take advantage of some momentary weaknesses of the warring factions and confront its need for internal reform, even though the formula for that reform was still lying on the table. Without outside help from its brothers, the Lebanese state fell prey to revived internal conflict and then to the emergence of the Palestinian issue in its midst.

The third period began when a new situation was created by the Israeli invasion and destruction of the Palestinian stronghold in Lebanon in June 1982, bringing an opportunity for a new peace initiative from the United States that was indeed seized but in a most unhelpful way. By launching a proposal that contained no incentives for any of the parties to participate, the United States missed a chance to sponsor an internal Lebanese settlement and start regional relations in a new direction. Syria and Israel collaborated in blocking the U.S. initiative, which was most effective in compromising the already-weak Lebanese government by hanging an albatross of a peace agreement with Israel around its neck. The

Reagan initiative destroyed its own ripe moment and consummated the collapse of the Lebanese state, when it could have focused on its reconstruction, taken advantage of the Palestinian removal, and negotiated partial, unlinked Israeli and Syrian disengagement.

When this failed, the fourth period of full state collapse set in, with a last opportunity for the U.S. and Arab states to arrest the process by salvaging the Geneva and Lausanne dialogues in 1984; they did not move, and the opportunity slipped through their fingers for another half decade. The alternative would have been a firm grip on the process through Syrian-Saudi cooperation, with U.S. encouragement, to impose and finance the implementation of the formula for reform on which there had been much agreement over the decade of the civil war. In the end, the conflict was brought under control by various degrees of external force, as Israel drove out the Palestinians and Syria imposed its control over the government system, sealed in the Taif agreement of 1989. With the Arab states' consent, Lebanon became a Syrian protectorate, cosmetic changes were made in the governing formula, and the internal conflict was managed by occupation and the external conflict by invasion, at great cost. In the earlier, missed rounds, the missing ingredient was a sense of commitment and urgency to overcome the resistance of some of the conflicting parties and a mistaken appreciation of the crucial importance of domestic political reform as the key to the ongoing crisis.

*January 1976: Militia stalemate and Arab League concern
provided an occasion to broaden a Syrian initiative and reinforce
the announced Constitutional Document while the civil conflict
was still in the hands of civilian politicians.*[4]

The first few months of the civil war were marked by Syrian efforts to mediate a quick stop to the bloody conflict. Arab League secretary-general Mahmoud Riadh and Syrian foreign minister Abd el-Halim Khaddam managed to obtain two cease-fire agreements in mid-1975, but they were very short-lived because they did not address the political and social elements of the conflict. After a lull in July and August, Syria encouraged the creation of a Committee for National Dialogue in which all Lebanese communities were represented, to discuss political reform. Sharp differences on the nature of this reform characterized the work of the committee during its nine meetings over October and November, each punctuated by escalating attempts to improve the parties' position through violence. Parties of the left called for reform plans as a precondition to ending violence, whereas the Christian right called for an end of violence as a precondition to constitutional discussion. "All but legally, . . . the country had fallen apart, and it needed a tremendous effort of will and imagination by all the sides concerned to put it together again."[5] Violence in Lebanon and negotiations in Syria followed over the next few months.[6]

The civil war took a new turn in January 1976, when the Palestinian militias became heavily involved in the war, and full-scale fighting broke out between the Palestinians and their leftist allies of the Lebanese National Movement (LNM) on one side and Christian militias of the Lebanese Front (LF) on the other. Syria became indirectly involved in the fighting when it sent soldiers of the Palestine Liberation Army (PLA), stationed in Syria, to cross the border into Lebanon and participate in the fighting, thus tilting the balance heavily against Christian forces. The political situation deteriorated further when on 18 January Lebanese prime minister Rashid Karami announced that he would submit his resignation to President Suleiman Franjieh. Citing the blockade of the Palestinian refugee camps, the counterattack by Muslim and leftist forces, and the offensive by rightists against the port in the Second Battle of Beirut, Karami stated that "all doors have been closed and I have no choice."[7]

Amid this chaos and escalation of fighting, the Syrian foreign minister started a new mediation effort. At the same time, the Arab League secretary-general called for an urgent Arab summit conference to end the civil strife in Lebanon and save the country from "a catastrophe."[8] The Syrian effort succeeded this time, and on 22 January 1976, the Lebanese negotiators, including Maronite president Franjieh, Sunni (acting) prime minister Karami, other Christian and Muslim leaders, and even, at that point, Druze and LNM leader Kamal Junblatt and PLO leader Yasir Arafat, with quiet U.S. support, announced their acceptance of a Syrian proposal for a new cease-fire and political reform. The Constitutional Document was announced on 14 February.[9] But its implementation hung in the balance, on both the political and the military fronts. Politically, it needed to be followed up by the formation of a national unity government and the enactment of measures provided in the document. Militarily, the Lebanese army needed to be reaffirmed in its national role and supported by a multinational Arab (even if largely Syrian) force.

In the light of the previous failures, widespread Lebanese acceptance of the Syrian proposal provided an appropriate opportunity for a broader Arab initiative to embrace the proposal and provide mechanisms to implement it with new political institutions, peacekeeping forces, and financial assistance. Syria was acting in a mediator role, on the invitation of the Lebanese government, and had not yet taken over as the protector of Lebanon. At the time of intervention, Syrian president Hafez al-Asad reaffirmed his opposition both to a partition of Lebanon into confessional ministates and to a victory of any side in the civil war.[10] As Syria clearly announced and had long maintained, it was not a neutral mediator in Lebanese affairs; it was a very interested party, as was to appear ever more strongly in the coming years, and Lebanon needed a counterbalancing involvement from the larger Arab community of states to protect its own interests. The conflict was still in an early stage in which the grievances of the various parties were easier to address and the politicians still had an important role. The previous five months of escalations had resulted in a stalemate among the militias, and the growing number of broken cease-fires could be used as a challenge to finally get it right and put the necessary resources into stopping a conflict that "could uproot the whole structure of society, . . . bring about a total revolution, [and] directly bear on the future of the Arab world," in Asad's prescient words.[11] The Arab League constituted the appropriate vehicle to endorse and implement the agreement.

In that scenario, the league's secretary-general would repeat his call in late January for an Arab summit in order to endorse the Constitutional Document and enforce the cease-fire. Most Arab countries would be willing to participate in the conference. For example, even though Syria had staunchly opposed "Arabization" of the Lebanese crisis, an Arab endorsement of the Syrian plan and Arab participation in its implementation would have made the conference acceptable to Syria. Egypt was also interested in playing a role with regard to Lebanon. Egypt had been unable to influence events in Lebanon after 1975, when Egypt's second disengagement agreement with Israel (and the absence of a second one between Syria and Israel) led to disagreement and personal bitterness between Presidents Anwar Sadat and Asad and strained relations with the PLO. The Egyptian-Syrian dispute was a principal obstacle to an Arab collective effort on Lebanon. On 26 January, however, Egyptian foreign minister Ismail Fahmy welcomed the Lebanese cease-fire, which was interpreted as an acceptance of the Syrian role in Lebanon.[12] Iraq would also be interested in attending the Arab League meeting because of its relationship with Palestinian and leftist groups in Lebanon. Other Arab countries, notably those of the Gulf and the Maghrib, would welcome any effort to end the war in Lebanon.

Out of the several overlapping issues in the Lebanese conflict, the intervention needed to separate the internal constitutional problem from the Palestinian dimension, a major challenge for substantive disentangling. The procedural answer would be to pose the issues seriatim and address the Lebanese internal problem first, since a restored Lebanese state was needed to handle the second issue and a formula for agreement was available in the Constitutional Document. The Arab summit would be called to endorse the principles of the Constitutional Document (essentially the same as those which were to end the war thirteen years later) and urge formation of a Lebanese government of national unity. The document reaffirmed the traditional formula for allocating "the three presidencies"—that Lebanon's president be a Christian Maronite, the prime minister a Sunni Muslim, and the speaker of the house a Shiite Muslim—but elevated the Muslim prime minister by having him chosen by parliament and not by the president. A new principle specified that the president would be responsible to parliament and that presidents, prime ministers, and ministers would be held accountable before a higher council for major offenses. There would be an equal distribution of seats in parliament instead of the historic Christians' six-to-five edge over Muslims; an end to the apportionment of civil service positions among religious communities, except for highest-ranking jobs; and the establishment of a merit system. It was (and was eventually to be) a modest reform, between Junblatt's call for total abolition of confessionalism and the Maronites' insistence on the status quo.

The Syrian intervention also provided for the establishment of a higher military committee, composed of Lebanese, Palestinian, and Syrian officers, charged with putting the new cease-fire into effect.[13] This body needed to reassert the role and unity of the Lebanese army as a defender of the state. In the event, a week before the Constitutional Document was announced, a scission began to open in the Lebanese army along confessional lines that was to provide another opportunity for escalation by the LNM of the left and the Palestinian militias. By mid-March the army had broken down into a number of confessional forces and had ceased to exist as a "unified functioning entity."[14] Thus, an outside military presence was needed to replace the Lebanese army if it could not be held together, deter escalations, and hold the parties to their agreement. Sending in an irregular army, the PLA, was "Track 2 intervention" at a time when state restoration was needed. The Arab summit would be called to provide for a multinational Arab force, with a large Syrian contingent, to monitor the cease-fire and guarantee the implementation of the accord.

The problem is expressed with habitual clarity by Henry Kissinger: "The anomaly was that the January 22 compromise was inherently shaky unless buttressed by outside military forces, which, if they were Syrian, would raise the specter of Syrian hegemony and involve the risk of Israeli intervention. And, if they were an Arab force as Egypt proposed, it would tilt toward the PLO, and Syria (and probably Israel) would surely resist."[15]

The answer should be "a little of both, but not too much of either to raise a reaction," that is, a predominantly Syrian Arab force limited in size and geographic location, again as was later mediated with great delicacy between Israel and Syria by the United States.[16] The intervention was not needed in the south, where a foreign military presence would have concerned the Israelis, but in central Lebanon where the fighting was located. At the same time, parties with historic ties to Lebanon—Jordan, Morocco, Saudi Arabia, backed by the United States and France—needed to join in pressing Franjieh and Karami, as well as the participating parties, for the formation of a national unity government. An Arab economic assistance plan for reconstruction and development of Lebanon, allocated in such a way that the various sectarian factions would benefit, would have provided the different parties with incentives to adhere to its provisions.

An Arab initiative failed to materialize for the simple but compound reason that its rejection by all the principal parties was not countered by the mediators. On the receiving end, Franjieh poetically declared Lebanon "would resist any Arab forces with all means and resources."[17] On the intervening side, Syria was suspicious of any Arab role in Lebanon, although less than six months later, in June 1976, it did accept the principle of Arabization of the conflict and participated in a special meeting for Arab foreign ministers that established an Arab (but principally Syrian) peacekeeping force. It took the collapse of the February initiative and the renewed outbreak of violence to bring Syria to seek greater involvement and Arab legitimization for its role. What was required, therefore, was the will to act consistently with the awareness that the parties—notably Asad—had of the impending disaster.

The proposed constitutional reform was indeed a "fifty-percent solution," but as such it was too much for the status quo politicians and too little for the Muslim revolutionaries. It was rejected, in turn, because all of the forces were hurting but none felt stalemated; although their escalations had reached an impasse in early 1976, they continued to look for an opportunity to escalate their way out, as the LNM had tried to do in March. The militias had invested too much blood in the conflict already to give in without some tangible benefit, and the proposed reform was considered too close to the status quo to be satisfying to them; they still had every expectation of overturning the status quo by force. Yet the proposed reform (as well as the violence) was too disruptive to the politicians, who had not yet lost. By not using the Constitutional Document as the basis for further discussion, within limits imposed by the Syrian-Arab force and with incentives provided by the Arab aid package, the mediators were unable to bridge the generation gap.

To be effective, an Arab initiative would have had to overcome these obstacles. Arab states' support for the essentially Syrian initiative could have bought their way into the process. The fellow Arab states also would have been useful in convincing the Lebanese militias to look more favorably on the reform package and at least begin a bargaining process over its details. French involvement would have been helpful to convince the Lebanese status quo parties, and French president Valéry Giscard d'Estaing had already indicated a willingness to play a role, even to the point of sending troops. No direct U.S. role was required, but U.S. encouragement for the effort and assistance in keeping its implications clear to the other Mideast parties would have been likely and helpful. "The conversation certainly demonstrated our central role in the area," noted Kissinger about a moment in the evolution of the situation two months later; "We alone were in touch with all the parties."[18] But "American officials, rather than having a grand policy for dealing with the Lebanon crisis or the Palestinians, were confused and perplexed by the internecine war in Lebanon. . . . Kissinger and Ford, quite simply, had no game in mind, other than to prevent a full-scale Arab-Israeli war. Apart from urging the evacuation of Americans in Lebanon, the US did little."[19]

Thus, the proposed reform package would have required international cooperation and coordination behind a process of patient negotiation, rather than a take-it-or-leave-it offer or a minimal try-it-and-drop-it effort at a mere conflict-managing cease-fire. The Syrians kept sending high-level missions over the period, but their unilateral efforts were by that very fact off-putting to many of the parties, including erstwhile allies such as Junblatt and the Palestinians at various times. The Syrian effort needed support and diffusion. It also would have required limits on alternative courses of action in the event that rejection were considered, that is, potential sanctions to lock the parties into a stalemate. The Syrian military engagement of 4,000 troops threatened in early April, decided at the end of May, effected on 1 June, and expanded five-fold at Riyadh in mid-October would have constituted a considerable threat, had it been issued in February.[20]

The stalemate continued to harden over the five months following February 1976.[21] As a result, an Arab summit in Riyadh decreed a new cease-fire for 21 October. Four days later, a follow-up summit in Cairo ratified the Riyadh decision and established the details for implementing the cease-fire, which included an Arab Deterrent Force (ADF) of up to 25,000 Syrian troops and a total of 4,000–5,000 troops from five other countries. But the military stalemate was accompanied by a political deadlock, with neither the reformers nor the transformers able to impose their will nor the conservatives able to eliminate their challenge, "leading to a vacuum at the centre of power."[22] Thus the civil war was suspended, until revived two years later by its Israeli-Palestinian dimension, but the basic problem of the deadlocked political system remained unresolved.

So the end of the war was only superficial and apparent, since the conferees at Riyadh and Cairo were only concerned with an end to the fighting but did not address the underlying issue of constitutional reform.[23] The principles agreed to in the Constitutional Document were not part of the Riyadh agreement, and so the management of the conflict was not linked to any effort at its resolution. Authoritative efforts to turn the sense of hurt into a sense of stalemate at the time that the Constitutional Document was available for further discussion and implementation would have put a purpose behind the cease-fire and begun to restore the Lebanese state.

November 1979: Withdrawals of external forces, weaknesses in militia leadership, and attempts at internal reform opened the potential for Arab and Lebanese efforts to restore the Lebanese polity.

The years following the Riyadh and Cairo agreements and the introduction of the ADF were punctuated by diverse external and internal attempts to settle the internal and external aspects of the Lebanese problem, with little coordination beyond rhetorical references between the two. In July 1977, representatives of Lebanon, the PLO, and the six ADF countries, including Syria, met to deal with the military aspects of the situation, such as a withdrawal of the PLO from the Israeli border area and its replacement by the Lebanese army and the ADF. But in September, the Israeli Defense Force (IDF) crossed the border to assist Christian militias in their fights with the PLO and the LNM militias, and then in mid-March 1978 Israeli forces invaded southern Lebanon. The UN Security Council called for an Israeli withdrawal and established the optimistically named UN Interim Force in Lebanon (UNIFIL), still in place more than a quarter century later.[24] The IDF partially withdrew from south Lebanon over the next months, leaving a proxy force of the "Free Lebanon Army" under Major Saad Haddad. In mid-October, the ADF parties again convened in Beiteddin and again called for the full implementation of the Riyadh-Cairo resolutions. But six months later, the five Arab components of the ADF went home, leaving the Syrians in charge. Between August 1978 and March 1979, the Syrian forces also withdrew from Beirut and central Lebanon and redeployed into the Beqa' valley and northern Lebanon. Throughout the same period and the coming year, Syria was weakened domestically by Islamist unrest and government repression.

Domestically, after the installation of Elias Sarkis as presidential successor to Franjieh in September 1976 and the selection of a government under Salim Hoss in December, a parliamentary committee representing all sectarian groups was created in October 1977 to devise a national reconciliation plan, and a Parliamentary Document was adopted on 24 April 1978 calling for the dissolution of the militias and the reconstruction of the army and its implantation in southern Lebanon. The consensus laid the groundwork for the reform of the army in the National Defense Law of 13 March 1979; it embodied some of the long-demanded reforms by reducing the president's powers and placing the army under the control of the government and a civilian defense minister. Still, the reconstituted army was unable to prevail against either the militias or the PLO, as the various internal and external declarations had called for. Sarkis continued to work on a constitutional document in consultation with the parties, finally producing his fourteen Axioms of National Reconciliation in March 1980.

During the same period, some significant changes in leadership were produced by internecine assassinations, throwing important organizations into debilitating struggles for succession. Kamal Junblatt was killed in March 1977, leaving his son, Walid, in charge of the Druze Progressive Socialist Party (PSP). But Kamal's assassination deprived the larger LNM of a leader for over a year; not until the fighting of 1982–1983 was Walid able to assert himself as full successor in his father's role.[25] Tony Franjieh, son of the president and head of the Maronite but pro-Syrian Marada militia, was assassinated by a Phalanx squad in mid-June 1978, consummating a bitter rift in the Christian camp as Bashir Gemayel drove to control the LF. And Imam Musa Sadr, founder of the Shiite Movement of the Disinherited, disappeared in Libya in August 1978, leaving the successor movement Amal in a leadership struggle until Nabih Berri was confirmed in 1980.

The challenge was to find a moment when internal and external efforts could take advantage of these developments and then to find an agent to coordinate the efforts. An Arab summit in Tunis in mid-November reaffirmed all previous conference declarations from Riyadh to Beiteddin while trying to heal the split in the Arab camp produced by the Camp David agreements and the Washington Peace Treaty between Egypt and Israel. Arab summits do not often produce much action, but it would have been an appropriate moment to follow up with constructive attention to the Lebanese internal situation. Economic conditions in Lebanon had improved over the three years since the Syrian takeover; the Israelis had been forced by international pressure to withdraw from the south and the Syrians to withdraw from the center and Beirut. Some of the new brand of leadership of 1980 had not yet been installed in the competing militias.[26] The opportunity for statesmanship was present.

Sarkis's own efforts to produce a document and Hoss's efforts to build a government of national unity could have been aided by an extension of the Riyadh, Cairo, Beiteddin, and Tunis conferences that would have focused on the internal reconstitution of the state. The formula for reform was already available and would be repeated each time until the final imposed agreement in Taif a decade later, and an indicative portion of it had already been prepared in the National Defense Law.

The agent was less immediately obvious, and that was the problem at the time. A catalyzer was needed to seize the opportunity and bring the external parties of the region to bear on the internal efforts at reconstitution. Saudi Arabia had been such an agent in the past and proved to be again in the future. From the outside, the Vatican's secretary of state Cardinal Agostino Casaroli was to appear on a conciliation mission in March 1980, soon after Sarkis's announcement of his fourteen axioms, and that mission could have been advanced to work on a November démarche. The UN Secretary-General and Security Council also had placed a challenge before themselves in creating UNIFIL, a peacekeeping measure that called for a peacemaking as its natural complement. As in other cases, temporarily effective peacekeeping lulled rather than goaded peacemaking. The UN force was initially effective but limited in its long-term impact in promoting Israeli withdrawal and Palestinian restraint and required a second round of effort to turn conflict management toward resolution. "Yet the United Nations did not activate a diplomatic response as long as the level of violence in southern Lebanon remained at a tolerable level and UNIFIL performed its buffer function relatively well."[27] Unfortunately, the United States was preoccupied with an election that November and with the Iranian cliffhanger that embittered its Mideast relations. The Arab states were pretty much on their own, and they missed the opportunity.

July–August 1982: The new unstable situation created by the Israeli invasion of Lebanon provided the opportunity for a different Reagan initiative than the one produced, focusing on the Lebanese problem, bringing in Syria, and working on an internal peace agreement.[28]

Despite the quiescent situation in Lebanon, the escalating conflict between the PLO and Israel finally burst into interstate war on 6 June 1982 as the IDF launched its blitzkrieg to Beirut—Operation Peace for Galilee. U.S. envoy Philip Habib mediated a cease-fire on 10 June just south of Beirut and the Beirut-Damascus road, but the Israeli army continued to press on, joining pincers across the strategic road on 20–22 June and penetrating particularly the Palestinian-dominated area of West Beirut. In addition to the 13,000 deaths among civilians and combatants, the most prominent political casualty was U.S. secretary of state Alexander Haig, who had given a yellow light to the invasion and was replaced by George Shultz at the end of June. Habib continued his mediation to the end of July, when he achieved the evacuation of the PLO camps of West Beirut and the establishment of a new security regime for southern Lebanon.

A number of events made a new policy statement imperative and imposed a deadline for it: the completion of the PLO withdrawal from West Beirut at the end of August, an impending Israeli cabinet meeting at the beginning of September, an upcoming Arab summit in Fez on 6 September. The initiative was both long and short in planning: the Reagan administration had been looking for a while for a comprehensive Mideast policy, but Shultz had only been appointed secretary of state on 25 June, his predecessor did not give up his activities until 5 July, and Shultz was installed only on 16 July, with a charge to produce a reassessment of U.S. Mideast policy.

However badly it may have done so, the United States seized the opportunity.[29] President Reagan's speech of 1 September outlined a number of elements that constituted the new U.S. policy initiative. Assuming that the Israeli invasion had settled the Lebanese question and "left us with a new opportunity for Middle East peace," Reagan proposed a settlement of the Palestinian question by joining the West Bank to Jordan (a position the Arab summit in Rabat had rejected in 1974). Under the "peace for security" formula of UN Security Council Resolution 242, Reagan indicated that the amount of security (territory) granted would determine the amount of peace gained and that settlements would be absolutely frozen and many given up in the end.

The speech came at an opportune time. The Israeli invasion had accomplished its primary goal by producing the PLO evacuation. American Jewish opinion, as well as public opinion in Israel, was deeply split by the invasion. Syria had been shown to be powerless to stop the Israelis, yet had retained its predominance in Lebanon. Syria had been relieved of its Soviet-supplied air force by the Israeli attack and abandoned by its Soviet supplier thereafter. "The Lebanese were ready for reconciliation. They were tired of fighting. Properly led and relieved of the domination of foreign armies and the interference of foreign intelligence services, they could perhaps have resolved their problems."[30] In a word, there was a mutually hurting stalemate, although as often happens, ripeness was a fleeting moment.

In addition, there was also a circle to square. The Israelis under Prime Minister Menachem Begin and Defense Minister Ariel Sharon were in a classical situation of entrapment, in no hurry to withdraw from Lebanon and unrealistically hopeful of extracting a peace treaty from Lebanon at gunpoint.[31] The Syrians were spoilers, eager only not to let the Israelis withdraw from Lebanon so that they themselves would not have to do the same. At the same time, the Syrians held the veto over the Israeli-Lebanese agreement by their own refusal to withdraw first, as Israel demanded, and to have their invited presence considered as equivalent to Israel's imposed presence on Lebanese soil. Incentives to Syria tended to be disincentives to Israel and vice versa. The Lebanese were in the throes of leadership change, in a new presidential election on 23 August by a parliament elected ten years earlier under a political agreement that was the subject of the civil war. The leading candidate from the rising generation, Bashir Gemayel of the Phalanxes, had cruelly destroyed his rivals for leadership of the Christian forces but was ambiguously tied to the Israelis and unambiguously at odds with the other Lebanese militia leaders.[32]

Reagan's initiative was a ham-handed attempt at peacemaking in the Middle East. By not addressing the parties' concerns, the administration let the moment slip from its hands and crash on the floor. By ignoring Syria in the speech and giving it scant attention in the subsequent negotiations, the United States gave Syria no incentive to drop its spoiler position and join the initiative. By telling Israel that if it played along, the next U.S. step would be to relieve it of the West Bank and Gaza and their settlements, the United States gave Israel no incentive to accelerate its withdrawal. By telling the parties that movement on Palestine would await progress on Lebanon the United States gave both Israel and Syria reasons to impede progress on Lebanon. By focusing subsequent efforts on an Israel-Lebanon peace agreement, the United States weighted down a contested Lebanese government (weakened all the more by the assassination of Bashir Gemayel on 14 September and the election of his weaker brother, Amin, on 23 September) with an unbearable burden for any national reconciliation. By introducing an unbalanced and unacceptable Israeli-Lebanese peace agreement that made Israeli withdrawal dependent on Syrian and PLO withdrawal, the United States added a new problem to the Lebanese account, not a new solution of any of the already present problems, blocking access to other initiatives, inciting new escalations, and bringing the state to full collapse.

Although the key objective of the United States was "the restoration of the authority of the central government of Lebanon,"[33] the opportunity was missed for a full focus on the Lebanese problem, with attention to the carrots and sticks—the positive and negative incentives—that the policy required. Lebanon needed above all a supportive agreement that would reinforce the position of its shaky government among the many sectors to which it was responsible. It is impossible to foreclose absolutely the chance of an idiosyncratic event such as Bashir Gemayel's assassination by a pro-Syrian before he even acceded to office, but an initiative focusing on Lebanese state reform and restoration and a more even-handed foreign involvement from the beginning might have had such an effect. For Israel, a better initiative meant avoiding mention of ultimate goals and next steps and concentrating on restoring a Lebanon that could function as a state and control the remaining Palestinians without a PLO, an Israeli interest. Tough language and assorted measures would be needed to produce the rapid withdrawal of Israeli forces that was the beginning of the process. Israel achieved removal of the PLO by its invasion; it could not expect to be paid several times for the same thing, by the removal of the Syrians as well. For Syria, a better initiative meant recognition of its role in the process and in the fate of Lebanon. Like Israel, Syria had legitimate interests in Lebanon and initially entered Lebanon in 1976 with U.S. acquiescence (more explicit than that assumed by Israel six years later).[34] The two countries' military withdrawal needed to be partial and not explicitly linked; Syria perceived its military presence to be the result of a Lebanese request and accepted by the other Arab states, whereas Israel's presence was the result of an invasion.

Furthermore, greater U.S. resources were required in the negotiations. Although Habib conducted negotiations for much of 1981 and 1982, he left the job to Morris Draper, his deputy, throughout the beginning of 1983 and returned only in mid-April; Secretary Shultz came to the area for the first time nearly two weeks later, in a region of the world trained to expect the attentions of the U.S. secretary of state and even the president. Shultz negotiated with tenacity but only between Beirut and Jerusalem, leaving Damascus for a notification visit after the agreement had been signed.[35] That kind of heavy weight behind a more balanced and initially limited agreement was what was required to get the bulk of the Israeli army out of Lebanon and restore a Lebanese state.

Commentators have wondered why someone as well versed in Arab affairs as Shultz could have designed such a flawed creation as a major U.S. initiative.[36] There was plenty of warning and dissent within U.S. government circles from before the announcement of the Reagan plan. On one hand, the winning consensus under Shultz, although much more pro-Arab than under Haig, was still opposed to making any payoffs to the Syrians, feeling that they were beaten and undeserving. On the other hand, supporters of the peace initiative felt that the moment was ripe for the larger initiative in late 1982, if only it could be concluded at the time. Both missed the point that Israel had no incentive to leave Lebanon, and when Israel was done blocking the agreement, Syria was ready to take up the opposition role. A confused sense of friends and enemies and of opportunities and incentives led the first hand to hide the second. As a result, when Bashir Gemayel was assassinated and his weaker brother elected president, the Israelis dragged out their withdrawal and overplayed their demands on a weakened Lebanon, the Syrians disdainfully rejected the peace agreement, 241 U.S. and 55 French troops of the Multi-National Force were killed in a terrorist bombing, and the United States gradually reneged on its assurances of support to Lebanon and retreated from the Middle East conflict, its tail between its legs.[37]

March 1984: Reconciliation sessions at Geneva and Lausanne
offered an opportunity for Saudi Arabia and the United States,
along with Syria, to add participants, incentives, and guarantees
to the Lausanne agreement.[38]

Syria followed up its denunciation of the Lebanese-Israeli peace agreement of 17 May 1983 with an organization of the opposition to Gemayel into a National Salvation Front in July. In the following months, after initial government success in taking over West Beirut, the Druze militia from the National Salvation Front inflicted defeats on Gemayel's Lebanese forces in the Shuf, and terrorists inflicted embarrassing casualties on the Americans, French, and Israelis. As a result, Gemayel was forced into a national reconciliation process, beginning with a series of meetings in Geneva in October and November. The conference was the product of an impressive effort of shuttle diplomacy by U.S. special representative Robert McFarlane, Saudi ambassador Prince Bandar, and Syrian intermediaries and was observed by U.S., UK, French, Italian, and Egyptian diplomats in the corridors. But it was preceded by a week by the 299 multinational force (MNF) casualties and was restricted in its composition by Syrian vetoes.[39]

When the Geneva meetings failed in their attempt to reach an agreement on the restructuring of the Lebanese political system, Gemayel told the delegates that he would meet with Reagan to find a solution to the problem caused by the 17 May agreement with Israel, which lay as a dead tree across the road to further discussion. The parties returned to fighting and Shiite militias took back West Beirut at the same time as the U.S. forces were "redeployed offshore" and the U.S. assurances of support were equivocated. The fighting between Shiite and Druze militia forces and the Lebanese army in West Beirut was described by Beirut residents as the most "intense and frightening" battles the city had witnessed since the beginning of the civil war.[40] At the beginning of February 1984, the Muslim ministers in government resigned under pressure from their respective communities, followed the next day by Prime Minister Shafik al-Wazzan.[41] Moreover, Shiite leader Nabih Berri joined Druze leader Walid Junblatt in demanding the resignation of President Gemayel and the abrogation of the May peace agreement.

The United States became part of the fighting on 6 February, when U.S. fighter planes and naval gunners bombarded the bases of anti-Gemayel militias in the hills overlooking the capital after U.S. marines at the Beirut airport had come under attack. The battleship *New Jersey* continued to fire hundreds of rounds at artillery positions of Syria and its Lebanese allies in Lebanon's eastern and central mountains throughout February.[42] At the same time, President Reagan ordered the 1,400 marines in the Beirut area to begin a phased withdrawal to Navy ships offshore.[43]

To arrest the deterioration of the political and security situation, the Saudis—in consultation with the Lebanese government—formulated a proposal to end the fighting. It included abrogation of the Israeli-Lebanese agreement, simultaneous withdrawal of all foreign forces including the Syrians and Israelis from Lebanon, introduction of political reforms, and the formation of a national unity government to implement this formula.[44] Gemayel accepted the Saudi proposal, but Syria rejected it, again on grounds that it represented a victory for Israel and an unfair equation of Syria with Israel in simultaneous withdrawal. The Americans also disapproved of the call for abrogation of the Israeli-Lebanese agreement that the United States had brokered and stated that they would not help bring the Israelis around to the proposal.[45]

The Saudis continued their mediation efforts in Lebanon despite the rejection of their plan. The Syrians gave the Saudis a counterproposal that included a promise to help the Lebanese president form a national unity government and call for the convening of a national dialogue conference, if he would promise to cancel the Lebanese-Israeli agreement. Again, Gemayel accepted the Syrian offer and on 5 March, the Lebanese cabinet abrogated the May 1983 agreement, clearing the way for a Syrian-backed cease-fire and renewed national reconciliation talks among the country's warring sectarian factions.[46]

The national dialogue conference started on 12 March in Lausanne with the participation of President Gemayel, eight factional leaders, and observers from Syria and Saudi Arabia. On 20 March, and after eight days of talks, the conference again broke up without any agreement on a new power-sharing formula or the formation of a national unity government, the two chief goals of the meeting. To save face and avert the appearance of a total failure, the participants issued a bland statement that left out all of the contentious points and called mainly for the creation of a higher security committee under the president to oversee the implementation of the shaky cease-fire arranged at the outset of the talks, the end of all defamatory press campaigns, the establishment of a thirty-two-member constitutional commission to submit proposals in six months, and continued consultations among the nine conference participants meeting upon request of the president.[47]

On return from Lausanne, a national union government was formed under Karami, which in turn issued a ministerial declaration on 23 May, reaffirming the provisions of the Constitutional Document of eight years previous and adding statements on neighboring relations. The search for internal reform continued, but "it foundered in the absence of active regional or international backing."[48]

The Lausanne national dialogue presented an opportunity for Syria and Saudi Arabia, with the support of the United States, to become actively involved in mediation to bridge the gap between the Lebanese factions and secure a successful agreement. This would have required three elements: creative proposals to bring together the different parties' positions, Syrian-Saudi cooperation and pressure, and expanded participation at the conference. There was a strong conviction among Muslim and Christian leaders that the National Pact of 1943 was no longer satisfactory in the light of political and demographic changes, but there was a wide gap in their perceptions of the nature and scope of changes needed.

Shiite leader Berri presented a proposal at the conference that stated that Lebanese society was unitary and therefore members of different communities should be treated equally on the basis of their merit and not their religious affiliation. The proposal called for the abolition of political confessionalism and an end to allocation of positions through a quota system based on religious affiliation. But it also called for the creation of a senate with equal representation for all major religious communities and a shift of power from the Maronite president to the Sunni Muslim prime minister. These proposals were rejected by the Christian leaders, who argued that the whole notion of nonconfessionalism was unrealistic because of the intense religious feelings on both sides and the Islamic theological position against full secularism. Furthermore, they argued that abolition of the confessional quota system would merely transfer appointments from intracommunal to intercommunal struggle.[49]

To break the impasse, Syria and Saudi Arabia would have had to join forces behind a compromise based on their previous proposals and already accepted by the Lebanese parties. It would have involved the restructured confessional elements of the Syrian proposal accepted by the Lebanese parties in January 1976, which confirmed the confessional allocation of "the three presidents," strengthened the Muslim prime minister, equalized parliamentary representation, and established a civil service merit system. These features could be paired with elements from the Saudi plan of February 1984, notably with ideas about a national unity government (which was to occur in April), political reforms, and Saudi commitment to help in implementing the formula. Other elements to be added to that proposal, which had already been accepted by the different parties, would include administrative decentralization, especially in designing and implementing social and economic development plans, as a compromise between the Christian demand for a federal state with autonomous cantons and the Muslim demand for a unitarian state. Additional components included disbanding the militias and reinstituting the Lebanese army on a nonsectarian basis, disseminating a culture of harmony and equality throughout the media and the educational system, and adopting a comprehensive reconstruction plan with the help of foreign donors, notably Saudi Arabia itself.

Some basic ideas about appropriate mediation that would have been useful to help the process were available at the time.[50] One was the need to include in the negotiations all parties who were capable of blocking them, particularly if they were to veto the result mainly because they were not included in its creation. Khaddam was firm about restricting participation to the militia leaders, but he erred on several counts: not only could the parties he excluded dash the results, but also in many cases the individuals excluded were politicians used to the art of bargaining and compromise more than were the militia fighters. Though representatives of major political groups and military factions were present in Lausanne, many of them, notably in the Christian side, represented the old guard. The two aging former Maronite Christian presidents participating in the talks—83-year-old Camille Chamoun and 72-year-old Suleiman Franjieh—as well as the 78-year-old Phalanx leader, Pierre Gemayel (who would die in August), were entrenched in the past and found it difficult to compromise on beliefs they had held for many years. Christian participation should have been expanded to include younger political figures and other Christian communities such as the Greek Orthodox, the Catholics, and the Armenians as well as Karami and an additional Maronite.[51] Their presence would doubtless have complicated the negotiations but, as on many instances, would have had a good chance of buying the opponents into the agreement and in any case would not have produced a worse result.

But it would have taken some negotiating skill, which the Syrian mediator Abd el-Halim Khaddam did not have. Perhaps the most surprising development was his inability to bring about a compromise. Khaddam had been expected to play a much more forceful role but seemed to waver in his support first for the Muslims' demands and then for the Christians' and proved unable to bring the two together. Although Syria entered the Lausanne talks as the dominant power in Lebanon after the abrogation of the May agreement, it nevertheless faced a big dilemma in a conference where every Lebanese party expected to be rewarded for its role in the abrogation. The Muslims expected to be rewarded for their early opposition of the agreement, but also President Gemayel and his supporters expected to be rewarded for accepting the abrogation. Therefore Syria was in a delicate but balanced position and did not exert enough pressure on the different parties to reach a compromise. Khaddam was "the master tactician, and the experienced mechanic in the cantankerous Lebanese machine."[52] But as a mediator, he proved to be weak and even offensive.

The other notion from mediation literature is that often "third parties need other third parties if they are to work efficiently and effectively in nurturing the conditions for peace."[53] The Syrian dilemma could have opened the door for other mediators to play a more active role. Even though the Syrians declined all efforts to cooperate with the Lebanese president, they could not say no to King Fahd, whom they considered a special friend. Saudi Arabia, notably in the person of Foreign Minister Saud al-Faisal, needed to be present, not merely sending messages from afar. Saudi Arabia would have completed the carrots-and-sticks functions of a mediator; Syria's 40,000 troops were an effective sanction, and Saudi Arabia's financial resources were a potential inducement—a combination of realpolitik and riyal politics.[54] Instead of playing the role of an observer in Lausanne, Saudi Arabia could have secured a more active role in the bargaining process, promising to provide financial assistance for reconstruction in case an agreement was reached, since it had already been part of the process leading to the conference and was the bankroller for poor regimes in the area (including Syria). Such a promise would have given the participants an incentive to take the talks more seriously and could have provided Saudi Arabia with more influence to exert on the different parties. For the militias, fighting had become a way of life and no longer painful, no matter how the population suffered, and so some combined persuasion, participation, and pressure would have been needed from the mediators. Despite a wary relationship, Syria and Saudi Arabia had worked together in the past, and Saudi Arabia was the main underwriter of Syria's weak economy. But Saudi Arabia needed to be pushed into a more active role and its efforts coordinated. U.S. participation in the Lausanne conference as an observer, by a more knowledgeable diplomat than special envoy Donald Rumsfeld, would have enabled greater coordination with the additional mediator while balancing the presence of the Muslim mediators, Syria and Saudi Arabia, and reducing the suspicions of the Christian camp. Besides its psychological impact, the United States could have also provided assurances for the implementation of any agreement and have promised to provide arms and training for the new Lebanese army and economic and technical assistance for the reconstruction of Lebanon.

The conference failed because Syria decided to delay action on reforms. Khaddam told his Lebanese counterpart Elie Salem that the participants at the conference were useless and that most did not represent the new Lebanon. The Syrian thought that it would be better to get the new generation of leaders together in some sort of dialogue and arrive at a general arrangement.[55] But, even though in a position of strength, he did nothing to pursue his own recommendation. The escalation of the Iran-Iraq war made the Saudis concentrate more on the situation in the Gulf and become less attentive to the situation in Lebanon. The renewed Lebanese conflict raged on for another three years, completing the destruction of parts of the country, until finally the two Arab countries called the parties to a conference in Riyadh and engaged new mediators, most notably Lakhdar Brahimi of Algeria, to produce an agreement that ended the war, confirmed Syria's protectorate, and instituted some of the reforms that had been on the table since 1976.

It is not merely lives of some 120,000 Lebanese (nearly 5 percent of the population) that earlier interventions could have saved, nor even the productivity and wealth of Beirut as the financial and commercial capital of the Levant. Lebanon registered zero population growth over the period of the war and a drop in gross domestic product (GDP) at the end of the war to less than a third of its 1975 level.[56] Although these considerations are of concern outside the country and its region because of the Lebanese diaspora and Lebanon's early integration into a globalizing economy, they are less important to the strategic thinking of the Cold War era and its post–Cold War prolongation than potential political advantages. If arrested within a year of its outbreak, the Lebanese civil war would have left an evolving society with a role to play in the incipient Middle East peace process, freer of both Syrian and Israeli dominance. Peaceful settlement of the internal distribution of power issue would have left the Palestinian issue to be dealt with on its merits, rather than fueling the domestic issue.[57] A different Reagan plan half a decade later, played with greater vigor, would again have produced a stronger Lebanese polity and, ironically, would have left the United States in a better position to pursue its other Middle East goals rather then having them all pull each other under. It also would have begun a process of wooing Syria by working on common goals, a process that did not take shape until a decade later in the third Gulf War. Serious diplomatic and military engagement behind the Lausanne and Damascus agreements in 1983 and 1984 would have extended U.S.-Arab cooperation at little cost, since the basic agreement had already been laid, awaiting implementation, and it would have left the United States in a much better position to pursue an Israeli-Jordanian-Palestinian peace agreement in 1985.[58]

Notes

1. I am grateful to Mohammed Kamal Shahda for his valuable assistance and to the following for their helpful comments: Graeme Bannerman, William Quandt, Adeed Dawisha, Iliya Harik, Michael Hudson, George Irani, Farid el-Khazen, Richard Parker, Elizabeth Picard, Harold Saunders, and Talcott Seelye.

2. Picard, "The Political Economy of Civil War in Lebanon."

3. el-Khazen, *The Breakdown of the State in Lebanon,* chap. 21.

4. Barry Crane, "Lebanon's New Order," *Newsweek,* 9 February 1976, 33; "Lebanese Cabinet Approves Reforms," *Facts on File,* 21 February 1976, 125A1; Dawisha, *Syria and the Lebanese Crisis;* Rabinovich, *The War for Lebanon.* I am grateful to Mohammed Kamal Shahda, Theresa Kuhn, and Julien Aubert for research assistance in this instance.

5. Salibi, *Crossroads to Civil War,* 140. State collapse was in fact only beginning.

6. Haddad, *Lebanon,* 45–49; Marius Deeb, *Militant Islamic Movements in Lebanon: Origins, Social Basis, and Ideology* (Washington, DC: Center for Contemporary Arab Studies, Georgetown University, 1986); Mary-Jane Deeb and Marius Deeb, "Internal Negotiations in a Centralist Conflict," in Zartman, *Elusive Peace,* 126–129; el-Khazen, *The Breakdown of the State in Lebanon, 1967–1976,* 315–317, 327–332; Dawisha, *Syria and the Lebanese Crisis,* 90–93.

7. *New York Times,* 19 January 1976, A1; 21 January 1976, A13.

8. *New York Times,* 22 January 1976, A1.

9. *New York Times,* 23 January 1976, A1; Henry A. Kissinger, *Years of Renewal,* 1026–1027; el-Khazen, *The Breakdown of the State in Lebanon, 1967–1976,* chap. 24; Rabinovich, *The War for Lebanon, 1970–1985,* 50, 217, and 201–236 for President Asad's account of the subsequent events, in his remarkable speech of 20 July 1976. By June, there had been twenty-three cease-fires since the war began.

10. Dawisha, *Syria and the Lebanese Crisis,* 120.

11. Kissinger, *Years of Renewal,* 1049–1050.

12. *New York Times,* 27 January 1976, A3.

13. *New York Times,* 23 January 1976, A1; Haddad, *Lebanon* 51. The PLA, although technically the armed wing of the PLO, was in fact the Palestinian auxiliary of the Syrian army even though Syria could not fully control its activities; Kissinger, *Years of Renewal,* 1026, 1039; Rabinovich, *The War for Lebanon, 1970–1985,* 49.

14. Dawisha, *Syria and the Lebanese Crisis,* 122.

15. Kissinger, *Years of Renewal,* 1040.

16. Ibid., 1045–1046; Quandt, *Peace Process* (1993), 246–249, 560; Dawisha, *Syria and the Lebanese Crisis,* 92.

17. Haley and Snider, *Lebanon in Crisis,* 277.

18. Kissinger, *Years of Renewal,* 1039. This is probably an exaggeration: Syria had good contacts with all parties, and France maintained its connections, considered by many to be more neutral than the Americans.

19. Quandt, *Peace Process* (1993), 248. This statement was omitted in the 2001 edition.

20. Michael Hudson suggested even earlier: "in the spring or summer of 1975 instead of a year later." "Domestic Content and Perspectives," 147.

21. el-Khazen, *The Breakdown of the State in Lebanon, 1967–1976,* 355–356.

22. Ibid., 367.

23. See Zartman and Kremenyuk, *Peace vs Justice.*

24. UN Security Council Resolutions 425 of 19 March 1978 and 426 of 20 March 1978.

25. Rabinovich, *The War for Lebanon, 1970–1985,* 99, 180–181.

26. On the new leadership and its social origins and political attitudes that differed from those of the preceding generation, see Nasr, Irani, and Sams, *Working Paper: Conference on Lebanon,* 42–44; and Picard, "The Political Economy of Civil War in Lebanon."

27. Weinberger, "How Peace Keeping Becomes Intervention," 163.

28. Part 3 of Parker, *The Politics of Miscalculation in the Middle East,* is a superb study. See also Young, *Missed Opportunities for Peace;* and Quandt, *Peace Process* (both the 1993 and the 2001 editions), chap. 8, another definitive study. I am grateful for the research assistance of Elizabeth Kime, Sasha Kishinchand, Safia Hachicha, and Walter Ferrara in this instance. Probably the greatest missed opportunity, in the sense of a wrong decision, was the green light given— or at least interpreted by—General Ariel Sharon for Operation Peace for Galilee, which delegitimated the Lebanese Front, Gemayel, and the United States in the eyes of many Lebanese people.

29. For affirmations of the window of opportunity, see Gerson, *The Kirkpatrick Mission,* 142.

30. Parker, *The Politics of Miscalculation in the Middle East,* 182.

31. Paul Meerts, "Entrapment, Escalation and Negotiation," in Zartman and Faure, *Escalation and Negotiation.*

32. Parker, *The Politics of Miscalculation in the Middle East,* 173.

33. Gerson, *The Kirkpatrick Mission,* 142.

34. Kissinger, *Years of Renewal,* 1043–1050, 1056.

35. Yaniv, *Dilemmas of Security; Los Angeles Times,* 11 May 1983.

36. In negotiations after a war between Israel and the PLO on Lebanese territory attributable to Israeli aggression, "provoked" or not, Shultz's comment to Lebanese foreign minister Elie A. Salem, "star[ing him] straight in the eye, 'Elie, I must remind you Israel won the war, you lost,'" indicated how skewed the supposedly pro-Arab mediator's perception was; Salem, *Violence and Diplomacy in Lebanon*, 28. Parker, *The Politics of Miscalculation in the Middle East*, chap. 10, gives a scrupulously careful and fair assessment of this question.

37. The gradual dilution of U.S. commitments is coolly recounted by Salem, *Violence and Diplomacy in Lebanon*.

38. Thomas Friedman, "Lebanese at Odds," *New York Times*, 19 March 1984.

39. Salem, *Violence and Diplomacy in Lebanon*, chap. 5.

40. "Rebels Capture West Beirut," *New York Times*, 7 February 1984, A1.

41. Bernard Gwertman, "Lebanese Cabinet Quits as Protests by Moslems Grow," *New York Times*, 6 February 1984, A1.

42. Richard Halloran, "U.S. Warships and Jets Pound Lebanon Targets," *New York Times*, 7 February 1984, A17; Herbert H. Denton and Bradley Graham, "U.S. Battleship Shells Gemayel's Foes," *Washington Post*, 9 February 1984, A1.

43. Bernard Gwertman, "Reagan Orders Marines Moved to Ships off Beirut but Widens Air and Sea Role," *New York Times*, 8 February 1984, A1.

44. See details of the plan in Salem, *Violence and Diplomacy in Lebanon*, 145–156; and Robin Wright, "Saudis Try Where US Failed in Lebanon," *Christian Science Monitor*, 13 February 1984, 1.

45. Jonathan C. Randal, "Syrians Reject Lebanon Peace Plan," *Washington Post*, 18 February 1984, A28; Judith Miller, "Saudi Diplomatic Efforts Settle Little, Please Few," *New York Times*, 26 February 1984, D4; Salem, *Violence and Diplomacy in Lebanon*, 14.

46. Salem, *Violence and Diplomacy in Lebanon*, 148–149; William Claiborne, "Lebanon Breaks Pact with Israel," *Washington Post*, 6 March 1984, A1.

47. David B. Ottaway, "Lebanese Conference Breaks Up; Cease-Fire Restated but Major Issues Left Unresolved," *Washington Post*, 21 March 1984, A1.

48. Nasr, Irani, and Sams, *Working Paper: Conference on Lebanon*, 87; see also 83–84. Salem, *Violence and Diplomacy in Lebanon*, 178, gave short shrift to the national union government and made no mention of the Ministerial Declaration.

49. Thomas L. Friedman, "Lebanese at Odds, Cancel a Session," *New York Times*, 19 March 1984, A10, and David B. Ottaway, "Compromise Still Eludes Lebanese," *Washington Post*, 20 March 1984, A1.

50. Stenelo, *Mediation in International Negotiations;* Pruitt, *Negotiation Behavior;* Pillar, *Negotiating Peace.* For a later summary of these ideas, see Hampson, *Nurturing Peace,* especially 207, 217, 233.

51. On the juvenescence of the leadership and the concomitant change in social origins, see the short but excellent section in Nasr, Irani, and Sams, *Working Paper: Conference on Lebanon*, 41–44; Elizabeth Picard, "Clients, Rents and Diaspora in the Lebanese War," in Arnson and Zartman, *Rethinking the Economics of War.*

52. Salem, *Violence and Diplomacy in Lebanon*, 191.

53. Hampson, *Nurturing Peace*, 233.

54. David Pollock, "Saudi Arabia's King Khaled and King Fahd," in Kellerman and Rubin, *Leadership and Negotiation in the Middle East*, 155.

55. Salem, *Violence and Diplomacy in Lebanon,* 162. Asad did get a "better" agreement from the militia leaders in the Tripartite agreement in Damascus in December 1985. That agreement went further to make Lebanon a Syrian protectorate than did the eventual Taif agreement, but the Tripartite agreement was rejected when the militia leaders returned home.

56. Nasr, Irani & Sams, *Working Paper: Conference on Lebanon,* 28.

57. Ibid., 87 passim, held that both the internal and external issues needed to be resolved at the same time. But there is no way the external—that is, the interlocked Syrian, Israeli, and Palestinian—dimension could be resolved short of a Mideast peace settlement, so to require an external settlement would be to render all efforts futile. The present discussion holds the opposite, that a concentration on an internal settlement centered about reform (as opposed to either status quo or transformation) would have provided an ingredient in an eventual overall peace settlement and in the process leading to it and that the admitted difficulties in extricating the internal issues from the external ones were all the more reason why a concerted cooperation between internal reform efforts and external mediation was so necessary.

58. See Quandt, *Peace Process* (2001), 260–265, for an account of a potential missed opportunity on the Jordanian-Palestinian front in early 1985 that fell victim to Shultz's disillusionment after the 1982–1983 events.

3

LIBERIA,
1985–1998

LIBERIA, ESTABLISHED BY THE UNITED STATES IN 1822 AS A HOME FOR FREED slaves, was ruled by their descendants, the Americo-Liberians, constituting a twentieth of the population, until 1980. At that time the regime of President William Tolbert was bloodily overthrown by Sergeant Samuel Kanyon Doe of the Krahn tribe of the indigenous African majority.[1] Although initially Doe turned to Libya and other radical regimes for support and companionship, he was gradually coaxed back into the close relationship with the United States that Liberia had traditionally enjoyed. As a result of its ties of historic responsibility with the United States—its colonizer-in-reverse—Liberia held an important position in the Cold War as the site of a diplomatic and intelligence telecommunications relay, a Voice of America transmitter, an Omega navigational station, and a strategic airfield and port and had enjoyed privileged diplomatic, political, and economic relations with past U.S. governments. Furthermore, Liberia had a more important position in the region than its small size would indicate: most of the indigenous ethnic groups had kinsmen across the borders, half of its porous boundary line was with Côte d'Ivoire and another quarter with Guinea, and its presidents had played a leading role in West African relations in the past.

Instead of preparing a democratic transition as promised, however, Doe increasingly consolidated his personal position, ran the country into the ground economically, instituted a repressive ethnically based rule, and squandered the broad support he initially had won for overthrowing the previous narrowly based regime. The new 1983 constitution, written by a broadly representative commission and accepted in a referendum, was gradually undermined by Doe's actions to perpetuate his rule, down to the point of arresting his opponents and falsifying his age by two years to

---

**Missed Opportunities:
Liberia, 1985–1998**

October 1985 Fraudulent electoral results after a U.S. warning provided the opportunity for U.S. decertification and support of the true count to end Doe's regime at a time when political forces were still intact and the army not yet cleansed of anti-Doe forces.

June 1990 A pause in the fighting provided both an opportunity for U.S. evacuation of Samuel Doe to safe retirement while Charles Taylor held off his attack on Monrovia and an occasion for influence with Taylor's NPFL.

April–July 1992 A holding cease-fire and an advancing mediation initiative offered the opportunity for inclusion of all factions and a stronger mediation role for the Carter Center's International Negotiation Network to provide details and monitored disarmament for the Yamoussoukro IV peace agreement.

July 1993 A new stalemate following intense fighting and a new framework agreement opened the opportunity for the Carter Center International Negotiation Network and the UN special representative of the Secretary-General to mediate a realistic disarmament and interim governance agreement.

July–October 1998 During a stalemate and rainy-season lull in the fighting in Sierra Leone, an agreement between the presidents of Sierra Leone and Liberia marked an opportunity to redeploy an augmented Economic Community of West African States Monitoring Group force along the common border and in the diamond areas of Sierra Leone.

---

meet the constitutional requirement of thirty-five years for presidential candidacy. At the beginning of 1985, Liberia defaulted on debt payments and the International Monetary Fund (IMF) declared it ineligible for IMF assistance; in June, Doe rejected IMF terms and conditions for new loans and was turned down by the World Bank for a structural adjustment loan. Doe's appointed Committee to Review the Present Economic Situation in Liberia reported that the country stood "on the brink of financial and economic collapse which would entail social and political chaos."[2] Voting in multiparty presidential and legislative elections in October 1985 was more or less free, but the results were rigged to give Doe a tiny majority. When Doe thus gave himself a fraudulently legitimized incumbency, the opportunity was present for the United States to decertify the results and have the true winner recognized. It did the contrary.

The U.S. decision not to sanction the removal of Doe by democratic means in 1985 left violence as the only means of political change. Dissatisfaction grew, despite repression, until Charles Taylor, one of Doe's former high officials, raised a widespread rebellion at the end of 1989. When the fighting led by Taylor's National Patriotic Front of Liberia (NPFL) hit a momentary stalemate after six months, U.S. officials moved to offer Doe an early retirement and then were suddenly pulled back from the effort, missing an opportunity for an early end to the conflict and a more gentle succession. The member states of the Economic Community of West African States (ECOWAS) intervened to save Doe and then, after his murder in September 1990, to protect the Interim Government of National Unity (IGNU) that they had established.

Fourteen separate rounds of negotiations ensued, each marked by superficial agreements that were soon broken. Toward the end of an extended round in Yamoussoukro in 1992, an agreement between the NPFL and IGNU was interrupted by the outbreak of a new rebellion by former Doe followers. There was an opportunity to make the agreement inclusive by bringing this group, the United Liberation Movement for Democracy (ULIMO), into the negotiations, but it was ignored on the grounds that new groups should not be encouraged to shoot their way into the negotiations. Similarly, a year later, another round of negotiations ending at Cotonou failed to provide the details necessary for the implementation of the agreement, leaving an opportunity for the mediators that was unfulfilled. Four more years of increasingly vicious civil war, regularly interspersed by incomplete attempts at conflict management, finally brought about an end to violence in 1996 and new elections in 1997. Threatening to bring back violence if he did not win, Taylor was elected in a relatively free election.

But the effects of the war had already spilled over into the neighborhood. Sierra Leone's diamonds—in addition to Liberian timber—were Taylor's source of wealth in the absence of a functioning economy, and Sierra Leone's own rebels, the Revolutionary United Front (RUF), were the source of rapacious anarchy in the absence of a functioning state. An agreement between the presidents of Liberia and Sierra Leone in mid-1998 during a rainy-season lull in fighting provided the opportunity for the international community, led by the United States, to hold the signatories accountable for implementation and to help their efforts. Instead, the agreement was taken to be self-implementing, and the wanton killing went on. A peace agreement signed the next year at Lomé brought the RUF into the government, but the rebels themselves broke the agreement by their behavior, alienated their people, and finally were brought under control by the UN Armed Mission in Sierra Leone (UNAMSIL) spearheaded by a resolute British contingent. Even though Sierra Leone returned to some superficial normality in the early 2000s, the basic causes of state collapse in the region remained unaddressed, and the deadly conflict broke out again in Liberia against the repressive government. When a succession of rebellions wracked neighboring Côte d'Ivoire after 1999, thugs and bandits from Liberia fomented dissidence in the bordering Ivorian regions. The same year, former ULIMO rebels began an invasion of Liberia from Guinea under the name of Liberians United for Revolution and Democracy (LURD), and together with other dissident movements finally forced Taylor into exile—ironically in Nigeria, former supporter of Doe—in March 2004. For want of effective diplomatic intervention at some very clearly indicated moments, the rot had spread, threatening the region.

Thus, among the many times when more peacemaking effort might have been effective, three groups of moments stand out clearly—one under Doe, three during the civil war, and one in the spillover of civil war into Sierra Leone.[3] All five would have changed the course of the unfolding conflict in the West African region, the first preventively and the rest by bringing civil war to an earlier end than actually occurred. The purpose of the interventions would have been the installation of a responsible, accountable state by first removing the egregious ruler who stood in the way and then by harnessing local forces under an international eye to build local institutions. The means would have involved focused and sustained diplomacy, with peacekeeping forces as well (as already employed). In all cases, an occasion for entry was present, but it would have taken some assiduous persuasion to have the parties perceive the pain of the stalemate in which they found themselves; instead, the egregious rulers and rebel leaders met a much more painful end than the way out offered by the intervenors. The agents of intervention were the same as were playing or were to play important roles in the conflict situation, but they did not invest enough skill and energy in the task, early enough and focused enough on the resolution rather than on just the superficial management of the conflict.

The first missed opportunity came in October 1985 at the electoral moment when Doe, against all pressure from the United States, confirmed the nature of his regime as a personal authoritarian structure resting on a narrow tribal base rather than the democracy his constitution promised. A U.S. decertification of the electoral results would have shown that the United States meant what it said; in the event, it showed that it did not. The lesson was to be repeated on many occasions (see below) over the next decade and a half. Decertification, accompanied by offers of asylum for Doe, would have suspended foreign aid, encouraged the opposition, and seated the legitimate winner in a democratizing regime. Instead, the rigged results closed the door for peaceful opposition and opened the way to two decades of repression and civil war.

Three strategic moments to bring that civil war under control occurred in the first half of the 1990s, in the midst of many other attempts at mediation. The agents—the U.S. government, fellow West African states, the Carter Center of Emory University—were already in place, and the moments were produced by short-lived opportunities in the course of the conflict. A crucial chance to provide asylum for Doe and a peaceful transition to a new government in June 1990 was let drop by an executive decision that U.S. interests did not warrant action; a long-standing cease-fire two years later gave involved NGOs the opportunity to bring in new players before they became spoilers and use conflict management measures to head toward conflict resolution; and again a year later a similar opportunity was available to the same parties to turn a stalemate into a resolution if the necessary tough mediation were deployed. In each case, the mediator declared satisfaction with a superficial conflict management agreement rather than focusing the parties' attention on the urgency of agreement, on inclusiveness in negotiations, on important details of resolution, and on unpleasant alternatives to nonagreement. Once these infrequent moments passed, the war went back to the bush, where it was difficult to grasp time, leaders, alternatives, and opportunities.

The fifth occasion came in the midst of the same type of situation in July 1998, when the Liberian war had spilled over into neighboring Sierra Leone. Again a momentary stalemate and a conflict-managing agreement between heads of state called for peacekeeping forces for implementation and sharp measures.

It is legitimate to ask, why count any effort to bring Charles Taylor into office a missed opportunity, when he subsequently became the new egregious ruler and the source of continuing deadly conflict? The argument is that seven years of war brought out his worst nature, made him more beholden to supportive predatory groups and child soldiers, and left him less susceptible to influence, if not control, from the outside and from his own civil society. Misread, the case may show the perfectionist wisdom of inaction; correctly read, it shows the practical need for early action.

*October 1985: Fraudulent electoral results after a U.S. warning
provided the opportunity for U.S. decertification and support of the
true count to end Doe's regime at a time when political forces were
still intact and the army not yet cleansed of anti-Doe forces.*[4]

There were a number of specific warning signs of malaise in Liberia just
preceding the 1985 elections. Former finance minister and World Bank official Ellen Johnson-Sirleaf, a leading figure in the opposition Unity Party
(UP), was arrested on 1 August for criticizing government officials in a
speech in Philadelphia and sentenced by a closed military tribunal to ten
years imprisonment. The U.S. government dispatched a special envoy to
express concern, the American ambassador informed the Liberian government that half of the $90 million in aid would be withheld unless all po-
litical prisoners were released and free and fair elections held, and Congress passed a resolution directing all aid to be suspended unless the civil
rights performance improved.

Johnson-Sirleaf was released in mid-September under U.S. pressure,
and Doe declared that U.S. conditions were met.[5] The two most popular parties, the United Peoples Party (UPP) of Bacchus Matthews and the Liberian
Peoples Party (LPP) of Amos Sawyer, were disqualified for spurious reasons, however. In the following month, opposition parties were harassed and
denied equal access to the media, but in the end electoral participation was
high and the voting peaceful, despite intimidation, irregularities, coercion,
fraud, and an absence of election observers.[6] Nonetheless, exit polls indicated a lead for the opposition Liberian Action Party (LAP) of 60–70 percent and a clear victory for its candidate, Jackson Doe (no relation to Samuel
Doe). On 16 October counting was halted, the ballot boxes moved to a
closed site, a special counting team appointed by the governmental electoral
committee chair, and after two weeks' delay, Samuel Doe's victory with
50.9 percent of the votes was announced. All observers agreed that, even
with the voting irregularities, the count was false. After some initial disagreement within the administration, the State Department hailed the beginning of a "democratic experiment" and congratulated Doe for claiming
only a bare margin "where incumbent rulers normally claim victories of
95% to 100%."[7]

Had the United States remained faithful to the original Reagan warning and acted as it was to do only six months later in the Philippines,[8] instead of embracing the false results, the course of events would have been
greatly altered. Continued implementation of announced U.S. policy in
September before the election, through insistence on the inclusion of the
UPP and LPP in the elections, would have been appropriate. It would have

been followed by the introduction— possibly imposition—of an election monitoring agency such as the Carter Center, National Democratic Institute (NDI), International Republican Institute (IRI), National Movement for Free Elections (NAMFREL), and official US delegations, as used in the Philippines. The presence of international observers would have encouraged Liberian civil society and opposition organizations in their efforts to obtain free elections.[9] Had the count been fair as a result, the U.S. aid on which Liberia depended for a third of its budget would have been restored and a new government would have been able to take on the task of restoring the state and the economy.

The remaining problem, as in the Philippines, would have been to provide a graceful retirement for Doe. By acclaiming him for removing the preceding narrowly based regime and then restoring democracy and by providing him with an appropriate retirement home, the United States could have overcome much of his opposition.[10] The military contained an important contingent of anti-Doe and reportedly pro-democracy forces and was not yet divided as it would be by the ill-conducted coup of the former armed forces commander, General Thomas Quiwonkpa, a month later.[11] Had Quiwonkpa been called back from exile to resume military leadership, it is most likely that the army would have supported the democratic transition, particularly if the increased stature and pay and the new constitutional protection against incrimination would have been maintained.[12]

Had the false count been maintained despite U.S. assertions and pressures, the continued aid suspension and Doe's earlier alienation from alternative sources of foreign support would have increased social unrest and weakened the regime's ability to resist;[13] Quiwonkpa's attempted coup to support the electoral results would have had better chances of succeeding if matters had gone that far. Even if the U.S. démarche had failed, it is hard to see how anything could have been worse than the ensuing events—rearrest of Johnson-Sirleaf, Jackson Doe, and others; assassination of media figures; bloody ethnic reprisals after the Quiwonkpa coup; and then the galvanizing rebellion at the end of the decade that utterly destroyed the country before its end seven years later. Of course, U.S. officials did not know of these events, but they were quite foreseeable, even if not specifically predictable.

But the United States did not move because it was not committed to pursuing the very conditions it imposed. Contrary to the standards announced to Doe, the State Department did not believe that free and fair elections were possible in the region or that a military ruler such as he would give up power under any conditions.[14] Liberia was not the Philippines, on the frontlines of the Cold War, with a strong and courageous election winner backed by an active civil society; it was seen to be a backwater with world telecommunications relay facilities, a strategic military airfield, and important U.S. investments that were perceived to be best held in the hands of a stable dictator with the modesty to win only slightly.[15] For this, the United States paid close to $1 billion during the 1980s, providing the largest U.S. per capita aid in black Africa.[16] The apparent stability, however, proved more and more illusory, until Christmas Eve 1989 when a small band led by Charles Taylor, a former official of the Doe regime who had been jailed in Boston on charges of embezzlement, repeated Quiwonkpa's venture more successfully and crossed the Côte d'Ivoire border to begin the Liberian civil war.

June 1990: A pause in the fighting provided both an opportunity for U.S. evacuation of Samuel Doe to safe retirement while Charles Taylor held off his attack on Monrovia and an occasion for influence with Taylor's NPFL.[17]

Contacts with the U.S. government by Taylor's NPFL were initiated almost immediately after the outbreak of the rebellion by "defense minister" Tom Woweiyu, although the United States was wary of a group that was Libyan-trained and Libyan-supported and perceived as unreliable.[18] There was never, throughout the entire Liberian conflict (and after), any illusion about the clean credentials or pure intentions of Charles Taylor, but it was felt that a quick end to Doe's exhausted regime and to the disastrous conflict would end the worst and possibly prepare for the better through new elections. By May 1990, the fortunes of Doe appeared unpromising, the NPFL appeared much more open to democracy and good U.S. relations, and a need began to appear to prepare for a possible evacuation of the 5,000 Americans in Liberia. The interagency Liberian Working Group in the U.S. government at the end of April decided "that a solution would have to begin with Doe's departure to a comfortable exile," followed by a negotiated transition to replacement elections.[19] President Gnassingbe Eyadema of Togo and later President Ibrahim Babangida of Nigeria agreed to grant asylum if requested by the United States. At the same time, Assistant Secretary of State for Africa Herman Cohen initiated the request for deployment of a Marine Amphibious Readiness Group (MARG) helicopter carrier from the Mediterranean to stand by in case of a need to evacuate American citizens, later amended to include posting a military C-130 airplane to Freetown, Sierra Leone, to evacuate Doe as well. Doe's wife and children fled to Britain in mid-May. The interagency Deputies

Committee on 24 May authorized deployment of the MARG, which arrived off Monrovia on the night of 3 June.

Conversations about Doe's deposition had begun in early May with U.S. Chargé d'Affaires Denis Jett and had moved back and forth across the realm of possibilities and the gamut of conditions, as the NPFL advanced to within 50 miles of Monrovia and then stopped at the major port of Buchanan. After a pause, the NPFL took Buchanan on 25 May, captured the Firestone plantation, and closed in on Monrovia. Discussions on Doe's evacuation picked up. Acutely aware of his lack of education,[20] Doe asked for assurances of a scholarship to Harvard or Cambridge, then asked to be flown with his family and followers to his home in Grand Geddeh County and at another time asked to have his evacuation include the transport of twenty-five cases of soft drinks. Former USAID administrator Peter McPherson, who had good relations with Doe, also contacted him and learned that Doe was also considering holding out in the presidential palace (a plan he eventually adopted). It was felt by the 4 June meeting of the Deputies Committee that a "final push" by a high level official was necessary to move Doe to accept early retirement, and Cohen prepared to travel to Monrovia with a plane ready to provide transportation to Togo, anticipating success in his mission. The rest of the scenario worked out by Jett involved Doe's replacement by his vice president, who would appoint Taylor as his successor and then resign in his favor; Taylor would be committed to holding new elections on the constitutionally mandated schedule, in October 1991. The date had been Doe's position in the earlier discussions, against Cohen's suggested date of October 1990 and the NPFL's preference for a later date.[21]

At the Deputies Committee meeting, Deputy National Security Adviser Robert Gates rejected any special U.S. responsibility or relationship vis-à-vis Liberia, and the representatives of other agencies (Central Intelligence Agency [CIA], U.S. Information Agency [USIA], and Defense) failed to support the "vital" and "critical" importance of the U.S. broadcasting, submarine, Coast Guard, and airfield facilities that they had endorsed in the previous Policy Coordinating Committee meetings. The day following the deputies meeting, the National Security Council (NSC) declared that the United States would not take charge of the Liberian problem and Cohen therefore should not travel to Monrovia, and the opportunity was dashed. Deputy Secretary Larry Eagleburger is reported to have said, "You don't tell a chief of state to leave unless you want to be responsible for what happens afterward." Instead, Doe was advised to reach an accommodation on his own with the NPFL.[22] In a classic summary of reasons for inaction, National Security Adviser Brent Scowcroft stated later, "It was difficult to see how we could intervene without taking over and pacifying Liberia with a more-or-less permanent involvement of US forces. Our attention was dedicated toward other areas most involved in ending the Cold War. You can only concentrate on so many things at once."[23] As a result, the United States was forced to concentrate on Liberia off and on again for the rest of the decade in more expensive ways.

The United States continued to look for retirement locations for Doe and announced it would help him there if he so requested.[24] Doe continued to toy with the ideas of resignation and of retreat to Grand Geddeh County and held discussions with the U.S. embassy but without closure or a high-level contact to make it happen. Secretary Cohen returned to mediation in preparing a cease-fire when he finally was able to get to the region in September but was told to "stop making peace" and was again reined in from further activity by the NSC.[25] An open opportunity to end the conflict and provide a smoother transition to normalcy had been deliberately scuttled.

At the same time, an important domestic effort at conflict management was taking place, and it accelerated with the collapse of the U.S. démarche. The Inter-Faith Mediation Council (IFMC) had been formed at the beginning of the year as a coalition of the Liberian Council of Churches (LCC) and the National Muslim Council of Liberia (NMCL). At a meeting with Doe's and Taylor's representatives in mid-June at the U.S. embassy in Freetown, the IFMC proposed a cease-fire, disarmament, interim government, and new elections. The effort collapsed over the NPFL insistence on Doe's prior resignation against Doe's insistence on remaining in power through the elections; the NPFL refused to participate in a follow-up session.[26] Had the United States remained in the process to support local initiatives, it would have encouraged local organizations such as the IFMC and the political parties to emerge from the Doe era and play a responsible role in politics. With the United States out of the peacemaking process, there was no influential mediator to support the grassroots initiative and press the parties to bridge the gap. There was no official backup to lower the parties' alternatives so that they would have less to gain by defecting from talks than by negotiating, and so the loss of the opportunity for an early end to the conflict was confirmed.

There is no guarantee that Assistant Secretary Cohen's visit would have convinced Doe to take early retirement, but since retirement remained an announced U.S. goal it was strange to deny the means to improve the chances of attaining it. There was little policy risk, as the United States was being blamed for inaction and held responsible for what happened afterward anyhow, and successful action to remove Doe would have opened up the possibility of a swift completion of the conflict before it began to devolve into ethnic massacres, splinter-group rivalries, child soldiering, and regional involvement. One resource appears to have been noted but never thought of in the plan: the use of shamans to counter the magician supplied to Doe by Eyadema. Among the anthropologists and political scientists who studied Liberia or the Liberian-American community in the United States, there were some who could have provided information on such practices, enabling the United States to provide its own magician to support its plan.[27]

Another resource was available and eager to move—the 2,100 marines of the MARG offshore. As in Haiti, an impending military presence could have helped Cohen's persuasiveness, and a number of specialists agree that the contingent was adequate for the job of evacuating the president as well as the American nationals.[28] Doe's evacuation to Togo or Nigeria—rapidly, before he changed his mind—would have been accompanied by continued contacts with the NPFL to limit reprisals against the Krahn tribe as Taylor took over Monrovia. Having facilitated that takeover and the end of the conflict, the United States would have been in a better position to assert its influence with Taylor, hold him to elections in either 1991 or 1990, save 100,000 lives, and use more productively the $900 million in official development assistance (ODA) expended over the course of the conflict. Nothing in this outcome assures good governance under Taylor, to be sure; but it does indicate a new situation as a result, with new opportunities for the United States to play a positive role in unfolding events and to avoid those events that were to occupy the decade.

April–July 1992: A holding cease-fire and an advancing mediation initiative offered the opportunity for inclusion of all factions and a stronger mediation role for the Carter Center's International Negotiation Network to provide details and monitored disarmament for the Yamoussoukro IV peace agreement.[29]

Following the withdrawal of active U.S. mediation, conflict management efforts were pursued by neighboring states in the region. At the annual meeting in Banjul at the end of May 1990 of the regional economic and security organization, the Economic Community of West African States, concern about the fate of its nationals caught in the civil war led to the formation of a Standing Mediation Committee (SMC) dominated by Nigeria, with Ghana, Gambia, Togo, and Mali. It proposed a cease-fire, Doe's resignation, an interim government excluding all warring faction leaders, elections within a year, and the establishment of an ECOWAS Monitoring Group (ECOMOG). The SMC convened a second meeting at Freetown on 12–19 July for the parties to sign the Banjul agreement, but now Taylor insisted on being named interim president to prepare the elections and accused ECOWAS of intervening at Nigeria's insistence to save Doe, Babangida's personal friend, not merely to protect its nationals.[30] At the third SMC meeting in Banjul on 6–7 August, the members decided to deploy ECOMOG on 24 August.[31] The ECOWAS decision gave Doe new courage; now that the U.S. initiative of June had collapsed, he withdrew his ideas of resigning and decided instead to serve out his term under the protection of ECOMOG.[32]

Other developments within the conflict worked to complicate conflict management efforts, as they would do in patterns to be repeated over the course of the civil war. When Taylor reacted to a military setback in April by executing the losing commanders, one of his lieutenants, Prince Yeduo (or Yormie) Johnson, broke away to form a splinter Independent National Patriotic Front (INPFL) and develop cooperative relations with the ECOMOG forces.[33] INPFL forces burst into the ECOMOG compound on 9 September to capture and then cruelly murder Doe, who had come on a diplomatic mission. Henceforth the conflict became a personal scramble for his succession, and its ethnic and desperate dimensions heightened. The Liberian Armed Forces (AFL) massacred some 200 people taking refuge in a church in Nimba County, NPFL forces killed Krahn and Mandingo civilians in their conquest of Buchanan, and ECOMOG (known popularly as "Every Car or Moving Object Gone") committed lootings and executions in Monrovia.

Negotiations and movement toward a cease-fire continued. The ECOWAS committee had convened an All-Liberian National Conference in Banjul from 27 August to 2 September 1990 to implement the Banjul-Freetown agreement. Delegates to the conference endorsed the election of an Interim Government of National Unity (IGNU) presided over by professor Amos Sawyer; they excluded the leaders of warring factions from elections, now set for October 1991.[34] Both provisions fully alienated Taylor and convinced him that ECOMOG was a Nigerian instrument.

Intense negotiations in connection with the ECOWAS committee meeting in Banjul on 22–24 October produced a cease-fire with its new allies, AFL and INPFL.[35] Further meetings with Taylor in Bamako on 28 November and Banjul on 21 December and the mediation of one of his backers and ECOMOG's most outspoken critic, Burkinabe president Blaise Campaore, brought Taylor to Lomé on 12–13 February 1991 to join the cease-fire agreement. It provided for disarmament of all troops and an all-party national conference, partially similar to the sovereign national conferences (CNSs) that were occurring within other states throughout the region. The conference began with the NPFL in March 1991 but ended with an NPFL walkout and Dr. Sawyer's election as interim president two weeks later.

The involvement of Taylor's French-speaking supporters was the key to balancing Nigerian dominance of the ECOWAS process and to bringing Taylor into an agreement. On the eve of the annual summit of ECOWAS at Abuja at the end of June 1991, Ivorian president Felix Houphouet-Boigny invited Taylor and Sawyer to a meeting with the Nigerian, Gambian, and Togolese presidents plus Campaore at Yamoussoukro and produced a new agreement on elections within six to nine months under a new Committee of Five (Côte d'Ivoire, Senegal, Gambia, Guinea-Bissau, Togo). The ECOWAS mediation then passed to a group of states closer to Taylor and moved to complement the Banjul-Bamako ceasefire with disarmament, encampment, and elections. After further rounds of negotiations at Yamoussoukro on 30 June and 29 July 1991, Houphouet-Boigny addressed Taylor's core concern at Yamoussoukro III on 16–17 September by providing for a reconfiguration of ECOMOG so that Taylor could disarm to friendly forces and not to Nigeria. Senegal had succeeded to the presidency of ECOWAS, and Senegalese president Abdou Diouf paid a state visit to Washington the same month, where a Senegalese commitment of armed forces and a U.S. commitment of financial support were worked out.[36] At the follow-up Yamoussoukro IV meeting on 29–30 October, the details of a settlement, including a buffer zone on the Sierra Leone border, a timetable for disarmament and encampment, repatriation of refugees and internally displaced people, and elections, were elaborated, even before the actual arrival of 1,500 Senegalese troops the following month.

The Banjul-Bamako cease-fire continued to hold throughout 1991, and progress continued on the track set out at Yamoussoukro. By January 1992, NPFL had reopened the roads leading to Monrovia, and INPFL had opened the road to its base in Cadwell; ECOMOG troops had inspected encampment sites throughout the country, including the NPFL "capital" of Gbarnga and the port of Buchanan. Taylor and Sawyer, meeting with some members of the Committee of Five in Geneva on 6–7 April 1992, confirmed these developments. They urged ECOMOG to implement immediately the Yamoussoukro decision to establish a buffer zone along the Sierra Leone border, the one place where no cease-fire was observed, and NPFL, ECOMOG, and Sierra Leonean representatives met to discuss the creation of the buffer zone.

It was this new development in the conflict, of the same type that had arisen a year earlier, that reversed the new-found NPFL cooperation and prevented progress to a final agreement. Krahn and Mandingo people of the northeast interior, who had achieved social promotion during the Doe regime and feared not only for their status but for their lives under Taylor, had organized in Sierra Leone behind a new military faction, the United Liberation Movement for Democracy, in June. ULIMO entered into combat in September 1991 in an area where fighting had already taken place since March between NPFL, its proxy RUF, and the Sierra Leonean army over diamond smuggling. ULIMO's activities were to receive additional support a year later by the takeover of the Sierra Leonean government at the end of April 1992 by Captain Valentine Strasser, who had served in ECOMOG and shared a dislike of Taylor.[37] NPFL had expressed its concern about the ULIMO breach of the cease-fire as early as Yamoussoukro IV in the previous October, and in December Taylor had indicated refusal to implement Yamoussoukro until ULIMO forces had withdrawn into Sierra Leone.[38] ULIMO was not invited to Yamoussoukro or to Geneva for fear of giving it status and legitimacy, nor was it included in the IGNU interim legislature. ULIMO was therefore fighting against exclusion from postwar Liberian politics when it opened a second front in the interior of the country. The only way to control it was to bring it into the cease-fire discussions; left out, ULIMO set out to destroy the growing cease-fire and in the process gave Taylor the valid excuse to do the same, a spoiler confirming its opponent as a spoiler too.

Two days after Geneva, ULIMO and NPFL both denounced the agreements, ULIMO declaring that they "effectively nullify all previous peace plans including Yamoussoukro IV" and announcing its intention to eliminate Taylor within three months. It improved its cooperation with ECOMOG and its operations against the NPFL, and ECOMOG began to regard ULIMO as a useful ally against Taylor in the back country, just as it was beginning to reopen its arms stocks to the AFL in the cities. In May, six soldiers of the newly deployed Senegalese unit to establish the long-awaited buffer zone were executed by NPFL when they discovered an NPFL arms cache along the Sierra Leone border in the area of ULIMO-NPFL combat. It was time to extend the conflict management efforts to ULIMO, bring them into the Yamoussoukro process, and remove the cause for Taylor's objections to proceeding with disarmament and encampment.

The opportunity for such an action came at two already-scheduled moments—either at the Geneva meeting itself in April, despite its small attendance, or at the annual summit of ECOWAS at Dakar on 27–29 July 1992. Both meetings provided the occasion to introduce appropriate revisions of the Yamoussoukro formula and present them to NPFL and ULIMO in an effort to address their conflict and grievances directly. The leaders should have stayed—or been kept—in session until a general agreement was reached and its details of implementation decided. Four elements in the current process needed revision. On the military level, a broader participation of African states was needed to reduce the Nigerian preponderance from 90 percent to around 60 percent of the forces and to provide the force needed to establish a neutral zone on the Sierra Leone border, lengths of which are along rivers. On the political level, IGNU, which did not function, needed to be replaced (as it was later) by a National Transitional Council including Taylor, Albert Kromah of ULIMO, and an additional figure, to govern until early elections at which all council members could be candidates. On the level of disarmament, a small UN force needed to be sent in to monitor the collection of arms and overcome the lack of bona fides of ECOMOG. On the level of guarantees, these agreements needed UN Security Council (UNSC) backing, including an arms embargo covering all forces in Liberia (not just "rebels"), UN military observers (UNOMIL) along with the ECOMOG buffer and disarmament forces, and direct sanctions against any force that did not comply with the disarmament and encampment agreement within a stipulated time.

The obvious agent for this intervention was ECOWAS itself, but ECOWAS was the party that was deficient in its functions.[39] Meaningful attempts at reconciliation such as the planned Harbel Prayer Meeting on Easter Sunday 1992, as well as efforts to rein in ULIMO, were simply blocked by ECOMOG, for whom ULIMO was an ally. The U.S. State Department's Africa Bureau—just when it was needed—was no longer involved in any form of mediation in Liberia, having twice been rapped on the knuckles by internal restrainers from higher levels in the department and the NSC. The moment was one where coordination was required between the United States and France, both to bring about UN Security Council action and to urge the outgoing and incoming chairs of ECOWAS—Senegalese and Beninois presidents Abdou Diouf and Christophe Soglo—to work out a plan that would bring Taylor into the management of conflict. France and the United States in the UNSC were in a position to insist on the inclusion of ULIMO, under the standard principle that "those who are part of the problem must be part of the solution." More than presence was required, of course; ULIMO needed to be included in the legislature in a new allocation of seats (including a larger portion for the NPFL) and in the disarmament, repatriation, and election provisions.[40] Such inclusions might well have been resisted initially by Taylor, but they were the key to his larger goals, control of hostilities on the northwestern front and accession to the Liberian presidency.

An additional agent was necessary. Former president Jimmy Carter was represented at Yamoussoukro I and was invited to participate in the negotiation process and monitor the unfolding electoral process. A representative of the Carter Center of Emory University met with IGNU president Sawyer, Taylor, and the Committee of Five leaders at the subsequent three Yamoussoukro meetings (but not at Geneva or Dakar) and off and on until the 1997 elections. One of Carter's operational guidelines is to engage with "unsavory characters," parties that others find it difficult to deal with, and this approach has enabled him to produce surprising results on occasion. Carter had sent an eleven-point proposal to the parties on the eve of Yamoussoukro IV; it was rejected as "weak" and "unrealistic" by ECOMOG and actually offended the IGNU side, causing problems for the Carter Center team on location, but it was in fact clear-sighted and even-handed in dealing with the Taylor-ECOMOG problem.[41]

A week after the Geneva meeting, in mid-April 1992, a delegation from the Carter Center's International Negotiation Network (INN) visiting Liberia nearly set up a face-to-face prayer meeting of Taylor and Sawyer on Easter Sunday at Harbel before it was vetoed by ECOMOG, but the ULIMO problem was neither mentioned nor addressed. The INN was to be made aware of the ULIMO problem from meetings in Washington in May if not before.[42] Carter met with Raleigh Seekie, president of ULIMO, during a trip to Liberia in mid-September, weeks before the NPFL 1992 Octopus offensive that destroyed the cease-fire; Carter discussed the fighting with ULIMO with Sawyer and called for a cease-fire and an ECOMOG buffer on the northwestern front, but the need to bring ULIMO into the Yamoussoukro agreements as a party did not appear (and a pressing airplane schedule prevented a detailed pursuit of issues). An earlier visit in April or July with a focus on the problem of ULIMO (another group of "unsavory characters") could have saved the cease-fire and reignited headway toward a settlement.

The Banjul-Bamako cease-fire, even if imperfect, gave mediators nearly a year in which to work. A solid agreement on terms for resolving the Liberian conflict at Geneva or Dakar would have benefited from the suspension of hostilities, seriously broken only in the northwest, and from the new ECOWAS team's working much more even-handedly to bring the conflict under control. It would have wound down the conflict before further splinter groups appeared to complicate the management process and before the fighting forces had dug too deeply into the reservoir of child soldiers that was to become their main source of recruitment. Had the intervention come in April, it would have preceded and doubtless precluded the execution of the Senegalese soldiers, which triggered a Senegalese decision to withdraw and undid all the efforts to broaden ECOMOG away from its Nigerian dominance. Furthermore, it would have brought settlement to the Liberian conflict before Taylor's counter-ULIMO in Sierra Leone, RUF, would have been able to consummate the collapse of Sierra Leone just as the Sierra Leonean government was poised on the verge of a first step toward democratization and reconstruction.[43]

The proposed efforts to seize the opportunity were not foreign to the subsequent events. In fact, on 14 August, Soglo invited ULIMO to Cotonou to participate in talks on Liberia, the first such invitation offered. ULIMO claimed that it was unable to attend because the invitation was received too late to assemble appropriate military as well as political leaders. Too late indeed it was: the same day NPFL declared its refusal to disarm and encamp as long as Sierra Leone and other ECOWAS countries continued to support ULIMO, and later in the month arms shipments ranging from rifles to tanks arrived for the NPFL in Robertsfield and Buchanan. Mid-July was certainly the last moment when ULIMO could have been fitted into the conflict management process and NPFL kept on board, and April would have been better. In October 1992, Taylor launched a massive Operation Octopus, which carried him back to the gates of Monrovia and in return brought ECOMOG into a full combat role, fully allied with ULIMO and AFL. An urgent ECOWAS summit in Cotonou on 20 October pleaded for a cease-fire and threatened NPFL (but not ULIMO) with sanctions if it did not accede. But a U.S. Embassy report indicated that Soglo "has thrown up his hands over Liberia. . . . Let them fight, he mutters often, until they are exhausted," as in fact they did.[44]

July 1993: A new stalemate following intense fighting and a new framework agreement opened the opportunity for the Carter Center International Negotiaton Network and the UN special representative of the Secretary-General to mediate a realistic disarmament and interim governance agreement.[45]

Over the following months, the war reached its greatest intensity between NPFL and ECOMOG with its Liberian allies. In response to NPFL's Operation Octopus, ECOMOG made sizable gains in its counteroffensive, capturing Robertsfield and Buchanan, and ULIMO made inroads into western Liberia. Yet neither party could eliminate the other. The UN Security Council reacted on 19 November 1992 with a call for sanctions against all parties except ECOMOG and for the appointment of an SRSG. Trevor Gordon-Somers was named SRSG, and ECOWAS also appointed former Zimbabwe president Canaan Banana as its liaison representative. Taylor welcomed the UN initiative and agreed to cooperate with it, but "never with ECOMOG."[46] Under the pressure of the stalemate into which he was being moved, Taylor accepted a meeting of NPFL, ULIMO, IGNU, ECOWAS, and Organization of African Unity (OAU) representatives in Geneva 10–16 July 1993 to work out a new agreement, then signed the agreement in Cotonou on 25 July.

The agreement moved the military and political aspects of a settlement to the same level. An expanded ECOMOG, including troops from Tanzania, Uganda, and Zimbabwe (the latter eventually did not appear because their price was too high), was to conduct disarmament, which a 300-person UNOMIL was to supervise. This meant that it was urgent for the additional forces and the UN observers to arrive, since the provision opened up a workable disarmament mechanism and overcame Taylor's refusal to disarm to the Nigerians alone. A Liberian National Transition Government (LNTG), replacing IGNU, was to be organized under a Council of State composed of both military faction and civil society representatives—an NPFL, a ULIMO, and an IGNU representative plus two more members selected by a panel of eminent personalities; a legislative assembly and a supreme court were to be reconstituted; and an expanded Electoral Commission from the Yamoussoukro agreements was prolonged for six months to prepare for elections in April 1994. A new cease-fire was to come into effect on 1 August. The Cotonou agreement took the necessary step of including the warlords, for the first time, in the governing council.

Yet so much was left undone. Details on the branches of government were left for further consultation; no mechanism was provided for filling the Council of State seats or resolving disputes in the process; there was no timetable for disarmament, encampment, and demobilization; and the relationship between disarmament and the installation of the Council of State was unclear. Sawyer contested the augmentation plan for ECOMOG, and the augmenting forces were slow in arriving. It took almost a year, until March 1994, before the council could be constituted, during which time the race for council and government seats led both NPFL and ULIMO to split and new rebel groups, the Lofa Defense Force (LDF) and the Liberian Peace Council (LPC), to emerge. The cease-fire began well but lasted only a month until being breached by factional fighting connected with the ULIMO. A new council was negotiated at Akosumbo in September 1994, leading new factions again to form; another LNTG formed at Abuja on 19 August 1995 was revised a year later, again at Abuja, after further fallout among the factions.[47]

The mediation of these agreements was weak and misguided. Gordon-Somers—and others—never understood the depth of Taylor's feeling toward a disarmament structured so as to be a surrender to ECOMOG, even though Nigerian accounts of the Liberian conflicts continually castigated Taylor for his opposition to ECOMOG and noted ECOMOG's single-minded hostility to Taylor.[48] Carter had a better understanding of the situation, although that made it more difficult for him to convince ECOMOG of his neutrality. His proposal for a power-sharing interim government, a reduction of ECOMOG forces and a monitoring of checkpoints by joint ECOMOG-NPFL teams, and monitored elections recognized these problems, even if it needed some fine-tuning and the inclusion of a more robust UNOMIL. During his September visit, Carter had negotiated the release of 508 ECOMOG troops taken hostage by NPFL in Monrovia three months earlier.[49] But the Carter Center's office in Monrovia had been twice sacked and closed, at great loss to an impecunious organization, and Carter's earlier proposals had offended Sawyer, leading the center team to opt for a low-key role when it reopened shop in March 1993.

Yet the situation provided an opportunity for a more vigorous and more perspicacious mediator as SRSG and for the stronger involvement of the Carter Center representatives. The Clinton administration had barred itself from an active role in Liberia until the end of its first term, in April 1996.[50] ECOWAS's turn to the UN and the Security Council's willingness to take up the conflict at the end of 1992 were positive moves. The SRSG mission had a positive beginning: the constitution of an executive council as a power-sharing institution that reflected the parties' strength on the ground met some of the realities of the conflict, even at the price of bringing in the warlords, and the adoption of the notion of safe havens—above all, Monrovia—would allow voting to take place even if other parts of the country were not yet disarmed.

But once the Council of State had been introduced, the SRSG left it as an agenda item and a prize to be fought over rather than as a body responsible for the transition process. A more forceful mediator was needed to freeze Council of State membership and get on with cease-fire, disarmament, and elections. The UN SRSG, a prestigious Carter Center INN representative, and the IFMC should have been ex officio observers on the Council of State (as, for example, the UN mediator and the Salvadorean Catholic Church had been placed on the National Commission for the Consolidation of Peace two years earlier in the El Salvador peace process).[51] A different personality was required as SRSG, and more financial support was required for a larger, more authoritative, and more active Carter Center presence. Had it come three years earlier, as knowledgeable observers had called for, the U.S. promise of $30 million in aid, contingent on progress toward elections, would have provided a carrot and stick rolled into one (as it did when finally made in 1996).[52]

Finally, a larger UN Chapter VI peacekeeping force was required to sanitize the process of arms collection—not a huge force, 1,000–2,000 would have sufficed. The UN Security Council, meeting after delays on Gordon-Somers's report and a request from the Secretary-General that pre-meeting consultations had considerably watered down, in the end welcomed the ostensibly successful ECOMOG offensive as a reason for not supplying the 350 UN peacekeepers and the 2,000-person ECOMOG expansion that Gordon-Somers had asked for a month earlier. An armed and uniformed UN presence would also have dampened the tendency to resort to armed jockeying for positions among petty warlords, even without its actually having to engage in fighting. The reversal of the NPFL Octopus Offensive created enough of a stalemate to favor revival of the transition.

By the time of Cotonou in 1993, the United States had spent $203 million in relief and $28 million for peacekeeping; Nigeria had spent half a billion dollars for ECOMOG. By the time of eventual elections in June 1997, those figures had doubled, plus another $1.2 million in the Cotonou Accords Trust Fund; UNOMIL cost another $100 million. Two-thirds of the 3 million Liberians were turned into internally displaced persons, three-quarters of whom at some point became refugees outside Liberia's borders; 150,000 were dead. Worse, the four years between Cotonou and the 1997 elections ensured the spread of regional rot into Sierra Leone and beyond, aggravated the predatory nature of Taylor's regime, entrenched the use of the child soldiers, and completed the destruction of the country. Yet after 1993 there was little that could be done in the absence of more vigorous mediation except to plod ahead with the transition process until every possibility of new warlords had been exhausted, and the population with it, so that Taylor could be elected, freely and fairly but by a people cowed by his threat of return to war.[53]

July–October 1998: During a stalemate and rainy-season lull in the fighting in Sierra Leone, an agreement between the presidents of Sierra Leone and Liberia marked an opportunity to redeploy an augmented Economic Community of Western African States Monitoring Group force along the border and in the diamond areas of Sierra Leone.[54]

Even though the Liberian civil war was being brought to a halt with the election of Charles Taylor as the winner, the conflict's spillover continued to devastate Sierra Leone. The RUF nearly took over the capital in 1995 before being repulsed by a private security firm, Executive Outcomes, and was again invited to share power after May 1997 when an army junta, the Armed Forces Revolutionary Council, overthrew the government until ousted by ECOMOG in February 1998. But ECOMOG forces only liberated the capital area, being too few in numbers to do more in the countryside. As a result, the RUF took advantage of the June–October rainy season to regroup and, in December, to relaunch its barbaric operations that again took it to the gates of the capital.

The RUF fed off three troughs: an arms lifeline through Liberia, originating in Burkina Faso and beyond that in Libya; the diamonds found in northeast Sierra Leone that funded its arms purchases, operations, and personal fortunes; and the unemployed youth of Freetown and beyond who provided its pool of recruits.[55] As a social protest movement with deep grassroots, the RUF was impervious to quick and military efforts at control, but that was not its entire nature. As a guerrilla movement with gruesome methods, RUF-type groups are vulnerable to a strategy of control: in this case, one that could cut their other two sources of supply, by blocking the borders and by occupying the diamond fields. Neither of these operations would be quick and easy. Both the diamond fields and the border— the same border as involved in controlling ULIMO on the Liberian side— consist of rivers and rain forests, difficult for operations during the rainy season. Although the roads are rudimentary, the mountainous terrain increases their importance for travel and makes interdiction conceivable. Thus, although it was true that "there [was] no purely military solution to the Sierra Leone conflict,"[56] a well-planned, -executed, and -sustained military operation could have cut off the movement from its vital lifelines, leaving it to wander around the bush without diamonds or new arms amid hostile (albeit cowed) populations. There it would still be capable of doing damage and invulnerable to total eradication, but no longer a threat to the heart of the country. The government would then be able to turn its attention in relative security to the socioeconomic problems of the country (a task at which it would need assistance and monitoring, to be sure).

There was an unpursued opportunity for such a policy following meetings between presidents Taylor and Tejan Kabbah of Liberia and Sierra Leone, respectively, at the instance of the UN Secretary-General and ECOWAS in Abuja on 2 July and in Monrovia on 20 July 1998. The communiqué of the second meeting again renewed a call for the deployment of ECOMOG and UN "observer units to the Liberian–Sierra Leonean border to assist the security forces of both countries in ensuring full compliance with UN[SC] Resolution 1132."[57] Although mere observers under Chapter VI would not be enough in the circumstances, the larger problem was the inadequacy of resources available to ECOWAS to field an appropriate number of troops. After the summits, ECOMOG commanding general Timothy Shelpidi expressed his conviction that his forces could "crush" the rebels "as soon as promised support from the international community arrives,"[58] sounding much like a bravely hopeful commander in a beleaguered outpost; the Nigerian ambassador to the UN importuned his colleagues for more military support. In June, the U.S. State Department emphasized the importance of security in Sierra Leone, and in October Congress urged military and logistic support.[59] In the latter half of 1998, ECOMOG had fewer than 10,000 troops in Sierra Leone, too dispersed and unprepared to withstand the RUF offensive when it came at the end of the year. An additional 5,000 troops from Mali and Gambia as well as Nigeria came in January but were too late and still inadequate to meet the challenge. Command and logistics continued to pose problems for the troops that were present, and inadequate finances kept more from coming. Instead, Nigeria began withdrawing its remaining troops from Monrovia at the beginning of 1999, to send to Sierra Leone, as reports of Liberian support for the rebels across the border became more frequent. New troops to patrol the border—from Senegal, Mali, and again Nigeria—were promised only after additional urgent ECOWAS summits at the end of 2000.

Yet the United States had promised financial support, which it did not send.[60] Such support was crucial and would have made the difference.[61] A larger number of troops than those that would have come from a single well-trained and -integrated force was needed, and assistance from some Western military advisers would have been helpful. A larger multinational ECOMOG force was required in two areas—along the Liberia–Sierra Leone border and in the diamond fields of Sierra Leone. International oversight would also have been necessary; Nigerian interests were less narrow and dominant at the end of the 1990s than they had been at the beginning, having been shaped by the Liberian experience, but the temptation to benefit from the diamond fields would have had to be kept in check. Such surveillance was no easy matter, as relations between UN-OMIL and ECOMOG had clearly shown.[62]

Sierra Leone itself is a complex story, replete with more deep tragedies than with clearly lost opportunities. Had the United States put money where its rhetoric was in the middle of 1998, the latest rounds of the RUF's barbarism and the bungled mediation of Jesse Jackson and Gnassingbe Eyadema to produce the Lomé agreements in June 1999 could have been avoided. Instead, the agreements gave the RUF butchers amnesty and brought them into a power-sharing arrangement, until they themselves broke the accord. The larger lesson lies in those considerations: once it began to roll, the collapse of Sierra Leone into repeatedly gruesome episodes was hard to control, but the place to have started was in Liberia at the beginning of the decade before it descended into its own abyss, pulling the neighbors with it.

Notes

1. I appreciate discussions during the preparation of the Liberian case study with the following: Ambassador James Bishop, Ambassador Kenneth Brown, Canon Burgess Carr, Assistant Secretary of State Herman Cohen, Monsignor Michael Francis, Viniucius Hodges, David Carroll, Ambassador Donald Petterson, John Prendergast, Victoria Reffell, Dr. Ellen Johnson-Sirleaf, Dayle Spencer, Dr. Amos Sawyer, and Dr. James Tarpeh. I am grateful for the research assistance of Peter J. Davis, Wendy Glickman, Nalinie Kouame, Alexander Lezhnev, Alexander Mundt, Kwaku Nuamah, Scott Pietan, Amber Rutland, R. Shpak, and Ugo Solinas.

2. Dunn and Tarr, *Liberia,* 127. See also Liebenow, *Liberia,* 307.

3. Sometimes when the slide to state collapse is clearly visible, it is nonetheless difficult to see any points where something could be or could have been done to stop the deadly conflict. Such is the case of Côte d'Ivoire, Africa's miracle of success during President Felix Houphouet-Boigny's reign, 1960–1993, and a catastrophic story of national suicide thereafter. A number of turning points in that slide can be identified, but none, it seems, where there was an opportunity to do something about it.

4. "The Voting Proceeds," *West Africa,* 21 October 1985; "SECOM: All Boxed In," *West Africa,* 28 October 1985; "Doe Makes History," *West Africa,* 4 November 1985; Kendall Wills, "Key US Legislators Favor Cut in Liberia Aid," *New York Times,* 1 December 1985; Inter-Press Service, 10 December 1985; Michael Massing, "General Doe, Our Autocratic Ally," *Chicago Tribune,* 30 January 1986.

5. "Freed in Liberia," *New York Times,* 15 September 1985.

6. Bill Berkeley, *Liberia: A Promise Betrayed* (New York: Lawyers Committee for Human Rights, 1986); "Liberia and United States Policy," U.S. Senate, Subcommittee on African Affairs, Committee on Foreign Relations, 99th Congress, 1st sess., 10 December 1985; Dunn and Tarr, *Liberia,* 115–122; Youboty, *Liberian Civil War,* chap. 11; Charles Powers, "Doe Wins Controversial Liberian Election," *Los Angeles Times,* 30 October 1985, 1:20. Election observers such as the National Democratic Institute declined to monitor an election deemed flawed from the start.

7. Chester Crocker, "Recent Developments in Liberia," *Department of State Bulletin* 86, no. 2107 (February 1986): 54–57.

8. Paul Wolfowitz, "After the Election in the Philippines," *Department of State Bulletin* 86, no. 2109 (April 1986): 69–71.

9. A succinct but comprehensive review of Liberian civil society is found in Toure, *The Role of Civil Society in National Reconciliation and Peacebuilding in Liberia.*

10. A federal "fellowship" to a U.S. university would have been an enticing inducement.

11. Larry James, "Quiwonkpa's Fatal Gamble," *Africa Report,* January/February 1986.

12. Liebenow, *Liberia,* 271.

13. A strategy detailed by the minister of state for presidential affairs, John Rancy, in a leaked letter in 1983; Dunn and Tarr, *Liberia,* 112–114; Mark Huband, *The Liberian Civil War* (London: Cass, 1998), 35–36.

14. Confidential interviews by the author.

15. A State Department official, defending the policy, said to the author, "It got us 5 years of support in the Cold War."

16. This amount included $400 million for the 1987–1988 management and consulting team of seventeen people funded by the U.S. Agency for International Development (USAID) that left "in extreme frustration" before its contract ended; Mark Huband, *The Liberian Civil War* (London: Cass, 1998), 42; N. Henry, "Doctors' Group Criticizes US for Not Intervening in Liberia," *Washington Post,* 16 August 1990, A17, A20; U.S. Department of Commerce, *Foreign Economic Trends and Their Implications for the United States: Liberia* (Washington, DC: Government Printing Office, 1988, 1990); U.S. General Accounting Office, *Report to the Hon. Edward M Kennedy, Liberia: Need to Improve Accountability and Control over US Assistance* (Washington, DC: General Accounting Office, 1987). Another $2.4 million was paid by the Overseas Private Investment Corporation (OPIC) to the rubber company Keene Industries in compensation for damages from political violence; L. D. Howell, *Keene Industries in Liberia* (Glendale, AZ: Thunderbird: American Graduate School of International Management, 1997).

17. *New York Times,* 31 July 1990; Kramer, "Liberia: A Casualty of the Cold War's End?" 8; Herman Cohen, "An Exit Interview with 'Hank' Cohen," *CSIS Africa Notes* (Washington, DC: Center for Strategic and International Studies, 1993), 7; Mary Curtius, "US Defends Actions on Uprising," *Boston Globe,* 2 August 1990; Clifford Kraus, "Liberian Officer Is Said to Desert," *New York Times,* 5 July 1990, A11; Cohen, *Intervening in Africa.* This instance is based in part on the account in Cohen, *Intervening in Africa,* 133–147.

18. State Department telegram to U.S. Embassy in Abidjan, 9 March 1990, cited in Cohen, *Intervening in Africa,* 133; on the Libyan training, see Abdullah, "Bush Path to Destruction," 1998.

19. Cohen, *Intervening in Africa,* 137.

20. Doe's search for the formal education that he lacked led to some important attempts to seal alliances. His close personal ties with Nigerian president Ibrahim Babangida were marked during Babangida's visit in December 1988 by an endowment of close to $1 million of a graduate program in international affairs at the University of Liberia, which Doe then named the Babangida School and where he planned to pursue a higher degree. Doe extracted from Secretary Cohen a promise to be commencement speaker at his graduation from the university in December 1990. See Emeka Nwokedi, *Regional Integration and Regional Security: ECOMOG, Nigeria and the Liberian Crisis* (Talence: Centre d'Etudes d'Afrique Noire, Institut d'Etudes Politiques, University of Bordeaux, 1992).

21. Charles Taylor, in *Financial Times,* 14 April 1990, 5.

22. Cohen, *Intervening in Africa,* 143–144; George Gedda, Associated Press dispatch, 6 June 1990.

23. Quoted in Kramer, "Liberia: A Casualty of the Cold War's End?" 1.

24. George Gedda, Associated Press dispatch, 6 June 1990; Margaret Tutwiler in Mark Huband, "Battle of Monrovia in Full Swing," United Press International dispatch, 2 July 1990; Richard Boucher in Mark Huband, "Report Doe Agrees to Resign," United Press International dispatch, 3 July 1990 and in Terence Hunt, "No Plans to Send US Troops," Associated Press dispatch, 30 July 1990; Robert Weller, "US Reportedly Refuses to Take Doe to His Home Province," Associated Press dispatch, 6 July 1990; Marlin Fitzwater, White House press briefing, 5 August 1990.

25. Cohen, *Intervening in Africa,* 153–156.

26. Sawyer, *The Dynamics of Conflict Management in Liberia,* 17–18; Cohen, *Intervening in Africa,* 145–146; Brown, "Mediation by Influence: American Policy Toward the Liberian War," 32; S. Elwood Dunn, "Liberia's Internal Responses to ECOMOG's Interventionist Efforts," in Magyar and Conteh-Morgan, *Peacekeeping in Africa: ECOMOG in Liberia;* Kofi Woods, "Civic Initiatives in the Liberian Peace Process," in Armon and Carl, "The Liberian Peace Process 1990–1996."

27. During a visit by a senior U.S. official, Doe offered to show the potency of a bullet-proof potion smeared on a guard by shooting at him; the official declined to witness the test.

28. Peter DeVos, "Searching for Peace in Liberia," in D. Francis, ed., *Mediating Deadly Conflict* (Cambridge: World Peace Foundation, 1998), 33; Herman Cohen, "An Exit Interview," 7; N. Henry, "Doctor's Group Criticizes US for Not Intervening in Liberia," *Washington Post,* 16 August 1990, A17.

29. *The Guardian,* 18 September 1991; Agence France Presse, 29, 30 October 1991; BBC 4, 6 November 1991; George Klay Kieh Jr., *The Obstacles to the Peaceful Resolution of the Liberian Civil Conflict*, Studies in Conflict and Terrorism, vol. 17 (London: Taylor and Francis, 1994).

30. For a good presentation of Nigeria's interests and perceptions in the conflict, beyond simply Babangida's friendship for Doe, including the NPFL attack on the Nigerian Embassy on 9 August 1990, see Terry Mays, "Nigerian Foreign Policy and Its Participation in ECOMOG," in Magyar and Conteh-Morgan, *Peacekeeping in Africa,* chap. 6.

31. Vogt, *The Liberian Crisis and ECOMOG.*

32. United Press International dispatch, 13 August 1990.

33. On additional ideological and ethnic reasons for the INPFL split, see Alao, *The Burden of Collective Goodwill,* 36.

34. The negotiations to July 1992 are well chronicled by Nnamdi Obasi, "The Negotiation Process," in Vogt, *The Liberian Crisis and ECOMOG.* The prohibition against interim government figures running for subsequent office, which came from the original IFMC plan, was not dropped until the Akosombo agreements of September 1994.

35. INPFL ended its participation in the conflict during the October 1992 Operation Octopus when Johnson was rescued by ECOMOG and spirited to Lagos, where the Nigerians have held him in pleasant captivity ever since; Mark Huband, *The Liberian Civil War* (London: Cass, 1998), 213.

36. Cohen, *Intervening in Africa,* 157–159.

37. Earl Conteh-Morgan and Shireen Kadivar, "Sierra Leone's Response to ECOMOG," in Magyar and Conteh-Morgan, *Peacekeeping in Africa,* chap. 8;

Vogt, *The Liberian Crisis and ECOMOG,* 160; Mark Huband, *The Liberian Civil War* (London: Cass, 1998), 205–209, 212; Alao, *The Burden of Collective Goodwill,* 25–26; Geraldine Faes, "Taylor perd du terrain," *Jeune Afrique,* no. 1652 (3 September 1992); P. Richards, "Rebellion in Sierra Leone and Liberia: A Crisis of Youth?" in Furley, *Conflict in Africa.*

38. Osisioma B.C. Nwolise, "Implementation of Yamoussoukro and Geneva Agreements," in Vogt, *The Liberian Crisis and ECOMOG,* 292.

39. In the rising debate over ECOMOG, a good critical analysis is found in van Walraven, *Containing Conflict in the Economic Community of West African States.*

40. At the Johns Hopkins–Carter Center Liberian National Reconciliation Workshop in May 1992, ULIMO was not invited, but when it appeared, NPFL had no objections to its participation. IGNU withdrew, officially, when it learned that FPFL was addressed as a "government" (NPRAG).

41. Carter Center letter of 26 October 1991 to ECOWAS heads of state; Agence France Presse, 1 November 1991.

42. The May 1992 Liberian Reconciliation Workshop organized by the Johns Hopkins University in Washington and the Carter Center heard an impassioned declaration of grievances from ULIMO, initially not invited, and reached impressive consensus from the three parties' and civil society representatives on problems and measures; Reed Kramer, "Peace Effort Is Revived in Liberia," *Washington Post,* 6 May 1992. A memorandum prepared for the Carter Center contained a sound analysis but little that would provide an intervention strategy; D. Ellwood Dunn and Ellen Johnson-Sirleaf, "Liberia; An Action Memorandum" (internal memorandum, Carter Center, Atlanta, GA, 15 January 1992).

43. The grassroots nature of the RUF is undeniable, but there is much debate about how much of a Liberian (or even Libyan) creation it was: "in June 2001, Omrie Golley, the Chairman of the RUF's Peace Council, claimed that until two weeks prior, Taylor had been in complete control of the rebels"; "Sierra Leone: Managing Uncertainty," International Crisis Group Report 35, 24 October 2001, 12. See also Paul Richards, Ibrahim Abdullah, P. Mauna, T. Stanley, and J. Vincent, *Reintegration of War-Affected Youth and Ex-Combatants* (Freetown: Sierra Leonean Ministry of National Reconstruction, Rehabilitation and Resettlement, 1997).

44. Cited in Peter da Costa, "Talking Tough to Taylor," *Africa Report,* January–February 1993, 21.

45. Richard Joseph, "Mending Torn Liberia," *Christian Science Monitor,* 9 August 1993, 19; Inter Press Service, 12 July 1993. I am grateful for helpful suggestions from Terrence Lyons in this instance.

46. Peter da Costa, "Mediators Hold Breath on Cease-Fire Agreement," Inter-Press Service, 26 July 1993.

47. Sawyer, *The Dynamics of Conflict Management in Liberia.*

48. For an appreciation of Gordon-Somers, see Alao, *The Burden of Collective Goodwill,* 118–120.

49. IGNU, "Report on the Visit of Former President Jimmy Carter to Liberia" (internal memorandum, Carter Center, Atlanta, GA, 12 September 1992); Vogt, *The Liberian Crisis and ECOMOG,* 370–371.

50. Cohen, *Intervening in Africa,* 160.

51. The IFMC was still active throughout the war; although it organized protests against the inclusion of warlords in the peace agreements in March 1995 and February 1996, its presence on the council would have provided a good balance.

52. Richard Joseph, "Mending Torn Liberia," *Christian Science Monitor*, 9 August 1993; briefing meeting at National Democratic Institute, Washington, DC, 5 August 1993.

53. For a discussion of Taylor's lost opportunity to embark on a process of reconciliation and national unity during his first year in office, see Anatole Ayissi, *West African Peacekeeping and Disarmament Project, Mission to Liberia 12–17 December 1999, Report* (Geneva: United Nations Institute for Disarmament Research, 2000).

54. The best work on this period is Hirsch, *Sierra Leone;* see also Kwaku Nuamah and I. William Zartman, "Sierra Leone,' in Lahneman, *Military Intervention.*

55. Abdullah, "Bush Path to Destruction"; Alie, "Background to the Conflict," in Ayissi and Poulton, *Bound to Cooperate;* Jimmy Kandeh, "Criminalization of the RUF Insurgency in Sierra Leone," in Arnson and Zartman, *Rethinking the Economics of War.*

56. David Pratt, "Sierra Leone: The Forgotten Crisis; Report to the Minister of Foreign Affairs," 23 April 1999, http://www.sierra-leone.org/pratt042399.html, 17 (accessed 20 December 2000).

57. http://www.sierra-leone.org/communique?html (accessed 20 December 2000).

58. http://www.sierra-leone.org/slnews0898.html (accessed 15 October 2002).

59. Principal Deputy Assistant Secretary of State for Africa Johnie Carson, "Testimony to the Africa Subcommittee, House Committee on International Relations," 105th Cong., 2nd sess., 11 June 1998; *Resolution 559 on Sierra Leone,* House of Representatives, 105th Cong., 2nd sess., 10 October 1998.

60. U.S. assistance was primarily in humanitarian aid and incidentally in military logistics, not in underwriting operations. It provided $55 million in humanitarian assistance to Sierra Leone in fiscal 1999; $3.9 million to ECOMOG in communications, transportation, and other logistical services through Pacific Architects and Engineers (PA&E) and their subcontractor International Charters, Inc., in fiscal 1998; and an additional $1.3 million to ECOMOG in medical supplies and equipment in 1999; see statements by Assistant Secretary of State Susan Rice before the Senate Foreign Relations Committee, African Affairs Subcommittee, 106th Cong., 2nd. sess., on 11 October 2000 on "U.S. Sierra Leone Policy" and before the House Committee on International Relations, Africa Subcommittee, 106th Cong., 1st sess., on 23 March 1999 on "Sierra Leone."

61. Natacha Scott and Larry Thompson, "An Invisible War in Africa," *Christian Science Monitor*, 29 July 1998, 12.

62. See the insightful analysis in Alao, *The Burden of Collective Goodwill.*

4

SOMALIA,
1988–1993

SOMALIA, A POOR COUNTRY WITH A STRATEGIC LOCATION AND TROUBLESOME irredentist pretensions, had been a football of the Cold War, tossed from one side to the other in reaction to similar passes by its larger neighbor, Ethiopia.[1] The breakdown of multiparty clan-based politics led to the military coup of Mohammed Siad Barre in 1969 and his search for support for his national irredentism in an alliance with the Soviet Union. When Ethiopia, part of whose territory (the Ogaden) fell within the Somali claims, changed sides to join the Soviet camp after the overthrow of Emperor Haile Selassie by the derg (military committee) of Mengistu Haile Mariam and defeated Somalia in the Ogaden War of 1977–1978, Somalia desperately turned to the United States for a new alliance partner. The United States obliged in part and gradually provided military and economic support to Somalia. But the military defeat and weakened health (notably after a car accident in 1986[2]) caused Siad Barre to turn increasingly paranoid, narrow his political base in the Darod clan to his immediate Marehan subclan and his Ogadeni and Dulbahante relatives (termed his M-O-D alliance) with some strategic ties with parts of other clans, and rely on repression to maintain his control.

By the mid-1980s Siad's state was clearly in the penultimate stage of collapse, a besieged subethnic bastion alienated from most of its population and governing little of its territory, supported largely by foreign aid given for Cold War purposes. In a government reorganization in January 1988, "Marehans took over the command of every ministry where money was to be made," and two years later Siad Barre could not find "a prime minister outside his charmed circle; none was foolhardy enough to accept."[3] A recently established regional organization, the Inter-Governmental Agency on Drought and Development (IGADD), in April 1988

77

**Missed Opportunities:
Somalia, 1988–1993**

October 1988 The Hargeisa massacre provided an opportunity for
UN Security Council, Organization of African Unity, and the Inter-
Governmental Agency on Drought and Development condemnation,
mediation of a monitored cease-fire, and convocation of a national
reconciliation conference under U.S.-USSR leadership.

May 1990–August 1990 The call for a sovereign national conference
offered an opportunity for U.S.–Soviet–Inter-Governmental Agency
on Drought and Development mediation of Siad Barre's resignation
and leadership transition.

March–June 1991 Cease-fire and a partial conference at Djibouti offered the possibility of success if complemented by earlier UN Security Council authorization of UN Operation in Somalia I with an
arms embargo and a more inclusive participation.

March 1992 A new cease-fire opened the opportunity for rapid UN
Security Council authorization of humanitarian intervention, peacekeeping monitors with extended rules of engagement, confidence-
building measures, and a reconciliation conference, under a broadened mandate for UN mediator Mohamed Sahnoun.

March 1993 The transition from Unified Task Force to UN Operation in Somalia II required a continuation of Unified Task Force
policies of grassroots institutionalization, agreement enforcement,
and policing.

October 1993 The confrontation between the militias and the Delta
Force was the opportunity for a firm reaction by U.S. forces in Somalia to deaths at the Aideed corral.

consummated a conflict management agreement between Mengistu and
Siad Barre on peaceful relations that had been initiated two years earlier
at its founding meeting in Djibouti. Ironically, a Somali dissident group,
the Somali National Movement (SNM), which had camped on the other
side of the border under Ethiopian protection, was thereby released and returned to northern Somalia to spark the revolt against Siad Barre's rem-

nant of a state. The brutal response of Siad Barre's army gave the international community an opportunity to condemn the regime and take steps for its succession, but that opportunity was allowed to pass.

By the end of 1990, Siad Barre's fall was evidently imminent, offering a last opportunity for a negotiated and consensual transition, but no mediator stepped forward to seize the moment. The collapse of the regime at the beginning of 1991 left a vacuum that rival clan militias fought savagely to fill. Exhausted, they declared a cease-fire in May and met perfunctorily in a conference in Djibouti in June. But little was resolved and the opportunity for a new beginning was again allowed to pass by weak mediators and slow UN action. By September, the militias were back at it again.

In the next two years, political militias and roving gangs fought to evict each other and foreign intervenors from their territories. A UN representative negotiated a new cease-fire in February 1992, but it took the UN Security Council another six months to respond to the opportunity for appropriate intervention to turn the cease-fire into a peace process. The UN Operation in Somalia (UNOSOM) I and then the U.S.-led Unified Task Force (UNITAF) were finally authorized, but their small successes were let drop by the new U.S. administration and the UN in the transition to UNOSOM II in early 1993, when the opportunity was present to continue peace building. In October, a UNOSOM unit was ambushed by rebels, and a U.S. retaliation raid produced publicly displayed casualties. The opportunity for a solid response was dropped, and instead the United States showed that it could be chased out of a conflict area by lawless bands. With that lesson firmly in place, ripeness fell away and the familiar soft, stable, self-serving stalemate took its place, leaving the many subsequent peace initiatives of the 1990s devoid of motive and momentum. Opportunity to end deadly violence and state collapse in Somalia did not begin to appear again until the next century.

The purpose of interventions in the later 1980s and early 1990s would have been to restore an institutional structure for responsible governance— a state—and in the circumstances this could only be done by building local orders and then building on them. More than in other cases (but perhaps closest to Lebanon), given the complex nature of Somali political society, overcoming collapse and conflict required handling both political and militia leaders and combining them into local institutions of law and order, rather than simply installing a national structure. The complexity of Somali political society makes getting it right exceptionally difficult for an external intervenor. In a segmentary society, of which Somalia is a prime example— characterized as "myself against my brother, my brother and I against our cousin, we cousins against the outside world"—solidarity is negative.[4] That means that intraclan conflict is basic and overcome only by an external enemy, either within the society or outside.[5] Intervention is prima facie a *casus foederis;* external support for one faction is a reason for solidarity of the others in opposition to it, and external targeting of one faction can either augment solidarity against it or be used by it to create solidarity against the intervenor. Hence an even hand was necessary, the maximum positive solidarity—state building—possible was a dynamic balancing of oppositions, and if targeting were to take place, it needed to be decisive.

The six moments of opportunity discussed here are of three types. Two were preventive, before the final collapse of the state and the flight of its saboteur, Siad Barre; three were constructive, during the diverse efforts to begin the state reconstruction process; and the last was quite different, a firm response required to make peace enforcers' threats credible. In the preventive cases, the stalemate was present in prospect, objectively, but the intervenors' challenge included producing a subjective awareness among the parties of their inability to fill the impending vacuum alone, as well providing attractive early retirement for Siad Barre himself. The entry point was negative in the first instance, provided by the Hargeisa massacre, and positive in the second, provided by the opposition manifesto. The next three opportunities took place within the ups and downs of the ensuing conflict, characteristically after a cease-fire had been achieved but was left unexploited by an absence of tough mediation to move toward conflict resolution. In all three instances, the missing ingredients were the same: rapid and decisive UN Security Council action, adequate peace enforcement (Chapter VII), military intervention for security and disarmament, police force training, and patient mediation on the ground and in convoked sessions. The last instance concerns another problem recurring in many cases: the refusal to deliver when the limiting threat to contain unacceptable behavior is challenged. Peacemaking should not have to be war-making for the intervenor, but to remain credible, it does have to make the parties' war-making a noncredible alternative, and that means blocking the pursuit of conflict, especially when conflict management is the announced policy.[6] Management of conflict requires conflict first to be stalemated, in a manner that hurts the conflicting parties, not the intervenor.

October 1988: The Hargeisa massacre provided an opportunity for UN Security Council, Organization of African Unity, and the Inter-Governmental Agency on Drought and Development condemnation, mediation of a monitored cease-fire, and convocation of a national reconciliation conference under U.S.-USSR leadership.[7]

The repressive nature of the Siad Barre regime could scarcely be questioned throughout the 1980s, but the invasion and massacre of 27–30 May

1988 was correctly characterized by the State Department as a surprise about which little information was available.[8] Especially the north (former British Somaliland) had long felt neglected and subject to discrimination by Siad Barre's narrowly clan-based regime, but most other clan areas had also been alienated by the regime. Repression of Isaaq clansmen in the north began in 1982 and intensified after 1985, with a curfew imposed in 1987. Former parliament members linked to the largely Isaaq SNM were given long prison sentences (some commuted from a death sentence by the president) in February 1988, but such actions were normal for the regime. The Somali-Ethiopian agreement of 3 April 1988 was greeted positively, but its side effects were unexpected; the SNM was certainly prepared to attack, considering the mere six weeks separating their agreement from their invasion, and Ethiopia, not one to leave its protégés out in the cold, helped in the preparations as compensation for the IGADD-brokered Djibouti agreement. In sum, Somalia was known to be an endemic disaster, but its flashpoint was unsuspected.

The SNM attack on northern Somalia quickly captured Burao and Hargeisa, Somalia's second largest city, which it held until mid-July. The Somali army response was brutal. Under the military direction of Siad Barre's son-in-law, General Omar Hajji Mohammed Siad Hersi "Morgan," Hargeisa was almost totally destroyed, civilians raped and massacred, wells poisoned, herds destroyed, and refugee camps wiped out. Since local Isaaqs and refugee Ogadenis from Ethiopia had been fighting over scarce land since the end of the Ogaden war, the attack also became a war between the SNM and the Ogadeni militias. As a result, 350,000 new (Isaaq) refugees were created, about two-thirds of the population of the two towns. The United States provided $1.9 million in disaster assistance to the victims of the conflict in 1988 and an additional $630,000 assistance and $18 million food aid in 1989, but it also provided the government with $1.4 million of small arms and ammunition that was shipped just before and saw use during the conflict. Siad Barre was scheduled for a state visit to Washington in mid-June, but the invitation was canceled because of the fighting.

In August 1988, Siad Barre appointed a committee to study the northern problem, which reported a number of broad measures of reconstruction and reconciliation at the end of the year, and his party politburo in January 1989 recommended reforms and a new policy of reconciliation and reconstruction in the north. A new committee was appointed in March to implement the measures, but the government had already lost control of the countryside and only held the destroyed cities as terrorizing army camps.[9] In the meantime, rebellion broke out in the rest of the country, removing important elements of Siad Barre's former support. A disaffected

Ogadeni group, the Somali Patriotic Movement (SPM) led by Colonel Ahmed Omar Jess, began attacks in the south, and a mutiny of Hawiye troops associated with the United Somali Congress (USC) in central Somalia brought military retaliation on the local population. The desertion of the Ogadenis was a serious blow to the regime. Spreading insecurity led the populations to carry the dynamic of Siad Barre's repressive policy to its conclusion and to seek protection within their clans, in opposition to the Marehan-based army and regime.

News accounts of the vicious fighting were plentiful, and the United States was aware enough of the massacres to cancel the state visit in the middle of 1988, a rather serious move. It was, however, only symbolic and needed to be followed up by concrete measures. The summer of the year, while the blood was fresh, was the appropriate time to intervene, even though the United States was busy at the time concluding the negotiations for the Namibia-Angola agreement to be signed in New York just before Christmas. The Somali situation provided an occasion to continue cooperation with the Soviet Union on African issues, and the Soviets were ready for further conflict management collaboration with the United States, including on Somalia.[10] A joint démarche in northeast Africa might have taxed the Africa Bureau of the State Department at the very moment it was celebrating its accomplishments in the southwest, but the cooperation created by the Namibia-Angola démarche provided a very propitious setting for further collaboration. The United States had a dominant role in Somalia and so would have to be part of any intervention, but the USSR's position as former patron gave it a role and interest as well.[11] The two superpowers would then turn to the UN Security Council with their program.

The action would begin with a condemnation of the massacres and a call for a cease-fire in place; even if the cease-fire did not take hold immediately, the subsequent steps would be pursued. An investigation into the Somali troops' massacre of their own population would be requested of the UN.[12] The desertion of the government by supporting subclans of the Ogadenis, Mijertein, and Dulbahante, which came in early 1989, would have produced a bandwagon effect if it had come in the midst of an international effort to move to a new regime; Somalis have a long history of crossing the aisle in times of opportunity. Diplomatic pressure from the two Security Council leaders, backed by the suspension of financial support for Somalia, including the very arms shipments that were in the pipeline, would be used to achieve the cease-fire. In the event, the U.S. ambassador, Frank Crigler, recommended freezing the arms deliveries in June and received State Department support but was overridden by the Defense Department, which remained fixed on Somalia's strategic position and proceeded with a joint training exercise (Bright Star) in August; smaller exercises continued over the ensuing months until riots in the streets and massacres of the opposition forced the practice to be canceled the following August.[13]

IGADD would then have the task of convening a national reconciliation conference, to be attended by all Somali political groups, as well as clan elders, religious figures, and education leaders. Such a meeting would give a larger role to the political leaders before the conflict was completely taken over by the military and would have afforded the parties a political rather than a military solution. Although this is a formula for a sovereign national conference (CNS), which was not invented until two years later in Benin, Somalia was especially well situated to provide its own model; its political culture included the *guurti* and the *shir*, long meetings of clan elders to make policy and manage conflict.[14] Such meetings follow their own agenda, but their dynamics would head them toward the formation of a government of national unity, the revision of government structures, the holding of new elections, and the retirement of Siad Barre.[15]

The organization of such a conference by IGADD, however, needed to be monitored with much patience by external parties—the United States, USSR, UK, Italy—so that the meeting would stay on track and not break up before appropriate decisions were made. The support of Italy and Egypt for Siad Barre needed to be contained by the other external parties. IGADD would also need help from the outside in keeping Ethiopia, Djibouti, and even Kenya from manipulating the talks toward an outcome designed to fit their parochial interests regarding their own Somali populations. The mixture of patience with a complex culture and insistence on results at the end of a long day is difficult to achieve, and its absence undid later efforts in Somalia. But it is necessary. "One would expect that in the absence of a democratic mechanism allowing for corrective measures, the international community would come to the rescue of the victimized population [in 1988,]" wrote Mohamed Sahnoun, without explaining how. "It did not, and this represents the *first missed opportunity*."[16]

Had the international community taken that step, it would have produced an ambiguous situation of the type so comfortable for Somali society. At a minimum, it would have identified the key constituencies and their leaders, thereby making later peacemaking efforts more effective. Siad Barre would certainly have continued to maneuver, but if an external carrot-stick such as continuation of development aid and international financial institution (IFI) creditworthiness would be tied to the achievement of a consensus result, a result could be obtainable. Siad Barre and his family would have needed a retirement home, such as Saudi Arabia could have provided. If the challenge had been met by a combination of internal dialogue and external attentions, Somalia could have bumped along to a new national political system, no worse than the states of West Africa that were to succeed with their CNS processes.[17] Indeed, in some respects Somalia might have done much better because of its cultural and religious coherence. U.S. interest in such action would have been part humanitarian but in large part strategic, as it moved to stabilize an ally that was still considered useful in 1988. If it were to fail, the efforts deployed would not have been costly, and Somalia would have fallen into civil war, which is what happened anyhow.

May 1990–August 1990: The call for a sovereign national conference offered an opportunity for U.S–Soviet–Inter-Governmental Agency on Drought and Development mediation of Siad Barre's resignation and leadership transition.[18]

Exactly two years later, on 15 May 1990, with the CNS movement growing in West and Central Africa, repression in full swing in Somalia, and the government reduced to the control of Mogadishu and a few other cities, 144 prominent Somalis led by members of the Abgal Hawiye subclan living in Mogadishu issued a manifesto calling for a Somali national conference and a broad agenda for reform.[19] Without the immediate public support they needed from the international community, dozens were arrested; when their trial opened, however, a massive crowd of local sympathizers surrounded the court in Mogadishu, and the reformers were released.[20] A second manifesto was issued in June, as opposition party endorsement grew and the parties became aware of the need for political cooperation through the summer. Italy quietly picked up the opportunity and tried to mediate between the Manifesto Group and Siad Barre throughout the year, but to no avail; following a preliminary meeting in Rome in November, plans for a conference the following month collapsed as Italy's move was perceived as an attempt to save Siad Barre. The United States also tried to promote internal negotiations. But all attempts focused on finding common ground between dying government and rising opposition, the same error that had doomed mediation attempts in Ethiopia during the past decade.[21] What was needed was an effort to bring the living forces of the country together, to set up a new political system to take over from the collapsed state.

At the end of August, Siad Barre announced new elections in six months, but the opposition only saw tricks in the proposal. In mid-October, he issued a new multiparty constitution and appointed an Isaaq prime minister in order to placate the SNM. Following victories by the USC militias in central Somalia in November, he declared a state of emergency. At the end of the year, Italy encouraged Egypt to conduct its own mediation, involving Boutros Boutros-Ghali as Egyptian foreign minister, but it was too late: the major opposition groups, sensing victory, refused. Assistant Secretary of State Cohen reported that "in 1989 and 1990, no analysts, to my knowledge, predicted the military demise of the Somali regime,"[22] which is surprising; the journal, *Horn of Africa*, for example, was replete with analyses of the "collapsed Somali State" and the "imminent fall of the regime," and expatriate Somalis and academic Somalia-watchers agreed that Siad was finished.[23] On 6 January 1991, U.S. and other diplomats left Mogadishu by helicopter in a nighttime evacuation. Three weeks later, Siad Barre left Mogadishu by tank in a daytime escape. Three days before, on 24 January, in a last desperate effort to save his regime, he had appointed a new government under another northern Isaaq, Omar Arteh Ghalleb, as prime minister, which then met with the Manifesto Group and called for a cease-fire, in vain.

By October 1990, the focus of coordination had turned to the military campaigns against the government. The "opposition groups ha[d] no common programme except to overthrow Siyad Barre" was the judgment of a commentator at the end of the year. "Once that goal is achieved it is most likely that they will turn their guns against each other. The civil war might continue. Only the enemy will be replaced."[24] The summer of the manifesto, however, had provided a window of opportunity while the parties were still thinking politically but needed help to think cooperatively. The Somali conflict had still been in the hands of politicians in the summer of 1990, not yet taken over by warlords (*warranleh*); a political process, once started, would have brought in other participants and created momentum. If a mediator had been able to rally factional leaders to the idea that the future was to be found in a CNS, many of Siad's supporters would likely have bolted, leaving him a lonely spoiler. The work of giving the final coup de grâce to the Siad Barre regime was being accomplished by the party militias; it was the challenge of bringing the competing politicians together to construct the replacement regime that needed help.

The resignation of the president and negotiated takeover of the capital were soon to be enacted next door in Ethiopia; the United States was barred from a role in the first event by the NSC Liberia decision, discussed in Chapter 3, but was active in the second. But there was a historic interest in Ethiopia that somehow, despite long and deep U.S. involvement, was not perceived in regard to Somalia, and the Gulf War, with the availability of other military facilities directly in the area of operations, suddenly caused Somalia to drop off the list of U.S. interests. There were other differences between the two cases, but none of them were insurmountable. In Ethiopia, there were clear-cut cohesive forces to engage and a history of U.S. dialogue with them, whereas in Somalia the U.S. engagement had been with the government itself.[25] An active U.S. role in preparing a Somali national conference would have created the domestic momentum for presidential succession, without direct U.S. involvement in the latter. Mediation would have been needed to help the parties come together before the military phase of succession had begun and coordinate their accession, an accession that it was clear from the outset no single party could (nor should) win.

Thus a U.S. involvement would have been necessary if collapse were to be stanched. An available partner in 1990 was the Soviet Union, Somalia's former patron that was involved in cooperative efforts in Ethiopia at the time; "US-Soviet cooperation was a White House priority."[26] England was another potential mediating partner, with some past contacts with opposition figures. Italy and Egypt were long-standing players in the Somali scene, and suspect; but both were knowledgeable and necessary to an eventual mediation. Both were seen as both linked to Siad Barre and motivated by an interest in keeping him in power, however, much as Nigeria was compromised at the same moment by a desire to save Doe in Liberia (Chapter 3). To be helpful, they would have had to be persuaded by the United States and the USSR to play the appropriate biased mediator's role, which is to deliver the party toward which the mediator is biased.[27] Only with an ostensibly powerful and neutral partner and a lot of careful orchestration could they constitute an effective mediating team.

Other external parties were in a more compromised position in regard to the internal multiparty conflict. Ethiopia itself was a knowledgeable party with ties to the SNM, but it was scarcely neutral in the conflict and generally taboo on the Somali scene, and it was in the final throes of its own civil war; Addis Ababa's selection as the prime venue for talks in the coming decade caused difficulties for attendance and outcomes. Djibouti, the other principal venue for negotiations, was so small in the equation as to be useful but weightless and could not have replaced the necessary collaboration of the United States, USSR, and the UK, working with Egypt and Italy.

Concerted efforts were required if the absence of a real stalemate was to be turned into a real opening. The ingredients of a positive international intervention are clear and were in the discourse and decisions regarding other similar situations at the time. The sovereign national conference and other measures called for in the manifesto provided a wise and workable formula for a transition, as practiced increasingly in other African countries. In West and Equatorial Africa, the CNSs took over from a functioning if weakened state, not from an already collapsed authority. These conferences, of course, were not convoked by an intervening power but by the internal political forces themselves. The role of the external coalition would have been to compellingly urge the parties to come together in a location such as Djibouti, closer to Somalia and more neutral than Rome, or Berbera or Obbia, on the opposition-occupied coast, to fill the opportunity of their accession and avoid the impending catastrophe of their disagreement.

In sum, it is clearer that there was an objective than a subjective moment, creating a need for assistance as parties not yet in a painful deadlock needed to be convinced that they were heading toward one and not toward the open door of victory. Something was missing to turn a moment into an opportunity.[28]

March–June 1991: Cease-fire and a partial conference at Djibouti offered the possibility of success if complemented by an earlier UN Security Council authorization of UN Operation in Somalia I with an arms embargo and a more inclusive participation.[29]

The overthrow of Siad Barre left a power vacuum in Somalia that no single party, faction, or clan could fill. The opposition groups were aware of this situation and—except for the SNM—sought both to find a solution for all of Somalia and to protect their clan interests.[30] Therefore, both convocation and war were used to fill the vacuum, and the convening of an all-Somali conference was the occasion for the search for both a solution for the country and an advantage for each party—a living chicken dilemma.[31] Attempts throughout the 1980s to counter the Siad Barre legacy and unite the fractioned clan opposition had failed repeatedly.[32] The predominant group outside of the north was a relative newcomer to the opposition, the USC, representing the Hawiye in the center of the country, but the Hawiye (like everyone else) were divided into competing subclans. When Siad Barre fled Mogadishu, Ali Mahdi of the Abgal subclan, a member of the Manifesto Group, was precipitously appointed interim president by the USC despite the fact that the Abgal had only jumped in at the last moment to overthrow the Siad Barre regime. Mahdi then appointed a government under Ghalleb, Siad Barre's last prime minister, that was predominantly Hawiye and contained many members of Ghalleb's previous abortive government. General Mohammed Farah Aideed of the Habr Gidir subclan, an off-again-on-again opponent of Siad Barre with a base outside Mogadishu, contested the selection. Not only personality but the rivalry of a sedentary versus pastoral way of life, respectively, between the subclans fueled their conflict. The state had become the principal means for clan enrichment; hence decisions at that point were vital.

Farther south, a complicated ballet typical of Somali politics was under way. Members of Siad Barre's subclan, the Marehan Darod, fled Mogadishu, regrouped to form the Somali National Front (SNF), and in February nearly retook the capital before being driven south beyond Kismayo by Aideed. There, under General "Morgan," they joined the alliance of Ali Mahdi against Aideed, where they entered into conflict with the Ogadeni Darod already organized in the same region as the SPM. Although the main Ogadeni faction of the SPM under Omar Jess was allied with Aideed in the military takeover of Mogadishu, another faction in reaction allied with "Morgan" and Ali Mahdi. Siad Barre himself fled only to another part of the Darod area in the south to regroup, amass huge supplies of arms, and twice return to attack Mogadishu and devastate the surrounding countryside, helping create the conditions for the resulting famine.[33]

To the obvious need for a national reconciliation conference, Mahdi's government responded with an invitation at the end of February 1991, repeated twice in the ensuing months, but major groups—notably the SNM in the north and the Aideed USC—declined to come. Ethiopia and Eritrea also issued invitations and were rejected. Finally, Djibouti agreed to host a conference with Saudi financial support in May, held at last on 5–11 June. The meeting was positive in that it allowed factions to meet and sound each other out and to reconvene on 15–21 July with a few more participants, but still with the SNM and the USC (Aideed) boycotting and the SPM repudiating its representative. The conference called for a cease-fire on 26 July, reaffirmed the 1960 constitution and the unity of Somalia (against the SNM, which had taken the north into secession as Somaliland on 17 May), and sought to allocate membership in Mahdi's government. The insistence on Mahdi's presidency and the fight for government seats exacerbated clan tensions and led to renewed hostilities between clans and then in November between the two USC factions in the second battle over Mogadishu, leaving another 30,000 dead by March 1992.

The fighting against Siad Barre and then among the opposition factions destroyed the country. Not only had the state collapsed but all logistics were interdicted and roads blocked, the feeble economy ruined, and anarchy imposed. The result was a famine that put 4.5 million people at risk, including half a million dead, 2 million displaced, and 1 million made refugees.[34] There was plenty of hurt but not enough sense of stalemate to fit the objective circumstances in mid-1991. In fact, the pain of all the others was seen by each party as a potential opportunity. The Djibouti conference was an expected and awaited event, but the parties were still stuck on their positions and unwilling to reach a larger agreement. Somalia was sick from its hostilities and dying of famine, but its clan leaders saw in that situation both a chance and a need to leap to the spoils of victory for themselves, rather than an opportunity to overcome the Siad Barre legacy. Each of the two USC factions held half of Mogadishu and after May observed an informal cease-fire until September, while more and more gangs of armed youths roamed in between beyond the control of either faction; "according to Mohammed Sahnoun, Aideed and Ali Mahdi were waiting for an outside mediator to broker a compromise."[35] They needed help.

Essentially, help had to come in the form of experienced mediation and authoritative constraints to stay at the table until the fundamental issues and their implementation were resolved. The Djibouti conference in June was run through with flaws—deficiencies both structural and processual. Structural deficiencies meant that the parties were not focused on a lasting settlement but were still jockeying for positions, testing their strength, and fighting for their own security. Only six movements were represented, and not all stuck to their commitments at the conference; they vied for each other's clientele among the clans and their internal organizations were shaky. The movements had only limited control over their militias on the ground, and the militias had not yet settled their own territorial limits. As a result, Chapter VI peacekeeping to monitor a stable and demarcated cease-fire was impossible.

Other deficiencies pointed to shortcomings in the process. Provisions were not made for the representation of all communities (including Siad Barre's own subclan), for equitable mechanisms of power sharing, or even for a way of determining what was equitable. Many ends were left hanging: attributions of ministerial portfolios, enforcement of the cease-fire, financing of the elections, among others. Each of the mediators carried its special bias, without being able to deliver the party toward whom it was biased: Djibouti, the host, was opposed to the SNM secession and its Isaaq base and tried to unite two small Dir parties—USF (Issa Dir) and SDA (Gadabursi Dir)—to challenge the SNM. Italy was opposed to Aideed's USC and tried to foster support for the candidates of two Darod parties—SSDF (Mijertein Darod) and Omar Jess's SPM (Ogadeni Darod). Egypt supported the USC, and Ethiopia, a player in the wings, also favored the two Dir and Darod alliances. The leanings of the mediators worked to exclude the two major actors—the secessionist Isaaq SNM in the north and the belligerent Habr Gidir Hawiye USC in the south—so that the conference became a search for support for Ali Mahdi and the Manifesto Group rather than a search for a solution for Somalia. Laudable though the Manifesto Group may have been, it

did not have the control of the situation on the ground that would have supported its claim to run the government.

Efforts to capitalize on the opportunity offered by the May cease-fire
and the June Djibouti conference and to remedy the deficiencies to make
Djibouti work needed to begin with the mediators themselves. Djibouti
had invited the UN to participate, but the Secretariat declined, without reasons; Under-Secretary for Political Affairs James Jonah, who was to mediate a cease-fire a year later, specifically discouraged UN involvement
and found Somalia a fractious backwater to deal with.[36] Yet the UN, in the
form of an experienced and prestigious SRSG such as Mohamed Sahnoun,
sent a year later, was the only agency with the authority and neutrality to
work out an agreement. A skillful mediator was needed to use the de facto
cease-fire to confirm the various factions' positions and foster a working
relationship among them. Skill was also required to overcome the presumption of Ali Mahdi's presidency so that the USC (Aideed) could attend. A more skilled mediator would have kept the parties in session for
the long discussions that Somalis enjoy, allowing them to work out the
necessary compromises and details, rather than cramming an incomplete
agreement into a short week.

But more than an SRSG was needed; the whole mechanism of the UN
was required, including a General Assembly resolution urging the parties
to an immediate settlement and a Security Council resolution defining the
SRSG's role. The weight of the UN was necessary to focus the parties' attention on the need to stop fighting and start rebuilding. The renewal of a
Western development aid program, whose termination in 1989 had exacerbated the conflict, would have been a powerful carrot for the mediator
to wield and would have helped provide alternatives to the loot-to-eat dynamics of the conflict.[37]

Instead of trying to propose a compromise and power sharing, Djibouti tried to impose a victor and a power grab where neither existed on
the ground. A follow-up agreement was signed at the beginning of August
to close some of the loopholes, but it did not deal with the major problems
of the conference. Instead, when Ali Mahdi announced his government in
October, it had forty-two ministers allocated to the six parties attending
the Djibouti conference and Ghalleb was still prime minister, despite an
earlier agreement to the contrary. The second battle of Mogadishu, between the two USC Hawiye factions, began in mid-November 1991.

A crucial question is whether mediation skill alone would have enabled the conference to succeed, or whether a military force—an earlier
but augmented UNOSOM I—would have been necessary and available.
Blakeley argued for a preemptive mission of 5,000–7,000 troops to secure

the cities, airfields, and ports; disarm the militias; and respond when fighting broke out. He pointed out that the militias were not yet well enough armed and organized to offer effective resistance to a smaller force than eventually constituted.[38] Even though the reasoning is correct, the questions remain, on one hand, whether any military force was necessary to the success of the mediation, and, on the other, whether a military force under a Chapter VII mandate—the type of mandate necessitated by tasks of disarmament and defense—was possible at the very moment (June 1991) when the UN-authorized ground forces were being withdrawn from the Gulf War arena.

A démarche as proposed should not be taken in ignorance of the possible need for military involvement, but neither should it be held prior hostage to all the eventualities that might ensue in the event of success or failure. Properly conducted, the diplomatic effort had a good chance of bringing success, and had it done so, a true Chapter VI cease-fire monitoring mission could have been possible. Had it run into difficulties, a new decision would have been required, either to abandon the effort without having incurred a major cost or raise the ante and put Chapter VII troops on the ground. The great powers and the United States first among them were still preoccupied with the recent Chapter VII exercise against Iraq and might well have authorized others but not have taken on an active role in the region themselves. What happened instead was a mixture of abandon and slightly raised ante, without having capitalized on the opportunity to try the diplomatic effort.

Although it would be hard to argue that Somalia represented a vital U.S. interest, particularly after its "strategic redundancy" was shown to be fully redundant in the Gulf War, there is no doubt that a U.S. responsibility was involved. Somalia was one of the largest recipients of per capita U.S. aid in both development and military assistance, its human rights situation was deemed worthy of U.S. attention, and its famine was finally to draw a strong response at the end of the administration of George H. W. Bush. Between Ethiopia and Kenya, two countries of serious U.S. attention, Somalia was worth a UN authorization to act in time. A Senate resolution introduced by Senator Nancy Kassebaum (R-KS) called urgent attention to the humanitarian crisis in Somalia in July 1991,[39] but Senate resolutions tend to be a cry in the wind. Instead, "Somalia dropped from our radar screens," observed Secretary Cohen. "The United States turned out the lights, closed the door, and forgot about the place" is the oft-quoted comment of Ambassador Crigler.[40] Had a UN-led mediation at Djibouti failed, the situation would have been no worse than what happened when Djibouti in fact failed. Had it started a process going toward a loose

power-sharing arrangement to keep Somalia together—or even if it had
kept all but the north together—it not only would have avoided the famine
and escalating war, which produced 1.8 million refugees, 300,000 civilian
deaths, and $11.7 billion in military and nonmilitary intervention costs,
but also would have made Somalia again eligible for a much-needed mul-
tisourced development aid program of $50–100 million per year.

March 1992: A new cease-fire opened the opportunity for rapid UN
Security Council authorization of humanitarian intervention,
peacekeeping monitors with extended rules of engagement,
confidence-building measures, and a reconciliation conference, under
a broadened mandate for UN mediator Mohamed Sahnoun.[41]

The second battle for Mogadishu, between the two USC factions, raged
throughout the rest of 1991 while famine and disease claimed an estimated
300,000 lives, immediately endangered 1.5 million others, and left an additional 3 million (adding up to over three-quarters of the 6 million Somalis) at risk. But it was not until 1992, when former Egyptian foreign
minister Boutros Boutros-Ghali became UN Secretary-General, that the
conflict drew meaningful attention from the international community. A
Department of Peace-Keeping Operations (DPKO) proposal the previous
October to outgoing UN Secretary-General Javier Perez de Cuellar to ask
the UNSC to facilitate relief deliveries had remained on his desk, and
Under Secretary-General Jonah was sent out to look for a cease-fire only
in the last week of Perez de Cuellar's term.[42]

   The subsequent story of UN intervention in 1992 was a slow-motion
opera of bureaucratic delays and political inefficiencies lasting eight
months, marked by mounting deaths from famine and fighting. It began on
11 January when Ali Mahdi's "government" again asked for UN attention
(a message only transmitted nine days later). The Security Council urged
a cease-fire on 23 January, called for an arms embargo under Chapter VII
in a country already awash with arms, and under pressure from the United
States resisted any mention of peacekeeping forces.[43] The Secretary-
General on 31 January invited representatives of the two USC factions to
New York to reinstate a cease-fire, accompanied by representatives of the
Arab League (LAS), the OAU, and the Organization of the Islamic Conference (OIC). The new cease-fire was agreed to in their meeting on
14–15 February and was followed by an implementation agreement medi-
ated between 29 February and 3 March in Mogadishu by Under Secretary-
General Jonah.

Two weeks later the Security Council supported the Secretary-General's decision to send a humanitarian assistance coordinator and an unarmed cease-fire monitoring team under chapter VI.[44] At the same time, the Secretary-General asked Mohamed Sahnoun to undertake an unofficial fact-finding mission in Somalia; the ensuing report at the end of March urged immediate action, and the UN team achieved agreement from Aideed and Ali Mahdi on mechanisms for cease-fire monitoring and arrangements for distribution of humanitarian aid in Hargeisa, Mogadishu, and Kismayo. More than three weeks later, toward the end of April, the Security Council under Chapter VI authorized the establishment of a UN-OSOM deployment of fifty UN unarmed observers to monitor the cease-fire (the United States blocked the 500 armed troops Boutros-Ghali had requested) and appointment of an SRSG, Sahnoun.[45]

It took two more months for Sahnoun to achieve agreement to the deployment of the UN observers, who then arrived in Mogadishu a further month later. At the same time, the Security Council approved the Secretary-General's request to expand the mission to cover four operational zones across the country and adopt a 90-Day Action Plan dealing with all aspects of the situation—humanitarian relief and reconstruction, cease-fire security, and reconciliation.[46] More than two weeks later, on 12 August, the Secretary-General reported the factions' agreement to the deployment of 500 peacekeepers of UNOSOM, but a month after the previous mission expansion, as the first Pakistani peacekeepers arrived, the UNSC approved a further mission expansion of 750-person units for each of the four zones, none of which were ever deployed.[47]

The entire eight-month period was marked by two clashing trends—a continued and interlocked degradation of the security and humanitarian situations, with 3,000 people a day dying while warehouses remained stocked, and an inadequate lagging response of the UN system hobbling slowly behind the galloping anarchy. Frustrated with an absence of support and cooperation within his own organization, Sahnoun resigned at the end of October. A month later, Boutros-Ghali outlined five possible remedies: continued UNOSOM chapter VI mandate, abandonment of UNOSOM and NGO relief agencies' reliance on their own means of protection, UNOSOM Chapter VII peace enforcement action, UNOSOM augmentation under a member state's leadership (in response to a U.S. offer), and UNOSOM augmentation under UN command and control. At the beginning of December, the Security Council authorized Chapter VII action "to establish a secure environment for humanitarian relief operations" and to accept the U.S. offer to lead the operation.[48] The first U.S. troops of the

UNITAF arrived a week later, on 9 December, and 25,000 troops were on the ground in another seven weeks.

Early action was the requirement of the Somali situation, picking up from the opportunity offered by the February–March 1992 cease-fire. The parties and the people were wearied of their war but fearful of losing control to others operating under the same fear. Paradoxically, such a security dilemma provides an opportunity for a credible and skilled mediator to build the conditions of stalemate and separation that dispel that fear.[49] The dimensions of the problem were well known: academic analyses, news reports, NGO testimony, and the experience of key actors all provided a good basis for understanding the gravity and complexity of the situation. Similarly, the ingredients of appropriate action are wide-ranging and have often been identified.[50]

The cease-fire was an occasion for immediate intervention involving an active mediator responsible directly to the UN Secretary-General, robust peacekeeping forces with a mandate covering security as well as relief, and mobilization and protection of Somali civil society for the job of state rebuilding.[51] That is indeed a tall order, at a time when a new Secretary-General had just come to the UN; when Chapter VII humanitarian operations had only recently been invented;[52] when the UN's peacekeeping (not even peace enforcement) budget was deeply burdened, particularly by its Bosnian mission; when the Somali famine had not yet reached its worst paroxysm; and when no advanced planning had yet been undertaken for any operation (and indeed the UN had been out of Somalia, to the Somalis' dismay, since 1988).

But houses do not catch fire when the fire engine happens to be cruising by, and crises do not wait for all to be ready before they occur. By March 1992, there was plenty of warning of the Somali situation that some people found difficult to hear. CARE, Humans Rights Watch, and other NGOs had raised the alarm. The Africa Bureau at the State Department and the Office of Foreign Disaster Assistance (OFDA) at USAID, the bureaus most directly responsible in regard to the Somali situation, had called for urgent measures, Andrew Natsios of OFDA in a strident appeal to the House of Representatives in January[53] and Secretary Cohen in a careful analysis to the Senate in March.[54]

Sahnoun was an excellent choice as an SRSG, "someone who talked to everyone, listened carefully, and worked hard."[55] His appointment at the end of March, when he submitted his unofficial report, with direct responsibility to the Secretary-General rather than working through three undersecretaries, would have been appropriate. He would then have been able to continue the talks with faction leaders that he had begun in his unofficial mission; getting the warlords' agreement to the deployment of UN troops was necessary if their mission was to be facilitated and bloodshed reduced, yet it needed to be accelerated. He also needed support from the UN, not only from the Secretary-General himself but also throughout the system. The row with the Secretary-General that broke out in October and brought about Sahnoun's resignation arose from the publicly voiced frustration of the SRSG and poor handling by the Secretary-General and left subsequent UN operations without any effective leadership by Sahnoun's two successors, Ismat Kittani and Jonathan Howe. The issue between the Secretary-General and his special representative, according to Boutros-Ghali,[56] was one of negotiation versus force, that is, whether UN access to Somalia should be dependent on the lengthy process of negotiation with the warlords (and particularly with Aideed, whom Boutros-Ghali distrusted, if not disliked) and on the unstable provision of protection by the militias. It was necessary to negotiate, however, since the UN did not have the means to do anything else.

Jan Eliasson, one of Sahnoun's chiefs as the able Under Secretary-General for Humanitarian Affairs just appointed by Boutros-Ghali in March, had been called to Addis Ababa in April from Burundi to deal with Sudan but was discouraged by UN headquarters in New York from going on to Mogadishu; when he finally got to Somalia in September, he was shocked into action by the degraded situation.[57] Had he been able to reach Mogadishu in April, the donors' conference called in October in Geneva, which led to the adoption of Sahnoun's proposal for a Hundred-Day Plan for Accelerated Humanitarian Assistance, could have come earlier. But it would have also required participation by Somalis—notably political and social leaders, other than faction chiefs—as finally occurred only at the second humanitarian conference in Addis in December 1992.[58]

The challenges faced by an SRSG, even with expanded confidence and autonomy, are not to be minimized. On one hand was the need to bring along not only the defensive UN internal bureaucracy but also the UNSC members, the latter the task of the Secretary-General but dependent in part on the performance of the SRSG.[59] On the other hand, he needed to develop the compliance of the fractious, obstreperous faction chiefs without, however, becoming dependent on them. For this, he needed solid support and open communications from New York more than ever, and autonomy for room to maneuver.

The rapid deployment of troops with an appropriate mandate was required. Not until the U.S. UNITAF troops arrived at the end of the year were there more than 500 lightly armed forces on the ground (and these only arrived in September), despite authorizations of 3,500, for a job that was to challenge ten times that number under UNITAF and eight times that number under UNOSOM II. Troops take a while to get on station and need a carefully coordinated command structure to be effective when there.[60] Although U.S. troops would not need to constitute the totality or even the bulk of the necessary force, U.S. political will would be necessary for an early and effective response. The U.S. government began to revise its position in July, so that an earlier turnabout on the availability of troops—although not out of the question—would have required some deft persuasion.[61]

The mandate was the other side of the question. The situation was composed of a shaky cease-fire and leaky relief deliveries. The problem in UN and official U.S. eyes was food and relief, but the problem for relief was its nondeliverability because of the war—not so much the fighting per se but the protection and extortion rackets the war engendered. It was blindly naive to consider the matter of relief without providing a realistic mandate for protecting its delivery and ultimately a political solution to provide the context for ongoing relief and development. The cease-fire was imperfectly in place and needed some help. Cease-fires need monitoring, and shaky cease-fires need monitoring with muscle.

The result should have been the UNSC authorization of a cease-fire monitoring and relief delivery protection mission beginning with the immediate deployment to Mogadishu of 500 armed troops and the rapid follow-up of up to 2,000, with a robust mandate to monitor the cease-fire and ensure the passage of relief supplies to cooperating areas, with similar deployments to other port cities (Kismayu, Bosasso, Berbera) to avoid the concentration of loot and power in Mogadishu. Optimally, the force should be large enough to remove the militia's heavy weapons and conduct the disarmament program requested by the Secretary-General—in other words, requiring a combat mission—although some have suggested that disarmament could have been accomplished without violence when UNITAF first arrived.[62] The expansion of arms and armed conflict, as well as the proliferation of informal militias beyond the control of the clan factions, was not as serious in the spring of 1992 as it was to become by the fall, so that a smaller force could have accomplished the mission.[63] The need for paid protection service from the militias could also have been replaced by the creation of a Somali security force as the nucleus of a reconstituted Somali police, as mentioned by Sahnoun before the Geneva donors' conference in October.[64] The security force would have to have been chosen carefully, optimally individually (although there are few Somali individuals, only clan members).[65]

The final ingredient, reinforcing the need for negotiations, was the provision of plans for state reconstruction, the misnamed "nation building" so often decried. The first step was taken by Sahnoun in convening a meeting of civil society leaders in the Seychelles in October, for which he was reprimanded.[66] This work needed to be pursued, working from the bottom up, building caucuses of both traditional and modern leaders, including political figures. There was a need to include military figures but also within a context of leaders of society. In 1992 (and even more so in 1991) there was still room for civilian and political participants in the state rebuilding process. By the time of the Addis Ababa conference a year later on 15 March 1993, the follow-up on the Seychelles meeting, the military faction leaders were the only participants, having taken over the political scene by force of arms, and civil society leaders were only allowed into the balcony. As in Liberia, "factions signed onto but failed to implement peace accords, in part because they had no interest in the implementation, and in part because they lacked the political capacity to enforce the accords they signed."[67] Building a peace process required the creation of incremental outcomes—food, roles, ongoing processes—that factional leaders would have an interest in buying into; the process would also need to develop the capability of continuing without some of the leaders if necessary—the assemblage of a train that was headed somewhere, that would leave the stations as planned even without some passengers, and that was protected against malicious derailment.[68] Such a project would take serious commitment and coordination in economic, social, political, and military engineering.

The overall proposal is not radical; it derives from a simple examination of the needs of the situation and contains only elements that were mentioned at the time. It was not adopted because of a focus on other, "larger" issues to the neglect of the Somali problem at hand. The International Organization (IO) Bureau of the State Department, thinking of limitations on the solution without thinking of the gravity of the problem, focused on legal and financial constraints; other parts of the U.S. government from Congress to the White House fell in line, until shaken by some strong voices, too late to keep the conflict from escalating beyond the ability of the outside world to bring it under control. Yet the Somali crisis hit the Cable News Network (CNN) screens in March 1992, at the right time to provide a background for building public support if the leadership was willing to do so. Balking at a timely humanitarian intervention because of the estimated cost of $7.5 million, the United States then incurred $2.2 billion in military costs and the UN an equal figure.[69] The UN too succumbed to its bureaucratic culture in New York, falling prey both to its internal bureaucratic turf wars and to its aversion to shirtsleeves diplomacy.[70] As a result, finally responding to the CNN effect, the United

States reacted at the end of the year, successfully providing protection for the relief workers but neither disarmament for the factions nor reconstruction of the Somali polity, and then made a bobbled pass of its functions to the UN.

March 1993: The opportunity for a seamless transition from Unified Task Force to UN Operation in Somalia II required a continuation of Unified Task Force policies of grassroots institutionalization, agreement enforcement, and policing.

When the Clinton administration came to Washington, its firm purpose was to get out of Somalia, with little regard for the implementation of the policies UNITAF had rather successfully started in the field. On the other side, the UN Secretariat had its own ideas about what should be done in Somalia but was curiously unconscious of its total lack of the means to do so and strangely uncomprehending of the goals that the U.S. administration—Bush before Clinton—had set for itself in entering Somalia. On one side, the U.S. administration simply dropped its own ball and ran away, and on the other side, the UN clearly did not have the means to pick up the dropped ball and run with it.[71] But on both sides, the willingness to recognize the gap in perceptions and to seek to cover it was surprisingly absent. Each clung to its positions and methods and wondered why the other did not understand. The UN was an inflexible bureaucracy and the U.S. a disorganized polity, and the twain never met.

Lost was the opportunity for better handling of several issues, all classic components of conflict prevention. Disarmament was an optimal goal in the situation, and had it been carried out as Secretary-General Boutros-Ghali wished, it would have gone far to reduce the violent conflict, throw the factions back into purely political competition, and helped rebuild the state. But not even the United States in UNITAF nor the international community in UNOSOM had the capacity to engage in the heavy fighting that forceful disarmament would have required. Boutros-Ghali himself bemoaned this lack of capacity in the UN and the absence of intentions by the United States, but he needed to recognize the same limitations on U.S. forces, or rather the same requirements that the well-armed Somali militias would impose on any forces.[72] "If the disarmament of the population becomes an objective, then there should be no mistaking the fact that the troops given this mission have been committed to combat."[73]

There was a substitute to coercive disarmament, and that was coercive or "encouraged" enforcement of the cantonment of heavy weapons as provided for in the Addis Ababa agreement of all parties on 15 January 1993.

But this in turn brought up the second subject of disjuncture between the United States and the UN. UNITAF forces used gunships and armor to enforce the cantonment agreement in the weeks after the Addis meeting. UNITAF rules of engagement were expressed as the Four Noes: no technicals, no banditry, no roadblocks, no visible weapons. "These rules, combined with the demonstration of overwhelming force by UNITAF, resulted in few challenges to forcible confiscation efforts—and surprisingly few challenges directed against US forces."[74]

But once the handover to UNOSOM took place, such vigorous enforcement was relaxed. As a result, Aideed became bolder, and the scene was set for the confrontations of June. Despite its experience in disarmament in Namibia and El Salvador, the UN had no plans for disarmament, demobilization, resettlements, and reintegration (DDRR) in Somalia, and disarmament of any kind essentially stopped after May 1993.[75] Agreements between conflicting parties are always only the beginning of conflict management and are never self-enforcing; the same firm hand is needed to keep them in place as it took to put them in place. That hand disappeared in the handover.

The same characteristic was evident on the political side. The new U.S. special envoy, Robert Oakley, through the same type of patient contacts that Sahnoun had shown, had created a joint security committee (JCS) in mid-December 1992 to provide Somali dialogue as the positive adjunct to international enforcement. Again, the JCS was not a solidly constructed locomotive that would lead the conflict into resolution on its own steam; it was only the framework for a process and needed constant tending and reaffirming by the peacemaking parties. It did set up the second Addis Ababa conference, held, after some delaying posturing by Aideed and his Somali National Alliance (SNA), in the midst of the transition. Although the conference involved only the representatives of the fifteen leading militias, Somali and international pressure secured the attendance of some 200 community leaders as observers. The conference produced an agreement on 27 March 1993 on a nationwide cease-fire and voluntary disarmament and a new government structure around a Transitional National Council (TNC).[76] Although the TNC was to include both militia and civil society representatives, militia representatives revised the accord after the meeting to close the local communities out of the selection process, and the UN representatives were unwilling to hold them to the original agreement. The cease-fire held for a few months, and district and regional councils were established. But with delays and disagreements within UNOSOM on how to implement and enforce the agreements, they never got very far beyond the signature stage. "After May 4, however, UNOSOM II did not continue the pattern of frequent meetings, the joint security committee withered away, and tension mounted."[77]

Two other UNITAF measures were also let lapse. The local police units mentioned earlier were actually formed under UNITAF and were on the streets of Mogadishu in mid-January 1993. Historically, the Somali police were trained by Britain and the United States in the early days of Somali independence, as the Soviet Union took over the formation of the army, and the police units had a higher reputation for integrity and non-partisanship during both Siad Barre's rule and the subsequent clan warfare. The units' creation and autonomy were negotiated with the rebel leaders in late 1992, and they were generally able to keep free of factional attempts at control. The 3,000 police in place at the time of the transition saw active duty in many instances, helping restore important elements of state authority and replacing the need for NGOs to rely on private hires—usually from unreliable factional irregulars—for their security.

But the UN in New York and Kittani in Mogadishu were unsympathetic to the efforts, preferring a top-down approach to institutionalization, and UN humanitarian coordinator in Somalia Philip Johnston was originally ordered to desist from what had become a personal initiative. The United States also opposed the program because of congressional restrictions on military training for police forces, after human rights infractions in Latin America, although there was no prohibition against police assisting and training other police. It was not until the end of 1993, after U.S. forces had withdrawn, that the Clinton administration made a presidential determination of an exception to congressional prohibitions and supplied equipment and training for the police force. A crucial year had been lost.[78]

Similarly, the district and regional commissions set up under the watchful prodding of UNITAF provided an important grassroots basis for state building (known officially for some reason as "nation building").[79] But "nation building" was mission creep and not part of the U.S. mandate; it was also opposed by Aideed's SNA (reorganized out of his USC in October 1992), since the local councils had their roots in the population and escaped his control. By October, 38 of the 61 district councils and 2 of the 18 regional councils were in place, even if sometimes contestedly so, but by that time the UNOSOM mission had been twisted first to a manhunt and then to collaboration, leaving its detractors encouraged and its supporters bewildered.

The transition between mid-March and 4 May 1993 was an opportunity to keep the UNITAF momentum going, and it was fumbled. It would have involved an active, committed UN SRSG with a loose leash from New York and a willingness to roll up his sleeves and get his hands dirty.

It would have involved a clear awareness of what UNITAF had done and what UNOSOM II needed to do to maintain continuity, in such crucial areas as enforced cantonment and follow-up measures, maintenance of coordination through the JCS, and support and expansion of the local police and the district and regional commissions. Many other measures would have followed; the point is not to detail all the next steps but to identify a spirit toward both the problem in Somalia and the transition from UNITAF. It is hard to make a sharp point of such soft elements as "a maximum of discussion, persuasion and patience,"[80] but they define the divide that separates peacemaking from disintegration.

Combined, such soft measures were designed to provide the material out of which the reconstruction process could be pursued. The reversal of efforts and results was so sharp in reality that a strong case can be made for progress toward the establishment of new institutions if the military and political efforts had been continued. Instead, the change in attitude, attention, and effort on the part of UNOSOM left the situation to degrade rapidly, particularly by leaving open opportunities for Aideed and his forces to assert themselves and prepare for the ambush of the Pakistani soldiers on 5 June 1993, provoking the UN's targeting of Aideed, and then the botched assault by the U.S. marines on 2 October 1993.

The reasons for missing the opportunity for a smooth transition are found on both the U.S. and the UN sides. Given the conditions of the original U.S. decision to undertake a Somali intervention at the end of the Bush administration, a broader set of rules of engagement—and hence a commitment of larger forces—to cover enforced disarmament was simply not possible at the time. But the policy of "encouraged" cantonment—the Four Noes—was a feasible step in the same direction and could have been continued until the presence of sufficient UNOSOM forces could take over the task. The Clinton administration was only interested in ending the operation and bringing the boys home, however, rather than providing the UN with the capacity to carry out the new Chapter VII mission for which the United States had voted. Four thousand troops remained under diverse commands, raising major coordination problems and further complicating the exercise of functions.

On the UN side, the office in the field was again split over tactics to be adopted, between the pursuit of and collaboration with the warlords, notably Aideed, and between cooperation with those warlords or with civil society leaders to create new state institutions working from the bottom up—much as the problem was posed in Liberia and Lebanon. In dealing with both "nation building" and with disarmament, the Secretariat was handed an expanded mission and a limited capacity to carry it out, and it pursued the mission in a centralized, bureaucratic top-down style that did not facilitate its accomplishment. But that is the way the UN had been trained to operate, as an organization coordinating states, even when faced with a situation where no state was present.

October 1993: The confrontation between the militias and
the Delta Force was the opportunity for a firm reaction by
U.S. forces in Somalia to deaths at the Aideed corral.

On 5 June 1993, a day after a follow-up conference between SNA and SSDF ended, following a status contest between Aideed and the UN over who called the conference, SNA forces ambushed a Pakistani unit of UN-OSOM and killed twenty-four soldiers. In response, the Security Council (including the United States) voted to change its mission and take "all necessary measures" to bring the responsible parties—naming specifically the SNA—to justice.[81] Over the following four months, the world organization and the local warlord waged a ranging war against each other. At the beginning of October, without notifying UNOSOM, the Delta Force of U.S. marines and army rangers—in its seventh attempt to find Aideed—raided an SNA site in Mogadishu, became trapped in a huge firefight, and ended up with 18 dead, 1 captured, and 78 wounded, for some 500–1,000 Somali casualties, including some 300 dead. The images of bodies of two U.S. soldiers being dragged through the streets and the U.S. helicopter pilot being bullied by his captors shocked public opinion.

Much more shocking was the empty inability of the U.S. administration to respond to the situation. Secretary of State Warren Christopher, Defense Secretary Les Aspin, and National Security Adviser Tony Lake met with congressional leaders the following day with no plans in hand and asked the audience for their opinions![82] In a typically contradictory statement, President Clinton announced that he was sending more troops and would withdraw all of them within six months. The purpose of the U.S. presence in Somalia and the robustness of the U.S. response were not conveyed. Indeed, at the very moment of the raid, U.S. policy was being torn between its official commitment to the capture of Aideed, as indicated in the UNSC resolution, and pressure to "seek peace" with Aideed. Having chosen a military encounter with Aideed, the United States was beaten and ran, without a sense of either purpose or commitment, sending a message to Aideed but also to other warlords watching in Haiti, Bosnia, and elsewhere that a few casualties could run the United States and the UN out of the country.

Whatever the merits in the abstract of the policy of pursuit rather than reconciliation, once previous opportunities for implementing a policy of disarmament and institution building had been missed, it was necessary to continue the established policy of confrontation. Reconciliation had been tried by the UN under Sahnoun and by the United States under Oakley; had it been pursued with persistence and commitment, as already indicated, it could have been effective, but by October 1993, it was clearly not an option on the ground, no matter how attractive in principle. "For the first time in the history of the UN, we left an operation without taking it to free and fair elections, or political reconciliation, or whatever it is that we had to do."[83] Nor was the October encounter enough to warrant retreat, either in the field or in the public's eyes. In the field, 4,000 U.S. forces and 24,000 UNOSOM forces were in place in Somalia, and if their lack of coordination reduced the effective number somewhat, a number of military participants and experts interviewed indicate that a better operation was possible, both on 3 October and thereafter. Similarly, the defeat in a battle called for a coherent response, both for the sake of the soldiers and for the broader public. The administration, by all accounts, had not focused on that.

Thus, the opportunity was missed for a last attempt at a coherent Somali policy and its sustained implementation. In the same year, representatives from Al-Qaida came from Afghanistan, joined forces with Aideed, and then used Somalia for transit and transshipment in preparing for the bombing of U.S. embassies in neighboring Nairobi and Dar es Salaam five years later.[84] But the second CNN effect, in which the audience is turned off, not on, followed the death of the Pakistanis and then of the American soldiers, when the United States and then the UN turned tail and ran. There still is no Somalia more than a decade later, but there are fewer Somalis by several hundred thousands.

It need not have been so. From the military outbreak of the final paroxysm of Siad Barre's regime to the direct clashes with UNOSOM II and U.S. forces by Aideed's militia, there were opportunities missed in Somalia. Initially, there were occasions to deploy diplomacy to convoke a sovereign national conference, beginning with the shock produced by the Hargeisa massacres in 1988 and the opening created by the manifesto in 1990. Then, cease-fires established in mid-1991 and early 1992 created moments when a strong UN SRSG in the field backed by a firm policy from New York was needed to keep the parties talking and to build up institutions around them to fill the vacuum left by the collapsed state. As these occasions were missed, early inaction led to higher cost opportunities and the need grew to deploy force along with diplomacy. That opportunity came with the cease-fire in early 1992 and then with the hand-off from UNITAF to UNOSOM II a year later; both needed broad and sustained state-building efforts to accompany them, with a maximum of discussion, persuasion, and patience.

By October 1993, the opportunity had been narrowed to simply a vigorous response to the clash with rebel forces, and even at that the United States and the UN failed.

Notes

1. In preparing the Somali case, I am grateful for interviews and review of the manuscript by Dr. Hussein Adam, Anatoly Adamishin, Assistant Secretary of State Herman Cohen, Theodore Dagne, Sunni Khalid, Dr. David Laitin, Jan Eliasson, Dr. Terrence Lyons, Ambassador Robert Oakley, John Prendergast, Ambassador Mohamed Sahnoun, and James Woods and for the research assistance of Wu Wei, Zoe Vantzos, and Madison Boeker. I am most grateful to Terrence Lyons for the use of his files.

2. Some have cited the accident as the last opportunity to press him for changes.

3. Quote on Marehans from Hirsch and Oakley, *Somalia and Operation Restore Hope,* 8; quote on Siad Barre from Ali Galaydh, "Notes on the State of the Somali State," *Horn of Africa* 13, no. 1/2 (January–June 1990): 27.

4. M. Fortes and E. E. Evans-Pritchard, eds., *African Political Systems* (Oxford: Oxford University Press, 1940); see also Lewis, *A Pastoral Democracy.*

5. It is frequently forgotten that Somalia hung together as a panethnic federation as long and only as long as the Ethiopian threat was clear and present; when the derg state collapsed in 1991 and its successor remained preoccupied with its own internal complexities, the Somali state lost its glue and collapsed too.

6. Jane Holl Lute, "The Use of Force for Peacemaking," in Zartman, *Peacemaking in International Conflict.*

7. Linda Feldman, "Rebels Create Havoc for US-Backed Somalia," *Christian Science Monitor,* 6 July 1988, 1; Amnesty International, *A Long Term Human Rights Crisis* (London: Amnesty International, 1988).

8. House Committee on Foreign Affairs, Subcommittee on Africa, *Reported Massacres and Indiscriminate Killings in Somalia,* 100th Cong., 2nd sess., 14 July 1988; Richard Greenfield, "Barre's Unholy Alliances," *Africa Report,* March 1989, 66.

9. Joseph Kelley, "Somalia: Observations Regarding the Northern Conflict and Resulting Conditions" (internal memorandum, General Accounting Office, 4 May 1989); Aryeh Neier, "Bloody Somalia," *The Nation,* 25 June 1988; Greenfield, "Barre's Unholy Alliances," 68. "Morgan" was the author of a Letter of Death in the mid-1980s that called for the extermination of the Isaaqs.

10. Anatoly Adamishin, interview by the author.

11. Cooperation with the Soviets over Angola was to get them out, as was incipient cooperation in Ethiopia; cooperation over Somalia would have the reverse motive, to stabilize a forward U.S. position, but the Soviets were interested as a symbolic recognition of their continuing role in a region of historic ties, at a time when their role was beginning to shrink fast.

12. Such a report was conducted for the Department of State a year later, however, based on research in Somalia, Ethiopia, and Kenya; Gersony, *Why Somalis Flee.*

13. David Rawson, "Dealing with Disintegration," in Samatar, *The Somali Challenge,* 173.

14. Lewis, *A Pastoral Democracy*; Kenneth Menkhaus, "Traditional Conflict Management in Contemporary Somalia," in Zartman, *Traditional Cures for Modern Conflicts,* 186, 190.

15. Offers of asylum for Siad Barre were reported to have been made by the United States and Saudi Arabia, but they do not appear to have been part of a concerted strategy if indeed they existed; *Africa Confidential* 29, no. 25 (16 December 1988): 20.

16. Sahnoun, *Somalia,* 6.

17. Zartman, *Governance as Conflict Management.*

18. Neil Henry, "Somali Civil War Slaughter a Legacy of Cold War Feud," *Washington Post,* 8 January 1991; "The Policy We Pursued in Somalia," *Washington Post,* 12 January 1991.

19. "An Open Letter to President Mohammed Siyaad Barre," *Horn of Africa* 13, no. 1/2(January–June 1990): 109–124.

20. Issa-Salwe, *The Collapse of the Somali State,* 78.

21. Marina Ottaway, "Eritrea and Ethiopia: Negotiations in a Transitional Conflict," in Zartman, *Elusive Peace.*

22. Cohen, *Intervening in Africa,* 202. He also recalled that after April 1990, the option of seeking the president's resignation and departure was excluded by the NSC decision in the Liberian case discussed in Chapter 3. The Congressional Research Service in May reported that the opposition groups "are likely to intensify their military campaign against the government" and that "desertions . . . might eventually lead to the demise of the Barre government," Theodore Dagne, "Somalia: Current Conditions and U.S. Policy," *CRS Report* 90-252 (12 May 1990), 6, 8. The Africa Watch report, *Somalia: A Government at War with Its Own People* (New York: Africa Watch), appeared in January 1990. A good background report is Bongartz, *The Civil War in Somalia.*

23. *Horn of Africa* 13, no. 1/2 (January–July 1990): 26–27; Laitin and Samatar spoke of a nascent civil war: *Somalia,* 154.

24. Bongartz, *The Civil War in Somalia,* 27.

25. Compare chapters 2 and 8 on Ethiopia and Somalia in Cohen, *Intervening in Africa.*

26. Ibid., 36–37.

27. Saadia Touval and I. William Zartman, "International Mediation in the Post–Cold War Era," in Crocker, Hampson, and Aall, *Turbulent Peace.*

28. I reach this conclusion despite the claims in Sahnoun, *Somalia,* 89, and Lyons and Samatar, *State Collapse, Multilateral Intervention, and Strategies for Postwar Political Reconstruction,* 28.

29. Anna Simmons, "No Exit from Somalia," *Washington Post,* 15 May 1991; "From One Dictator to Another," *Washington Post,* 12 June 1991.

30. After much debate, the SNM opted for its own solution and sought recognition as its own state. U.S. State and Defense Departments wanted to deal with but not recognize Somaliland, but the NSC was not interested.

31. On the chicken dilemma game (CDG) and the problems of coordination, see Steven J. Brams, *Negotiation Games.*

32. Daniel Compagnon, "The Somali Opposition Fronts," *Horn of Africa* 13, no. 1/2 (January–June 1990): 35–40.

33. "Somalia: Where Do We Go from Here?" *Africa Confidential* 32, no. 3 (8 February 1991): 1–2; Issa-Salwe, *The Collapse of the Somali State,* 82–84; Samatar, *Somalia.*

34. U.S. Committee for Refugees, *World Refugee Survey* (Washington, DC: U.S. Committee for Refugees, 1995), 74–75.

35. Hirsch and Oakley, *Somalia and Operation Restore Hope,* 15; for a similar informal cease-fire, also involving the untiring efforts of Sahnoun, in Congo-Brazzaville where the United States and the UNSC neglected to seize the opportunity, see Zartman, "An Apology Needs a Pledge"; on the militia situation the following year, which was not dissimilar, see Said Samatar, "Why the [14 February 1992] Mogadishu Cease-Fire Will Not Hold," *Horn of Africa* 13, no. 3/4 and 14, no. 1/2 (July 1990–June 1991): 140–141 (note that *Horn of Africa* often appears late).

36. Thomas Callahan, "Some Observations on Somalia's Past and Future," *CSIS Africa Notes* 158 (9 March 1994). A number of commentators supported the need for a UN role at this point but without indicating its content; Lyons and Samatar, *Somalia,* 29; Sahnoun, *Somalia,* 10; Callahan, "Some Observations on Somalia's Past and Future," 1994, 2–3; Jonathan Stevenson, "Hope Restored in Somalia," *Foreign Policy* 94 (1994):144; Ray Bonner, "Why We Went," *Mother Jones* 18, no. 2 (March–April 1993): 55.

37. Curiously, Mike Blakeley suggested that an earlier moment of intervention had occurred in 1989 when maintenance of foreign aid would have eliminated the trigger for the war of succession. Yet it was Siad Barre, not the loss of foreign aid, that was the problem and the cause of state collapse. See "Somalia" in Brown and Rosecrance, *The Costs of Conflict,* 75–90.

38. Ibid.

39. *Horn of Africa,* S Res. 155, 102nd Cong., 1st sess., introduced 25 April, voted 26 June 1991.

40. Cohen, *Intervening in Africa,* 203–204.

41. Rakiya Omaar and Alex de Waal, "Who Prolongs Somalia's Agony," *New York Times,* 26 February 1992, A21; Nancy Kassebaum and Paul Simon, "Save Somalia from Itself," *New York Times,* 2 January 1992, All.

42. Hirsch and Oakley, *Somalia and Operation Restore Hope,* 18.

43. UN Security Council Resolution 733 of 23 January 1992.

44. UN Security Council Resolution 746 of 17 March 1992.

45. UN Security Council Resolution 751 of 24 April 1992; *New York Times,* 26 April 1992, A22; response from Ambassador Thomas Pickering, "Letters to the Editor," *New York Times,* 1–22, 9 May 1992.

46. UN Security Council Resolution 767 of 27 July 1992.

47. UN Security Council Resolution 775 of 28 August 1992.

48. UN Security Council Resolution 794 of 3 December 1992. On the U.S. decision, see the excellent study by Maryann Cusimano, *Operation Restore Hope,* and see Coll, *Operation Restore Hope.*

49. On security dilemmas, see Barry Posner, "The Security Dilemma and Ethnic Conflict," in Brown, *Ethnic Conflict and International Security.*

50. Sahnoun, *Somalia;* Lyons and Samatar, *Somalia,* 35; Hirsch and Oakley, *Somalia and Operation Restore Hope;* Clarke and Herbst, *Learning from Somalia;* Samuel Makinda, *Seeking Peace from Chaos* (Boulder, CO: Lynne Rienner, 1993); Thomas and Spataro, *Peacekeeping and Policing in Somalia;* Hampson, *Nurturing Peace.*

51. Sahnoun (*Somalia,* 28), in a report near the end of his mission, dated the appropriate moment of action around October 1991, between the previous moment analyzed above and the March date discussed here; although this supports the urgency of the situation under analysis, there does not seem to have been an appropriate entry point at that time.

52. The chapter VII humanitarian operations were set up for Operation Provide Comfort to Kurds in April 1991.

53. Andrew Natsios, "Statement Before the House Select Committee on Hunger," *The Humanitarian Tragedy in Somalia,* 30 January 1992, 102nd Cong., 2nd sess.; see also Jane Perlez, "Somalia Self-Destructs and the World Looks On," *New York Times,* 29 December 1991; Rakiya Omaar, "Somalia: A Fight to the Death?" *News from Africa Watch,* 13 February 1992.

54. Herman J. Cohen, "Statement before the Senate Committee on Foreign Relations," 19 March 1992.

55. Callahan, "Some Observations on Somalia's Past and Future," 3.

56. Boutros-Ghali, *Unvanquished,* 56–59, 96–97; the issue is not mentioned by Sahnoun, *Somalia.*

57. Hirsch and Oakley, *Somalia and Operation Restore Hope,* 27–28. Eliasson pointed out in an interview with the author that at $1.5 billion, the UN military costs in Somalia had become ten times bigger than the humanitarian program of $163 million.

58. Hirsch and Oakley, *Somalia and Operation Restore Hope,* 29, 33.

59. For an account of the Sahnoun mission and its relations with UN headquarters, see Sahnoun, *Somalia,* 15–41, and Hirsch and Oakley, *Somalia and Operation Restore Hope,* 21–23, 29–33.

60. See the careful, if controversial, study on Rwanda by Kuperman, *The Limits of Humanitarian Intervention.*

61. Cohen, *Intervening in Africa,* 209. The State Department Bureaus of African Affairs and Human Rights called for military action, against opposition from the State Department International Organization Bureau, the Defense Department, and NSC. Cohen noted, "Our public statements were designed to undermine official policy" (7), but it took another six months to do so.

62. Private communication by UNITAF participant in interview with author.

63. Sahnoun saw deployment as late as early September as sufficient: *Somalia,* 38.

64. Ibid., 29.

65. See Thomas and Spataro, *Peacekeeping and Policing in Somalia.*

66. Sahnoun, *Somalia,* 40.

67. Menkhaus, *Somalia,* 193.

68. See Stephen John Stedman, "Spoiler Problems in Peace Processes," in Paul Stern and Daniel Druckman, eds., *International Conflict Resolution After the Cold War* (Washington, DC: National Academy Press, 2000).

69. *New York Times* editorial, 28 April 1992; Brown and Rosecrance, *The Costs of Conflict,* 84.

70. Compare two different appreciations of the Kittani mission: Boutros-Ghali, *Unvanquished,* 57, and Hirsch and Oakley, *Somalia and Operation Restore Hope,* 32. Kittani had indicated from the start that he would only serve for a few months and in any case was away from his post for medical treatment much of the time; Hirsch and Oakley, *Somalia and Operation Restore Hope,* 96, 110.

71. On the need to have ends and means in balance, see Walter Lippman, *U.S. Foreign Policy: Shield of the Republic* (New York: Pocket Books, 1943), 4.

72. The disarmament issue is discussed in Boutros-Ghali, *Unvanquished,* 59–60; Secretary-General's letters to UNSC, 29 November and 19 December 1992; Secretary-General's letter to President Bush, 8 December 1992; Hirsch and Oakley, *Somalia and Operation Restore Hope,* 94–99, 103–106.

73. Allard, *Somalia Operations: Lessons Learned,* 90.

74. Ibid., 36–37. See also Lyons and Samatar, *Somalia,* 47; "Report of the Secretary-General, S/25354" (UN internal document, 3 March 1994), par. 6.

75. When foreign or refugee soldiers are involved, the process is referred to as disarmament, demobilization, repatriation, resettlement, and reintegration (DDRRR).

76. The Addis Ababa agreement of 27 March, like all the others, can be found at www.incore.ulst.ac.uk/CDs/agreements/somalia.html.

77. Hirsch and Oakley, *Somalia and Operation Restore Hope,* 58. See also Rosegrant with Watkins, *A "Seamless" Transition,* 3–4. On Addis Ababa II, see Lyons and Samatar, *Somalia,* 47–57; Hirsch and Oakley, *Somalia and Operation Restore Hope,* 96–99; Boutros-Ghali, *Unvanquished,* 94; Kenneth Menkhaus, "Traditional Conflict Management in Contemporary Somalia," in Zartman, *Traditional Cures for Modern Conflicts,* 192–194.

78. On the police, see Hirsch and Oakley, *Somalia and Operation Restore Hope,* 61, 69, 87–92, 134; Martin Ganzglass, "The Restoration of the Somali Justice System," in Clarke and Herbst, *Learning from Somalia.*

79. For an evaluation of the district and regional councils, see Bernard Helander, "Building Peace from Below," report to the Life and Peace Institute, Uppsala University, Sweden, April 1995.

80. Hirsch and Oakley, *Somalia and Operation Restore Hope,* 158.

81. UN Security Council Resolution 837 of 6 June 1993. Others have suggested a number of missed opportunities between June and October. "Aideed could have been picked up on June 6 in a Chevy pickup truck," declared U.S. special envoy Robert Gosende, "because at that point, he thought he could get away with killing 24 Pakistanis"; cited in Rosegrant with Watkins, *A Seamless Transition,* 7.

82. For reports on the "spectacle worthy of Abbott and Costello," see Sidney Blumenthal, "Why Are We in Somalia?" *New Yorker,* 25 October 1993, 51; Ann Devroy, "New Deployment Raises Confusion on US Goals," *Washington Post,* 6 October 1993; Callahan, "Some Observations on Somalia's Past and Future," 7.

83. Elizabeth Lindenmayer of the Secretary-General's office, quoted in Rosegrant with Watkins, *A Seamless Transition,* 19.

84. *Washington Post,* 4 November 2001; Ken Menkhaus, "Terrorism in Somalia: Threat Assessment and Policy Options" (paper presented at the United States Institute of Peace Workshop, May 2003); Menkhaus, *Somalia*; International Crisis Group [ICG], *Somalia: Countering Terrorism in a Failed State,* Africa Report 45 (Brussels: ICG, 2002).

5

ZAIRE,
1991–1996

ZAIRE (PREVIOUSLY CONGO AND SUBSEQUENTLY DEMOCRATIC REPUBLIC OF Congo) has been an important African ally of the three states who are its major partners in trade and investment—the United States, France, and Belgium, termed the Troika.[1] Zaire had been Belgium's largest colony, initially the exploited personal property of the Belgian king, and after independence the subsequent shared love-hate relationship was marked by fits of pout and pique on both sides. But Congo was also big business for Belgium, and its many political exiles operated from the former metropole. Congo was also big business for France and the southern anchor of its active zone of influence in sub-Saharan Africa that stretched north and west along the coast and interior to Mauritania.[2] French elites, starting with the Elysée, maintained intimate personal ties with Mobutu Sese Seko, who was a regular participant in the Franco-African summits and a strong supporter of French African policy. The United States, however, was responsible for putting Mobutu into power in 1965, in the hopes of ending five years of initial instability after independence,[3] and Mobutu repaid the debt with arrogant declarations of autonomy and useful cooperation with U.S. Cold War policies in times of need. Zaire's location in the heart of Africa on the borders of nine other states, its political support, and its economic potential made it a major focus of interest throughout the Cold War.

In twenty-five years in power since 1965, Zairean president Mobutu Sese Seko had drained the economic riches of the country into his bank accounts, to be used for his personal investments and for cooptation of the political class, creating a political vacuum around himself and those whom he corrupted. At the beginning of the 1990s, as African political systems were being shaken by the overthrow of the single-party regimes in Eastern Europe and the end of apartheid in South Africa, U.S. secretary of

> ### Missed Opportunities:
> ### Zaire, 1991–1996
>
> *September 1991* Soldier and civilian riots brought French and Belgian troops to Kinshasa, providing an opportunity to bring Mobutu to hand over power to the Sovereign National Conference.
>
> *January–February 1993* Soldier and civilian riots brought French troops to Kinshasa, and the killing of the French ambassador provided an opportunity to bring Mobutu to hand over power to the Sovereign National Conference or to arrest him when he went to France for dental treatment.
>
> *September 1993–January 1994* A number of occasions on the diplomatic and internal Zairean level offered opportunities for U.S. mediation of governmental reform.
>
> *July 1995* Warnings of pogroms in Masisi provided an opportunity for an international effort to halt ethnic violence and move and disarm Rwandan refugee camps in Zaire.
>
> *March 1996* Renewed warnings of pogroms against another Tutsi population, the Banyamulenge, provided a last opportunity for the UN, the Organization of African Unity, and the Carter Center to mediate to protect the population.

state James Baker urged Mobutu to introduce democracy to his 45 million people. The following month, in April 1990, Mobutu announced the establishment of the Third Republic, with a radically altered political landscape composed of multiple parties and a free press. Surprised by the expressions of widespread discontent that emerged, Mobutu sought to reassert his control of the political space. Hundreds of new parties were founded, many of them fronts for Mobutu loyalists, in order to undermine popular opposition parties such as Etienne Tshisekedi's Democratic Union for Social Progress (UDPS). Zairean sociologist Mondonga M. Mokoli stated that "instead of leading post-1990 Zaire to the rise of sustainable democracy and socio-economic development at the grass roots level, [the] failed transition [has] rather been a political mechanism to sustain the status quo and the kleptocracy in the best interest of Zaire's lord and his vassals, but at the expense of their serfs. [It] has moved that social formation from the state of chaos . . . to one of a complete collapse of socio-economic and political institutions."[4]

Following the pattern of events set in Benin and other French-speaking African states in 1990, a Sovereign National Conference (CNS) of 2,000 representatives of all segments of civil and political society—civic and nongovernmental organizations, religious groups, and opposition politicians—was finally convened in Kinshasa in August 1991. Mobutu, however, had closely observed the fate of his colleague across the river, Congolese president Denis Sassou Nguesso, and was determined not to suffer similar humiliation at the hands of the peoples' representatives. The Zairean societal forces, on the other hand, were equally determined to make a fresh start without Mobutu, although they suffered sharp divisions among themselves, and Tshisekedi's UDPS was particularly unwilling to share power with other parties. Tshisekedi himself was stubborn and haughty but at least had a movement for change behind him. Political maneuvering by the president brought the activities of the CNS to a stalemate almost from the start, a deadlock that continued throughout the rest of the decade.

The countries of the Troika operated under the assumption of "Mobutu or Chaos."[5] All three feared the effects of chaos, erroneously seeing in it a repetition of the fissiparous tendencies of Congo's early years and thereby also missing the fact that Mobutu *was* chaos. As a result, they dodged repeated opportunities to secure a smooth transition from his dying reign, support an extraordinary movement born of civil society, and contain repeated exercises of ethnic cleansing. There were a number of such opportunities, of which five stand out. Three were moments when the CNS process could have been strengthened and Mobutu retired. On two of these occasions, in September 1991 and January–February 1993, troops of the Troika were in Kinshasa following serious riots and a CNS government component was in place, giving external powers an occasion to tilt the balance in favor of a transition government; and in late 1993 a more complex opportunity unfolded in the same direction. Two other were times when ethnic pogroms in eastern Zaire called for an international response to remove the trigger for the subsequent revolt that brought in the regime of Laurent Kabila at the expense of the democratic movement.

The first two moments were marked by an entry point created by the breakdown of public order and the actual presence of Troika military forces on the scene; the democratic forces were in a position of momentary ascendancy. In the third moment, the political forces were stalemated, again temporarily; the United States was called into entry in any case, and it needed a better plan. In all three cases, rapid action was required to seize the carefully balanced moment, and that in turn required a clear-sighted appraisal of the situation and a strategy. Thereafter a combination of active diplomacy and limited military action was called for in the first two instances, and simply diplomacy in the third. In all three instances, the Troika states hoped against all evidence that Mobutu could be reformed and could lead his country into the democracy that would replace him and correct his kleptocracy, and so the country slipped back into the morass he had made. They feared a vacuum and so they helped make one, as Kabila's advent showed.

The last two moments involved the eastern region, which untended became the site of continuing warfare for the next decade. The issue was the removal of Zairean citizenship from a historic group of immigrants from the region. When they began to protest and then fight for their civic and human rights, they became a pawn in layers of conflicts, from local disputes between farmers and herders, to international war of existentialist dimensions centered on Rwanda. Zaire's policies made these people enemies instead of citizens, and they then became the agents of his overthrow and of the subsequent War of the Zairean Succession. Had the Troika intervened to throw a spotlight on the ethnic repression and to handle the spillover of the Rwandan genocide—after having failed to react in time to the genocide itself—the seeds of the ensuing Great Lakes War could have been kept from sprouting. Instead, they found Mobutu helpful in handling the Rwandan refugee flow, of *génocidaires* (ethnic cleansers) not of victims, and so shielded their eyes from the real problem.

By persistently working to legitimize Mobutu, the source of the problem, the Troika turned down measures to fill the vacuum he had created and help strengthen the elements of a succession. Then, they watched bewildered when a radical relic of the 1960s arose to oust a moribund Mobutu and deepen the chaos they had feared. The chance of saving a deep-rooted democratizing movement and effecting a transition from predatory autocracy to pluralist accountability was lost. It took another two years before the Congolese political system removed Kabila in its own way, by assassination, and installed his son Joseph, a totally unknown quantity who gradually worked to assert his predominancy as a step toward creating a new state.

September 1991: Soldier and civilian riots brought French and Belgian troops to Kinshasa, providing an opportunity to bring Mobutu to hand over power to the Sovereign National Conference.

Public frustration with a deadlocked CNS and with hyperinflation up to 1,000 percent a year brought the political order to the point of total collapse in September 1991 and Mobutu to his weakest moment.[6] Although the precise moment came as a surprise, explosive expressions of popular frustration and dissatisfaction, with the forces of order looking on, had already burst out as warning signs in Kinshasa and other cities in December 1990 and May–June 1991. On 23 September, dissatisfied unpaid soldiers from the Thirty-First paratroopers' brigade mutinied and looted the capital, followed by other troops of the Zairean Armed Forces (FAZ) in the provincial cities. The rampaging soldiers were soon joined by the impoverished urban population; during the few days of countrywide looting, about 90 percent of Zaire's modern economy was destroyed. The government took refuge in the Intercontinental Hotel and Mobutu on his yacht on the Congo River at Nsele. The next day, U.S. planes transported 2,500 French and Belgian troops into Brazzaville to go on to Zaire to evacuate 20,000 foreign nationals. Once on the scene, the troops had an opportunity to make a decisive show of support for CNS leader Tshisekedi, put pressure on Mobutu to step down, and let the Sovereign National Conference take its course.

But the Troika did not consider evacuation of Mobutu. Among the members of the Troika, France was not in favor of measures to ease Mobutu out of power; Belgium was more favorable. France and Belgium rejected the idea of freezing Mobutu's assets. The consensus of a U.S. Inter-Agency Group on Zaire was that there would be no progress with Mobutu in power and that it would be best if he were to go; Under Secretary of State Lawrence Eagleburger blocked any further thinking in that direction with the reasoning that no one could know what would happen afterward, saying, "Do not even think of it."[7] The U.S. position therefore continued to favor power sharing and moving Mobutu to a symbolic position, as eventually took place, but from which he was able to recover all the levers of control, block the work of the CNS, and—repeatedly—fire Tshisekedi.

Enforced retirement of egregious rulers was not a policy foreign to France, although most of its armed interventions in Africa—1964 in Gabon, 1977 and 1978 in Zaire, 1977 and 1991 in Djibouti, 1983–1988 in Chad, 1986 and 1991 in Togo, 1991 in Benin, 1990 and 1993 in Rwanda, 1993 in Burundi—were to support the incumbent rulers, some of them egregious, rather than to remove them. The exceptions were Operation Barracuda in Central Africa in 1979 and the French assistance in removing Jean-Claude Duvalier from Haiti in 1986.[8] It obviously would have taken a major policy shift to move Zaire from the first category to the second, as the situation warranted, but the action itself would not have been incompatible with French practice or with French policy values as just enunciated in the "democratic contract" of the Franco-African summit at La Baule in 1990.

Instead, the basic ingredients required for the task were a small additional complement of troops; money to finance a cooperation agreement with the Israeli-trained elite Special Presidential Division (DSP) and to ensure demobilization of the unpaid, disorganized, partially French-trained FAZ; emphatic support for the CNS as it set up new government institutions and prepared elections; and assistance to facilitate Mobutu's escape into retirement (along with gentle intimation of seized assets if he did not go peacefully). Earlier, he was reported to have already made an emergency plan to flee the country if the situation became untenable and had investigated the possibility of asylum in France and Switzerland; Madame Mobutu was to arrive in France on 1 October and earlier other members of the family had already gone to Brussels.[9] Without any need of heavy foreign interference, the situation itself in September 1991 left Mobutu bereft of military and political support and made personal security his prime concern. This deep vulnerability was not to last long, and it provided a clear moment of opportunity.

The opportunity's window was narrow and would have required earlier contingency planning. Failure to take advantage of it restored Mobutu's confidence in his ability to run though Western divisions and to manipulate his opponents. In August, the CNS had demanded Mobutu's resignation and moved to create an interim government and a new constitution, with elections in prospect. At that point, Mobutu was defiant, claiming that it was unconstitutional to fire him and that France and Belgium "want my head at any price. I will not accept this kind of ultimatum. Nobody will tell me how to behave."[10] His objective position was much more vulnerable a month later, with his army out of control and Troika troops in his capital; a Western ambassador found him on his boat with his head in his hands moaning, "What's going on? What's going on?"[11] But diplomatic efforts would still have had to face a cornered fox, even if not a lion. Firmness, direction, coordination, an honorable departure with a helpful push, a clear understanding with the DSP and FAZ leaders, and a quick transition to CNS rule were the ingredients of the move.

Decisive action was arguably in the interest of all three members of the Troika, who bore the responsibility for having kept Mobutu in power over the previous quarter century, and particularly of the United States, who bore the responsibility for having put him there. It was also in line with the declared policy principles of the three countries to support a democratic upsurge and one that would provide a legitimate, functioning institution to fill the gap that would be left by Mobutu's departure. Military action by the

Troika troops, however, was the key ingredient, necessary to overcome pervasive Zairean reticence induced by decades of Mobutu's control. French officers had in fact contacted Tshisekedi through the intermediation of Cléophas Kamitatu, urging him simply to take over and he replied, "That wouldn't be legal."[12] With Western troops already on the ground, a decisive move would have involved little additional exposure. But the troops would have been there to support the diplomatic initiative, not to fight the Congolese army. With the connections the French had with the FAZ and especially the DSP, and the dissatisfaction of the troops with their conditions, the Zairean military would most likely have joined the newly winning side in their own interest, a habit that years of Zairean politics had taught them. Instead the Troika walked away from the opportunity.

Had the move succeeded, it would have put the country's government in the hands of the rising multiparty—perhaps even democratic—movement and an inexperienced Tshisekedi, opening up an unstable period of transition. The Troika, reasonably united at the time, would have helped restructure the army with the aim of keeping it out of politics, and bumpily but positively, the economy would have picked up. Mobutu would doubtless have been plotting a return from his exile, but away from power and as long as internally generated money kept flowing within the country, his blandishments would have lacked luster. A pledge to stay out of politics, usually extracted from early retired leaders, would be monitored by France, in support of its own engagement behind the new policy. The Zairean evolution would also have given a healthy boost to the democracy movement in the rest of the continent. Neither in Zaire nor elsewhere in Africa would that evolution have been smooth nor uniquely positive (as subsequent events from Angola to Zambia indicate), but such is the nature of democratic transitions, or of democracy itself, and the direction would have been preferable to more Mobutu. Had the move failed, it would have left Mobutu offended, Tshisekedi weakened, the various military forces at odds with each other, and the Troika with little control over events in Zaire—a situation scarcely different from the one that obtained in reality.

Once the moment of crisis had passed without decisive action by the Troika, Mobutu was able to rebound, strengthened by the missed opportunity. On 29 September, Mobutu and the opposition moved to reluctant agreement that Tshisekedi would form a transitional coalition government, which was only able to be constituted two weeks later. Mobutu also appointed a general of greater integrity and loyalty, General Mahele Liyeko, on 1 October to reorganize the FAZ. Although the president was to occupy only a symbolic role, "like the Queen of England," and governing power was to be exercised by the prime minister, Mobutu soon demanded control of military and foreign affairs, and the United States urged understanding of his position. Three weeks after his appointment as prime minister, Tshisekedi was fired.

The obstacles to a firm policy were resistance and timidity within Western policy and bureaucratic routines. As one senior Western diplomat stated, "It is not in our interest that Mobutu suddenly disappear. What may replace him is unclear, and meanwhile, the situation could prove chaotic."[13] Specifics behind this general fear included reluctance to penetrate the "sovereignty barrier," uncertainty over the political capabilities of the Zairean opposition, and close ties between Mobutu and parts of the French establishment, including presidential adviser on African affairs Jean-Christophe Mitterrand, Madame Danielle Mitterrand, and fundraisers for the French Socialist Party. Despite a quarter century of dealing with Mobutu, Washington, Brussels, and Paris felt against all evidence that he could be convinced to trade power for position and preside benevolently over a transition, providing stability against jolts.[14]

The United States' initially tough stance soon translated into a more symbolic decision to restrict Mobutu's freedom to travel by denying him visas to the Troika countries, a sanction that did not hurt the sanctioners; France and Belgium opposed freezing assets. This was proof to Mobutu that economic issues remained more important to his former Western allies than democratic process. With this knowledge, he was encouraged and free to continue manipulating the process in the years to come.

Once the Troika decided not to press for Mobutu's exit from the political arena, it effectively passed control over to him. "Faith in preventive diplomacy translated into faith in Mobutu's keeping his end of whatever bargain was struck," a profession of naïvete that is incredible given Mobutu's past political record.[15] There was a paralyzing fear of disruption in Zaire and of crisis on the hands of the Troika capitals, all of which is exactly what took place as a result of the inaction. The first of a series of opportunities to cut through the dilemma perceived as "Mobutu or chaos" became an occasion to pick Mobutu and chaos at the same time.[16]

January–February 1993: Soldier and civilian riots brought French troops to Kinshasa, and the killing of the French ambassador provided an opportunity to bring Mobutu to hand over power to the Sovereign National Conference or to arrest him when he went to France for dental treatment.

Following a "comprehensive political compromise" negotiated in July–August 1992 between Mobutu and the CNS, by which the president would remain in charge of security forces while the CNS would appoint a prime minister (Tshisekedi), the end of the year brought to new heights the tensions between Mobutu and the CNS transitional parliament (PT), the High Council of the Republic (HCR).[17] The continuing confrontation was itself ample warning of popular explosions whenever the match was struck. HCR charges that Mobutu was guilty of crimes against humanity were supported by a European Parliament resolution urging all member states to confiscate his assets until he would surrender to criminal investigation. On 11 December Mobutu suspended the HCR, which retorted on 15 January 1993 by declaring Mobutu guilty of high treason for preventing the country's institutions from functioning. Most members of the HCR gathered under the flag of the united opposition the next day to launch a four-day general strike directed against Mobutu. The strike was accompanied by large demonstrations in Kinshasa, with calls for the resignation of Mobutu and the liberalization of television and radio broadcasting.

Ten days later, on 28 January, Kinshasa again underwent city-wide riots, in reaction to the 65,000 new 5 million zaire notes (worth about $2) used to pay the army, which Zairean merchants—at Tshisekedi's urging—refused to accept.[18] The next day, 700 French paratroopers again entered Kinshasa from Brazzaville to protect and evacuate foreign nationals, and additional Belgian troops stood by across the river, barred by Mobutu from crossing. The riots were put down by DSP units who entered Kinshasa the following day and took over the looting themselves. The riots resulted in casualties estimated at as high as 1,000, among them French ambassador Philippe Bernard, killed while watching the violence from his embassy office. HCR president Monsignor Laurent Monsengwo Pasinga asked for an international military intervention in order to strengthen the Tshisekedi government.

Mobutu's response to international pressure to yield all power to the prime minister and the HCR was defiance: he blamed Tshisekedi for the riots and again dismissed him as prime minister. Tshisekedi, however, refused to leave his office and stated that, having been appointed by the High Council of the Republic, he could not be dismissed by Mobutu. Belgium supported Tshisekedi's stance, refused to ship the controversial 5 million zaire notes, and denied visa requests from Mobutu. Because Tshisekedi's government did not request impounding, however, the currency notes were allowed to return from Brussels to their source in London after a week and eventually found their way to Zaire. France granted Mobutu a visa "for medical reasons" on 19 February to allow him to undergo dental treatment while he stayed at his villa at Roquebrune Cap-Martin on the French Riviera.[19]

There were two moments in early 1993 when there were opportunities for decisive diplomatic action. The first was at the end of January, when French troops were essentially in control of Kinshasa, the DSP was outside the city, and Mobutu was up the river in his palace at Gbadolite. Rapid reinforcements of the French contingent and a firm diplomatic stand, consistent with Troika policies at the time, supporting the HCR as the government of Zaire, would have produced an important power shift. It would have to have been followed up with an agreement negotiated with the DSP to bring it into support for the HCR government and out from Mobutu's control, to avoid combat between the foreign troops and the DSP. The French had trained parts of the FAZ and actually commanded certain units until 1989 and so were in a potentially influential position. The strength of the situation lies in the fact that there was a legal, constituted government in place and that parliamentary leaders were actually calling for foreign intervention.

The final piece of the action, and probably the greatest challenge, was to secure Mobutu's retirement from Zaire, out of range of reentry into politics. Friends such as Morocco's king Hassan II and French presidential adviser Jean-Christophe Mitterrand would need to be mobilized to use their influence. There were incentives to be presented for Mobutu's retirement, such as the HCR's and European Parliament's willingness to drop any charges against him should he agree to go into exile and not return to Zaire, or foreign governments' willingness to drop threats to seize his assets. The United States might have lifted travel restrictions to allow Mobutu and his family to travel freely. King Hassan, whom he had just visited before the January riots, being a good friend, could well have offered Mobutu and his family exile to their properties in Morocco.

The second opportunity came when Mobutu arrived in France three weeks after the riots. His presence in Roquebrune Cap-Martin resolved the challenge of the previous occasion: Mobutu was now out of the country. France had every reason to detain him as responsible for the assassination of the French ambassador; the HCR would have had no trouble in waiving his presidential immunity, as required by the 1969 Vienna Convention of the Law of Treaties. His physical detention in French hands would have weakened his control over the DSP and would have left the HCR in legal and effective control of the country.

Although the February occasion gave Mobutu time to regroup his forces and recover from the effects of the riots, in other ways it had all the strengths and overcame all the weaknesses of the January occasion. In February 1993, Mobutu's fortunes were at a critically low point, formally accused by the HCR and by the European Parliament of having committed crimes against humanity and threatened by a U.S. call for sanctions. Troika officials responsible for Africa, meeting in Brussels on 2 February, agreed that there would be no banknotes and no haven or visas for Mobutu's family and that the family's foreign assets would be inventoried; they issued a statement again calling on Mobutu to transfer military, budgetary, and monetary powers to the HCR government. When the United States agreed to seizure of his assets, France declared it would have to consult in Paris. So there was no follow-through or implementation. Even impounding the currency would have weakened the regime and opened it to further mutinies.

Success in removing Mobutu at either moment would again have left the government in the hands of the democracy movement, by now having some experience in the paths and pitfalls of government. It was riven with divisions and its path would not have been smooth, but it would have been heading in a more responsible direction, with more assured chances for a new constitution and elections than actual events permitted. Again, the democracy movement throughout the continent would have benefited. There were a number of different ways in which the interventions could have failed. A badly executed military augmentation in January could have led to a confrontation with the DSP and a need to either defeat or retreat militarily. Either eventuality would have been disastrous, a pre-Somalia or pre–Congo-Brazzaville in a worse place, and would have necessitated good military and diplomatic execution to avoid it. Mobutu could also have refused to retire, either from the country or from politics even when abroad, requiring either very convincing pressures at the beginning or vigilant controls over his exile activities at the end. Still, had careful and intense efforts not been able to avoid any one of these possibilities of failure, the resulting situation would scarcely have been any different than the reality of the 1990s.

Early retirement was not Troika policy at the time, and decisive action would have required policy change as well as implementation. A State Department paper dated 11 February warned, however, that Zaire was developing into "Somalia and Liberia rolled into one, with vast potential for immense refugee flows, regional destabilization and humanitarian disaster," a presciently accurate analysis. The State Department paper said that seizing "personal assets . . . would send a strong message to him."[20] Other steps that were discussed included suspension from the International Monetary Fund, an arms embargo, and a ban on Zairean exports. The Belgian foreign minister and the U.S. secretary of state, meeting in Washington two weeks later, spoke heavily of sanctions "in the next few days," although their nature was not decided and IMF expulsion was ruled out.[21]

The United States stepped up pressure on the day of Mobutu's arrival in France, calling on Mobutu to "transfer all authority to the transitional government" and "to 'stop interfering' in its efforts to prepare a democratic transition."[22] State Department spokesman Joseph Snyder confirmed that "the United States backed Tshisekedi's transitional government and urged Mobutu to give up power. . . . We're dealing with [the HCR] as a government, as a transitional authority, and by making statements like this we're supporting their effort. . . ."[23] The chairman of the U.S. House of Representatives Foreign Affairs Committee, Congressman Lee Hamilton, had already urged President Clinton to "impose tough economic and political sanctions against . . . Mobutu." Hamilton emphasized that Mobutu had "undermined his country's movement toward democracy . . . and that the United States should consider pressuring Mobutu to leave the country."[24]

But all the firmness on the part of the Troika was on the level of "we hope he gets the message." There was no follow-through. In the United States, the Clinton administration, newly installed, was reeling in the aftermath of the Somali exercise and, to distinguish itself from its predecessor, was taking no action on any foreign policy front. In Belgium, a weak coalition government faced a pro-Mobutu opposition and a threat of early elections, although the business community was wearied of Zaire.[25] But any government faces an opposition, and a resolute U.S. position would have carried Belgian support. It was the French position that had changed since 1991, showing enormous tolerance toward the murder of its own ambassador and the rejection of the Troika's appeals. Yet providing a smooth transition was the clearly announced policy of all three countries, and it was just as clear that a weak and ailing Mobutu was unable to furnish that result. Even for policy based on personal attachments, the kindest thing to do for Mobutu would have been to give him a comfortable retirement and a place in history for helping his country work its way out of his heritage of chaos.

Given the international community's reluctance to act quickly and decisively, another chance to influence Zaire's progress towards democracy effectively was wasted. Upon Mobutu's return to Zaire, the HCR boycotted joint meetings, thereby giving the president the opportunity to regroup his troops. While assuring U.S. assistant secretary of state Herman Cohen that he would keep his hands off "finance," which was particularly important for U.S. concerns over good governance, Mobutu soon reinterpreted the agreement to refer to the largely symbolic Ministry of Finance while keeping tight control over the Central Bank where the money was. By the beginning of April, Mobutu had once again recovered from his brief lapse from power and had appointed Faustin Birindwa from

Tshisekedi's own movement as the head of the Government of Broad National Union and Public Salvation, thus effectively splitting the opposition.[26] As a result, the HCR lost momentum, and Mobutu was once again firmly back in the seat of power.

September 1993–January 1994: A number of occasions on the diplomatic and internal Zairean level offered opportunities for U.S. mediation of governmental reform.

After nearly three decades of Mobutu's politics and three years of Tshisekedi's "premiership," a number of judgments were clear, even if not universally shared. (1) Any arrangement that left Mobutu in any office would leave him the room to undermine any other parts of the same arrangement that might seem to promise reform. (2) Although Tshisekedi, thrice stymied as prime minister, had actually never served in office more than two weeks, any arrangement involving him would be captive to his now proven and worsening political incompetence. (3) Elections for the presidency before other positions were filled would legitimize and prolong Mobutu's rule; only elections that began at the local level would allow the CNS and civil society structures to have an impact. (4) Elections would take a year or two to prepare, during which Mobutu could manipulate the system and players as he wished. (5) Despite his continued ability to subvert transition arrangements, Mobutu was clearly on his last legs, able to block but not able to build; the state was in collapse and the economy in implosion. These were absolute incontrovertibles and the only reason to deny them was a fixation on the object—Mobutu, the CNS, elections—and inattention to its consequences. Even after having missed the two previous clear opportunities, policymakers contemplating Zaire should have been on the alert for an opportunity to deal decisively with the situation a new time. The future, as usual, was unknown, but Mobutu was well known.

After February 1993, two men—Etienne Tshisekedi and Faustin Birindwa—claimed to be prime minister in charge of preparing the elections. Tshisekedi considered his dismissal by Mobutu to be unconstitutional since he had been elected by the Sovereign National Conference. Birindwa's appointment split the opposition and resulted in the revival of the old National Assembly as a transitional parliament. Mobutu's personal interest in elections waxed and waned. In October at the Franco-African summit at Mauritius, he signed an agreement with President Mitterrand to proceed with elections and to leave government to a prime minister.

On 11 January 1994, representatives of both the Presidential Movement of Mobutu and much of the opposition (denounced by Tshisekedi)

signed a Protocol of Accord providing for a "national reconciliation government" and a new parliament of the merged HCR and transitional parliament (HCR-PT) to prepare the elections in 1994. Within the week,
Mobutu made overtures to the United States and asked President Clinton
for U.S. help to prepare the first multiparty elections in Zaire.[27] Washington's response to Mobutu's approach was cautious: a State Department official confirmed, in a rather tail-chasing statement, that "the United States
would help with elections in Zaire only if the voting was fair."[28] The Clinton administration welcomed "any concrete steps toward resolving Zaire's
social and political crisis,"[29] but State Department officials also voiced
skepticism in regard to Mobutu's sincerity, given his long history of broken promises. "None of Mr. Mobutu's recent moves tackle[d] the fundamental source of the disorder, the Zairian President himself," State Department officials recognized.[30] At the same time, France's newly elected
conservative government grew tired of the intransigence of Tshisekedi and
began to look for a "third way" to bring better governance to Zaire independent of Mobutu.

Over the last quarter of 1993, there was an opportunity for the United
States and the other members of the Troika to become actively involved in
preparing an alternative transition out of Mobutu's regime, although the
opportunity was fuzzier and the steps more subtle than in the previous two
openings. A strategy was needed to seize occasions to reinforce the CNS
government and promote an accelerated election timetable for the huge
country to provide a bridge into the post-Mobutu era. An initial step to be
taken was the seating in September 1993 of the Tshisekedi delegation to
the UN General Assembly rather than the Birindwa delegation. Support
for the Tshisekedi delegation would have solved no problems, but it would
have helped produce the hurting stalemate out of which solutions emerge.
Instead, the United States joined a brief discussion in the General Assembly in support of the Birindwa delegation.[31]

Second and third steps were mediation among the parties to unite the
Zairean opposition and pressure on the president to ensure that the electoral
timetable was kept, rather than negotiating yet another agreement that provided yet another way of keeping Mobutu in power. The convocation of a
meeting in a nearby country by an American NGO—for example, the National Endowment for Democracy (NED) or one of its offspring—to bring
all the opposition together and enhance their organizational capacities
would have been helpful. The meeting could have been a resurrection of
the CNS in a new phase or a session of the HCR without the PT, and U.S.
attention would have responded to complaints of the HCR-PT president,
Monsignor Monsengwo, that lack of U.S. support was the cause of the

democracy movement's failure. Thereafter, any promise of U.S. and European electoral assistance needed to be contingent upon reinstatement of a CNS government and upon actual fulfillment of conditions during the election preparations. Contingent promises alone would have little meaning to Mobutu and would need to be accompanied by credible threats, notably to seize personal assets abroad (which were indeed the product of the Zairean state and people, appropriated by the president).

The only Zairean figure with the stature and integrity to lead a transition was Kisangani Archbishop Monsengwo, president of the CNS and then of the HCR-PT. Like all the other figures in the transition process, Monsengwo had lost some of his aura in the infighting and frustration of the past years and was being reined in by the Vatican's concern over his involvement in temporal politics. Nonetheless, he was an authority figure in both Mobutu's and Tshisekedi's eyes and in the minds of much of the population and a diligent mediator among the parties. There are questions as to whether he would have had the heart to lead an interim effort to organize, schedule, and conduct elections, starting from the bottom up, and in the event he soon withdrew from formal politics, although continuing his interest behind the scenes. But Monsengwo had what any other new prime minister lacked—an independent political base in both society and in institutions, and committed international support could have kept him on track in leading a transition.

By implicitly withdrawing support from the elected prime minister and by not putting on pressure to stick to the electoral timetable, the Clinton administration communicated to Mobutu that he would not have to fear much more than strong words from his friends in Washington, as in Paris. Instead, the United States helped mediate agreements on a new government, consistent with the Transition Accord negotiated among the factions on 9 April 1994, followed by another Protocol of Agreement postponing elections for a year, on 16 June and 18 July 1994, respectively. Through skillful maneuvering, Mobutu positioned Leon Lobitch Kengo wa Dondo as the HCR candidate for prime minister and had him elected by a minority vote in the absence of a quorum. Kengo was of part Polish and part Tutsi descent, with no possible chance of building a political base of his own, and therefore no threat to Mobutu's presidency. He was supported by the Troika in the vain hope that he would work with Tshisekedi to provide the economic discipline the parliamentary leader lacked and that he would gain autonomy and leverage vis-à-vis Mobutu by bringing the international aid and legitimacy that the president needed. Even though he presented himself as the opposition candidate, Kengo had been loyal to Mobutu during many years of service, first as minister of justice in the late 1960s, after which he was accused of implication in the 1969 massacre of university students, then from 1982 to 1985 and from 1988 to 1990 as prime minister, periods that the CNS later cited in charging him with embezzlement. He was, however, presented as a moderate who could bring economic discipline to the Zairean state, and his defenders quipped that his honesty was guaranteed by the fact that he had already squirreled away his personal fortune from his previous posts and needed no more.

Kengo wa Dondo, a smooth and skillful diplomat, easily convinced the Clinton administration that he was independent of Mobutu and a true reformer. As a result, the administration's Africa strategists were "working to support Mr. Kengo so he [could] develop a power base independent of Mr. Mobutu."[32] Critics of the administration's policy, however, said that "the strategy of backing Mr. Kengo and hinting at economic aid will strengthen Mr. Mobutu's hand because the longtime ruler can point to it as a sign of acceptance by Washington. These critics also argue that embracing Mr. Kengo is misguided because he is at worst a puppet of Mr. Mobutu and at best largely dependent on him."[33] The hope of his cooperation with Tshisekedi was flawed from the start, not only personally by personality clashes but also structurally because Kengo was sitting in the chair Tshisekedi claimed as his own.[34]

The details of electoral organization are beyond this discussion, but a few points are worth noting. Funding for the estimated $250 million cost was available through a European Community commitment in addition to Zairean sources (although some from both sources had already been consumed by inflation and predation).[35] Furthermore, the electoral process would have required a voter registration, but not a census as is sometimes suggested. Nor would the vote have been dependent on a prior constitutional referendum; an argument could even be made that constitution making should be left to a newly elected parliament in preference to the hybrid texts on the table. Above all, the electoral process would need to have been scheduled from the bottom up, beginning with local offices, and with legislative offices grouped on a second ballot, before a third ballot on the presidency, lest—if the order were reversed—the last position determine all the rest. This was the sequence provided by the CNS but reversed by the January 1994 Protocol of Accord.

The international community's lack of interest and pressure on Mobutu during the early months of 1994, and then its reliance on Mobutu's assistance in dealing with the aftermath of the Rwandan genocide and the Burundian instability, resulted in his re-legitimization and aided his political longevity. Having embraced Kengo as the legitimate prime minister, the international community weakened the Zairean opposition and thus delayed the democratization process, particularly the important step of national elections. In June 1995 the HCR-PT extended Mobutu's presidency of the transition another two years, by which point he had been finally removed by Laurent Kabila's Alliance of Democratic Forces for the Liberation of Congo (AFDL). It is hard to see any diplomatic opportunity after 1994 to ease out Mobutu and create a legitimate succession. The focus of diplomacy necessarily turns to the sources of civil conflict.

July 1995: Warnings of pogroms in Masisi provided an opportunity for an international effort to halt ethnic violence and move and disarm Rwandan refugee camps in Zaire.

Since the Rwandan genocide of 1994, the refugee camps in northeast Zaire had posed a major humanitarian and security challenge and a major opportunity for righting the record of inaction by the West. The Masisi region of North Kivu near the border with Uganda and Rwanda was the scene of intense violence in 1993 against the Banyarwanda (people of Rwanda, both Hutu and Tutsi) who had migrated to Zaire at various times from the seventeenth and eighteenth centuries until the 1930s and 1940s, the latter migration on invitation of the Belgian administration, and again in the 1960s. As the special rapporteur for human rights in Zaire, Roberto Garreton outlined in a UN report[36] the violence that culminated in the killing and expulsion of tens of thousands of Banyarwanda, particularly Tutsi, at Masisi had its roots in decades of Zairean history that should have left no attentive observer unaware of the building crisis, above all after the Rwandan genocide of the previous year. The 1964 constitutional provision that granted citizenship to all those living in Zaire at the time, including the Banyarwanda immigrants, was partially revoked in 1972, when citizenship was removed from those who had immigrated into Zaire after 1960. The nationality law of 1981 was even more restrictive, in providing citizenship only for those who could prove Zairean ancestry back to the time of the Berlin Conference of 1885. Indigenous Hunde and Nyanga groups destroyed local archives to make it impossible for any Banyarwanda to prove their ancestry in the country.

As Zaire deteriorated economically, the battle for arable land became fiercer in eastern Zaire, and animosity against "the Rwandans," as all Banyarwanda were called, irrespective of their origins, was on the rise. Banyarwanda villages, both Hutu or Tutsi, were often attacked by local armed bands indigenous to the Kivus, with FAZ units looking on or joining in the lootings and killings; unpaid Zairean soldiers confiscated Banyarwanda cattle in this rich agricultural area and sold them on the Kisingani market. A spate of intense violence in March 1993, which caused casualties variously estimated at 6,000 to 40,000 deaths, was followed by a truce of fatigue. The personal intervention of Mobutu and the institution of "town meetings" (*journées de réflexion*) in November and in February 1994 and higher-level arbitrations brought a good deal of progress toward reconciliation.[37]

This situation of precarious peace was broken a year later by the effects of the Rwandan genocide of April 1994. After the influx of the Rwandan refugees, among them some 40,000 Interahamwe (Hutu militia) and ex-FAR (Rwandan Armed Forces) of the overthrown Habyarimina regime (referred to as *génocidaires* for their role in the killings), the attacks were increasingly perpetrated by the Rwandan Hutu refugees, who wanted to continue the Tutsi eradication that they had not completed in Rwanda and to establish an ethnically cleansed sanctuary from which to regroup and return to Rwanda.[38] A culture of impunity as well as small arms proliferation throughout Zaire's population led to an upward spiral of violence, with up to 10,000 deaths in April 1994.

The HRC-PT at the end of April 1995 called for all "Rwandans" to be expelled from Zaire and "returned" to Rwanda. Those targeted included Banyarwanda who had lived in Zaire for decades, if not for centuries, as well as recent 1994 refugees. Rwandan Hutu bands joined with local groups to kill and loot Zairean Tutsi in Masisi, with a signal outburst of violence occurring in June 1995.[39] In response, FAZ units were sent in to limit the violence, but they only protected or appropriated it. Rwanda warned that if the violence, particularly the attacks by Rwandan refugees, were not stopped, Rwanda might intervene against the camps; as early as December 1994, in a speech at the Free University of Brussels, Rwandan general Paul Kagamé warned of the option of hot pursuit, the first of a number of such warnings.[40] Yet the international community did not respond.

The situation required official UN Security Council condemnation of the violence and the complicity of the Zairean government in the killings and expulsions in June–July 1995, while the ethnic cleansing was visible but before it became a localized massacre and an irreversible escalation in November. U.S. and European governments had an occasion to voice their outrage at the violence in part tolerated, in part perpetrated, by agents of the Zairean state. More actively, the moment required that the "refugee" camps be moved westward, away from the border, as refugee practice required; that the "refugees" be disarmed, as the first groups were when they arrived in 1994; that the ex-FAR and Interahamwe be separated from their civilian hostages; that a UN/OAU peacekeeping force of military observers be stationed in the buffer area and along the border; and that the Masisi massacres be stopped.[41] Vocal official condemnation at the height of tension would have resulted in media coverage and increased international pressure and would have signaled an active Western policy in the crisis region. Such actions would have reduced the danger for those Tutsi who remained in their home regions in Masisi and would have averted further violence in both Kivus. The latter measures dealing with the Rwandan refugees and their *génocidaire* elements would have required military intervention of the type that was finally proposed by Canada and France to the Security Council a year later, pleaded for by Secretary-General Boutros-Ghali, and opposed by the United States.[42]

By November 1995, the violence in Masisi had escalated dramatically. By June 1996, more than 250,000 people had been uprooted, thousands of Tutsi killed, and over 15,000 Tutsi forced across the border into Rwanda. Zaire barred journalists from the region.[43] Refugee camps in northwest Rwanda spread like a blue carpet for miles between Gisenyi and Ruhengeri. Through the many warning signals in the media and the work of the UN agencies on the ground, UN agencies were well aware of the situation and the causes of violence in eastern Zaire. The apparent complexity over who was chasing whom that covered the mixture of true refugees and *génocidaires* merely underscored the need for good professional analysis and clear forward-looking policy decisions that concentrated on removing causes for future collapse and conflict.

It is amazing that growing awareness of Western complicity by inaction in the Rwandan genocide of 1994 did not impel a late corrective in response to the signals of alarm from Masisi. UN Secretary-General Boutros-Ghali's proposed peacekeeping force of 5,000 in the Kivus in November 1994 was rejected by the Security Council after the figure was termed too low and only one country responded to the call for troops. Instead Zaire agreed on 27 January 1995 to send 1,500 FAZ troops to police the camps, putting the foxes in charge of the chicken coops (and the foxholes). The Security Council did take action in August 1995 when it lifted the arms embargo against Rwanda but went no further to deal with the core of the problem.[44] The measure taken actually complicated the problem by assuring its escalation rather than removing its cause. Zaire started forcibly repatriating the refugees on 19 August, then stopped five days later upon pressure from the international community and turned instead on its own "Rwandans" in Masisi.[45] The United States, which had talked down Security Council resolutions that would have sent additional troops to halt the genocide in Rwanda in April and June 1994 and which above all feared involvement in any military action in Africa, saw no national interest in the region.

This context in mind, it is not surprising that neither the Security Council, nor the United States, nor the European Union voiced criticism of Mobutu's regime in respect to the Masisi crisis but rather was grateful to Zaire for providing a haven for the Rwandan refugees. On the other side of the same logic, it is shocking that the Security Council members who apologized for their inaction in regard to Rwanda did not seize the pogroms against the Masisi as an occasion to make good on their guilt and put their apologies into action.

There was no cost to a visible and vocal condemnation of the massacres, although the more tangible actions on the ground under Chapter VII would have required troops and funding, whether as a UN or a multinational force (MNF). U.S. logistical support but no U.S. troops would have been involved. NGOs who would have been involved in servicing the camps as they moved westward called for the measures in question. The most difficult part of the job was disarmament, but it would have been immensely facilitated by the westward displacement of the camps at the same time. Tens of thousands of lives would have been saved, and a good deal of the subsequent tension among the states of the Great Lakes seriously reduced. Handling the *génocidaires'* situation would have removed the pretext for Rwandan interference in Zairean and then Congolese politics for the rest of the decade. But nothing was done, and when local actors, notably Rwanda and Kabila's AFDL, took matters in their own hands, as they warned they would, there was a righteous public outcry that further tied Western policy in "nots."

Absent any vocal international outrage against the violence in North Kivu, measures taken in December by the Zairean Interior Ministry to regularize the nationality of the (remaining) Banyarwanda in Masisi were not applied. Mobutu's administration in South Kivu, as well as local and Rwandan Hutu militias, felt free instead to increase their pressure against another Banyarwanda group, the Banyamulenge ("the mountain people"), a community of Tutsi who had migrated from Rwanda into Zaire in the eighteenth century. A lack of international attention on North and South Kivu led to civil war and finally to Mobutu's overthrow a year later.

March 1996: Renewed warnings of pogroms against another Tutsi population, the Banyamulenge, provided a last opportunity for the UN, the Organization of African Unity, and the Carter Center to mediate to protect the population.

As the Zairean economy declined into the mid-1990s, so did xenophobia increase, particularly in North and South Kivu in eastern Zaire. The April 1995 HCR-PT resolution revoking the Zairean nationality of the Banyarwanda demanded the expulsion of all people of Rwandan origin, even those whose entry preceded the existence of a Zaire (or even of a Congo). Thus the Banyamulenge in South Kivu, who had crossed the mountains in the late eighteenth century, were put into the same category as the Rwandan refugees—civilians, militias, and military alike—who had entered Zaire in 1994 and suddenly found themselves stateless. After most of the Tutsi in North Kivu had been killed or driven out of Masisi, the FAZ and government officials both in the capital and in the province concentrated their violent propaganda on the Banyamulenge.[46]

UN Human Rights Observer Garreton in January 1996 warned of an escalation of the conflict in the Kivus and pointed to the roots of the violence.[47] Among many others from the region who braved arrest to write to various authorities alerting them of the problem, Muller Ruhimbika, a Banyamulenge leader from Uvira in South Kivu, had already called the nationality issue and the danger faced by the Tutsi minority in South Kivu to the attention of Garreton in November and the Carter Center in Atlanta in August 1995. Preoccupied with a larger initiative of its own through the Great Lakes region, the Carter Center did not respond to the request, which in addition had been mislaid, and Ruhimbika and other leaders of his Milima Group were detained and questioned by the Zairean authorities after the Garreton interview. March–April 1996 was probably the last period at which the war in eastern Zaire, and the eventual campaign of the AFDL, could have been prevented by vigorous action by the international community.[48]

The plea for help by Banyamulenge spokesman Ruhimbika, first to the Carter Center and then to the UN, through Garreton, was a warning and an opportunity for action and should not have remained without response. Former president Carter had launched an important démarche to create a regional dialogue in 1995, culminating in the Cairo summit of the regional heads of state at the end of November, a second summit in Tunis in mid-March 1996, and eventually the whole Burundi peace process taken over by the former presidents of Tanzania, Julius Nyerere, and South Africa, Nelson Mandela.[49] In May 1996 President Carter also floated the idea of a demilitarized zone in Zaire along its eastern border with Burundi and Rwanda to help combat arms trafficking and to accelerate the return of refugees, an idea already raised in Cairo in November and Tunis in March.[50] If the Tunis summit itself could not have been focused more specifically on the mounting pogroms in Kivu, a high profile visit to South Kivu, in March after the summit, could have drawn world attention to the situation of the Banyamulenge and, with diplomatic backup from the Troika, impelled the Zairean government and parliament to reexamine their nationality policy (the prime minister himself was a quarter Rwandan Tutsi).

The matter of the Banyamulenge was one of sovereign rights of citizenship, but it needed to be linked to the international side of the same problem by measures to deal with the ex-FAR and Interahamwe in the region, as detailed in the previous section. Mobutu was sick, absent, and at his weakest in the spring of 1996, in a vulnerable position before a coordinated policy involving both the second track efforts of President Carter and his willingness to deal with "unsavory characters" and the first track efforts of the Troika states to deal firmly with the Hutu-Tutsi problem in eastern Zaire. But coordination between the two tracks was as difficult to achieve as consensus within the Troika. When Canada proposed to send in a UN force to handle the problem at the end of the year, it was too late, even before the United States withdrew its support for the proposal in the UN.

Instead, already deeply involved in searching for a resolution for the conflicts in the area, President Carter saw the Ruhimbika appeal as a distraction to the main effort of dealing with the region through multilateral concertation, which required Mobutu's cooperation. Mobutu signed the Tunis declaration and appended a statement deploring the activities of the refugees, which to Zaire meant or included the Banyarwanda, and Carter's strategy was to work with Mobutu—the unsavory character of the moment—and bring him to a subsequent summit in May in Atlanta.

Although diplomatic and press observers were taken by surprise at the evolution of events in eastern Zaire and the rise of Kabila's Alliance, there were plenty of early warning signals. Preparing for a genocide with Nazi-like precision, Zairean officials began a series of measures to be taken against the Banyarwanda. The April 1995 parliamentary resolution included provisions for the arrest and expulsion of a list of people, cancellation of immigrant sales or transfer of assets, and banning of Banyarwanda from all official positions. In mid-September, the Uvira District Commissioner ordered a census of all Banyamulenge property, cessation of all Banyamulenge construction, and notification of the Banyamulenge community of these actions.[51] A directive from the South Kivu administration a month later indicated that the leaders of "an unknown ethnic group of Zaire called the Banyamulenge" would all be expelled, including their bishop.[52]

But xenophobic propaganda grew fiercer, as if the reverse lesson had been the one learned from the neighboring genocide of 1994. September 1996 saw the intensification of the anti-Banyamulenge campaign and the application of the measures of expulsion.[53] The vice governor of South Kivu, Lwasi Ngabo Lwabanji, warned the Banyamulenge in a radio broadcast that they would have to leave Zaire within a week, or they would be exterminated: "We will begin cleaning up," he stated in an interview with an American delegation two days before the broadcast.[54] The statements of the governor and vice governor were remarkably similar to the extremist Hutu messages broadcast during the Rwandan genocide.[55] In late September, mortar fire was exchanged between Rwanda and Zaire over several days.

The lesson of Masisi in 1995 was taken to heart by the Banyamulenge, who decided not to remain inactive in the face of danger.[56] Since the international community ignored the mounting conflict in South Kivu, Kinshasa was taken by surprise when different rebel movements joined forces and, with support from friendly governments in Rwanda and Uganda, started a movement that swept across the nation and finally overthrew Mobutu's government. The failure of the international community to act in April 1996 is part of the cause of ever increased xenophobia and ethnic conflict throughout Zaire, but particularly in the Kivus, that continued over the subsequent decade. Tacit international support for Kabila's movement accomplished one of the goals of the international community: it rid Zaire of its dictator. But if the primary goal for Zaire was to bring democracy to its people, implicit support for Kabila did nothing to achieve this. To the contrary, the Zairean political opposition was outlawed, the efforts of civil society were undermined, and state collapse continued from where Mobutu had left off. When Kabila was murdered by his bodyguard in January 2001, and his son Joseph took over, the country remained divided into rebel fiefdoms, despite an improved style in Kinshasa. Efforts to reassert the primacy of Kinshasa over the rebel forces and regions, with the support of the Troika, have also been accompanied by continuing tribal violence in the east and utilization of ethnic groups and loose *génocidaires* by the government, the rebels, and neighboring states for their own purposes of ascendancy. Some opportunities were seized by the international community to bring the second phase of the War of the Zairean Succession that began in August 1998 to a negotiated agreement in Lusaka in July 2000, in Sun City in 2003, and in Pretoria in December 2002, and any opportunities that were missed in the 2000s were general policy directions rather than clear moments.[57]

Five opportunities presented themselves, for the most part very sharply, in as many years. The first two moments in late 1991 and early 1993 were clear opportunities when Troika troops, with good contacts with the Zairean military, were already on the ground, the problem— Mobutu himself—clearly recognized, and a legal democracy movement partly in charge of the government; in addition, a few weeks later in 1993 Mobutu was out of the country, in France, posing even less of a problem for action. But the Troika, in varying degrees, preferred the devil they knew to a venture, however promising, that was, like all futures, unknown. The third opportunity was more diffuse, but it provided several occasions when the United States and other Troika members could have put their actions behind their announced goals but were busy elsewhere, despite announced lack of confidence even in the devil they knew. The last two of the series—and the last of the decade—arose because of the ethnic cleansing taking place, with clear and mounting warnings, in eastern Zaire. Diplomacy and some UN military presence would have been required, at a moment when the Troika members were criticized and apologizing for not having exercised diplomacy and military support in the previous Rwandan genocide.

The costs of half a decade of neglect and irresponsibility by external actors were felt throughout Zaire before it became Congo again under the Kabilas. Battle-related deaths numbered between 5,000 and 10,000, with 30,000 to 100,000 deaths from other related causes, in addition to some 50,000 internally displaced persons (IDPs) and 150,000 refugees over the 1990s. The total population loss from conflict and its broader effects, such as famine and disease, however, was 3.2 million between 1996 and 1999, continuing toward 4 million into the 2000s.[58] For Americans and Europeans, the cost was economic, in aid and investment losses, and above all opportunity costs, in the tremendous potential of Zaire (Congo) for a role as the pole of central African development. Three billion dollars in ODA in the first half of the decade and another $3 billion in UN Consolidated Inter-Agency Appeals were spent in keeping the collapsed economy's head above water and its leaders' pockets filled.

Notes

1. In preparing the Zairean cases, I am grateful for discussions with Ambassador Richard Bogosian, Jacqueline Bisimwa, President Jimmy Carter, Assistant Secretary of State Herman Cohen, Dr. Rick Coolsaet, Vincent Farley, Dr. André Kapanga, Monsignor Laurent Monsengwo, Dr. Joyce Neu, Ambassador Rethoré, Dr. Filip Reyntjens, Leon-David Saur, Deogratias Symba, Etienne Tshisekedi, Dr. Herbert Weiss, Dr. Jean-Claude Willame, and Ambassador Howard Wolpe. I am grateful for the research assistance of Katherina Vogeli, Eavan O'Halloran, Wei Wu, Yuko Sano, and Raf Goovaerts.

2. See I. William Zartman, "The French Connection," in Arlinghaus, *African Security Issues;* Rouvez, *Disconsolate Empires;* Bayart, *La politique africaine de François Mitterrand.*

3. See, for example, Schraeder, *United States Foreign Policy Toward Africa,* chap. 3, especially 74–80; Forbes Pachter, "Our Man in Kinshasa," 107.

4. Mondonga M. Mokoli, *The Transition Toward Democracy in Post-1990 Zaire* (Bethesda, MD: International Scholars Publications, 1997), 12.

5. Schatzberg, *Mobutu or Chaos?;* Forbes Pachter, "Our Man in Kinshasa."

6. Sabakinu Kivilu, "Pauvrete et misere," and Martin Pongo, "Memoire de la Violence," *Canadian Journal of African Studies* 33, no. 2–3 (1999): 459–472, 549–566.

7. Confidential interview by author with group participant.

8. Chipman, *French Power in Africa;* McNamara, *France in Black Africa;* Rouvez, *Disconsolate Empires;* Stephen Smith, "Le jeu des interventions," in Dumoulin, *La France et la sécurité en Afrique subsaharienne.*

9. "Zaire: Mobutu Looks Ahead," *Africa Confidential* 31, no. 10 (18 May 1990): 4–5; "Zaire: Mobutu Takes to the Water," *Africa Confidential* 31, no. 12 (5 June 1990): 1–3; *Le Monde,* 3 October 1991, 6.

10. Associated Press, Kinshasa, 27 October 1991, cited in Herbert Weiss, "Zaire: Collapsed Society, Surviving State, Future Polity," in Zartman, *Collapsed States,* 163.

11. Interview by author.

12. Confidential interview by author.

13. Kenneth B. Noble, "Zaire's Dictator Agrees to Share Power with Foe," *New York Times,* 30 September 1991, A1.

14. Forbes Pachter, "Our Man in Kinshasa."

15. Steve Morrison, "Zaire: Looming Disaster After Preventive Diplomacy," *SAIS Review* 15, no. 2 (Summer-Fall 1995): 39–52.

16. Schatzberg, *Mobutu or Chaos?*

17. Monsignor Monsengwo cited the 100,000-person March of the Believers in February 1992, when Zairean security forces killed thirty of the marchers, as another missed opportunity. The march dispersed with much wailing but no action, however, and external intervenors would have had to appear in force out of the blue to overthrow the regime. There was no Zairean action to support and therefore no opportunity to lose.

18. Rake, "Mobutu Fights for His Life," 42; "Zaire: Mobutu's Monetary Mutiny," *Africa Confidential* 34, no. 3 (5 February 1993): 4–5.

19. Riding, "Mobutu Visits France for Medical Treatment."

20. Noble, "U.S. and Allies Discuss Sanctions to Force Mobutu to Yield Power."

21. Ibid., A2; "West Raises Pressure."

22. State Department spokesman Joseph Snyder, reported in Reuters, 23 February 1993.

23. Reuters RLR, 23 February 1993; Riding, "Mobutu Visits France for Medical Treatment," 16.

24. "U.S. Sanctions Urged Against Zaire," Reuters RLR, 23 February 1993.

25. European Community commissioner Etienne Davignon, cited in *LeMonde,* 26 September 1991.

26. Misser, "Two Governments," 32.

27. Kenneth B. Noble, "Mobutu Is Said to Make Overtures," *New York Times,* 16 January 1994; confidential interviews by author.

28. *New York Times,* 15 January 1994, A9.

29. Kenneth B. Noble, "Mobutu Is Said to Make Overtures," *New York Times,* 16 January 1994.

30. Ibid.

31. United Nations, "First Report of the Credentials Committee, A/48/512," 20 October 1993.

32. Steven Greenhouse, "U.S. Trying New Tactic with Zaire," *New York Times,* 8 November 1994, A9.

33. Ibid.

34. For an evaluation of Kengo's government, see McCormick and White-house, "Zaire at the Crossroads"; "Zaire: Whose Man in Kinshasa?" *Africa Confidential* 35, no. 25 (16 December 1994): 1–4.

35. Republique du Zaire, Commission Nationale des Élections, *Budget estimatif des élections au Zaire 1997* (Kinshasa: Republique du Zaire, Commission National des Élections, 1996).

36. Roberto Garreton, UN Document ECOSOC, E/CN.4/1996/66, Geneva, 29 January 1996.

37. U.S. Committee for Refugees, *Zaire Issue Brief* (Washington, DC: U.S. Committee for Refugees, 1996); Willame, *Banyarwanda et Banyamulenge,* 66–68, 124–131.

38. Reyntjens, *La Guerre des Grands Lacs,* 16–20; Jeff Dumtra, "Zaire's Haven for Murderers," *Washington Post,* 14 July 1996, CO1.

39. BBC, 12 June 1995; Joseph Mutambo Jondwe, *Les Banyamulenge* (Kinshasa: St. Paul, n.d.).

40. Journalist Philip Gourevitch dated Kagamé's decision at February 1995 and his warnings to U.S. Defense Department officials in June.

41. Yett, *Masisi, Down the Road from Goma.*

42. Since disarmament was involved, it would have to have been a Chapter VII intervention.

43. McKinley, "Stoked by Rwandans, Tribal Violence"; "Rwanda Calls for Immediate Response"; UN High Commissioner for Refugees, *Zairean Refugees from Masisi* (Washington, DC: UN High Commissioner for Refugees, 1996).

44. UN Security Council Resolution 1011 of 16 August 1995.

45. Ngangoue, "Refugees Pawns in Mobutu's Gamesmanship."

46. See the excellent study of Willame, *Banyarwanda et Banyamulenge.*

47. Roberto Garreton, UN Document ECOSOC E/CN.4/1996/66, 29 January 1996, 2.

48. *Report on the Twelfth Meeting of the Burundi Policy Forum, Search for Common Ground* (Washington, DC: 1996).

49. The text of both meetings' declarations may be obtained from the Carter Center.

50. Reuters textline, May 29, 1996.

51. "The Conflict in South Kivu," press release, UN Department of Humanitarian Affairs, Integrated Regional Information Network Briefing, 7 October 1996.

52. Robert Garreton, UN document ECOSOC E/CN.4/1996/66, 29 January 1996, para. 35.

53. "Zaire: Conflict in South Kivu," Africa News Service, 7 October 1996.

54. Consortium for Elections and Political Process, *Strengthening, Report on Election Preparation in Zaire* (Washington, DC: Consortium for Elections and Political Process, 1996).

55. Chris McGreal, *Mail and Guardian*, 1–7 November, 1996.

56. The Banyamulenge merely put into effect the "people's self-defense" measures recommended by an NGO conference in Kinshasa in June 1993, in the absence of effective public defense; "Auto-defense populaire," *AZADHO Périodique des Droits de l'Homme,* no. 10 (March 1994): 4.

57. Weiss and Carayannis, "The Enduring Idea of the Congo."

58. Roberts et al., *Mortality in the Democratic Republic of Congo.*

6

YUGOSLAVIA, 1989–1998

THE VIOLENCE THAT BEGAN IN 1990 LED TO THE DISINTEGRATION OF THE Federal Republic of Yugoslavia (FRY), killed 300,000 and wounded a million people, and created the worst European refugee crisis since World War II.[1] The compound cause of the Yugoslav state collapse can be found in the rise of the constituent republics' nationalism occasioned by the disappearance of the common Communist ideology and organization and the concomitant competition for economic resources.[2] Just at the time when structural adjustment caused the richer republics such as Croatia and Slovenia to want to protect their wealth and poorer republics such as Serbia to share in it, the uniting beliefs and organizational structures of the Communist federal republic disintegrated along with the Cold War, and political leaders took refuge in strident ethnic nationalism. Faced with this multiple collapse, the West was of no help.

Yet the preservation of Yugoslavia was the policy of the West at the end of the Cold War, and it was not so much reversed as simply displaced by narrower considerations—such as Germany's recognition of Slovenia and Croatia—or overtaken by events. The continuation of the Yugoslav state made sense in terms of U.S. and European states' interests and values. Had the maintenance of boundaries enunciated in the Helsinki document of the 1975 Conference on Security and Cooperation in Europe (CSCE) and repeatedly used as the justification for maintaining the boundaries of the secessionist republics been applied to the Yugoslav state itself, as it was to the reuniting German state, the strained Sudanese state, or, earlier, the endangered Nigerian state, the Western states would have had a consistent platform for blocking secession, restraining deadly conflict, and helping the republics find a new constitutional framework under which they could live together. A major state in the Balkans would have

137

Missed Opportunities:
Yugoslavia, 1989–1998

October 1989–March 1990 Croatian, Slovenian, and Serbian insistence on maintaining a (con)federal Yugoslavia provided the opportunity for an international conference under U.S./European Community and Conference on Security and Cooperation in Europe auspices to work out a satisfactory solution and provide economic support.

March–July 1991 Impending threat of independence provided the occasion for European Community reaffirmation of minority rights conditions for recognition of Croatia and insistence on (con)federal Yugoslavia, with U.S. support within the Conference on Security and Cooperation in Europe.

February–March 1992 and January 1993 Two UN and European Community démarches, the Cutileiro and Vance-Owen plans, were successive opportunities for the United States and the European Community to guarantee Bosnian integrity.

September–November 1996 Dayton agreements provided an opportunity to enforce standards of democracy and ethnic treatment that would help prevent violence in Kosovo.

October 1998 Kosovo Liberation Army and North Atlantic Treaty Organization pressure created an opportunity only halfway pursued for meaningful negotiations between the Kosovar and Milosevic on a transitional status for Kosovo.

---

been preserved and Western interests in peace, democracy, and economic stability would have had an institutional framework in which to be pursued. The NATO states did not want to sponsor a precedent that might hasten a disorderly breakup of the Soviet Union, but they made disjointed and mutually undercutting moves that cleared the way for intense campaigns of violence and inhuman expressions of viciousness, reopening wounds and reconfirming hatreds that would render reconstruction and normalcy impossible for decades. It was the West's greatest moment of foreign policy incompetence in the postwar era.

During the Cold War, Yugoslavia's "friendly communism" and its independence from the Soviet Union gave it a pivotal role between the East and the West. For the United States, the strategic value in Yugoslavia lay especially in denying Soviet interests there and sustaining an icon of independence among Communist countries. Once the Berlin Wall had fallen and Communist regimes had begun collapsing, however, that purpose was gone. In Europe, the historically most influential country in the Balkans, Germany, was busy with the political and economic ramifications of its own reunification. Historic ties with Croatia and Slovenia, as well as a support for the principle of self-determination, meant that Germany and Austria supported recognition of the independence of the separate Yugoslav republics, contrary to the rest of the European community, who saw a breakup of the federation as a threat to European security.

Although present rivalries in the Balkans cannot be attributed to medieval history, the Yugoslav republics are all new states with long histories and longer memories. Serbia is unique among countries in having a national festival that commemorates a lost battle, at Kosovo Polje in 1389, "only" 287 years after Croatia lost its independence to the Hungarians in 1102. A Russian foreign policy expert, in response to the remark that Bosnians were merely responding to Serb atrocities, retorted that Serb actions were a justified response to Bosnian atrocities, perpetrated in 1578. Serbia became independent in 1878 at the Congress of Berlin, Croatia was reborn after World War I after a millennium of absence as an independent entity, and Bosnia-Herzegovina enjoyed only ambiguous sovereignty for 500 years before being absorbed into Yugoslavia after World War I.

Under the long rule of Marshal Tito (Josip Broz), from 1945 to 1980, an enormous effort had gone into suppressing the ghosts and carnage of the past. But on his death the taboo was broken, and mass graves began to be exhumed in fact and in memory by all sides in order to ceremoniously rebury the victims.[3] In 1989, the Serbs even went as far as digging up the bones of King Lazar, who died at the battle of Kosovo Polje, carrying them around the country to arouse the Serbian spirit of nationalism and convoking all the other republic party leaders to the Serbian party's mammoth celebration of the 600-year anniversary of the battle. During this event, Slobodan Milosevic delivered a speech invoking the need to fight for Serbian rights again, a statement understood as a direct threat by other Yugoslavian ethnic entities. The Croatians on their part did not remain idle. Franjo Tudjman revived the past by rehabilitating the Ustasha, the fascist movement that committed unspeakable atrocities against neighboring populations—and especially against minority Serbs—during and immediately after World

War II.[4] In the breakdown of the Yugoslav Communist system, ghosts and vengeance provided an answer to the search for new legitimization for power, especially by Serbian leaders whose seat was in the federal capital.

Constitutional talks were held in the early 1980s between the Communist party leaders of the six Yugoslav republics—Slovenia, Croatia, Serbia, Bosnia-Herzegovina, Montenegro, and Macedonia—and the two autonomous regions of Vojvodina and Kosovo. Most of the participating politicians, regardless of origin, agreed that the system on which the federation was based needed fundamental reform, although Slovenian and Croatian delegates were the most vocal proponents of change and Serbs the least.[5] During the twelfth Communist party congress in 1982, however, all proposals for organizational reform were rejected by the centralists; by blocking the demands for reform, they radicalized them.

After Milosevic had come to power as party chief in Serbia, in 1986, a new Serbian constitution, passed by less than a majority of its assembly in March 1989, curtailed the autonomous status of Kosovo and Vojvodina (abolished completely in September 1990). In response, Slovenia passed fifty-four new amendments to its constitution in September 1989 and added a promise of multiparty elections by early 1990. Contrary to the 1974 federal constitution, the republic claimed the right to nullify any unwanted federal legislation and to secede from the federation without the consent of the other republics. It subsequently declared that it would cut its budgetary payments to the federal government but began sending aid directly to other parts of the federation, especially Kosovo. The Serbian leadership responded by calling for a federal boycott of Slovenian consumer goods.

Many authors agree that the Balkan conflict erupted as a result of badly deteriorating economic conditions facing the volatile ethnic environment.[6] Yugoslavia had become heavily indebted in the 1970s. A substantial drop in the agricultural base was not matched by growth in the industrial base. The balance of payments deficit amounted to $3.6 billion, and in 1983 debt service rose to $4 billion with foreign exchange earnings of only $10–15 billion.[7] The dinar fell into hyperinflation because of overvaluation that favored imports over exports. Finally, in 1988 the new federal prime minister, Ante Markovic, instituted an economic reform program that stopped the inflation and pegged the dinar to the dollar. The austerity program proved impossible to implement, however, because of the rigid requirement of consensus under which the federal presidency operated and the decentralization established by the 1974 constitution. The harmonization of interests that was so badly needed within the federation was especially difficult because of the high level of development in Slovenia and Croatia in relation to the rest of the republics. Eager to plunge into new economic opportunities, the two richer republics found themselves held back economically by having to provide for the poorer republics.

The fourteenth Federal Party Congress in January 1990 has been identified as the final breakdown of the Yugoslav federation. Slovenia introduced a proposal for a looser federation with an economic "asymmetric union," explaining that it was not prepared to pay for a repression of the Kosovo Albanians. When their proposal was rejected by the centralists, the Slovenians walked out. Because the four Milosevic votes (Serbia, Montenegro, Vojvodina, and Kosovo) then outnumbered the votes of the remaining three republics, the Croatian delegates refused to continue without the Slovenians. The federal party would never meet again.

As an effort to try to save the federation, Prime Minister Markovic attempted to initiate elections in order to replace the Communist-dominated federal assembly. Paradoxically, it was not the undemocratic Serbian leader that opposed such elections (as he favored the principle of one-person-one-vote), but rather the more democratic Slovenia, which successfully insisted that republican elections take place first and continued to block any attempt to have a countrywide referendum decide the country's future. Had federal elections preceded elections in the republics and had the federal economic reforms attempted by Markovic been implemented, things might have been different. Because the non-Communist parties organized first in the republics, however, they were compelled to reach out to localized nationalist interests rather than to a countrywide multiethnic electorate. In the end, "Yugoslavia perished, without its citizens ever being permitted to cast their vote as Yugoslavs."[8]

Yet there were some last-minute opportunities to try to save Yugoslavia as some sort of federation and to prevent—or at least delay—the scarring violence, leaving space and time for further action. The goal would be to manage peacefully the transition of Yugoslavia from under Communist rule, on the basis of rising awareness of the danger of deadly conflict born of state collapse. One opportunity arose at the turn of the decade, when the United States and what was then the European Community (EC), working within CSCE, could have called an international conference such as had marked Yugoslavia's twentieth-century history, while strong feelings for the preservation of some form of federation still remained. Another moment for the same type of action came when the CSCE Conflict Prevention Center opened in March 1991, before the threatened declarations of independence of the first breakaway republics took place in June.

When these last opportunities were allowed to fade in inaction, the possibilities shifted to the central area of conflict, Bosnia, where the visible threat of deadly conflict brought conferences, competing plans, and indecision. At least two of these—the EC Cutileiro Plan of early 1992 and the UN-EC Vance-Owen plan a year later—would have offered a real possibility if the convening states had swung behind them in support. Instead they pursued their various ideas and avoided commitment, allowing for two and a half more years of the worst civilian massacres before the United States finally elbowed its way into muscled mediation at Dayton.

The train of conflict and collapse then plowed into Serbia-Yugoslavia itself, where its internal nature had previously left little room for opportunity. There was a chance in late 1996 to send a message that cooperation over Bosnia had not bought a license to kill in Kosovo, but that chance was ignored by Washington. Instead, economic sanctions were lifted following unfree and unfair elections in Bosnia and Serb refusal to recognize opposition victories in its own municipal elections. When that opportunity to signal credible toughness was let slide, the last chance to bridge the positions of increasingly militant Kosovar and increasingly obdurate Serbs came in the negotiations of mid-1998, where mixed messages, partial efforts, and unbelieved threats brought the area to failed conferences and punishing bombing instead. Across the decade, options narrowed and carnage expanded, yet both the options present and the carnage impending were clearly identified at the time, and lack of decision, leadership, commitment, and attention left the peacemakers in the end with no choice but to show that they too had the will to cause casualties.

October 1989–March 1990: Croatian, Slovenian, and Serbian insistence on maintaining a (con)federal Yugoslavia provided the opportunity for an international conference under U.S./European Community and Conference on Security and Cooperation in Europe auspices to work out a satisfactory solution and provide economic support.

As usual, there was plenty of early warning of impending catastrophe. The steady erosion of autonomy for Kosovo between autumn 1988 and autumn 1990 was ample warning to the West of the motives of the Belgrade dictatorship. In 1989, Ambassador Warren Zimmermann and his staff warned Washington that Yugoslavia might break up along national lines and do so violently. Kosovo had become one of the most serious human rights problems west of the Soviet Union, raising strong concerns in the U.S. Congress and within the administration. The Vienna Follow-up Meeting of the CSCE had concluded in January 1989 with a document reaffirming that a government's treatment of its own citizens was a legitimate subject for international scrutiny.[9] Although Yugoslavia was not explicitly mentioned in the document, the message was quite clear. After the first elections in the republics beginning in April 1990, the U.S. embassy began to predict the disaster that was to follow, and in the summer of 1990, the CIA came out with an analysis forecasting that Yugoslavia would cease to exist within two years.[10] Instead of a warning for prevention, it became a self-fulfilling prophecy.

The first six months of Markovic's economic "shock therapy" produced impressive improvements in economic conditions. The annual inflation rate of almost 3,000 percent in 1989 went to zero in 1990, bringing promises of future support from Western creditors and governments. In an effort to encourage continued economic reform and stability, the European Commission even indicated in the summer of 1990 that Yugoslavia might be the first Eastern European country with which it would negotiate an association agreement, and in mid-December (four days before the Slovenian independence referendum) the EC expressed confidence that association negotiations were on track.[11]

Yet, in the same year confidence in the dinar again began to deteriorate, the domestic money supply expanded, and inflation restarted. High interest rates and heavy tax burdens on all levels, combined with a complete end of state subsidies, made it difficult for enterprises to pay wages, and industrial output dropped by 11 percent for the first half of 1990. But it was Milosevic's actions that gave the deathblow to the economy. On the eve of its elections, Serbia took half of the drawing rights of the entire federation—$1.5 billion worth of dinars—without authorization and used them to pay back wages, pensions, and bonuses to state enterprise and government employees.[12] Further, in every republic, beginning with Croatia and Slovenia in the spring, governments ignored the monetary restrictions of the stabilization program in order to win voters, thereby destroying the economic achievements. By now the EC governments were beginning to realize that appeals to good behavior and threats of economic sanctions had little effect.

Alerted by danger signs of the breakup of Yugoslavia, Western states needed to seize the opportunity to underwrite and reconstruct its existence by giving economic support to the federal government and convening a conference dedicated to devising a flexible type of federation that would meet the various needs of the situation, notably nationalist and economic, held together within a looser but reaffirmed type of sovereignty. Yugoslavia had already been the product of similar conferences at Versailles in 1918 and Yalta in 1944, as had Serbia at Berlin in 1878, and the exercise in 1990 would only have been a more modern version in a series, dealing with constitutional matters as well as sovereignty. There would have been a number of elements to piece together for such action, including timing, agency, and content. Serious thinking about necessary action should have begun in October 1989, when Markovic visited Washington and was assured of U.S. support for "Yugoslav independence, unity, and sovereignty, market-oriented economic reform, and democratic pluralism."[13] Markovic received enthusiastic verbal endorsement but no economic or democratic assistance to keep his reforms and electoral base in place; instead, he was saddled with prospective sanctions for human rights violations in a republic where he was fast losing control, with Congress not understanding that this action was helping Milosevic and hurting Markovic, who had nothing to do with the violations in Kosovo.[14] When he wanted to return to Washington for further consultations in 1990, the administration discouraged the visit and refused to issue an invitation.[15]

At this point, an economic study of Yugoslavia under Markovic's structural adjustment was needed, with an evaluation of supportive measures in trade and finance to keep the program on track and particular attention to softening the effects on the poorer republics and preserving the advantages of the richer republics, which were to tear the federation apart. The EC's promise of an association agreement needed to be implemented with concrete measures.[16] A strategy was needed, based on making it profitable for the republics to keep their destiny tied to the maintenance of the federation. The economy was the substance around which the nationalist appeals were wound, and it needed attention. Europe had enormous economic leverage over Yugoslavia, since it absorbed 40 percent of all Yugoslav exports. This window of opportunity for Europe would not come back; once violence had started and the republics' independence was recognized, the leverage that the Europeans had to change the direction of the conflict disappeared.

As in the case of economic reforms, political reforms opening opportunities for pro-democracy forces needed money behind the message. Yugoslavia deserved to receive the same pro-democracy attention and assistance that was being directed toward other countries of Eastern Europe. "An inexpensive program of technical assistance, sending some three hundred technical advisors to the political parties throughout the country and observers on media freedom during 1990, might have created an entirely different atmosphere of transparency, international interest and equal opportunity."[17]

In addition, the international community needed to focus multilateral attention on the political framework for an evolving Yugoslavia, in order to keep it from falling into the violence that was widely predicted. That too required a strategy, and one of multilateral coordination. Although there were plenty of institutional venues on hand, however, none of them provided the ready-made basket required. Part of the problem was the fact that the European states were reluctant to take up their responsibilities in regard to Yugoslavia on their own, so a common U.S.-EC initiative—which the United States did not want—was required. But no common institutions were in function; the most appropriate one, the CSCE, was not to hold its "Charter of Paris for a New Europe" meeting where it created its conflict prevention center until November 1990, and the center and other CSCE institutions were not actually in place until March 1991. It was just this sort of problem for which CSCE was created, with the advantage of having the Soviet Union or Russia as a member, but it was not yet operative. A debate on a peacekeeping operation during the Paris meeting was crippled by the CSCE's unanimity rule, which gave the FRY an effective veto to any such undertakings.[18] The Western European Union (WEU) and the Council of Europe were European organizations without a mandate for the task, and NATO as a military alliance was scarcely appropriate for a peaceful conference and was busy trying to reorient its activities as well as open its doors to new Eastern European members. The task was beyond the mandate and capabilities of the UN.[19]

The only venue left was one made up for the occasion, a jointly called U.S.-EC initiative to consider the Yugoslavian question, like the UN-EC International Conference on the Former Yugoslavia two years later in August 1992. The Soviet Union would have to be invited and, given its own internal troubles at the time, would have been on acceptable behavior. The formula for an agreement is not obvious but not beyond imagination. A secessionist and a centralist position can be squared through a unified-but-decentralized formula that loosens the federation without shifting sovereignty (including UN membership) to the component units of a confederation. Other matters such as allocation of resources and even consideration of boundaries would also have been meat for debate. The importance of the issues is not to be minimized, but they were not beyond solution, and a search for one under conditions of support for the federation, as outlined above, would keep minds off secession, which would lurk in the wings as a threat to keep the focus on federation. The conference would have created its own occasioning stalemate, by temporarily suspending the independence option.

An advantage of early action was not only that it would have avoided the bloody conflict which ensued among the Yugoslav parties, but also that it would not have necessitated military intervention from the outside. The eventual provision of monitors might have been required, especially if the boundary question were to be addressed (or if not), but the presumption of peaceful observers would have been far more tenable as a result of an all-party conference under Western supervision than in the conditions under which EC peacekeepers arrived a year later or the UN peacekeepers eventually appeared two years later, in March 1992.

There was no specific target date on which to anchor a conference, but a time during the first quarter of 1990 would have been appropriate. The period provided several favorable conditions for action to reverse the disintegration of the federal government. At the time of the first republic elections in Slovenia in April 1990, polls indicated that nearly 60 percent of the Slovenes were still in favor of a federal rather than a secessionist solution, even though few were willing to grant primary power to a federal body.[20] In August the Slovenian prime minister made a careful distinction between sovereignty, which he espoused, and independence from Yugoslavia, which he did not find necessary.[21] In Serbia and Montenegro, more than 80 percent of the population wanted to keep the federation. By the December 1990 referendum in Slovenia on whether to remain in the federation or not, however, 95 percent of the voters opted for independence.[22]

Similarly, popular support for Markovic was remarkable in 1990 until the middle of June. In all Yugoslavia, his popularity was higher than any other politician at almost 80 percent, with a majority in every republic but Kosovo. From a slim majority in Slovenia of 59 percent, his support in Serbia, Croatia, and Bosnia-Herzegovina was at 81, 83, and 93 percent respectively.[23] Markovic's time as prime minister offered one of the last opportunities for the rest of the world to prevent the breakup of the federation.

The conference would have filled the enormous hole in the center of U.S. policy and on the flanks of European policy on Yugoslavia. U.S. policy, as presented by Ambassador Zimmermann on 28 May, was contained in a "hope that no constituent unit of Yugoslavia will seriously consider separation, just as we hope that no consideration will be given to using force to preserve unity."[24] Between those two negative hopes, however, lay no positive policy for deterring separation and preserving unity without force. When Lawrence Eagleburger visited Yugoslavia in 1989, he also said that the United States supported territorial integrity, independence, and unity of Yugoslavia but would not hold Yugoslavia together by force. The Slovenian leadership took that statement as tacit support for secession, whereas the Serbs were also convinced that the United States had an interest in keeping the federation together.

The official line in Washington about Yugoslavia was that the United States would work with those who worked for democracy and that the Yugoslav authorities should be informed about this policy.[25] But democracy was an ideological preference, not a policy, and in any case was the wrong policy in Yugoslavia at the beginning of the 1990s.[26] In supporting democracy without insisting on an appropriate state structure for its exercise, the United States and Western Europe contributed to the demise of the center in Yugoslavia. The ambiguity with which the West handled the Balkan problem thus had the effect of giving the green light to all parties to pursue their unilateral objective. Economic sanctions or enticements had no—even undesired—effects. A conscious diplomatic effort to examine and ratify alternatives was required.

For the United States, the problem was not a crowded schedule—the Gulf War had not yet loomed on the horizon, despite intelligence warnings—but a matter of focus. A view prevalent in the Bush administration was that the problems in Yugoslavia stemmed from the fact that it had not made a clean break with its Communist past.[27] Democracy was seen as the only recipe for curing the political ills of communism, regardless of the problems that the country was actually facing. Another attitude sought to explain the conflict as "ancient ethnic hatreds" rather than something that was caused by modern economics or politics; U.S. policymakers were thus able to rationalize inaction by declaring the conflict unresponsive to outside influence. Eagleburger, who earlier had warned about the dangers of a breakup of Yugoslavia, now defended U.S. passive policy by explaining the conflict as irrational: "There is no rationality at all about ethnic conflict. It is gut; it is hatred; it's not for any common set of values or purposes; it just goes on. And that kind of warfare is most difficult to bring to a halt."[28]

The United States and Western Europe were busy dealing with German reunification and the creation of the European Union (EU), as well as the possible breakup of the Soviet Union. A major element behind the European inaction was the difference of opinion among the Europeans themselves. European cooperation in the Balkans was darkened by the shadow of the past: ancient European partisanships toward the various Yugoslav republics' complicated cooperation. Repeated warnings from diplomats, scholars, and intelligence agencies about the dangers of "Lebanonization" were largely dismissed, not because they were unconvincing but because the prospects did not seem to present any threats to the major European powers. Yet the one place in the entire area between the Soviet Union and the European Community with any real possibility of destabilization, against a background of historic conflict, was Yugoslavia. A modicum of contingency planning could have been expected.

March–June 1991: Impending threat of independence provided the occasion for European Community reaffirmation of minority rights conditions for recognition of Croatia and insistence on (con)federal Yugoslavia, with U.S. support within the Conference on Security and Cooperation in Europe.[29]

Elections took place within the republics between April and December 1990, successfully bringing nationalists to power in almost all cases. The elections helped "snuff out the very flame of democracy they had kindled."[30] A CIA report leaked in November 1990 again predicted a violent breakup of Yugoslavia.[31] Specific warning came with the Slovenian referendum of 22 December 1990, which called for independence within six months unless there were agreement on a loose confederal structure for Yugoslavia.[32] The tension was most visible in Croatia, where ethnic Serbs began to form paramilitary units and seal off predominantly Serb-populated areas from Croatian control, while Croatia was building up military forces for the purpose of targeting the Yugoslav National Army (JNA). Troop movements in Croatia in January 1991 drew a promise from Ambassador Zimmermann that the United States would not support the use of force to hold the country together. In February Slovenia and Croatia suspended federal law on their territories, and a series of summit meetings began between the federal presidency and the republican presidents to discuss how the federation could peacefully dissolve.

The battle over the FRY was carried to the federal presidency in the first half of 1991. At a meeting of the collective presidency in January, the Serbian member, Borisav Jovic, together with the defense minister and functional head of the JNA, General Veljko Kadijevic, attempted to gain enough votes to order the federal army to intervene against the paramilitary units in Croatia and Slovenia. The Serbian move failed to gain a majority, however. Despite clear messages to both Jovic and Tudjman that Washington would isolate those who used force to carry out their objective, Milosevic's campaign was not over. In mid-March, the Serbs "hijacked" the members of the presidency and took them to a military headquarters but again failed to gain a majority; Milosevic withdrew Jovic from the presidency, "resigned" all the other members under his control, and declared "Yugoslavia finished." In a belligerent address, he announced that Serbia would no longer respect federal Yugoslav authority and was prepared to fight if it had to: "If we don't know how to work and do business, at least we know how to fight."[33] With no presidency, the JNA would not have a civilian authority to prevent a move against the rebel republics.

Milosevic's coup was not long lasting, however, and when the four remaining presidency members gathered with the support of Markovic a week later, Jovic and his allies returned. It is likely that sharp foreign reactions and strong warnings from the United States worked to refrain Milosevic from deploying the army at this time. The final act in the presidential breakdown came in May 1991, when Serbia and satellites within the collective presidency blocked the rotation of the presidency to the representative of soon-to-secede Croatia, Stipe Mesic.

As the political game was played out in the corridors of Belgrade and in the separate republics, opposition was beginning to take shape among ordinary Yugoslavs in Belgrade and elsewhere. In the middle of the contentious week of 11–17 March, a mass rally in the heart of Belgrade fifty years after the Nazi takeover of the city protested against Milosevic's control of the press. Some 30,000 participants demanded Milosevic's resignation and voiced clear support for Prime Minister Markovic's government.[34] In an interview with the author, Sabrina Ramet presented this moment as the last chance to remove Milosevic, as massive demonstrations took hold of Belgrade's streets for several days, Serbian police forces killed two protesters and injured 100, and the federal army intervened for the first time in an internal dispute. Had the opposition been sufficiently encouraged by the West, it could have mounted a considerable challenge to the Milosevic government at its weakest moment. Such action—like that of the JNA—would have been internal interference, however, unless combined with specific efforts to arrive at a political solution for the federal state on the way to collapse.

In a word, the West—the EU states and the United States—should have been shepherding as large and important a state as Yugoslavia through its post-Communist transition rather than standing by as a curious observer. Instead, the international community's support of the federal government during the spring of 1991 became increasingly inconsistent. While the United States and EC members were still verbally supporting economic reform and federal unity, financial support was dwindling rapidly, further destabilizing the fragile political situation. After a failed attempt to show unity on the Gulf War, the unity of the Europeans on the FRY began to crack in early 1991. Various European bodies developed different positions. Although until early November 1991 the twelve EC foreign ministers kept their pledge that recognition of individual republics would be considered only within the framework of a general settlement,

the European Parliament resolved as early as mid-March that "the constituent republics and autonomous provinces of Yugoslavia must have the
right freely to determine their own future in a peaceful and democratic
manner and on the basis of recognized international and internal borders."[35] The EC Declaration of 26 March on future membership of Yugoslavia in the European Community referred to both unity and democracy, overlooking the reality that they had become logically incompatible
in Yugoslavia. The European Troika—former Council president Gianni
deMichelis of Italy, current president Jacques Poos of Luxembourg, and
designated president Hans van der Broek of the Netherlands—pointedly
met only with federal officials during their April visit, but commissioners
met with republic officials in Brussels in February and in Belgrade in
May. Yet implicit insistence on unity, along with explicit mention of
human rights, constitutional structures, and economic reforms, was reiterated in the latter visit and in EC communiqués and letters in the first half
of June.[36] Then, at the last minute, two days before Croatian and Slovenian independence, the European Council declared it would refuse any contact with republic officials and any acknowledgment of independence declarations, only to be contradicted by its chairman saying the whole matter
was subject to negotiation.

The United States offered the same confusion. A State Department
statement on 26 June said "the US opposes the use or threat of force." The
next day, in Belgrade, Secretary of State James Baker said that the United
States "could support greater autonomy, some sort of sovereignty for the
republics of Yugoslavia." When Baker visited Yugoslavia in late June
1991, at the last minute before the breakup, he told Markovic, "If you
force us to choose between unity and democracy, we will always choose
democracy."[37] These contradictions as well as the paralysis of the West
were interpreted as permission to promote ethnic agendas without price.[38]
"[I]nternational diplomacy did not bother to push seriously for a confederal restructuring of the country that would have been acceptable to the
non-Serb republics at a time when there still may have been a chance for
it (namely, in the winter of 1990–1991)."[39]

Yet the opportunity was present for a concerted effort before the last
minute, before the declarations of independence in June. A date was available, and an institutional framework as well. The CSCE Conflict Prevention Center created in November 1990 opened its doors in Vienna on 18
March 1991.[40] An appropriate focus of its opening ceremonies would
have been the convocation of a meeting to address the Yugoslav constitutional issue and engage energies in talking among Yugoslavs in a Western

forum instead of killing each other at home. The idea that Yugoslavia would serve as the "test case" for the new European security organizations was already present. European actions in Yugoslavia would serve to legitimize the CSCE and a new unifying Europe, with Yugoslavia being the vehicle for European unity rather than simply its beneficiary. The mandate of the CSCE in these areas would have allowed it to tread where other organizations such as the UN could not without being accused of interference in internal affairs. CSCE meetings during the year were to grapple with issues of human rights and sovereignty.[41] Notably, the CSCE foreign ministers met in Berlin in mid-June to hear an account of the crisis from Yugoslav foreign minister Budimir Loncar and create emergency procedures to circumvent the CSCE unanimity rule, which they did with a qualified majority rule, regardless of the consent of the state concerned, worked out between Baker and Soviet foreign minister Andrei Gromyko. The CSCE praised the accomplishment and ended with the adoption of a resolution that called for the "democratic unity and territorial integrity of Yugoslavia" and a continued dialogue between all parties. Loncar returned to Belgrade assured that the CSCE would stand behind the federal government.[42]

Touval noted that "it might occasion some surprise that the Western intervenors did not try to mediate among the Yugoslav parties" and that such mediation was avoided because Western countries felt that it might imply acceptance of the two breakaway republics.[43] But in March, no break had yet occurred, and the warnings were abundantly clear. Markovic had refused a CSCE Good Offices Mission, but that was in an earlier context. As the above record shows, meetings were frequent events during the period, so the convocation of a formal event in mid-March would not have been unusual. The difference between such a meeting and the many others that took place would have been an external presence operating under a body of Helsinki principles. What would have been unusual in the circumstances was a clear objective, coordinated efforts, and strong follow-up. It would have been necessary to sort out the contradictory messages the Western countries had been sending, by focusing on a single goal, developing a strategy of carrots and sticks, and setting steps for implementation. Each of these three—objective, efforts, and follow-up—requires further development.

Out of the multiple goals the West was pushing, such as democracy, economic reform, state integrity, human rights, and an end to armed conflict, it was necessary to do some prioritizing and some calculations on cause and effect. Democracy was posited as an immediate goal rather than a gradual effort, in complete misunderstanding of the nature of the process. Encouraging democracy as a principle inherently discouraged state integrity in the current context of nationalist mobilization, but the reverse was not necessarily true.[44] Economic reform was working to the destruction of Yugoslav integrity and stability and fueled the fire of demogogery, and so needed cushions to be built into its efforts. Human rights as an absolute (as it so often is among human rights advocates) left the other goals in the dust. Yet basic to all of these was the restoration of a functioning state, as a source of law and order and as a framework for reform and, eventually, democracy and human rights. Instead of thinking through these elements as a process and a progression, the Western parties either grabbed hold of one value as an overriding goal without working out its relation to the others or posited several values as simultaneous goals without considering the contradictions they posed for the others.

To put some order into thinking required leadership. The United States was just emerging from the Gulf War, with a diplomatic effort behind the wartime Gulf War coalition every bit as impressive as the military effort behind Operation Desert Storm. To pick up another campaign and organize it, even if only on the diplomatic level, was seemingly out of the ordinary. Ambassador Zimmermann voiced the standard judgment in saying, "Even a great superpower has difficulty in dealing with more than one crisis at a time."[45] But there is more to be considered: early enough, the situation was not a crisis; Secretary Baker was being prepared for a later visit anyhow; and there was a European Bureau in the State Department that was presumably doing its job. Former secretary of state Kissinger has noted that Middle East policy in the late 1970s "needed to be reinvented every day for the better part of a year—while we were simultaneously conducting Latin American and Southern African diplomacy."[46] Strategizing for more than one area at a time is normal diplomacy, especially for a great superpower.

There was a model for discussion on the table, to be called the Confederation of Independent States (CIS), designed as the fig leaf to cover the breakup of the Soviet Union. The move to its creation began on 17 March 1991 with the all–Soviet Union referendum on the preservation of the integrity of the USSR, the results of which were declared to be favorable, and continued through the failed August putsch to the signature of the Belovezhskaia and Almaty agreements in December, setting up the CIS. It occupied sixteen summit conferences of ex-Soviet leaders and eventually proved to be ephemeral, but it allowed dissolution to take place rather peacefully.[47] The goal in Yugoslavia would have been on the other side of the crest of sovereignty, to adopt as loose relations as possible within a single sovereign state (which could then reassert its unity gradually in the coming years). It was not the end point that was the necessary goal at this moment, however, but rather the selection of a process that would lead away from the clouds of war. For these purposes, a CIS process could have served as the initial motion, open for discussion.

Despite the harsh relations among the republics' leadership in the spring of 1991, proposals for a restructured federation were made repeatedly, and the presidents met under their own auspices in six summits of the republics between late March and early June, without external assistance. They came to an agreement in the fifth summit in late May on a power-sharing plan to serve as the basis for further negotiations. Indeed, as late as the beginning of June, there was a majority among the Yugoslav republics for a confederal arrangement. Bosnian president Alija Izetbegovic and Macedonian president Kiro Gligorov presented a joint proposal somewhere between federation and confederation, which the Serbs first rejected and then three days later at the sixth summit of the republics accepted conditionally for discussion. But without outside help and pressure, it was too late.[48] When the Slovene and Croat call for asymmetric unity was rejected by the Milosevic camp, the two republics withdrew and eventually declared their full independence on 25 June. Had the Western powers been more intimately involved in Yugoslav constitutional politics, they could have used the opportunity to coach the parties through further negotiations at this point.

The main obstacle to an effort at unity was to be Germany, which under domestic pressure gradually moved from support of Yugoslav unity up until the middle of 1991 to a position of recognition for Croatian and Slovenian independence.[49] German motives were in many ways self-interested but in other ways very sincere in seeking a way to limit the spread of conflict and violence and—in between the two—to avoid siding with Milosevic's Serbs, seen as the root of all Yugoslav evil.[50] But in the first half of 1991, when the trends were clear and the dangers impending, German positions had not yet crystallized in favor of secession, and pro-integrity countries such as Britain and France still had time to bring the EC to play a positive role in maintaining Yugoslavia intact and furthering economic and political reforms.

As Germany's argument was to evolve, it seemed a logical extension of the German experience: self-determination was sacred because it united Germany and so should be honored even if it broke up Yugoslavia. That the pieces that broke off first—Croatia and Slovenia—were old allies of Germany only rooted the logic in history. But the logic would have been easy to turn on its head, if a strong public statement about unity as the prime value and the condition for democracy had been made by a prominent figure, notably American; the United States owed little to Germany in the Gulf War and so such a statement would not have been difficult. Unity brought Germany together peacefully, for spiritual and economic satisfaction; unity should hold Yugoslavia together, for the same benefits.

Four days before Croatian and Slovenian independence in June 1991, when the CSCE held a ministerial meeting in Berlin, the emergency mechanism for handling disputes was put into place. Despite visible tensions in Yugoslavia, however, the European foreign ministers expressed only "friendly concern" about the situation and called for democracy and the rights of minorities, as well as the preservation of territorial integrity, an inadequate measure at this point in the conflict. The resources of the European Community and the CSCE to provide credible carrots and sticks were unexplored.[51]

But carrots and sticks were needed. Economic incentives were being offered to the federal government to proceed with its reforms, but economic incentives and disincentives were never mentioned to the separatist republics to dissuade them from secession. Yet as much as their own emotional nationalism, it was the economic attraction of Europe and the desire not to subsidize the poorer republics that underlay the arguments of Croatia and Slovenia for independence. Such stands were an invitation to a Western threat of tough economic sanctions and total political rejection if the republics persisted on the path to secession without first entering into serious negotiations. Those stands were also a call to consider compensations and incentives for remaining within the federation, the other side of the coin of sanctions and disincentives for leaving. "Whoever by 1991 continued to demand that Slovenes and Croats remain together with the Serbs in a Yugoslav state asked for a sacrifice on their part that would have to be justified explicitly and carefully, and for which something would have to be offered in return."[52] The secessionist republics, most notably Croatia, did have real grievances, as did Serbia as well, which could have been addressed positively in the spring of 1991, before it was too late.

In addition, Croatia and Slovenia could be put on notice that they would be held responsible for triggering the anticipated violence.[53] The CSCE itself had no military or economic leverage, but its members did, and they were free to apply incentives and disincentives on their own in support of CSCE goals and actions. The EC in fact had substantial leverage over the republics in the beginning of the conflict, so that early action could have influenced the very character of the dispute and broadened the scope of domestic political options, both at the federal and republican levels.[54] Instead, the EC economic sanctions that extended beyond the early stages of the conflict were aimed at other goals than unity. They were very meaningful to Milosevic and could have been used with effect if tied to an effort to keep the country together. These were matters that could have been discussed at the CSCE meeting in March. They were not.

Three months later—a day earlier than scheduled—Slovenia declared its independence on 25 June and quickly moved to take control of the Slovenian border posts. The ease with which the Slovenian fighters shook off the Yugoslav army from their territory encouraged Croatia to take the same step as Slovenia.[55] Gathered for a ministerial meeting in Brussels at the end of June, two days before Slovenian and Croatian independence was declared and the war started, the EC decided not to recognize any declarations of independence. The following day the EC signed an agreement with FRY on a loan of 700 million European Currency Units (ECUs) until 1995, conditional on the country's continuing unity.[56] The EC Troika made several futile proposals for a cease-fire, then imposed an arms embargo on both parties to the conflict and at the behest of Germany cut off all aid to Yugoslavia, the body that was being dismantled.

The EC Troika's ministers finally on 7 July won a cease-fire agreement at Brioni, but it had run out of opportunities either to save Yugoslavia as a framework for peaceful change or to deter violence in a new framework. The EC, it was claimed, had "created the conditions" for peaceful negotiations.[57] Slovenia and Croatia agreed to suspend their declarations of independence for three months, Yugoslavia pledged to send JNA troops back to their barracks and allow Mesic to occupy the presidency, the parties accepted a CSCE monitoring mission focused on Slovenia and possibly extended into Croatia, and serious discussions about the future of Yugoslavia were to begin in The Hague in August. Translated, this meant that Slovenian and Croatian independence was not rejected, and Serbia got three months to regroup the JNA in Serb territories of Croatia and Bosnia-Herzogovina where its interests were centered. As an added disincentive to the parties to hold the agreement, the Troika promised that if there were full compliance it would not continue mediation efforts.[58]

The cease-fire was broken everywhere, the JNA withdrew from Slovenia in order to prepare its all-out attack on Croatian forces, the EC was unable to field forces that could prevent the violence, and when Dubrovnik was shelled by the JNA, British naval units offshore refused to fire for fear of being fired upon.[59]

It is again not clear what size military force would have been needed at this point to give teeth to the negotiations, but numbers would not have

been large, especially if associated with an agreement to suspend movement on the ground by the republics' forces and the JNA. There was no
consensus for intervention, either in the United States or in Europe.[60] When
on 19 September, a Franco-German proposal was made for the deployment
of a peacekeeping force between Serbs and Croats in Croatia itself, within
the WEU framework, this was opposed by the British who, with their experience of military involvement in Northern Ireland and Cyprus, warned
that great caution had to be exercised in interposition operations. In the
end, the European Council refused military intervention and declared that
a committed cease-fire was a precondition to the deployment even of a reinforced monitor mission, confusing the conditions for a Chapter VI with a
Chapter VII intervention, to use UN terms. The logical gap was flagrant: at
"German insistence, . . . an end to the fighting was an essential prerequisite
for continuing the search for a political solution,"[61] yet fighting was the republic's way of looking for a political solution in the absence of compelling
efforts by the Europeans to find alternatives.

EC mediation during this time centered on a peace conference, finally
convened on 7 September. Shuttle diplomacy by its chairman Lord Peter
Carrington at last focused attention on the Brussels peace commission's
drafting of a constitutional document on Yugoslavia's future that could be
presented for negotiations. Carrington was held back by conflicting European states' interests, the EC members' reluctance to use force, and the
emerging competition of other mediators as a result of the increasing involvement of the UN and the United States. After eighteen failed cease-
fire attempts in Croatia under Carrington and after the JNA had occupied
nearly a third of Croatia, the parties finally agreed to the nineteenth cease-
fire attempt in February 1992 under UN special envoy Cyrus Vance, the
withdrawal of the JNA, and the deployment of 10,000 peacekeepers in
Croatia.[62] Lord Carrington was later criticized for his ineffective methods
of not leaving enough room for the disputants to work out their differences. On his part, he noted bitterly that the German recognition of Slovenia and Croatia in December 1991 had "torpedoed" his peace conference.[63] On the eve of the December EC meeting, Paris and London had
argued for the use of the UN Security Council to contain German pressure
to recognize Croatia and Slovenia. Since Germany did not show any signs
of budging, however, France gave up in favor of EC unity. The last half of
1991 since Brioni had been frittered away in European irresponsibility.
The opportunities shifted to the remaining republics, above all Bosnia-
Herzogovina, which held the key in turn for a settlement in Croatia and for
conditions of stability in the neighboring republics.

February–March 1992 and January 1993: Two UN and European Community démarches, the Cutileiro and Vance-Owen plans, offered successive opportunities for the United States and the European Community to guarantee Bosnian integrity.

Like Croatia, Bosnia showed early warning signs of what was to come. Ethnic relations had worsened ever since 1989, and between October 1990 and March 1992 the four Serb "autonomous" regions received a steady infusion of arms, tanks, and heavy artillery. In October 1991 Milosevic and the Bosnian Serb leader Radovan Karadzic had met to coordinate plans for the takeover of Bosnia. Soon after the cease-fire in Croatia in January 1992, the war began in Bosnia-Herzegovina, where the JNA moved the troops withdrawn from Croatia. Bosnia-Herzegovina was covered by the general arms embargo that had been imposed on the Yugoslav successor states in September 1991, leaving the Bosnian Muslims (Bosniacs), who were thus unable to obtain military hardware, practically defenseless against the well-armed JNA and Serb militias. President Izetbegovic asked for European monitors in Bosnia, which he got, and UN peacekeepers, which were refused; Vance, concentrating on the urgent need for peacekeepers in Croatia, held that peacekeepers should be employed after and not before a cease-fire, again confusing Chapter VI with the needed Chapter VII.

Both Serbs and Croats in Bosnia, urged on by Milosevic and Tudjman, were looking to separate their national territory from Bosnia and join their protector republics. Only the Muslim Bosniacs were really interested in seeing a unitary state with borders unchanged. On 10 January 1992, in response to Izetbegovic's December call for international recognition of Bosnia, the Bosnian Serb parliament proclaimed the creation of its own autonomous Yugoslav state, the Republika Srpska, with a claim on 60 percent of the land (even though Serbs constituted only 31 percent of the population).[64] The Serbian Democratic Party (SDS) in Bosnia declared a boycott of the announced referendum on independence in early February, barricades went up in western Herzegovina, violent clashes occurred between refugees from the Croatian war and army or local militia units, and villages mobilized for self-defense. In the event, the referendum on Bosnia's independence on 29 February–1 March was boycotted by most Bosnian Serbs, but Muslim and Croat voters supported independence with 62.7 percent of the total eligible voters. Violent demonstrations and barricades followed in Sarajevo. Two days later, on 3 March 1992, Izetbegovic declared Bosnian independence. The evil cycle of revenge had begun.

In the early months of 1992, the Europeans discussed the creation of an interposition force in order to be more effective in achieving a cease-fire in Croatia, but no such force was available.[65] The United States opposed the plan, and when the Europeans took it to the UN, the Soviet Union, afraid of a possible precedent for its own country, cited the UN charter and the need to respect the territorial integrity of sovereign states. The United States insisted on the same treatment for all the republics and therefore in January argued that Bosnia-Herzegovina and Macedonia had to be recognized like all the others. The United States argued that recognition could stabilize the situation in Bosnia and allow the governments to take independent action to prevent the spread of the conflict. The Europeans were reluctant, after their previous ill-chosen decision to recognize Slovenia and Croatia for the same reasons and the EC's Badinter Commission ruling that Bosnian independence should be recognized only if approved by a majority from each of the three nationalities in a referendum.

February and March 1992 offered an invaluable opportunity for political negotiations to head off a crisis in Bosnia-Herzegovina. A series of EC-brokered diplomatic initiatives to forestall war in Bosnia-Herzegovina began in Sarajevo on 13 February under the auspices of Portuguese foreign minister José Cutileiro, and ten days later—a week before the Bosnian referendum—produced an agreement in Lisbon among the three Bosnian parties to maintain the existing borders of Bosnia-Herzegovina as "an independent state consisting of three constituent states, to be called either regions or provinces."[66] The constituent states were not necessarily contiguous, and their boundaries were not yet provided. The agreement was broken in two days by Bosnian defection, but new talks began on 7 March in Brussels.

When initial progress on a proposal for a federal constitution stalled, the delegations returned to Sarajevo and on 18 March agreed on a further document outlining the political principles of a republic composed of three constituent units based on national, "economic, geographic and other criteria,"[67] each with veto power over central legislation and wide authority over its own affairs. This resulted in signatures by Karadzic for the Bosnian Serbs, Mate Boban for the Bosnian Croats, and Izetbegovic for Bosnian Muslims. One week after the agreement, Boban reneged, however, feeling that more negotiation could get Croatia more territory. He was joined by Izetbegovic, who felt that he could get recognition for his sovereignty instead and saw the plan as a step to partition.[68] Izetbegovic sensed less than enthusiasm for the plan in Europe and opposition in the United States, and the Croats joined only to maintain their alliance of the moment with Bosnia.

Cutileiro's was one of the two plans that objectively could have worked in Bosnia, providing the initial basis for a successful peace effort.[69] It was vague in some places, notably on the dimensions of the national regions and their division of powers with the central government, which controlled defense and monetary policies. It had been subject to much negotiation and needed more to balance the various contradictory claims. But its main problem was that the parties, above all the Bosnian government, felt they could do better with U.S. recognition than by adhering to the agreement. The United States may not have explicitly encouraged such thoughts, although Zimmermann was later accused of urging Izetbegovic to reject the Lisbon agreement when he should have been complimenting the politician for his achievements.[70] More important, the United States did not explicitly discourage such perceptions and make plain its support for the project. Instead, the United States urged the EC on 10 March to extend "collective recognition" to Bosnia, which Europe did a month later.[71]

The recommended alternative is not complicated: it would have required clear support for the Cutileiro démarche and firm advice to the parties, but above all to the Bosnians in this case, to sign and join. The moment the negotiations took place, at the very edge of the last minute, provided the United States and the European countries with the opportunity to wield a powerful carrot and stick in one—recognition. It was no longer a question of saving Yugoslavia through constitutional engineering, but of shaping the constitution of Bosnia in such a way as to avoid the horrible killing and structural disabling that ensued. The United States and the EU could have firmly established the limits of the negotiations by showing that there was no alternative to the plan. Making recognition contingent on agreement on a stable institutional arrangement, rather than making that arrangement the outcome of bloody civil war, was the opportunity offered and missed.

The United States played the same role in March 1992 in regard to Bosnia as Germany had in regard to Croatia and Slovenia a year and a half before, warning against the consequences of not recognizing the remaining states. Thomas Niles, assistant secretary of state for European affairs, said that there was a real possibility that intercommunal violence could erupt at any time in Bosnia-Herzegovina and used the same arguments as Germany had used in favor of recognition: "Recognition is seen as a way to reinforce stability, especially if the outcome of the Bosnian referendum clearly favors independence."[72] Both Gligorov and Izetbegovic had warned earlier, even before the recognition of Croatia, that it could be destabilizing if the United States recognized other republics but not theirs.[73] Others, including

Vance, expressed concern as early as December that recognition would be detrimental to the stability in Bosnia-Herzegovina. The Europeans (including Germany) also had doubts about whether recognizing Bosnia-Herzegovina was the best policy.[74] As a compromise, as in the case of Germany's recognition of Croatia, the EC made recognition conditional on Bosnia's human rights record—over which Bosnia had little control—rather than on the achievement of a settlement on its constitution. Recognition without an institutional structure was as disastrous for Bosnia as the earlier recognition of Slovenia and Croatia under the same conditions was for Yugoslavia. It effectively dealt a blow to the EC's own peace efforts, prolonged the war, and reduced the alternatives to action left to the international community.

Baker clearly had a choice. He could have capitalized on the opportunity for compromise, not tried to convince EC governments about recognition, and thereby worked to avoid another three years of terrifying war.[75] In July 1992, the EC and the UN finally agreed that the war in Bosnia-Herzegovina had to be stopped by a political agreement that would include what they called the "three warring factions."[76] Trapped between the aspirations of the state republic and the component nations, negotiations in Geneva in August 1992 worked on a constitution that would include both: self-determination for the different national communities and proportionally shared political power and jurisdiction for all three groups.

In this environment, the new EC mediator, Lord Carrington, found his work stifled by an inconsistent mandate and the ambiguity that the EC showed toward its own political objectives and competing political principles, such as the unwillingness to commit military forces against the Serbs after having identified them as aggressors.[77] By September 1992, Serb units controlled about two-thirds of Bosnian total territory and had besieged all major cities. The effect of European indecision and U.S. inaction shifted the locus of diplomatic activity to the UN, as reports of systematic atrocities, such as rape and ethnic cleansing, came to the attention of the Western media.

The second plan that provided an opportunity for arresting the Bosnian conflict was the Vance-Owen proposal that grew out of the UN-EC International Conference on the Former Yugoslavia (ICFY) in London on 26–27 August 1992. Vance and David Owen, appointed to serve as UN and EC mediators, respectively, soon found themselves unable to mediate. Instead of recommending forceful military action to halt aggression, they recommended that parties should engage in meaningful peace negotiations in good faith, in the absence of cease-fire or any curtailment of genocidal policies or ethnic cleansing. They rejected the Cutileiro idea of three national units as inviting ethnic enclaving and cleansing because of the intermingled populations and instead improved on it by opting, out of a menu of five options, for "a centralized federal state with significant functions carried out by between four and ten regions" based on the Cutileiro criteria, with agreement by all three parties necessary to establish the regions.[78]

Since the parties could not agree, the two mediators finally worked out their own plan of ten constitutional principles and a map of the ten regions and submitted it to the parties on 2 January 1993. The plan was tinkered with over three more meetings until the end of the month, when the three parties signed the constitutional principles, but then the map was again altered unilaterally by the mediators at the beginning of February in the light of objections by the parties.[79] The next meeting a month later reaffirmed the deadlock but produced agreement between the Bosnian Croats and Muslims on internal governance.[80] More changes were made in the map during the last round, between 16 and 25 March, but at the end the Bosnian Serbs refused to sign unless their regions were turned into one contiguous state.[81] Repeated negotiations over the next five weeks produced changes that allowed Karadzic to sign *ad referendum* on 5 May, the day of Vance's resignation, but the signature was annulled by the Bosnian Serb assembly the next day.

The Geneva conference on the Vance-Owen plan inherited the violent consequences of the Croatian cease-fire and the Serb disappointment over the failure of the Cutileiro plan. With completely incompatible agendas, the three parties set out to grab as much land as possible, with the Serbs taking a steady lead because of their military advantage. The problem (mainly for the United States) with the Vance-Owen plan was that by dealing with the current situation, it inadvertently rewarded Serb aggression and conquest of land.[82] Rather than seeing the conflict as one between a legitimate government and two insurgents, the conference saw it as three warring factions, thus placing the Bosnian government at the same level as the Serb dissidents. But unless the mediator was willing to commit itself to the rearmament of that government and the absolute destruction of the rebel forces, a negotiated settlement where the government was a party among others with a veto was the only path to the end of the conflict. Such debates are rendered sad and moot by the subsequent events, which piled on enormous costs in order for the mediator to arrive at the conclusion it previously denied.

During the negotiations, the fighting raged unabated among all three parties, despite the initial agreement between Bosniac Muslims and Croats. The UN Security Council imposed its most comprehensive mandatory sanctions ever on Serbia/FRY,[83] but negotiations continued under competing EU and U.S. auspices until mid-July 1994, undercutting each other with vigor.

The one result was the solidification of the March 1993 Bosnian-Croat agreement into a federation on 1 March 1994, the first stepping-stone to the eventual negotiation of the Dayton accords eighteen months and hundreds of deaths later.

What was not done and what could have been done in the case of the two plans are the same side of the coin. In both the Cutileiro and the Vance-Owen initiatives, the negotiators devised a reasonable formula for constituent relations within Bosnia and pursued the matter assiduously with the parties. Their efforts may have been incomplete, but therein does not lie the problem. Their insufficiencies came from their absence of leverage and, behind that, from the absence of unity and support given to them by the United States and the members of the EC.[84] The main constraint on the talks still lay in the quarrel within the Western alliance, which allowed the opportunity at hand to be let slide.[85] Both plans depended on strong support from the United States and the UK, yet the mediators had worsening relations with their home governments.

Both the Cutileiro and Vance-Owen plans were lacking in important components and elements of implementation. The Europeans seemed to be unaware of the fact that the different parties had different ideas about cantonization. Left open were the shape and form of the cantons, how they should be created out of the present territorial situation, and how the project should be carried out practically. Owen and Russian foreign minister Andrei Kozyrev did, however, discuss an idea of a partial or gradual implementation through the establishment and expansion of safe areas under UN control, with economic incentives, which could have had a good chance to succeed, since economic assets were behind some of the strategic thinking of the warriors.[86] Bosnian Croats and Muslims were still on the same side, although their relations were crumbling, and international action could have helped avert their coming war. A program of progressive implementation could also have allowed for the participation of UN peacekeepers (50,000–70,000 were envisaged), refocused the agenda, created safe areas, and dampened the flames of war.

The lack of support also relates to the inconclusive nature of the negotiations. The mediators were flexible to a fault, continually open to unilateral revisions that their own rules had excluded in order to achieve a fit with the parties' incompatible positions, but theirs was an exercise in cartography, in which, having no ability to enforce the boundaries on the ground, they were unable to call closure and establish a deadline because they had no sanctions to impose for defection. Again, the mediators needed the confidence and backing of the United States and the EC.

The issue that overshadows all others when it comes to these opportunities is the question of the use of force, which had already come up at this point. Had the Western powers been willing to back up their political diplomacy with military force through NATO, the CSCE, or the UN, many new moments for a negotiated settlement would probably have appeared. Neither the United States nor the EC/EU countries were anywhere near this point in 1992.[87] With Sarajevo on the brink of starvation in June, Baker finally took the initiative to discuss with National Security Adviser Brent Scowcroft the possibility of using the only remaining instrument that might change the course of the war—Western military intervention.[88] A game plan was designed that would justify any action for the purpose of delivering humanitarian relief to Sarajevo.[89]

French foreign minister Roland Dumas complemented this plan with a call for the creation of an air-exclusion zone over Bosnia in order to ease humanitarian flights into Sarajevo as well as to deny the Serbian absolute military advantage in the air. Baker said that the only way the Bosnian conflict could have been prevented or reversed would have been through the application of substantial military force early on, with all the costs, particularly in lives, that would have been entailed, although there was a debate about how costly a military intervention would have been, with many observers of previous Defense Department estimates arguing that casualties would have been much lower.

After January the U.S. approach changed considerably as Clinton came to the White House. The onus for the failure of the Vance-Owen plan belongs at the feet of Clinton and the new administration, who refused to give it assent, assuming (incorrectly) that it was unacceptable to the Bosnian side.[90] Despite Clinton's early statement that a failure to act in Bosnia would be to "give up American leadership," the new administration's early attempts to lift the arms embargo and use air power to "pin the Serbs down" were never carried through. Although the Europeans rejected Warren Christopher's proposal in May 1993 to "lift and strike" after the United States had repeatedly made and withdrawn threats of air strikes, the heart of the problem was domestic: Clinton had a distaste for force and was simply not strong enough internally or politically to override the Pentagon's opposition to the commitment of U.S. military forces.[91] Christopher, just as Eagleburger had done earlier, stated in a press conference that Bosnia was a "European issue" and represented "ancient hatreds." Further, he excused U.S. inaction by its allies' rejection of the lift-and-strike plan.[92]

After the recognition of Bosnia and the Serb military advances and ethnic cleansing, it was simply not possible to get any agreement until an inside force was able to equilibrate the holdings of the three ethnic polities and an outside force—such as NATO, eventually—was willing and able to punish infractions. A mutually hurting stalemate on the ground had to be created.

September–November 1996: Dayton agreements provided an opportunity to enforce standards of democracy and ethnic treatment that would help prevent violence in Kosovo.

After creating the Washington agreement setting up the Croat-Bosniac Federation in March 1994, U.S. mediators hosted the Geneva and New York meetings establishing the Basic Principles of 8 and 26 September 1995, respectively, and the Dayton negotiations of 1–21 November drawing up the Paris agreement of 14 December 1995. Despite wistful glances at perfection, it is certain that the tough mediation produced the best meeting point possible at the time between incompatible demands, ending the conflict and tracing a creative if uncertain path toward its resolution. Also despite hopes for the desirable over the impossible, it is equally certain that the Kosovo question could not have been included in the Dayton negotiations without upsetting the chances of any agreement at all.[93]

Kosovo was the mirror image of Bosnia as a problem. International intervention was needed to support—indeed, create—a Bosnian government; intervention in Kosovo was needed to restrain the Serbian government. The challenge in Bosnia was to protect the territorial integrity of the state against irredentist tendencies of its neighbors; the challenge in Kosovo was to protect the population of a formerly autonomous region against repression by the state.[94] There is a world of difference. Richard Holbrooke noted that the Dayton negotiations had effectively prevented the Bosnian conflict from spreading into Kosovo to become one single theater of war, but the problems in Kosovo still remained after the Dayton negotiations and the Belgrade bombing, on their own.[95] The feeling that the big problems were over after the Dayton meetings was mirrored in the non-U.S. part of the West; the working groups of the EU-UN ICFY, sidelined by the U.S. initiative at Dayton, were withdrawn from Kosovo and other parts of the FRY for lack of money, just at a time when their attention was needed. Although the last working group contacts with Serb leaders at the end of 1995 indicated a Serb willingness to show flexibility on Kosovo as a part of Belgrade's eagerness to achieve acceptance in Europe, the contacts were let drop.[96] It took the humanitarian outrages over the

Serb forces and the radicalization of Kosovar nationalism from a Democratic League (LDK) to a Liberation Army (KLA) to force international efforts to search for a solution.

There were plenty of indications that Kosovo was a hot spot already after 1987 when its autonomous status granted under Tito began to be revoked under Milosevic. Some 50,000 Serbs left Kosovo for other Yugoslav republics in the 1980s, partly due to the pressure of the political climate but also because of the attraction of better economic opportunities elsewhere. This provided a good opportunity to produce a nationalist campaign, and Milosevic used the Serb depopulation as well as the nationalist memorandum of 1986 to charge Muslim genocide of Kosovo's Serbs and to consolidate his power. Starting with riots in 1981, the opinion that Kosovo might lead to a broader Balkan clash was widespread.[97] Throughout 1991 and 1992, state repression dramatically increased in Kosovo. Its most egregious examples included the shooting of protesters, beatings, tortures, arbitrary arrests, the jailing of political dissidents and human rights activists, mass firing of Albanian (Kosovar) workers, and the closure of Albanian schools and cultural institutions, including the Albanian-language university in Pristina.[98]

Outgoing President Bush warned Milosevic at the end of 1992 that the United States would consider a war in Kosovo to be a direct threat to the national interest and would be obliged to act, a "Christmas warning" repeated by his successor and by Secretary of State Christopher in February 1993, without any further measures.[99] Yet it is doubtful whether there were any opportunities—missed or otherwise—to deal directly with the Kosovo question before the end of the decade. Other than through an all-Yugoslav conference in the early 1990s, as discussed above, there was no justification for entry into a sovereign territory without a serious provocation. The missed opportunities for dealing with Kosovo were indirect, in not conveying to Milosevic the impression that Europe and the United States meant what they said—including the Christmas warning—when they said it.

Following the declarations of independence of Slovenia and Croatia in 1991, Ibrahim Rugova of the largest party of the independence movement, the LDK, declared that Albanians would not remain in a truncated Serb-dominated Yugoslavia. In a referendum in September 1991, an overwhelming majority voted for separation from Yugoslavia. Rugova's combination of pacifist strategy and maximalist demand gradually solidified into a stalemate that presaged either negotiation or violence. With the emergence of the KLA in 1997, pressure exploded for a more aggressive strategy, as the KLA called on the citizens of Kosovo to reject Rugova's pacifist approach and to pursue a liberation struggle against the oppressor.

The Kosovo problem is complicated both practically and legally. The province contained a shrinking Serb minority (from more than a quarter of the population in 1960 to less than a tenth in 1995[100]), attempts to import Serbs from Krajina after the Dayton negotiations had little effect, and expulsions of the Kosovar would have to be extraordinarily massive—even for the Serbs—to be effective. Yet Kosovo was the heart of Milosevic's nationalist message and the springboard of his political success. By the reigning principle of state succession and the rejection of population transfers, if not outright ethnic cleansing, the province was not entitled to secession, but by the principle of national self-determination, it should have become independent immediately (or perhaps part of Albania, for which there was little support). Alternatives to full independence included separating the populations and incorporating the northern fringe into Serbia proper; placing the Serb enclaves, the Kosovo Polje battlefield, and the great monasteries of Kosovo under permanent Serb control and United Nations guarantees within an enlarged Albania; or instituting a rebalanced Yugoslav federation consisting of Serbia, Kosovo, Montenegro, and Vojvodina.

The West reflected the same ambiguity as the Serbs, a problem that has dogged Western efforts from the beginning to an end yet to come. Although not wanting to encourage secession, particularly by the KLA's violent means, Western policy did not want to condone Kosovo's integration into Serbia with the repression of the Kosovar that endorsement of Milosevic's policy would entail. Despite fears expressed at the time, an enlarged Albania was on no party's agenda. Return to the status of autonomy that Kosovo enjoyed under the FRY's 1974 constitution until 1987 would be ideal, but it depended on a multirepublic Yugoslav federation that no longer existed; autonomy was a worn-out solution in the Kosovar's eyes, having failed and been outrun by nationalism. In an admittedly difficult situation, without a clear goal, neither the United States nor the EU had a clear policy. Clinton's reiteration of Bush's Christmas warning had lost all credibility, as the lead-up to the 1999 bombing was to show.

In the absence of a prominent and desirable outcome, the next best policy goal would be to convince Milosevic that only one trade-off was possible: Serbia could only hope to keep its territory intact if it would cease repressing its people. Standing in the way of any such clear message to Milosevic were the feelings that his goodwill was earned and needed by the Dayton agreement and that in any case the Dayton negotiations had solved the Yugoslav problem, giving place to China and NATO enlargement on the policy agenda of the new Clinton administration. Having gained his primary goal of lifted sanctions and proven himself necessary to the Dayton settlement, Milosevic returned to cooperation with the

Bosnian Serb hardliners without fear of Western pressure; Radovan Karadzic and other indicted war criminals roamed freely in Bosnia under the uncocked guns of the NATO force, which counted the days to its promised June 1998 departure.

Two days before the 1996 U.S. elections, an unusual opportunity to deliver a double-barreled message to Milosevic began to unfold. An opposition coalition organized by three politicians as the Together (Zajedno) Movement won municipal elections in the major cities of Serbia, including Belgrade; the government refused to recognize the results, instituted legal challenges, and closed down independent radio.[101] Serbs by the hundreds of thousands took to the streets of Belgrade, joined by demonstrators in other cities, and stayed there, off and on, until mid-February in a sustained demonstration for democracy. There was no State Department condemnation or threat of action until mid-January 1997, two and a half months later. Other than one visit to Washington, Zajedno had no contacts with any senior U.S. officials, and no administration official went to Belgrade lest Milosevic turn their visit to support for himself.

Zajedno needed urgent and massive support from the democracy movement in Washington. The National Endowment for Democracy, the International Republican Institute, and related NGOs—"the children of NED"—needed to mobilize not just immediate support for the movement and other democratic parties (for example, the Civic Alliance and the Democratic Party) but also training in running and presenting a political organization in the elections, and then in governing municipal affairs. NGOs' programs did not start until mid-1997, when the opportunity was long gone. Such support from Washington to the field and in publicized visits in Washington could have given momentum to the movement and the other democratic parties of the opposition toward sustained pressure for competitive democracy and a vigorous campaign in the upcoming FRY elections. "But Washington missed the chance to affect these events," Holbrooke noted,[102] and instead the three leaders of Zajedno turned against each other and by June 1997 brought down the movement in internecine conflict.

The other barrel should have been a vigorous pursuit of the perpetrators of ethnic violence already identified in Bosnia. Although Western officials expressed their concern about developments in Kosovo and repeatedly urged Milosevic to restore the rights of the Kosovar Muslims that he had revoked in 1989, the past record conveyed instead the message that such concerns would remain purely verbal and not pose any limitations to the Serbs' actions in a place as important to them as Kosovo. By treating Milosevic as an ally after the Dayton meetings and ignoring its own commitments in Dayton to hunt down the ethnic cleansers, the United States signaled that, despite past rhetoric, Kosovo was a Serbian problem to be dealt with by Serbian methods. By letting its diplomatic efforts on Kosovo drop, the EU signaled its disengagement from the problem. With these messages, it is no wonder that by 1999, the West had an impossible job of convincing Milosevic that this time it meant business.[103] Had a stronger message been sent in preparation, the Serb-Kosovar talks in New York and then the talks of Secretary of State Madeleine Albright with Milosevic in Belgrade in May would have had greater chances of dealing effectively with Kosovo before the nationalist movement turned military. A clearer message would at least have made the signals more credible three years later in 1999 and might have made them unnecessary.

October 1998: Kosovo Liberation Army and NATO pressure created an opportunity only halfway pursued for meaningful negotiations between the Kosovar and Milosevic on a transitional status for Kosovo.

Although the KLA came into formation throughout the mid-1990s, the most important event in its preparation came from next door with the collapse of the Albanian state in March 1997 and the resultant flood of arms into Kosovo.[104] The KLA began military operations in the latter half of 1997, to which the Serb/Yugoslav armed forces responded by directly attacking civilians, provoking mass displacements that rose from 75,000 to 300,000 during July and August. The KLA was impatient with the nonviolent political approach of Rugova's LDK and took up arms for an independent Kosovo. When Milosevic sent his troops and tanks into Kosovo in March 1998, he fulfilled the international community's worst predictions for the conflict and confirmed their beliefs about his disastrous intentions. As a result, the Kosovar had less and less to lose in seeking independence by violence. An unemployment rate of over 90 percent and the enforcement of martial law made Milosevic's least favorable outcome of secession most attractive to the Kosovar.

At the beginning of 1998 the Contact Group of France, Germany, the UK, Italy, Russia, and the United States urged Serbs and Kosovar to negotiate a solution between status quo and independence. A major confrontation between the KLA and the Serb police and JNA began at the end of February and lasted for a week into March in the Drenica region, leading the Contact Group ministers to call Spanish foreign minister Felipe Gonzalez Marquez to mediate. A week later, Holbrooke was asked by Rugova to mediate "without conditions."[105] But Milosevic refused to see Gonzalez and also the U.S. special envoy Robert Gelbard, and it took six weeks of internal U.S. debates before Holbrooke was appointed. A month after an official referendum in April confirming that Kosovo was a purely internal issue, Yugoslavia initiated talks with the Kosovar leadership in order to avoid international interference. These soon collapsed and Milosevic accepted Holbrooke's and Gelbard's mediation for talks with Rugova on 22 May.[106]

The four results of the meeting were mixed: the smiling picture of Rugova after the meeting weakened his standing with the KLA, the regular low-level talks the summit was designed to produce were rare and unproductive, Milosevic's agreement to U.S. mediation (by U.S. ambassador to Macedonia Christopher Hill) was denied in practice, but diplomatic observers were allowed to visit Kosovo to observe conditions.[107] Indirect negotiations by the State Department team followed over the summer, focusing first on procedure and then on substance. The procedural question concerned the participation of the KLA, which the United States accepted in late June in meetings with KLA representatives but was then unable to operationalize into a common Kosovar Albanian negotiating team.

The substantive question concerned the formula on which negotiations would center. Between status quo and independence lay autonomy (partition, the other option, being excluded by the precedent of Dayton),[108] and the Contact Group in early July decided to flesh out the concept with the parties as an interim measure, leaving a final solution for later. "[R]uling out independence condition[ed] the negotiations in Milosevic's favor," but not ruling it out kept Kosovar hopes unreasonably high.[109] Two months later, Hill announced Milosevic's and Rugova's acceptance of the formula of interim autonomy. KLA leaders did not join the agreement, but they acquiesced in most steps of the discussions after mid-July, including deferral of independence. Compromising Rugova and dividing the Kosovar was doubtless a goal of Milosevic, into which the others played willingly.

At the same time, the Serb army launched a major offensive, crippling the KLA and wounding the Kosovar population at the end of July. The Security Council did not begin to react until a month later, despite horrendous tales of the offensive's ravages, and against Russian opposition to any mention of enforcement,[110] passed UN Security Council Resolution 1199 calling for cease-fire and negotiations only on 23 September. The next day, the NATO defense ministers' meeting and the North Atlantic Council issued an activation warning (ACTWARN), the penultimate step in preparing NATO air strikes.

As Serb atrocities continued, the United States sent Holbrooke and Hill back to Belgrade to make a last-ditch effort to revive negotiations and emphasize the conditions for avoiding airstrikes. To these goals, Holbrooke added the installation of verification systems to monitor compliance, eventually through an unarmed civilian Kosovo Verification Mission (KVM) and aerial surveillance. As the talks dragged on, Holbrooke cleverly used the delays to extract an action order (ACTORD) from the NATO Council and the ACTORD to extract an agreement from Milosevic, both on 13 October. Two days later, the NATO command and the Yugoslav army made an agreement to allow aerial surveillance; the next day the Organization for Security and Cooperation in Europe (OSCE) and Yugoslavia signed an agreement to deploy the 2,000-man KVM; a week after, the Security Council applauded the progress and demanded immediate implementation on the remaining agreements.[111] On 27 October, NATO confirmed "substantial compliance" with the provisions for military and police withdrawal from Kosovo.

But in the absence of any enforcement capability to back up verification, the Yugoslav withdrawals were an open opportunity for the KLA to rebound to fill the vacuum. Since the agreement was made without the KLA, it lasted for only about a week (in practice) and fell apart when fighting between the KLA and the Serb forces broke out again. Milosevic felt betrayed by an agreement that allowed the KLA to rebound, and he fired his moderate advisers and assembled a group of conspiracy theory hardliners who were to guide him through the eventual NATO bombings.[112] In November, Yugoslav withdrawals were reversed, and the Serbs decided on an operation—nicknamed Horseshoe—that would eliminate the KLA and clean out the Kosovar.[113] The rising brutality of the Serb forces, culminating in the Racak massacre of 15 January 1999, galvanized NATO into calling a final negotiation—"designed to fail," in the words of a commentator[114]—and engaging in seventy-eight days of intense bombing.

Talks began on 6 February 1999 at Rambouillet, France, with a ten-point framework that both sides were told by the Contact Group to accept as the framework for the accords. The issues that the Contact Group determined would be discussed included autonomy for Kosovo and a withdrawal of all Serbian paramilitary and army units except some border troops. Contact Group members determined that the two dozen "basic elements" presented at the beginning of the conference were "nonnegotiable principles," since they felt that the parties had implicitly accepted them by agreeing to come and further negotiations would only constitute delaying tactics.[115] This was a major mistake on the part of the Contact Group, who left little room for the parties to own their agreement. The two sides of the conflict needed more opportunity to change and amend the different points of the framework that had been determined by the Contact Group.

From the beginning, there was little incentive within the proposal for the Yugoslavs to sign. Yugoslav territorial integrity would be violated by foreign troops whose leaders had constantly denounced Yugoslav actions, so that the prospects of ending the rebellion and confirming Serb sovereignty in Kosovo were highly diluted. The main incentives were outside the agreement, in the opportunity to avoid the bombing that the Yugoslavs did not expect to occur and in the promise of seeing sanctions lifted again and Yugoslavia accepted into Europe. But these carrots were considered bland, and the sticks reedy. Much of the rest of the framework to the talks was acceptable to the Serbian delegation, but not to Milosevic, and constituted much of the same framework as the final agreement signed by the Yugoslav parliament on 3 June 1999.

The Kosovar also had difficulties with the Contact Group draft. The main goal of many in their delegation was full independence from Yugoslavia, not three years of autonomy and an uncertain future thereafter. At the least, the Kosovar delegation demanded a referendum to decide the future after the three years. This was still not allowable to the Contact Group, since it wished to maintain the territorial integrity of republics and discourage other national minorities from rebelling in hopes of achieving their own state.

Two weeks after the talks ended at Rambouillet, the negotiations reconvened in Paris. The Kosovar had decided to accept the Rambouillet accords and signed two days later, but the Serbs issued new proposals for peace that were completely different from the accords and refused to take part in the closing ceremony. Soon after the end of the Paris talks, Holbrooke went back to Belgrade in a last attempt to try to convince Milosevic to sign the document. Milosevic, still without any incentive to sign, refused, and soon after Holbrooke left, the bombing of Kosovo and the FRY began. The NATO countries had assumed that there would be no need to bomb Yugoslavia for more than a "relatively short period of time" for Milosevic to give in and that he would capitulate once he saw that NATO meant business.[116] This was a false hope, and NATO fell into its own trap, believing that it could dictate to a dictator and forgetting that it had taught him in the previous years that bombing threats were empty or at least subject to long delays. NATO initially had only about 200 targets to bomb, enough for about one week of sustained bombing, not the seventy-eight days, some 8,000 strike sorties, and the identification of new targets that the campaign actually took. Milosevic was determined not to give in and set out to fracture the NATO alliance.

After weeks of NATO bombing, the Russians continued to try to hammer out an agreement more favorable for the Yugoslav government and then, unable to rally international support to end the NATO bombing, worked to get Milosevic to sign an agreement that would offer peace and yet not include the unfavorable parts of the Rambouillet accord. The Russians asked a close ally of Boris Yeltsin and Viktor Chernomyrdin, Peter Castenfelt (a Swedish financier who helped the Russians secure IMF funding in 1993), to deliver the framework for this new deal. He was then able to convince Milosevic that Moscow would not come to his aid and may have also offered Milosevic a carrot or two in the form of individual financial incentives. Castenfelt paved the way for Finnish president Maati Ahtisaari and Chernomyrdin to finalize the peace agreement in Belgrade in late May.

The entire year was occupied with two crossing tracks. The diplomatic track held the formula for autonomy that changed only in details, no matter how important, in the time between the first proposals in the summer of 1998 and the agreement of June 1999; the military track bore the competing efforts of the Yugoslav government and the KLA to eliminate each other in Kosovo—the Serbs by military extermination and the Kosovar by military provocation until independence would be granted. Until the two competing efforts at elimination had firmly checked each other, on the ground and above all in the two parties' minds, the parties would not engage on the first track toward an agreed outcome. Unfortunately, as often happens when decisions are based on subjective perceptions, one party's view that the other is blocked is seen as an occasion to press one's own advantage, unless that party sees its own efforts as blocked as well. Thus, the challenge to the mediators was not merely to devise a formula agreeable to both sides, since the bargaining zones of the two simply did not overlap, but to convince both parties that they had no alternatives and that their competing efforts to eliminate each other in Kosovo would not work.

Convincing the parties of their lack of alternatives was achieved partially and sporadically throughout the first half of 1999 with enormous effort. The Kosovar at Rambouillet did not agree that they had no other alternative, only that the Rambouillet accord represented the best alternative for the moment. It took two and a half months of bombing and concerted convincing by Chernomyrdin to persuade Milosevic that he had no alternatives left. Could the same thing have been accomplished earlier, without the costly bombing?

There were a few moments when the opportunity to do so was present. The earliest during this period came in March 1998, when the Drenica offensive by the Serb police and army should have galvanized the outsiders into action. The Drenica action killed nearly twice as many civilians as the Racak massacre the following January that triggered the call for Rambouillet. A forceful démarche at this time, responding to Rugova's invitation, would have come before the KLA had been able to gather steam and before the Serb offensive in May, and would have strengthened Rugova if progress toward a stable status for Kosovo could have been made.[117] The United States was disorganized in getting its mediation team appointed and in action. Neither objectively or subjectively was there a stalemate, but there was warning aplenty that both hurt and stalemate were in the offing. Neither side could be sure of winning when the war broke out in earnest, so that it would be worthwhile cutting losses early if a preferable outcome could be devised.

Despite Milosevic's continued refusal of international mediation, all parties shared an interest in producing a positive result that would undercut and forestall the rising KLA.[118] The KLA's inclusion would be hard to arrange because of their disorganization, but it would engage them before they became either dominant or defeated on the ground. Nothing at this point made a decision on the substantive question any more obvious except the unacceptability of the two zero-sum positions, so full autonomy for an interim period under international supervision was the likely end point toward which to work. Above all, it would have been necessary to rehabilitate the Christmas warning and repolish its credibility and to hold off preparations for a Serb offensive as well as KLA attacks.

May–July presented less of an opportunity, despite the mediators' efforts. A major Serb offensive began right after the Milosevic meeting and the two sides fought hard until the Serbs declared their summer offensive over in late September. During this period, KLA political leadership had not crystallized as yet, nor had any sense of stalemate until the offensive was over.

The best moment to seize an opportunity was during the Holbrooke-Hill mission in October 1998, when some agreements were extracted from Milosevic before he changed his advisers and decided on Operation Horseshoe to eradicate the KLA.[119] Although Holbrooke complained that "this guy is not taking us seriously" in the first few days of the mission, by the end of the mission Milosevic appeared to have changed his appreciation of the dangers.[120] This appreciation quickly dissipated when the KLA resumed its attacks and the verifiers were not able to enforce the agreement. In fact, the ACTWARN, ACTORD, and actual bombing decisions appear to have been as much a process of NATO's screwing up its own courage to finally send a military force to Kosovo (KFOR) as it was a constraint on Milosevic. Yet reports indicate that NATO members expected Holbrooke to return in October with a request for troops, and it was the U.S. administration that was afraid to make the military decision that was the logical component of its diplomatic accomplishment.[121] To compound the error, the October agreements gave Milosevic 2,000 unarmed KVM civilian hostages, tempering the very threat that had made Milosevic temporarily change his mind, even though the Bosnia experience had shown the risk of having observers on the ground when aerial operations are contemplated.

But keeping Milosevic on the diplomatic track depended on keeping the KLA there too, and that involved bringing the KLA into the negotiations, something the Hill-Holbrooke mission did not attempt. Holbrooke has indicated that he focused "all leverage" on Milosevic because "there was no Albanian leadership to negotiate with us."[122] Whether this perception is a fault of the intelligence services or a tactical misjudgment is not clear; two months before the October agreement the KLA had announced a "political representative" and six other leaders, and KLA figures had been in contact with the U.S. delegation since May.[123] Four months later, Hill and his mediation group had shaped a Kosovar delegation to come to Rambouillet, motley to be sure, but broadly representative.

But bringing the KLA and other Kosovar onto the diplomatic track depended on their awareness that the process was meaningful and that other alternatives—the military track—were blocked. The knowledge that they would have a meaningful role in the October talks would have been a powerful incentive to the Kosovar to pull a delegation together. That awareness in turn depended on the same element as on the Yugoslav side, the enforcement of the cease-fire and withdrawal terms through the presence of NATO troops. Like Milosevic, the KLA leaders got serious with the NATO mediators when they felt that the mediators were serious with them. But above all, the political indecision in Washington left the tremendous diplomatic efforts in the field unsupported and undermined, confirming both sides' impression that the Western diplomacy was only words, even when—at the end—it no longer was.

The formula for agreement was relatively straightforward even in October: withdrawal of most Yugoslav forces and police, stationing of NATO enforcement forces along with aerial and land verification missions, autonomy status for a period of time with representative and accountable institutions, and a mechanism for determining a final status at the end of the interim period. Obviously these Contact Group principles covered many devilish details, but the key to their determination lay in the military measures and political determination that indicated convincingly that there was no military track and no alternative.

Had the effort succeeded, it would have spared the world in general and the Serbs and Kosovar in particular a disastrous series of events that embittered relations the world around. It has been claimed that the October agreement as it was enabled the Kosovar to get through the winter before being evicted and saved some 30,000 lives, which a better October agreement would also have accomplished.[124] It has also been claimed that the Rambouillet negotiations were successful in showing that force was necessary for diplomacy and that diplomacy had to be exhausted before force was used.[125] But these are lessons that fill history books and should not have to be repeated each time the question arises. The greatest lessons of the Yugoslav experience underscore the need both for early diplomatic action when warnings of catastrophe are loud and clear, considering interests as a long-term calculation, and for constantly tending the credibility of the threat of force, putting one's military where one's mouth is. If the states of the West (or, indeed, most states) can be considered reactive and inertia- or status quo–oriented in their foreign outlook, they had no concerted policy either to preserve the status quo in a disintegrating Yugoslavia or to guide its evolution to a more stable future.

Notes

1. I am grateful for the assistance of Tova Norlen, Hynd Bouhia, and Joseph Brinker in preparing this case and for discussions with Martti Ahtisaari, Liam Mahoney, James O'Brien, Sabrina Ramet, Daniel Serwer, Haris Silajdzic, and Saadia Touval.

2. Gow, *Triumph of the Lack of Will;* Christopher Cvic, "Yugoslavia: The Unmaking of a Federation," in Larrabee, *The Volatile Powder Keg.*

3. Almond, *Europe's Backyard War,* 3.

4. Beloff, *An Avoidable War;* Zimmermann, *The Origins of a Catastrophe,* 77.

5. Ramet, *Balkan Babel,* 10, 16.

6. The policies needed would especially have to target unemployment and inflation rates and the slow growth of the GDP. In 1985 crime soared and inflation was at 50–100 percent per annum. Unemployment was higher than 20 percent in all republics except Slovenia and Croatia, and there was a growing gap between the cost of living and real wages; Woodward, *Balkan Tragedy,* 45, 46, 73–74, 79–80; Ramet, *Balkan Babel,* 23–45; Gow, *Triumph of the Lack of Will,* 20.

7. The Economic Intelligence Unit, *Country Profile, Yugoslavia, 1991* (London: The Economic Intelligence Unit, 1991).

8. Zimmermann, *The Origins of a Catastrophe,* 56; see also Woodward, *Balkan Tragedy,* 118.

9. *Concluding Document of the Vienna Follow-Up Meeting of the CSCE* (Washington, DC: Commission for Security and Cooperation in Europe, 1989).

10. Zimmermann, *The Origins of a Catastrophe,* 84; *New York Times,* 7 July 1990; Cohen, *Broken Bonds,* 219.

11. The Economic Intelligence Unit, *Yugoslavia Country Profile 1990-1991 (Recent History Since 1918),* (London: The Economic Intelligence Unit, 1990); Woodward, *Balkan Tragedy,* 128; Touval, *Mediation in the Yugoslav Wars,* 31.

12. Lampe, *Yugoslavia as History;* Woodward, *Balkan Tragedy,* 129.

13. Warren Zimmermann, "Yugoslavia: 1989–1996," in Jeremy Azrael and Emil Payin, eds., *Conference Report: US and Russian Policymaking with Respect to the Use of Force,* CF-129-CRES (Washington, DC: RAND, 1996), 4.

14. Touval, *Mediation in the Yugoslav Wars,* 25–26.

15. Ibid., 23.

16. The Economic Intelligence Unit, *Yugoslavia Country Profile, 1990–1991 (Recent History Since 1918),* (London: The Economic Intelligence Unit, 1991).

17. Susan Woodward, "Costly Disinterest: Missed Opportunities for Preventive Diplomacy in Croatia and Bosnia and Herzegovina, 1985–1991," in Jentleson, *Opportunities Missed, Opportunities Seized,* 148.

18. Eyal, *Europe and Yugoslavia;* Woodward, *Balkan Tragedy,* 199–200, 274–275.

19. Woodward, *Balkan Tragedy,* 150, 158, 179, 273, 285. Some argued that the only institution that had a clear mandate was the UN; the French wanted to use the WEU where the United States was not a member.

20. Cohen, *Broken Bonds,* 90; Zimmermann, *The Origins of a Catastrophe,* 30–32.

21. Foreign Broadcast Information Service (Eastern Europe), Washington, DC, 1 August 1990, 58; Cohen, *Broken Bonds,* 118–121.

22. Lampe, *Yugoslavia as History,* 351–352; Woodward, *Balkan Tragedy,* 139.

23. Woodward, *Balkan Tragedy,* 128–129.

24. Warren Zimmermann, "Yugoslavia 1989–1996," in Jeremy Azrael and Emil Payin, eds., *Conference Report: US and Russian Policymaking with Respect to the Use of Force,* CF-120-CRES (Washington, DC: RAND, 1996), 5–6.

25. Bert, *The Reluctant Superpower,* 133.

26. In a discussion with Ambassador Zimmermann, Federal Defense Minister General Veljko Kadijevic said that democracy was the wrong prescription in Yugoslavia in the 1990s and that it was leading to bloodshed and was an "abyss to the Yugoslav people." Woodward wrote that in bringing democracy to birth in Yugoslavia, the West helped "strangle it in its cradle"; see Zimmermann, *The Origins of a Catastrophe,* 90; Woodward, *Balkan Tragedy,* 117–125; Gow, *Triumph of the Lack of Will.*

27. Bert, *The Reluctant Superpower,* 135.

28. Eagleburger quoted in ibid., 102.

29. Lewis, "How to Stop a Civil War."

30. Zimmermann, *The Origins of a Catastrophe,* 68; see also Lampe, *Yugoslavia as History,* 351.

31. *New York Times,* 28 November 1990, A7.

32. Unlike homogeneous Slovenia, Croatia was made up of 11.5 percent Serbs, who showed their resentment by boycotting the referendum. In a similar poll among the Croatian Serb residents of the Krajina on 12 May, however, an overwhelming majority had voted to join Serbia in the event of a breakup of the federation; Bert, *The Reluctant Superpower,* 133.

33. Milosevic's quote from Zimmermann, *The Origins of a Catastrophe,* 102–103; see also Woodward, *Balkan Tragedy,* 141.

34. Zimmermann, *The Origins of a Catastrophe,* 108; Ramet, *Balkan Babel,* 48–49, 201.

35. Woodward, *Balkan Tragedy,* 158.

36. Touval, *Mediation in the Yugoslav Wars,* 32.

37. Baker, *The Politics of Diplomacy,* 137.

38. Bert, *The Reluctant Superpower,* 68.

39. Libal, *Limits of Persuasion,* 5.

40. Although the Organization for Security and Cooperation in Europe (OSCE) meeting occurred two days after the European Parliament declaration referred to above, it would have been helpful if that statement could have been held off pending the results of the OSCE conference.

41. Woodward, *Balkan Tragedy,* 174. Article VII, Report of the CSCE Meeting of Experts on National Minorities in Geneva on 19 July 1991 reads: "The members of the CSCE . . . categorically and irrevocably declare that the commitments undertaken in the field of the human dimension of the CSCE are matters of direct and legitimate concern to all participating States and do not belong exclusively to the internal affairs of the State concerned. They express their determination to fulfill all of their human dimension commitments and to resolve by peaceful means any related issue, individually and collectively, on the basis of mutual respect and cooperation. In this context they recognize that the active involvement of persons, groups, organizations and institutions is essential to ensure continuing progress in this direction." The third CSCE Conference on the Human Dimension in Moscow, 10 September–4 October 1991, emphasized that issues related to human rights, fundamental freedoms, democracy, and the rule of law are of international concern. These meetings took place after the proposed March date but indicate the tenor of opinion within CSCE during the year.

42. Eyal, *Europe and Yugoslavia,* 15.

43. Touval, *Mediation in the Yugoslav Wars,* 37; see also Zimmermann, *The Origins of a Catastrophe,* 146–147; Gow, *Triumph of the Lack of Will,* 304; Ramet, *Nationalism and Federalism in Yugoslavia; Europe,* no. 5484 (6–7 May 1991): 1; *Europe,* no. 5490 (13–14 May 1991): 3; *Europe,* no. 5505 (1 June 1991): 7.

44. Almond, *Europe's Backyard War,* 42.

45. Zimmermann, *The Origins of a Catastrophe,* 137.

46. Kissinger, *Years of Renewal,* 1043.

47. Valasova, "Facing the Dilemma of Re-Integration Versus Independence in the Transitional Period"; Staravoitova, *National Self-Determination: Approaches and Case Studies.*

48. Cohen, *Broken Bonds,* 216.

49. Libal, *Limits of Persuasion;* Wynaendts, *L'Engrenage.*

50. Pedraq Avramovic, "Recognition of Former Yugoslav Republics" (M.Phil. thesis, University of Cambridge, 1996), chap.2; Sabrina Ramet and Letty Coffin, "German Foreign Policy Toward the Yugoslav Successor States, 1991–1999," *Problems of Post Communism* 48, no. 1 (January 2001): 48–64.

51. Woodward, *Balkan Tragedy,* 155, 160–161, 175; Zimmermann, *The Origins of a Catastrophe,* 133, 139–140.

52. Libal, *Limits of Persuasion,* 9.

53. Zimmermann, *The Origins of a Catastrophe,* 71.

54. *Cespi Report: Yugoslavia* (Rome: Centro Studi di Politica Internazionale, 1993), 5, 15; an example would be when the EC got Slovenia and Croatia to agree to suspend their declarations of independence for three months in the July 1991 Brioni Declaration. Leo Tindemans et al., *Unfinished Peace: Report of the International Commission on the Balkans* (Berlin: Aspen Institute, 1996), 43–44; Cohen, *Broken Bonds,* 233–234.

55. Sremac, *War of Words,* 66.

56. Almond, *Europe's Backyard War,* 48; Woodward, *Balkan Tragedy,* 160.

57. Gow, *Triumph of the Lack of Will,* 52.

58. Leo Tindemans et al., *Unfinished Peace: Report of the International Commission on the Balkans* (Berlin: Aspen Institute, 1996), 43; Libal, *Limits of Persuasion*, 20–21.

59. Cohen, *Broken Bonds*, 234.

60. This situation illustrates the paradox of preventive diplomacy: it is rarely possible to win support for preventive action at a time when the circumstances that unambiguously justify such action have not yet arrived; see Zimmermann, *The Origins of a Catastrophe*, 140.

61. Libal, *Limits of Persuasion*, 55.

62. UN Security Council Resolution 743 of 21 February 1992.

63. Almond, *Europe's Backyard War*, 246.

64. Sremac, *War of Words*, justified this with the explanation that Bosnian Serbs were farmers and therefore occupied bigger portions of land than the Muslims, who mostly resided in the cities. They were therefore also in need of larger land areas for survival.

65. Woodward, *Balkan Tragedy*, 174.

66. Ibid., 196; see also George Rudman, *Bosnia Peace Talks 1992–1995* (Washington, DC: School of Advanced International Studies, The Johns Hopkins University, 1996), 13–14.

67. "Statement upon Principles for a new Bosnia-Herzegovina," cited in Mladen Klemencic, *Territorial Proposals for the Settlement of the War in Bosnia-Herzegovina*, Boundary and Territory Brief, vol. 1, no. 3 (Durham, UK: Intentional Boundaries Research Unit, 1994).

68. Woodward, *Balkan Tragedy*, 197; Cohen, *Broken Bonds*, 243.

69. George Rudman, *Bosnia Peace Talks 1992–1995* (Washington, DC: School of Advanced International Studies, The Johns Hopkins University, 1996), 12–23.

70. Touval, *Mediation in the Yugoslav Wars*, 110. Both Baker and Zimmermann had been quite open in their support for immediate recognitions. Zimmermann, writing about his meeting with Izetbegovic in Sarajevo upon his return from Lisbon, said that he told Izetbegovic "if he wasn't happy about the agreement he shouldn't have signed it." Woodward, *Balkan Tragedy*, 281, 495n13; see also Gow, *Triumph of the Lack of Will*, 85.

71. Baker, *The Politics of Diplomacy*, 641.

72. Ibid., 639.

73. Ibid., 640.

74. Woodward, *Balkan Tragedy*, 277.

75. Ibid., 283.

76. Ibid., 211.

77. Almond, *Europe's Backyard War*, 244; Woodward, *Balkan Tragedy*, 179–180. Even when five EC monitors were killed after their helicopter had been targeted by a federal jet, the Europeans refrained from issuing condemnations but only referred to it as the "accident."

78. Owen, *Balkan Odyssey*, 62.

79. Ramet, *Balkan Babel*, 249.

80. George Rudman, *Bosnia Peace Talks 1992–1995* (Washington, DC: School of Advanced International Studies, The Johns Hopkins University, 1996), 36.

81. Ibid., 37–39; Touval, *Mediation in the Yugoslav Wars*, 121.

82. Gow, *Triumph of the Lack of Will*, 217; Ramet, *Balkan Babel*, 249–250; Woodward, *Balkan Tragedy*, 213. Ramet noted that one of the most important

weaknesses of the Vance-Owen plan was that it broke with past diplomatic practice and in one swoop annulled a key principle of international law, known as *uti possidetis, ita possidetis* (you may keep what you had before). Applied when colonial possessions become independent or when existing states break up, it stipulates that internal administrative borders should be treated as legitimate. Arguably, therefore, Vance-Owen opened the door to the partial recognition of conquests.

83. UN Security Council Resolution 820 of 17 April 1994.

84. Touval, *Mediation in the Yugoslav Wars,* 131. On mediators' leverage, see ibid. as well as Touval and Zartman, *International Mediation in Theory and Practice.*

85. Woodward, *Balkan Tragedy,* 198; Owen, *Balkan Odyssey,* 69, 107–108; Baker, *The Politics of Diplomacy,* 642–643. Baker mentioned that one of the top priorities at that time was to prevent the conflict from spreading into Kosovo and to monitor Serb breaches against the CSCE principles there.

86. Gow, *Triumph of the Lack of Will,* 211; Woodward, *Balkan Tragedy,* 308–309; Zimmermann, *The Origins of a Catastrophe,* 213.

87. Gow and Smith, *Peace-Making, Peace-Keeping.* For a general discussion about the U.S. administration and the debate over the use of force, see Warren Zimmermann, "Yugoslavia: 1989–1996," in Jeremy Azrael and Emil Payin, eds., *Conference Report: US and Russian Policy Making with Respect to the Use of Force,* CF-129-CRES (Washington, DC: RAND, 1996), 12–13.

88. Baker, *The Politics of Diplomacy,* 646–648.

89. Ibid., 651. For the first time the United States showed resolve by demonstrating a willingness to conduct multilateral air strikes as necessary to create conditions for delivery of humanitarian relief. It moved an air force carrier into the Adriatic, set up a naval blockade, and cut the main oil pipeline to rump Yugoslavia, the states remaining after the departure of Croatia, Slovenia, Macedonia, and Bosnia.

90. Warren Zimmermann, "Yugoslavia: 1989–1996," in Jeremy Azrael and Emil Payin, eds., *Conference Report: US and Russian Policymaking with Respect to the Use of Force,* CF-129-CRES (Washington, DC: RAND, 1996), 12; this complicated the situation on the ground, wrote Zimmermann, since Bosnians then expected more forceful help from the United States.

91. Cohen, *Broken Bonds,* 282–285.

92. Warren Zimmermann, "Yugoslavia: 1989–1996," in Jeremy Azrael and Emil Payin, eds., *Conference Report: US and Russian Policymaking with Respect to the Use of Force,* CF-129-CRES (Washington, DC: RAND, 1996), 12–13; *Washington Post,* 17 October 1993, A29.

93. *Kosovo Dialogue,* 2; R. G. Hurner, "Bosnia and Kosovo, or the Two Sides of the Same Balkan Coin," in AIIS, 113.

94. Martin Sopta (at Croatian Center for Strategic Studies), "Kosova: How Can We Prevent Another War," in AIIS, *Democracy and Security: Kosovo on the Agenda,* 116, 120–123.

95. Holbrooke, *To End a War,* 357.

96. Ahrens, *Negotiating Ethnic Conflict in Former Yugoslavia.*

97. Ivanov, *The Balkans Divided,* 73. *Kosovar* (both singular and plural) will be used here to refer to the Albanian (Muslim) population of Kosovo.

98. Janusz Bugajski, "Kosova Between War and Independence: Implications for International Security," in *Democracy and Security: Kosova on the Agenda* (Tirana, Albania: Albanian Institute for International Studies, 1999), 57.

99. Bush quoted in *New York Times*, 28 December 1992, A6; Warren Christopher, Department of State dispatch, vol. 4, no. 6 (8 February 1993), 69.

100. Leo Tindemans et al., *Unfinished Peace: Report of the International Commission on the Balkans* (Berlin: Aspen Institute, 1996), 114.

101. On Zajedno as a social movement, see Tarrow, *Power in Movement*, chap. 6.

102. Holbrooke, *To End a War*, 345. Russia, on the other hand, opened contacts with the opposition and cooled its relations with Milosevic in the lights of the regime's "signs of cracking;" Levitin, "Inside Moscow's Kosovo Muddle," 134; for Russia's "lost opportunities," see 135.

103. Daalder and O'Hanlon, *Winning Ugly*.

104. Tim Judah, *Kosovo* (Princeton, NJ: Princeton University Press, 2000), especially 115–136.

105. Ibid., 144.

106. Weller, "The Rambouillet Conference on Kosovo," 219.

107. Daalder and O'Hanlon, *Winning Ugly*, 38–39.

108. *Kosovo Dialogue*, 5–6.

109. Ibid., 6.

110. On Russia's tactical delays, see Levitin, "Inside Moscow's Kosovo Muddle."

111. UN Security Council Resolution 1203 of 24 October 1998.

112. Daalder and O'Hanlon, *Winning Ugly*, 58; Milosevic developed the impression that the United States said it would handle the KLA (although that was never stated by the U.S. delegation), further adding to the feelings of betrayal.

113. Ibid.

114. Barnaby Mason, "Rambouillet Talks 'Designed to Fail,'" BBC, 19 March 2000.

115. Weller, "The Rambouillet Conference on Kosovo," 225–226; Daalder and O'Hanlon, *Winning Ugly*, 77–78.

116. Secretary of State Madeleine Albright, 24 March, cited in Daalder and O'Hanlon, *Winning Ugly*, 91.

117. On Rugova's continuing status despite the rise of the KLA, see Judah, *Kosovo*, 146.

118. *Kosovo Dialogue*. This was the same situation as had obtained in Oslo five years earlier, where Hamas had provided all sides with a common incentive to agree; Zartman, "Explaining Oslo."

119. R. Jeffrey Smith and William Drozdiak, "Serbs' Offensive Was Meticulously Planned," *Washington Post*, 11 April 1999, A1, A26–27.

120. Martin Walker and Richard Norton-Taylor, "Kosovo Crisis: How a Fragile Peace Was Won," *The Guardian*, 14 October 1998, 15.

121. Daalder and O'Hanlon, *Winning Ugly*, 54–56.

122. Ibid., 57.

123. *Kosovo's Long Hot Summer* (Washington, DC: International Crisis Group, 1998).

124. Daalder and O'Hanlon, *Winning Ugly*, 59.

125. Ibid., 84–89.

7

HAITI, 1991–1996

HAITI IN THE POST-DUVALIER ERA WAS A CASE OF CONFLICT AND COLLAPSE THAT directly touched U.S. interests in a number of ways.[1] In the U.S. backyard (only 950 kilometers from Florida), Haiti contributed 1.5 million citizens and permanent residents or one-sixth of its people to the U.S. population, largely in New York, many of them businessmen and professionals, and threatened to send hundreds of thousands more as boat people fleeing economic and political conditions at home. It had been a site of U.S. investment in earlier, more stable days. More important to U.S.—and hemispheric— interests was the political situation. From a repressive dictatorship, Haiti suddenly became an open battlefield between a U.S.-created and -trained army that wanted to perpetuate repressive rule and a home-grown democracy movement that finally saw its hour. When the Organization of American States (OAS) took a principled position on this type of confrontation, in the Santiago Commitment to Democracy and Development and the Renewal of the Inter-American System of June 1991, Haiti became its first test case and the United States was faced with an opportunity to come to the support of its most basic values—democratization and the rule of law—and help create stability south of its coast.

The case has been made convincingly that state collapse occurred in Haiti under "Papa Doc" François Duvalier or at many earlier points, even beginning with independence, and that the United States at one point, between the two world wars, spent two decades in an ill-starred occupation of the half-island trying to deal with its problems but only making matters worse. Thereafter, it is unlikely that there was any significant opportunity for effective intervention before the exile of "Baby Doc" Jean-Claude Duvalier in February 1986 or during the rest of the decade. The possibility has

Missed Opportunities:
Haiti, 1991–1996

October–December 1991 Organization of American States sanctions offered an opportunity for UN Security Council support and negotiation of the coup's reversal and for tightening sanctions during the Cartagena meeting to reverse Aristide's overthrow.

January–February 1992 Organization of American States mediation gave an opportunity for pressure on the Dominican Republic to close borders and enforce sanctions to force the junta to withdraw.

August–October 1993 The Governor's Island agreement provided the opportunity for a conclusive action through maintenance of the sanctions and insistence on the *Harlan County's* landing and observance of the agreement.

January–July 1996 Maintenance of the constitutional rules for succession opened a last opportunity for a U.S.-led dialogue program among government, parties, business, and civic groups to create momentum toward reconstruction programs.

been raised of an intervention during the euphoric months after Duvalier's departure, capitalizing on the National Congress of Democratic Movements in January 1987 and the approval of the Constituent Assembly's new constitution in a referendum in March and triggered by the army's brutal massacre of peasants and voters between July and the aborted elections of November.[2] Neither on the U.S. side nor on the part of the rest of the hemisphere, however, was there any proclivity to support the direct military involvement that would have been necessary to bring the Haitian army under control and give the democracy movement the space it needed. It would have taken armed election monitors and a new police strong enough to hold off the army to keep the system open at that point. Unfortunately, the polity needed time to start shaking off the effects of thirty years of the Duvaliers, and the other members of the OAS needed to evolve out of the Cold War mentalities to envisage the necessary measures.[3] The rigged elections of January 1988 provided no alternative to the heavy-handed army rule.

The opportunity for a positive initiative opened for a brief half-decade in the 1990s with the election of Jean-Bertrand Aristide on 16 December 1990 by 67 percent of the vote in the country's first—perhaps only, to date—free and fair elections. The fact that the elections were monitored by the OAS and the UN, as well as the Carter Center, contributed to their fairness and to the subsequent sense of responsibility and engagement of the international organizations as well.[4] Filling the political vacuum left by the collapse of the Duvalier state proved difficult for the new regime, even with the benefit of electoral legitimization, and on 30 September 1991, less than eight months after his inauguration, Aristide was overthrown by a military coup, his followers massacred, and his supporters from the urban slums chased to the countryside. The military government merely deepened the collapse of the state. Although the actual events of the coup took Aristide by surprise, in that he was not able to take sufficient measures to stop it, he and the surrounding international community were well aware of its potential imminence and even its preparations.[5]

The initial reaction of the international community was swift. The OAS, in the first test of its Santiago Declaration of the previous June banning military overthrow of democratically elected governments, adopted a resolution—nonbinding, however—on 3 October calling on member states to suspend economic activities with Haiti and another one five days later to freeze Haitian government assets and impose a trade embargo.[6] The sanctions immediately proved leaky, however, and the initial contacts between Aristide in exile in Venezuela and the junta led by General Raoul Cedras in power in Haiti foundered on the latter's intransigence and the third parties' irresolution. Efforts by the OAS and the UN Security Council members soon shifted from an attempt to reverse the coup in 1991 to two years of effort to find a middle ground between the illegitimate participants in the coup and the freely elected president, until after March 1994 the United States finally turned to a committed policy of reversing the coup and restoring the constitutional order.[7] Three years after the coup, almost exactly, on 19 September 1994, agreement was finally implemented on the departure of the junta from Haiti and the return of Aristide. But that waiting period could have been shortened or eliminated, had successive U.S. governments and the international community grasped a number of opportunities to put their declared policies into action and restore the institutions of democracy. These actions needed to include not only the return of the elected president but the reinforcement of the other branches of government, the strengthening of the whole democracy movement, and the rebuilding of relations between sectors of society. Arguably, there were at least four such moments, when a more effective response to the coup could have been undertaken in order to restore the legitimate elected ruler rapidly and set up the institutional and political structures that a functioning state requires.

The first opportunities came with two OAS initiatives immediately after the coup. Both the OAS visit to Port-au-Prince, Haiti, in October and its mediation between Aristide and a Haitian delegation in Cartagena, Colombia, the following month ended precipitously in the midst of mediator timidity and indecision, instead of decisive action that would have caught the newly installed junta off guard. At the beginning of the following year, another OAS mediation needed to back its diplomatic efforts with an effective quarantine both at sea and along the Dominican border. A carrot needed a stick, but in the absence of the latter the former shriveled. Similarly, in the fall of 1993, when international pressure brought the junta to Governor's Island, New York, to negotiate an agreement for Aristide's return, the precipitous lifting of sanctions and the fearful recall of the *Harlan County* told the junta that it need not live up to its agreement. In all of these instances, a committed response could have capitalized on the opportunity of the moment to bring the junta to an end and reinstate legitimate government.

But restoring a president is not a surrogate for restoring a state. In each instance, the president needed to be surrounded by the other institutions of the state to establish a balance of powers and protect him from the dictatorial tendencies that are part of the Haitian political heritage. Despite the fact that his own Lavalas (avalanche or flood) movement split, Aristide was able to outmaneuver the multifarious opposition and dominate the other governmental institutions while playing on the deep divisions within Haitian society. His return to the island posed the need and opportunity for an external intervention to build bridges among social groups as the basis for an effective state. But the intervenors felt that Haiti was on track with the reinstatement of its president and the moment slipped by.

Such initiatives would have saved lives, restored a state and an economy, and started the process of reconstructing a society. Had they been taken and failed, the result would still not have been as bad for all as were the years 1991 to 1994 in Haiti and then the decade thereafter. In the process to which the delay and indecision contributed their bit, Haiti by the end of the decade was back again in a state of collapse, and in 2004, Aristide had to be rescued from rebellious gangs and mobs by the United States, the same intervenor who had put him back into power a decade earlier.[8]

October-December 1991: Organization of American States sanctions
offered an opportunity for UN Security Council support and
negotiation of the coup's reversal and for tightening sanctions during
the Cartagena meeting to reverse Aristide's overthrow.[9]

Two opportunities presented themselves to the OAS to pursue its declarations with action in the first few months after the September 1991 coup. The first came the day after the organization's meeting at the beginning of October, when a delegation of seven foreign ministers, a U.S. assistant secretary of state, and the OAS secretary-general arrived in Port-au-Prince for two days of talks with the junta and then returned without results. The next day, the military forced the Haitian parliament to approve the coup and replace the president. In the middle of the month, the UN General Assembly condemned the coup, but neither the assembly nor the Security Council supported the OAS sanctions.[10] The second occasion for action occurred after 23 November, when a Haitian parliamentary delegation and President Aristide opened talks in Cartagena under OAS auspices; after only a few days, they adjourned in disagreement, an outcome underscored by the fact that a Colombian tanker carrying the first load of oil since the coup ran the embargo with impunity in the midst of the talks. Neither delegation contained any high-ranking military officers to deal with the military junta, in a country of proverbs where a predominant saying was "constitutions are paper but bayonets are steel."

The moment for action in the initial stalemate came between October and November 1991. The situation required UN Security Council support for the regional organization's sanctions from the beginning and OAS (U.S.) enforcement of sanctions through the Cartagena meeting. It also required longer negotiations and insistence on acceptable terms—agreement on a new prime minister, amnesty and exile for the junta, and firm arrangements for Aristide's return.[11]

The moment provided an opportunity and a difficulty for the same reasons: both sides were suddenly, precariously, in a new situation, their positions not yet consolidated, and both their strengths and those of the external parties not yet demonstrated. By provoking an immediate confrontation and keeping the cost of holding out high, the international community represented by the OAS would show who was weakest. In the event, it did just that and picked itself for the weaker role, setting the stage for confrontations without credibility over the next four years. But for the same reason, the two Haitian sides resisted concessions, since they had just made their move and lost the round, respectively, and had everything to lose by giving in. Objectively, the international community was strongest; it had little to lose in holding firm, and by applying and enforcing the sanctions, it would gain leverage in the subsequent negotiations. Oil sanctions at this point were necessary, accompanied by "smart" or targeted sanctions against the junta, which in the event only came in part in May–June 1994.[12] The purpose of the OAS sanctions themselves in the short run was not to cause enough pain to force the junta to capitulate but to furnish a symbol of the holding power of the intervening third party. In reality, that symbol was hollow until given content by the UNSC's limited sanctions twenty months later.

The other element that was necessary in the intervention strategy was a way out for the parties. Intervention had to provide a graceful escape for the junta and a magnanimous reentry for Aristide and had to convince both that such modified outcomes were in their interests and that they owed their safety to the international community—the UN and the OAS. It was necessary to hold firm on the return of the constitutionally elected president to his office, but it was equally necessary to show flexibility on the details of that return. They included acceptance of Réné Théodore, the parliament's candidate and head of the Communist Party, as prime minister, and amnesty for the junta, along with a comfortable retirement home. These elements—prime minister, recognition of Aristide as president, amnesty—were finally included in an agreement three months after the Cartagena meeting; they needed to be complemented by a provision for the president's early return, before the two sides became locked in their positions. As it was, the Washington agreement of 23 February 1992 only showed the willingness of the mediators to compromise, and the junta arranged to have the supreme court declare it unconstitutional a month later.[13] The agreement lacked a firm date for the return of Aristide and maintained Cedras as commander in chief of the armed forces.

A combination of these three elements was required during the opportunity provided by the visit of the OAS ministerial delegation in October. On one hand, the tougher OAS stand that was voted after the collapse of the ministerial visit was needed earlier, before the delegation arrived, with full endorsement by the UN Security Council. These sanctions would have required no U.S. forces on the island, an eventuality feared by the United States, the rest of the hemisphere, and even Aristide; if forces would be required, they could have come from other American countries.[14] Although some have suggested that the original OAS position itself was too strong,[15] and others have suggested that a peacekeeping force was needed immediately,[16] a proper balance is important. An immediate invasion—clearly a Chapter VII, not a Chapter VI exercise under the UN Charter, as in fact later occurred—would have been rash, counterproductive, and dangerous, but a stronger backup for the mission was needed; at this point, a naval presence or a public statement of military readiness if needed and a high-ranking officer in the delegation would have been sufficient.[17] On the other hand, wiping the slate clean with an amnesty and safe conduct, before the junta's crimes began to multiply, was necessary to get the junta to back down and would allow the delegation to play a good cop against the sanctions' bad cop regime. Toughness and speed were important before the parliament was forced, literally at gunpoint, to support the coup and replace Aristide with an interim president. The security of none of the friends of Haiti—the United States, France, Venezuela, Canada—was endangered by events in Haiti, but the flow of political refugees exerted considerable pressure on the United States.

A firm and inflexible alternative—as the United States had shown in a much more dangerous Caribbean crisis over Cuba thirty years before—would have helped the junta understand that holding to the coup was an untenable option, before they had a chance to settle in, psychologically and politically, just as the OAS had proclaimed. The offer of safe conduct would open a different alternative, not leaving the junta with its back against the wall but giving it a way out that could only be attractive once the precariousness of their hold on power was conveyed.

Had this failed, the November opportunity was even clearer. Again, on one hand, more time was needed to work out the agreement that came later—not the three years of conflict that occurred in fact but more days of negotiation in Cartagena. The flexible elements were coming into place, but no agreement could be made under such circumstances in two days. Parties need time to stomp and posture, if only for themselves, and then time to climb down from their high horses, a basic truth about the negotiation process that is so often ignored. On the other hand, it was absolutely necessary to enforce the blockade, which had brought fuel supplies down to only a week's reserves by the end of October.[18] The ignominy of a Colombian tanker succeeding in the first test of the blockade while the Colombian meeting was going on was a blow to the process and scuttled it for years.[19] An interception of the tanker, which could only come from U.S. naval action, was required to show that embargo meant embargo.[20] Instead, the event proclaimed the embargo a paper tiger and began the process of showing the junta that the United States and the OAS did not mean what they said. The United States was sending the same flabby message as it was issuing on Somalia, Yugoslavia, and Liberia at the same time.

The junta's situation was that of a hostage taker, and the name of the game in hostage negotiations is to shift the terms of trade from "hostages in exchange for demands" to "hostages in exchange for safe conduct."[21] To do so depends on conclusively showing that the first terms are blocked but that the second are conceivable. Tactical delicacy and time are required for such a strategy to operate successfully—delicacy so that the hostage takers do not feel challenged or threatened by the blocking measures, and time to allow them to consider and work out the alternative. Time does not mean elapsed time since the trigger event but interaction time within an intervention; the more immediate the intervention after the coup, the shorter the interaction time needed, but a few days is not enough. Both tact and time were needed in the fall of 1991.

As in October, November firmness in holding the blockade would have conveyed a situation of tightening grip, showing that the international community meant business as it did in Cuba in 1962 or as the NATO bombings finally did in Bosnia in 1995. The firmness shown against the junta would have been useful in turn in persuading Aristide to agree to safe haven for the junta, as he did and then reneged on in the coming months, in exchange for a date for his own return. At least, even if not immediately successful, such measures would have reversed the direction of events, setting the agenda for an eventual return of Aristide, as occurred in fact three years, hundreds of boat people, and several thousands of deaths later.

In reality, the October strategy was not decisive enough because of divisions within the ministerial delegation and because of the Latin American states' desire to begin at a low level of pressure, leaving room to increase pressure, as they did. The delegation was also intimidated by a military riot and fear for their personal safety, although there are claims that an agreement—sincere or not—was close.[22] In addition, the delegation was not backed by a strong UN resolution, despite Western and Russian efforts, because of U.S. official ambiguity about Aristide and because China was opposed, India was chairing, and Third World members were afraid to breach the sovereignty barrier. By November, the OAS conditions had hardened but the anti-Aristide forces in the United States had had time to sow stories about his record and stability, leading Aristide to harden his position. "[T]he tanker incident [w]as a turning point in the OAS-led diplomacy."[23]

January–February 1992: Organization of American States mediation provided an opportunity for pressure on the Dominican Republic to close borders and enforce sanctions to force the junta to withdraw.

The OAS's failure to give teeth to sanctions proved to the junta that it could get away with its coup, that there was no worse alternative to threaten its current course of action, and that the international community feared sanctions more than did its targets. It also allowed right-wing groups in the United States to malign Aristide and right-wing groups in Haiti to intimidate anyone with moderate tendencies, including the new prime minister, Réné Théodore. Yet OAS efforts to mediate persisted, finally bringing Théodore and Aristide together to negotiate and on 23 February 1992 to sign the Washington agreement that left an amnestied army in place and a frustrated Aristide still awaiting return.[24]

The junta played a cat-and-mouse game with the agreement, alternately supporting and rejecting it and then leaving it to the parliament to rally opinion against it and finally to the compliant Haitian Supreme Court to declare it unconstitutional on 27 March. On his side, Aristide played into the junta's hands by reneging on the promise of amnesty the day after the agreement was signed, since it said nothing about his return. The previous six months had shown the OAS to be powerless to impose any costs on the junta for maintaining the coup, therefore providing Aristide with little hope for an effective solution. The United States had even withdrawn unilaterally from the embargo at the beginning of February and at the end of the month announced that Ambassador Alvin Adams was to work to create a government of consensus with the junta as well as with Aristide, thereby putting the two sides on the same level of legitimacy.

Yet the OAS mediation provided an opportunity for decisive action, the last one in the early part of the crisis. Over the first three months of 1992, as the OAS worked to bring the two negotiating parties together, it needed to strengthen its other hand by effectively closing the blockade that it had failed to implement in 1991. Now, six months later, the challenge was much greater, the task more difficult, and the results less likely to be as immediate. The blockade needed enforcement on sea, where it had become a sieve. It also needed enforcement on land, along the Dominican border, where old roads were used and new roads built to circumvent the sanctions; as a prelude to pressuring the target country, its neighbor also needed to be persuaded and induced to join the sanctions and to allow OAS monitors to seal the border. A complete embargo in the early period would have had a good chance of success without giving the elite the possibility of trading and stocking at the expense of the people; the embargo also needed to be sharpened with targeted sanctions that further hit the elite without hurting the people.

The position that had unanimous backing in late 1991 faced cold feet and defections among the international community by early 1992; without extrahemispheric participation and with regional defections, the OAS secretary-general said that it was "not possible to implement the embargo" by the end of January.[25] In addition, the playing field had tilted, psychologically, as the junta saw that its gamble had won the first international tests and that it had been able to consolidate its hold on the Haitian body politic. Action in this period was therefore more difficult. In January 1992, new OAS measures were required to consolidate the blockade, by means of a naval encirclement around the Haitian maritime perimeter and a monitoring mission along the Dominican border, as an adjunct to the mediation mission of the organization, before the United States defected from the quarantine.

The United States, to the contrary, was confused by the "noise" of the continuing crisis, unable to see through the arguments about the boat people, the dangers and fears of invasion, the specter of Aristide's character defects, and the fears of various parts of the Haitian population for their lives under various regimes. Rather than opting clearly for the removal of the military and the restoration of democracy, which would put it in a strong position to moderate Aristide's innate authoritarian radicalism, the United States after the beginning of 1992 sought to find a middle way that would please everyone, with the formula of a coalition of unfriendly forces that therefore would leave the military essentially in charge. By seeking to mediate when it should have focused on evacuating the junta and restoring Aristide, the United States betrayed its own initial purpose and tied its own hands.

The result was to prolong the crisis, ruin the country economically for both business and peasants, and cause thousands of deaths, often in atrocious ways. It has been estimated that earlier and firmer diplomacy would have involved less than half the cost—$2 to $2.3 billion—compared to the $5 billion spent on Haiti over the three-year period of the junta's rule.[26] Although the latter figure was of course not known at the time, it was fully foreseeable given the half-hearted efforts of the period: it costs more to deploy inadequate measures over a longer period of time than it does to allocate the necessary efforts to achieve early success. The above scenarios do not involve military interventions, and so much of even that reduced cost would have been saved. In Haiti itself, where the per capita GNP is less than a tenth of the Latin American average, the economy in the five years after 1991 lost about $1.3 billion in GDP from its level throughout the 1980s and received $1.9 billion in ODA (or $1.3 billion above its level in the 1980s, in constant dollars). The losses represented by the general breakdown of the economy, society, and infrastructure, which would have been prevented by an earlier restoration of the state, were incalculable.

August–October 1993: The Governor's Island agreement provided the opportunity for a conclusive action through maintenance of the sanctions and insistence on the Harlan County's landing and observance of the agreement.

A year later, insistent efforts from February through June 1993 by OAS/UN and U.S. special representatives Dante Caputo and Lawrence Pezzulo, respectively, brought the junta to an agreement on Governor's Island on 3 July. "The process of bringing the Haitian army to the negotiating table was largely the result of steps that both fine-tuned and expanded sanctions."[27] Notably, when the two representatives' trips to Haiti produced no results, the United States imposed sanctions targeting eighty-three individuals or institutions that supported the junta. When additional UN sanctions were being proposed, the Haitian parliament recognized Aristide's legitimacy as president and asked him to name a new prime minister. Cedras then announced that he would attend negotiations only if sanctions were lifted, whereupon the UN Security Council on 16 June imposed a fuel and arms embargo; in five days, Cedras agreed to meet Aristide to negotiate.

When the Governor's Island agreement was signed, with the United States, Canada, France, and Venezuela as guarantors, there was a sense of triumph among the mediators, even if not in the Aristide camp. Yet most of the provisions established the terms for an effective restoration.[28] Much of the time in negotiations was taken up by the question of timing in lifting the successful sanctions, Cedras calling for their removal once the new government of Robert Malval had been confirmed by the parliament and Aristide insisting on their maintenance until his actual return, on 30 October. He was right. In the event, the former position prevailed, the effect of the well-orchestrated sanctions was undone, and the junta was able to replenish its stocks, organize local resistance, renege on its agreement, and defy the international community.

When, on 11 October in accordance with the agreement, the troopship *Harlan County* approached the dock in Port-au-Prince with 200 U.S. and Canadian military instructors, it feared nasty riots on the dock by the Front for the Advancement and Progress of Haiti (with the fearsome acronym FRAPH) and sailed home, without notifying the UN or the guarantors, fearing a rerun of Mogadishu, where eighteen U.S. rangers had died the previous week (as discussed in Chapter 4).[29] The UN troops already ashore, including fifty Royal Canadian Mounted Police, were ordered not to clear the dock and prepare for landing but rather to leave that up to the Haitian military, who were instigating the riots. The next day, the justice minister was assassinated in broad daylight and Cedras refused to resign, as he had agreed to in the Governor's Island agreement. "The message . . . was unmistakable: You can push us around easily. The United States Government is so afraid of its public opinion after Somalia that even you can intimidate it,"[30] confirming the same message the United States had given the week before in Somalia and Bosnia. Once again, as in the case of the Colombian tanker two years earlier, the carefully arranged diplomatic measures were completely undermined by Washington's loss of nerve. A full year was lost in the process.

The missed opportunities stand out in sharp light. The premature lifting of sanctions on 27 August was the first mistake, without which the junta could not have heightened its reign of terror and assassination in Haiti and made a show of resistance on the dock. Thereafter, instead of turning tail and running, an affirmative reaction was needed at Port-au-Prince on 11 October, as in Mogadishu. The *Harlan County* needed to enter and stay in the harbor, backed by a U.S. message to the junta with a time limit "to call off its goons."[31] The blockade needed reinforcing, as in fact occurred on 13 October. Since the 200 military instructors on the *Harlan County* were not armed to fight their way ashore, military reinforcements needed to be brought up alongside the ship, as an indication of worse alternatives available if the junta pursued its defiance. There is little likelihood that the reinforcements would have had to fight their way across the dock; "the FRAPH demonstrators would almost certainly have dispersed at the first sign of US and Canadian troops willing to defend themselves and their Mission."[32] These various measures worked a year later, after the embargo and other measures had been restored, but they all could have been applied with decisiveness a year earlier to save the Governor's Island agreement. It is estimated that the five weeks of lifted sanctions gave the junta another three months of supplies, notably petroleum, while at the same time impoverishing the population and further destroying the poor country's forests and topsoil.

The failure to carry out military action had another important effect on the Haitian situation, in that it now clinched the conviction of the junta and its followers that the United States and the world community would never go beyond words into action. Threats had lost all credibility. Even when a full embargo was applied by the UN six months later, the junta brushed it off as not serious. "After 32 months of measuring Washington's resolve," declared a military analyst of the Haitian situation, "Haiti's army leadership is convinced that no intervention will take place, and nothing short of military action will change their minds."[33] Six months later, after the diplomatic intervention during invasion plans that finally secured the junta's agreement to withdraw and allow Aristide to return, members of the persuasion team led by President Carter complained that "the difference between a credible threat, which was essential to reach an agreement, and the actual use of force, which in this case was counterproductive," was not respected.[34] News of the invasion in September 1994 broke up the negotiations for a peaceful entry, which were then put back on track only with difficulty. But without the tangible evidence of the will to invade, full agreement was not able to be reached.[35] The repeated loss of opportunities and the emptying of threats by the international community over the preceding three years made diplomacy without coercion impossible. Indecision had increased its own chances of failure.

There is no doubt that the Governor's Island agreement was flawed, and not only by its self-negation through the premature withdrawal of sanctions.[36] The notion that military and police trainers—some of the *Harlan County* passengers were simply military engineers—could create a nice police force and army while the junta leaders were still in place was only one of the elements of hopeful naïvete or duplicitous indecision that characterized U.S. policy in the period. Most of the trainers were unarmed and the rest had only side arms, with orders to "run the other way" in case of trouble.[37] The agreement lacked deadlines and enforcement, and agreements without commitments to enforce are agreements that the parties sign without intention to observe.

More important, Governor's Island was a shortsighted agreement on the restoration of a government, with not a glance at what would happen afterward. In a deeply fissured society and polity, no provision was made for the sort of dialogue and reconciliation measures that were an important part of the Nicaraguan, Guatemalan, and Salvadoran processes.[38] While providing for the return of the leading figure of the regime, it ignored both the rest of the institutions of government—legislature, judiciary, local government—and the society of the governed—business, labor, peasants, technocrats, and diaspora. The need for reconciliation was not between the usurpers and the elected, but within the remaining and restored elements once the usurper had left. That, of course, could not be negotiated between the parties at Governor's Island. The agreement provided enough of a framework that, had its timetable been respected, it could have been the basis of a restoration of Aristide and the amnestied exile of the junta. But it was only the initial step in the solution and needed a large complement of dialogue and reconciliation.

In addition, there was an enormous failure of intelligence, human understanding, and logic among the U.S. policymakers. On one hand, the feeling was often expressed that the junta and its "goons" were nice, well-intentioned people capable of cooperation: "I have confidence in the Armed Forces of Haiti [FAd'H]," said U.S. colonel James Pulley, commander of the UN military contingent, on 13 October; "if they [FAd'H] are smart, they will cooperate," opined U.S. chargé d'affaires Vicky Huddleston the same day.[39] But they were smart enough to know that if they would not cooperate, nothing would happen to them. On the other hand, the several hundred armed demonstrators, whose main weapon was their official impunity, were viewed as a dangerous force, irresistible against an augmented military unit, and totally insubordinate to the very junta leadership invoked the same day. Just after giving the order to retreat, with all its consequences, President Clinton "strongly condemned" the murder of Justice Minister Guy Malary and said, addressing the wrong suspect, "The people of Haiti would be sadly misguided if they think the United States has weakened its resolve."[40] Caught in such contradictions, the U.S. foreign policy leadership gave the "goons" another year to kill and terrorize and to make reconstruction and reconciliation that much more difficult when it finally came. In so doing, they also provided many reasons for the followers of Aristide to harden their opposition to any concessions and thus make any negotiated agreement even harder to find.[41]

The premature lifting of sanctions was a serious tactical mistake and its reversal would have cost nothing to the international community, including the United States. Backing up the *Harlan County* with seaborne troops and then landing them the next day, with a mandate to protect, might have run some small risk of bloodshed. Unarmed and even armed troops might well have been harassed, but the risks of loss were minimal, and as events showed a year later, the population would have rapidly sided with the U.S. forces against the thugs of the junta, once they saw where greater protection lay. The more the United States recoiled before the junta's threats, the more it increased the chances of the junta's intransigence and the risks of bloodshed in a final confrontation. In the end, those chances were enormous but the risks nonexistent.

January–July 1996: Maintenance of the constitutional rules for succession opened a last opportunity for a U.S.-led dialogue program among government, parties, business, and civic groups to create momentum toward reconstruction programs.

Restored, tightened, and targeted sanctions (to be lifted only upon Aristide's return), preparations for U.S. troop landings, and the last-minute persuasion of President Carter produced an agreement on 14 September 1994 much similar to that of Governor's Island a year before.[42] On 19–23 September, 15,000 U.S. troops landed to supervise security on the half-island; the junta leaders left on 13 October, and Aristide returned two days later. He had little more than a year left on his elected term; unable to succeed himself, he was followed by Réné Préval, elected in December 1995, and Aristide came back to office in 2000. The 1995 election was a crucial event along the uncertain path of Haiti's democratization, for it established—at least formally—the constitutional provision on term limits and—incidentally—split Aristide's Lavalas party.[43] A decade later, the need for a U.S.-UN intervention to protect Aristide against gangs and mobs led to his exile rather than his protection to fill out his term of office. Had the provision of electoral legitimacy been maintained, in 2004, the principle of democracy would have been strengthened.

The entire strategy for the restoration of legality to the Haitian political system was focused on the return of the president, as if there were no other institutions of government or parts of society. Aristide's (and his predecessors') heritage was a society torn and divided, with the parts convinced of each others' illegitimacy, each seeking not merely to defend its position but to eliminate the others, in a true zero-sum situation. Opposition parties feared the Lavalas's monopolist tendencies, while the Lavalas saw the opposition as leftover juntists and Duvalierists. Business was seen as profiteering and supportive of the ancien régime, whereas the masses were viewed as vengeful and violent. No side saw the legitimate role of the other in society and politics. After the decades of the Duvaliers and then the junta, Haiti required a huge effort of state and society rebuilding.

The Clinton administration was so busy defending its belated accomplishments in Haiti that it made little provision for measures to secure the results. Much of its attention beyond a vigorous touting of its success was centered on determining the amount of time U.S. troops should remain in the country. But a bigger need opened up after the restoration of Aristide and deepened after the election of Préval, for which there was no policy. Senator Sam Nunn, part of the 1994 persuasion team, returned from a visit to Haiti six months later with the comment, "We have a one-year plan for a ten-year challenge."[44] Even though there was a good deal of international assistance in setting up some of the institutional pieces of the new state—courts, police, parliament—something was needed to combine the component parts to make the machinery work.[45] The pieces of the polity and society needed to be brought together into a dialogue about their country's future in which each would be able to see the role of the others and its importance to their own plans.[46] No one in Haiti had the authority to call such a dialogue, since each was part of the problem. Even the presidency was not in a strong and neutral enough position to follow through on its own appeals and convoke the mechanism of a national reconciliation, even if it had thought to do so.

A dedicated external convenor with quiet, neutral authority was required to schedule a program of dialogue sessions among representatives of government, political parties, civil society, and the population at large and to focus their attention on some basic questions: What kind of Haiti would you like to see in five years? What are the obstacles to that outcome? How can those obstacles be overcome? These questions have been used in other similar situations by a variety of organizations working among disparate political groups to inaugurate discussions.[47] In some cases, the agent can be a private institution of "track two" diplomacy, although its job would generally be limited by its need to build up status to a long-term effort.[48]

In Haiti, a semiofficial agency was already present through its work as a monitor of the election processes, with a good record of contacts and meetings and a sound reputation for fairness and independence—the International Republican Institute, one of the "children of NED (National Endowment for Democracy)."[49] Any of the agencies funded by the NED could have done the job, had they proposed it, but the particular importance of the IRI proposal lay in its usefulness in presenting a bipartisan foreign policy to a critical Republican-dominated Congress. IRI had submitted proposals in this direction since before the 1995 elections, but the Agency for International Development (AID) was uninterested in anything that offered alternatives to the budding Lavalas single-party rule; IRI funding for the election observation mission ran out in March 1996. It was only after the April 1997 legislative elections, where even the 5 percent participation figure was likely an exaggeration, that AID again became interested in a Haiti program working with political parties and civil society, and only a year later that a town hall program was funded. It was eventually to be run out of Haiti by Lavalas goons' harassment after a year of operation, in June 1999. To the surprise of pro-democracy elements, there was no U.S. reaction to the intimidation. The International Peace Academy conducted a series of five consultations between January 1998 and June 1999, mainly outside Haiti, a later, smaller, more distant effort that showed the promise inherent in a larger project.[50]

A broader, more intensive program of dialogue beginning right after the 1995 presidential elections would have made a major impact on the tone of discourse and the political dynamics in Haiti. At best, it would have permitted political, social, and economic sectors of society to communicate with each other, get to know each other's visions of Haiti and its future, and move toward a common language and common program. These goals sound banal in the extreme, which is only an indication of how sundered society in a collapsed state can become and how necessary very simple goals and measures can be. If the broader goals would not have been attainable because of being rejected and seen as a threat by the group in power, at least the possibility of establishing communications among the opposition parties, as actually began to occur too late several years later, was an available outcome that would have increased the chances of pluralism and credible alternatives. A major part of the effort would have been to sell the idea to the Haitian government as a non-threatening opportunity, which would have been facilitated in turn by support from the U.S. government.

Earlier, a larger effort backed by the United States and winning Haitian government approval and cooperation could have made the difference in changing attitudes among the component parties within the country. As it was, the United States operated in Haiti driven by a constant search for an exit strategy, which took the form of a personalized presidency and a fixation on elections, rather than a convinced insistence on the idea that democracy was accountability, pluralism, institutionalization, and communication between the government and the governed, the necessary basis of state restoration.

Notes

1. In preparing the Haitian cases, I am grateful for interviews with Marc Bazin, Lakhdar Brahimi, Georges Fauriol, Chetan Kumar, David Malone, Robert Maguire, Ian Martin, Johanna Mendelson-Forman, James Morrell, and Michael Zarin. I am grateful to Martin Wikfalk for the information on costs.

2. Maguire et al., *Haiti Held Hostage,* 17; Kumar, *Building Peace in Haiti,* 86.

3. It is interesting to compare these conditions with those in Liberia (1985) and Somalia (1988) that made different responses envisionable.

4. Carter et al., *The 1990 General Elections in Haiti*.

5. Aristide, *Aristide;* Perusse, *Haitian Democracy Restored*, 15–19.

6. Organization of American States–MRE, Resolution 1/91.

7. The best account of this process is Malone, *Decision-Making in the UN Security Council*.

8. See ibid., 147, 149; David Gonzales, "8 Years After Invasion, Haiti Squalor Worsens," *New York Times*, 30 July 2002, Al, A8; Hagman, *Lessons Learned*, 3.

9. Howard French, "Haiti's Exiled Chief Seeks to Punish Coup Plotters" and "Haitian Talks Near Crucial Point," *New York Times*, 17 and 28 December 1991. I am grateful for assistance from Rodolfo Higaredo, Katerina Vogeli, Julius Clark, Juan Osvaldo Cruz, Nicole Nolan, and Sandra Polaski in preparing this case.

10. Malone, *Decision-Making in the UN Security Council*, chap. 4.

11. Editorial, *Washington Post*, 2 October 1991; French, "Haiti's Exiled Chief Seeks to Punish Coup Plotters" and "Haitian Talks Near Crucial Point." There was much debate over the element of amnesty and impunity, part of a larger debate over peace versus justice; Michael Kelly, "Letter from Washington: It All Co-depends," *The New Yorker*, 3 October 1994; see Kremenyuk and Zartman, *Peace vs Justice*. Although a judgment on the issue depends in part on circumstances, it is argued here that amnesty was necessary to get the junta out; there are any number of Haitian institutions not signatory to the agreements that could have pursued the junta in justice after the restoration; Maguire et al., *Haiti Held Hostage*, 100–101.

12. UN Security Council Resolution 917 of 6 May 1994; U.S. Executive Orders 12920, "Prohibiting Certain Transactions with Respect to Haiti," and 12922, "Blocking Certain Property of Haitian Nationals," of 9 and 22 June 1994.

13. On the Washington agreement and its aftermath, see Perusse, *Haitian Democracy Restored*, 30–35; Malone, *Decision-Making in the UN Security Council*, 68, 220n70.

14. Thomas Friedman, "The OAS Agrees to Isolate Chiefs of the Haitian Junta," *New York Times*, 3 October 1991, 1–2.

15. Stephen Horblitt, "Multilateral Policy: The Road Toward Reconciliation," in Fauriol, *The Haitian Challenge*, 71.

16. Editorial, *Washington Post*, 2 and 6 October 1991. Randall Robinson claimed that Canada, Venezuela, and Jamaica were ready to join the United States in putting troops on the island to restore Aristide; *Washington Post*, 15 October 1994.

17. See the discussion in Malone, *Decision-Making in the UN Security Council*, 172.

18. Ibid., 68.

19. For similar threatened sanctions that were undercut by their wielders, see the South African events in 1978; Zartman, *Ripe for Resolution*, 199–201.

20. Editorial, *New York Times*, 30 January 1992.

21. Zartman, "Negotiating Effectively with Terrorists," 163–188. See also George and Simons, *The Limits of Coercive Diplomacy*, 279–282; Hansen, *Haiti*, 2 passim.

22. Perusse, *Haitian Democracy Restored*, 24–25; Maguire et al., *Haiti Held Hostage*, 31; Stephen Horblitt, "Multilateral Policy: The Road Toward Reconciliation," in Fauriol, *The Haitian Challenge*, 71.

23. Maguire et al., *Haiti Held Hostage,* 33. On the shift in the U.S. position in February 1992, see Malone, *Decision-Making in the UN Security Council,* 70.

24. Its eight points were presented in Perusse, *Haitian Democracy Restored,* 31–32.

25. Canute James, "Haiti's Junta Tries," *Financial Times,* 28 January 1992, sec. 1, American News, 5.

26. Blakeley, "Haiti," 101–107.

27. Maguire et al., *Haiti Held Hostage,* 35.

28. Text of the Governor's Island agreement is found in Georges Fauriol, *The Haitian Challenge.*

29. Pezzulo claimed his advice that the *Harlan County* troops should land despite the resistance was vetoed by Secretary of State Warren Christopher; Perusse, *Haitian Democracy Restored,* 82. In another account, Christopher, Pezzulo, Vice President Al Gore, and National Security Adviser Anthony Lake favored military action, but Defense Secretary Les Aspin opposed it; Thomas Masland et al., "How Did We Get Here," *Newsweek* 124, no. 13, 26 September 1994, 19.

30. Anthony Lewis, "The Road to Panic," *New York Times,* 22 October 1993, A29.

31. Ibid.; Amy Wilentz, "Choke Haiti's Thugs," *New York Times,* 13 October 1993, A2.

32. Malone, *Decision-Making in the UN Security Council,* 95. The FRAPH leader later claimed prior approval of the CIA station chief for the demonstration, a claim that was implicitly accepted (222n99).

33. Howard French, "Haiti's `Generals Remain Defiant," *New York Times,* 23 May 1994, A1.

34. Pastor, "A Short History of Haiti," 24.

35. Pastor, "With Carter in Haiti," 6, claimed that just before the news of the invasion came to the group, "they had convinced the Haitian generals, for the first time, that force would be used against them if the talks failed." But there were still "some details that needed to be negotiated, and time was running out," thus still no completion of the negotiations.

36. Perusse, *Haitian Democracy Restored,* 51–52, 56; Ian Martin, "Paper Versus Steel: The First Phase of the International Civilian Mission in Haiti," in Henkin, *Honoring Human Rights,* 95; Martin, "Haiti: Mangled Multilateralism," *Foreign Policy,* 85; Schulz and Gabriel, *Reconciling the Irreconcilable,* 46–48.

37. Howard French, "Haitians Block Landing," *New York Times,* 12 October 1993, A1.

38. Kumar, *Building Peace in Haiti,* especially 87.

39. Howard French, "US Move Angers Diplomats," *New York Times,* 14 October 1993, A8.

40. "US Presses," *New York Times,* 15 October 1993, A1.

41. Elaine Sciolino, "Clinton's New Policy on Haiti Yields Little Progress," *New York Times,* 18 May 1994, A1; Howard French, "Haiti's Generals Remain Defiant," *New York Times,* 23 May 1994, A1.

42. For accounts of these negotiations, with particular emphasis on the use of force and persuasion, see Robert Pastor, "With Carter in Haiti," *Worldview* 8, no. 2 (Spring 1995): 5–7, and "A Short History of Haiti," *Foreign Service Journal* 72, no. 11 (November 1995): 20–25.

43. Some have made a reasonable case for the contrary, that the spirit of the constitution granted Aristide five years in office, and so his term should have been extended to make up for the three years lost to the junta and should have been used by the United States to establish close cooperation and increased institutionalization.

44. Cited in Pastor, "A Short History of Haiti," 25.

45. In Hagman's comprehensive stock-taking report, *Lessons Learned,* for example, there is no mention of parties or parliament or local government.

46. Pastor, "A Short History of Haiti," 21, 24; Chetan Kumar, "Peacebuilding in Haiti," in Cousens and Kumar, *Peacebuilding as Politics,* 41–42, 44.

47. Examples of such groups are the Liberian Reconciliation Workshop, the Carter Center, and The Johns Hopkins University School of Advanced International Studies (see Chapter 3); the Reconciliation Workshops organized by the U.S. embassy and the Ministry of National Reconciliation in Côte d'Ivoire in June 2003 and March 2005; the Montfleur Scenarios in South Africa in 1992; the Institute for Multi-Track Diplomacy (IMTD); and Mitchell and Banks, *Handbook of Conflict Resolution.*

48. Nadim Rouhana, "Interactive Conflict Resolution," in Paul Stern and Daniel Druckman, eds., *International Conflict Resolution After the Cold War* (Washington, DC: National Academy Press, 2000); Ronald Fisher, "Interactive Conflict Resolution," and Herbert Kelman, "Social-Psychological Dimensions of International Conflict," in Zartman, *Peacemaking in International Conflict;* Saunders, *A Public Peace Process.*

49. International Republican Institute, "Proposal to USAID," 24 July 1996.

50. Kumar and Cousens, *Peacebuilding in Haiti;* Kumar, *Interim Report on the Project on Policy Advocacy and Facilitation in Haiti;* Kumar and Gélin-Adams, *Project on Policy Advocacy and Facilitation in Haiti.*

8

Seizing Opportunities

CONFLICT PREVENTION AND MANAGEMENT ARE MATTERS OF CRITICAL CHOICE, not of unequivocal rules of operation. At every step of the way there are difficult decisions, involving courage, leadership, and risk. It is always safest to follow the bureaucratic reflex and do nothing, hoping that something might happen to remove the challenge on its own. Often, however, things only get worse, again posing the challenge to choice. This alone goes far to explain why intervention so often occurs too little and too late, with no follow-through. When action finally becomes unavoidable, the situation has deteriorated, become more difficult to manage, and caused enormous losses for the intervenor, the population, and the economy. Clear lessons on preventing conflict and collapse from entering into a severe, violent phase emerge inductively from this examination, some reaffirmations of current understanding and others new or reversals of elements of current "wisdom" on intervention and conflict management.

• The most important finding is that early diplomatic action is more effective and more efficient, and less costly and less constrained, than delayed action. The costs of delay are enormous. The more the intervenor waits, the greater the danger of losing control, narrowing the available options for action, and increasing both the intervention costs and the irreparable losses for the conflicting parties, thus making positive action and reconstruction even harder. External intervenors will be compelled to take action later anyhow, when worsening human destruction and the disintegrating regional situations brought on by state collapse and deadly conflict make intervention unavoidable. Even if the suggested early action failed, the situation would be no worse than what actually eventuated.

• The greatest cause of preventive failure once action has begun has been intervenor fatigue and premature satisfaction with results. Conflict managers need to take the time it takes to finish their job; whether as peacemakers or as peacekeepers, they should leave as soon as they can but stay as long as they must. Cease-fires are only conflict management measures, opportunities that need to be exploited for conflict resolution lest they be used to launch new rounds of conflict. Stopping at a cease-fire wastes momentum and misses opportunities.

• Parties in conflict need help in order to emerge from their conflict. Mediation is required to assist parties achieve solutions that they are not able to find on their own. In internal conflict, this means convincing the government to recognize that a rebellion is a sign of grievance and a return to legitimate governance means opening the political system to participation by the rebels.

• States in collapse need help in bringing the conflicting parties together to fill the vacuum of authority. Convocation of both warlords, who need to be contained, and civil society leaders, who need to be empowered, is required to reconstruct the political system and begin resurrecting its institutions.

• Egregious rulers guarantee subsequent chaos if not replaced before rebellion takes hold. Deposition becomes an advisable option when the incumbent is the cause of conflict and collapse, but a legitimate successor or mechanism for finding one must be available. The experience of Taylor, Aristide, and Laurent Kabila has shown that unless the welcome successor to an egregious ruler is encased in a responsive institutional structure, he becomes—like Darth Vader—the image of his nemesis.

• Intervenors must be armed with both carrots and sticks. It does no good to offer a better alternative if a worse alternative is not available for comparison. It takes a hurting stalemate to get conflicting parties' attention. If parties have learned to live with the status quo, they must be assured that it cannot continue as a measure for judging better outcomes; it takes the threatening prospect of a worsened status quo to makes an alternative look good. Intervenors must make good on threats if they are ignored, for the sake of their own credibility and for the credibility of other threats at other times and places. Sanctions (enacted threats) should not be lifted prematurely before the action demanded has actually been accomplished; early recall of the sanctions allows sanctioned parties to recall their promised compliance.

• Conflict is not over until responsive and accountable state authority has been rebuilt. Preventive action is only halfway done when violence ends; rebels need responses to what they were fighting for. Governance is conflict management. Deadly conflicts are not brought under control until a functional state is restored to manage ongoing relations among parties. Restoring the state is as important a response to conflict as is ending violence.

Early Awareness and Early Action

The huge attention and efforts devoted to early warning have not produced either the corresponding conceptual advances or desired policy benefits.[1] On one hand, almost all opportunities, as noted in the case studies, were preceded by ample early warning. Official observers as well as academic analysts noted deteriorating conditions and warning signs of conflict and collapse. Aristide knew of his impending overthrow, even if not to the day and the hour. Siad Barre and Doe took active measures against the deposition they feared, thus making it more likely. The unraveling of Yugoslavia carried its own warnings at each step. The possible exceptions are the beginnings of the crises in Lebanon and Zaire, where the artificiality and corruption of the system were often noted, but the early events of its collapse came as a surprise, even to the participants. The various schemes for calculating an early alert would have added nothing, however, to the general awareness of instability already present among observers.

On the other hand, the early warnings available were often discounted and dismissed in the instances studied. The fragility of the six political systems considered here required contingency plans, alternative scenarios, ready responses, that were not evident in the event. The characteristic policy attitude seems to have one of gaining time on inevitable evolutions rather than preparing to guide them in desired directions. Officialdom was taken by surprise by unsurprising turns of events and was unprepared to greet early warnings with early awareness and take early action.

The strongest reason for early action is that the costs are less and options are still possible. Later action is more expensive for the intervenor, and choices are limited; continued inaction is costly in its consequences and, in the end, unacceptable. In all of the cases, the United States—but also the EU and the UN and other organs of the international community—was obliged to enter the conflict in its final paroxysms, at great cost and with limited options, after having missed opportunities to take lesser action at earlier moments. Although the argument is usually made that the loss of 216 marines in Lebanon in 1982, or 18 rangers and special forces in Somalia in 1993, or the Dutch and Senegalese troops executed in Bosnia and Liberia, respectively, in 1993, or the threatened danger for the policemen aboard the *Harlan County* in 1993, or for the Troika's troops offshore from Kinshasa in 1991 and 1993, or for British sailors offshore from Dubrovnik show the cost of intervention and the proof of its inadvisability, that argument is upside down. These costs showed the need for earlier action to preclude them and for better action if earlier action was not taken. Detailed estimates of intervenors' costs are even more uncertain than estimates of intervention's political effects, but an unusual and authoritative study led by Michael Brown and Richard Rosecrance permits an appreciation of some orders of magnitude in the cases studied.[2] Intervention in early 1992 in Bosnia would have incurred a cost estimated at $10.8 billion for a four-year period, compared with actual costs of $53.7 billion, not counting ongoing costs of rehabilitation or of the effects of actual Bosnian policy on the subsequent crisis in Kosovo. In Somalia, intervention in 1989 or again in mid-1991 would have involved an estimated cost of $1.5 billion, compared to the actual costs of the conflict and intervention of over $7 billion, not including the continued downturn of Somali fortunes. In Haiti, early intervention in early 1991 or 1992 would have cost half of the actual costs of $5 billion, counting only until the middle of the decade.

By the time later policies were finally adopted, the costs of the conflict had become enormous. The death toll had already consumed tens—and in some cases hundreds—of thousand lives, with larger numbers displaced within or outside the country. Many of the deaths and displacements were accompanied by frightful human abuses—systematic rapes, indiscriminate massacres, destruction of homes and places of worship, and other brutalities.

These losses had even greater secondary effects that need to be calculated into the decision not to act. Socially and psychologically, they left deeply scarred and wounded people, unprepared for any subsequent reconciliation and reconstruction. Where groups previously were mobilized by memories of atrocities from the past, these wounds now came from the present, carried out by individuals currently living among or beside their victims. Turks, Ustashe, Tonton Macouts, Hutu and Tutsi, Banyarwanda, Ogadenis-Marehans-Dulbahantes, Krahns, Gios and Manos, and others stepped out of history and became real, confirming the myths of the past, some of which had become dim and distant. Reconciliation then became an additional burden for the conflict resolution process, justice vied with peace, and trust and cooperation lay dead with the victims.

Society was also shattered by the conflict. Population displacement destroyed the social tissue; traditional norms of respect and authority were trashed; social institutions such as church and school were left in ruins. Social geography, patterns, and structures were seriously altered, usually in unproductive and further conflictual ways; generally societies underwent leveling and proletarianizing, with a massive influx into the cities. A new leadership tended to emerge from this social restructuring, to which it appealed and from which its support came. Youth was torn from its social moorings in all of the countries, with heavy implications for the future:

families were sundered; education was interrupted; unemployment became endemic; drugs took hold; child soldiers underwent a scarring experience in their formative years. This is not just a litany of the evil effects of civil strife; it is a specific list of social dislocations resulting from a conflict left to run its course, through missed opportunities for its management.

Furthermore, the conflicts consumed national as well as personal economies. It was not simply that some buildings were destroyed and needed rebuilding or that some people lost their jobs or even savings. The entire national economic systems of the six countries were demolished. Haiti was set back decades, denuded of its industry and topsoil; the Lebanese GDP in the early 1990s was less than half its level two decades earlier, in 1974, and the Lebanese pound lost nearly 10,000 times its value.[3] Liberia's economic and social indicators have been among the lowest in Africa (the lowest continent in the world), and GDP growth was consistently negative for a quarter century after the arrival of Doe to power, which accounted in part for Taylor's reliance on his diamond habit. Zaire's formal economy virtually collapsed during the same period, the remaining part of its infrastructure that had not disintegrated from mismanagement and neglect was destroyed in the riots of the early 1990s, and anything left or added since was again demolished in the civil wars of 1996–1997 and 1998–2002. Although the prosperous parts of Yugoslavia hived off to enjoy themselves alone in the early 1990s, the rest have continually disintegrated. Somalia, never well-off, has simply returned to subsistence. The countries or parts of them that had known successful development in the preconflict period, such as Yugoslavia (particularly Slovenia and Croatia) and Lebanon, were able to rebound from their disasters, but the countries originally poor became subsequently miserable.

Normally the list of costs stops here, or earlier, but there is a third sector whose collapse also bears heavy consequences—the political.[4] Despite the increasingly bypassed and outmoded nature of the state,[5] it still serves some important purposes. As a source of services, order, authority, identity, representation, allegiance, and international relations, it cannot be beat. When the state is privatized, as in Zaire/Congo and Liberia, or pulverized as in Somalia, or drawn and quartered as in Yugoslavia, or contested as in Lebanon, or hijacked as in Haiti, it loses its legitimacy as well as its ability to function. Collapsed states are not simply rebuilt like a fallen statehouse portico; they need reconstruction from the foundations. Not only is that a long and complex job, but it leaves a void until its completion that foreign forces and international institutions cannot adequately fill. There is no one to conduct state business as usual during remodeling. The problem with state reconstruction—unlike economic and even social reconstruction—is not state reconstruction per se but the fact that there is no state to hold activities together while reconstruction is going on. And that means that some external agency must fill the role until an indigenous state is rebuilt.

The point of this enumeration of multilayered damage is not simply to emphasize the humanitarian costs for the victims of conflict but to show the depth of the task involved in state reconstruction, by society and intervenor alike. Ending the conflict does not involve simply ending the conflict, as is too often thought and practiced, but staying around for a long time to help society, economy, and polity get back on their feet enough to proceed alone. The conflict was not ended when Cedras was retired and Aristide reinstated, or when Doe was removed and Taylor elected, or when Mobutu or Siad Barre were eased out, or when the old order changed in Yugoslavia; with these actions, the ending had only begun. Thereafter came the long process of reviving participation, rebuilding institutions, restoring production, renewing sanitation and education, and reconnecting society. That process takes huge efforts and resources from the international community to help the local community. If these are not allocated, the conflict is certain to return within the decade, as it did in fact in Haiti, Liberia, and the Democratic Republic of Congo, if not simply continue, as it did in Somalia.[6]

The rapacious practices of Mobutu, Duvalier, Siad Barre, and Doe meant that it was hard to find successors with a civic spirit and a sense of government, so a Kabila, Aristide, Aideed, and Taylor were predictable, if not inevitable. The legacy of the Gemayels' militarily won elections and then dual government meant that the eventual restoration of the state had to be Syrian-imposed and so not Lebanese at all. The succession of military autocrats who followed the two decades of the Duvaliers left an institutional vacuum and no checks and balances when Haiti finally got a legitimately elected president. The narrow clan base of Siad Barre's regime meant that he left no legitimacy and no institutional structure standing to fill when he fled. Even in the successor states to Yugoslavia, the writ of the government simply did not run to the Serb and Croat portions of Bosnia or to Kosovo in Serbia. For a short while, the UN supplied the necessary state structure to Haiti and Somalia, and for a longer period, NATO has been operating protectorates in Bosnia and Serbia (Kosovo). Although the process of state collapse began well before the periods examined in these cases and early action was not really early in that process, actions at the beginning of the time span covered here, when a replacement was on hand, would still have saved much loss in the political area and provided the successors with a state less fully collapsed than they eventually inherited.

In all of these cases, not only was it expensive to delay effective external action in the conflict; at some late point, it became impossible to avoid involvement, with further expensive consequences. After the United States and Europe had dithered through the evolving Yugoslav disintegration in the early 1990s, the United States was unavoidably drawn in to handle the consequences in Bosnia, Kosovo, and Macedonia in the second half of the decade. After the United States pursued its contradictory appreciations of the Haitian crisis in the early 1990s, it was finally obliged to enter in full force toward the middle of the decade, then declare victory and go back home, only to return a decade later when the cycle of conflict and collapse required a new intervention. After the United States and its Troika partners avoided decisive measures at the beginning and into the middle of the 1990s in dealing with Mobutu's Zaire, they then found themselves obliged to reckon with an intransigent, paranoid successor and then a rebel-wracked country in dealing with Laurent and Joseph Kabila's Congo. After the international community only looked on, shocked, at the final paroxysms of Siad Barre's regime, it felt compelled (as the anguished discussions at the end of the Bush and the beginning of the Clinton administrations show[7]) to engage in even more shocking events in the successor situation. If external actors could have successfully ridden out the worsening courses of conflict and collapse in world trouble spots, then the missed opportunities would only be humanitarian losses. But since the United States and other outside players feel obliged to be involved at a later point when the situation is worse, early engagement becomes a matter of interest.

Interest

Need is not opportunity, but opportunity is not interest. For an opportunity to be seized, or missed, there must be an interest in involvement on the part of the third party. The enormous losses that missed opportunities entail, and their effect on regional or global relations, provide a humanitarian interest in intervention. Despite what realists may say, humanitarian interest is not a negligible concern for the United States. Whether in the Cold War or in regional conflicts, states have acted to protect and advance their values, not just their structural position, and without values, structural positions are untenable. The importance of human life to the U.S. system of values gives humanitarian interest a special salience. As Western shame over inaction on genocide and official attempts to avoid the "G-word" in Rwanda in 1994 as in Sudan a decade later show, humanitarian interest and the value of human life anywhere are not absolute, but they are strong. Joseph Nye has indicated that "a democratic definition of the national interest does not accept the distinction between a morality-based and an interest-based foreign policy. Moral values are simply intangible interests," and former British foreign secretary Robin Cook has denied the distinction between "promoting our values and pursuing our interests."[8]

Incredibly, the fate of Lebanon, Somalia, Zaire, Yugoslavia, Liberia, and Haiti has on crucial occasions not been considered of interest to the United States, Europe, or their own regions, nor has the importance of their announced collapse to the fate of their region in general been deemed worthy of motivating U.S., European, or neighbors' early involvement. If the cost of 500,000 Yugoslav lives, 500,000 Somalis, 150,000 Liberians, 120,000 Lebanese, 100,000 (and indirectly, 3.5 million) Zaireans, and 5,000 Haitians as direct killings at the hands of their own countrymen does not provide a compelling humanitarian interest, it is not because these losses were not foreseeable and foretold. The proposed interventions span the period from the early outbreak of violence to the time of the worst killings, that is, a period when the holocausts were already visible on the horizon and were the subject of frequent warnings. If humanitarian interest was not enough of a motivation, the importance of each case in regard to U.S.—and other Western—foreign policy values such as good governance and democracy, regional stability, economic accountability and access, and external responsibility should have been.

Even for those who hold to the distinction between values and interest, there is a national or strategic interest in managing deadly conflict and state collapse. Collapsed states tend to be vacuums, drawing in outside forces to fill the empty political space. That space is then occupied by regional conflict, perpetuating the state collapse, exacerbating the domestic conflict, encouraging terrorism, extending the regional conflict, and forcing extraregional powers to take sides against their interests. Where there is no state to contain conflict, conflict pours into the vacuum and also wells out to engulf the region.

The six cases are notable examples. The conflict in Liberia was a domestic revolt within the regional context of sustained confrontation between Nigeria, as the regional hegemon, and Francophile states, under France, the extraregional protector. It spread along the West Coast, from southern Senegal (Casamance) to Côte d'Ivoire, in the latter case destroying one of the anchors of stability and Western interest in the region. The final collapse of the Mobutist state opened the War of the Zairean Succession, drawing nine surrounding states into military confrontation within the Democratic Republic of Congo. It also spilled over into six of them, destabilizing their security through insurgencies, alliances, and refugees. The collapse of the Lebanese state was caused by and escalated the competition among Syria, Israel, and the PLO for the Lebanese political and geographic space, finally ending in the eviction of the latter two and the predominance of Syria. But Syria, Israel, and the PLO fought not only over Lebanon; they fought from Lebanon, carrying their war, often by proxy, into each other's territory. Finally, if Yugoslavia did not become an open East-West battleground, it was because the Western (U.S. and EC/EU) reactions to the Yugoslav state collapse were tempered by a constant care not to open too overt a conflict with Russia, protector of the Slavs. Within a narrower region, however, the Bosnian vacuum became the poaching ground for Croatia and Serbia, and the Kosovar and north Macedonian areas outside of central authority became the battleground for Albania and Serbia or Macedonia. Even in Somalia, where the proud xenophobic forces of anarchy were unappetizing to outside predators, Egypt, Ethiopia, Eritrea, Kenya, Libya, and Italy all engaged in competitive maneuvers to fill the vacuum in their favor.

Only the insularity of Haiti (and the weakness of Cuba, the potential support against the United States) prevented the power vacuum from drawing in a contest of outside forces. But outside forces—not regional security rivals but globalized drug networks—appeared nonetheless to profit from the vacuum. Haiti has become the major Caribbean hub for the flow of Andean drugs into the United States. The Presevo Valley in Kosovo is an important node along the Balkan connection between Istanbul and Belgrade that provides 25 to 40 percent of the U.S. heroin supply.[9] Drug production and trade underwent a dramatic increase in Lebanon over three decades beginning in the mid-1970s, concomitant with the escalation of the civil war.[10] It is in the interest of outside powers to restore stability to the state so that it can control its own territory and to dampen and deter the neighborly as well as global contests for exploiting political vacuums.

This argument is sometimes turned on its head to justify support for dictators, who supposedly block the way to state collapse. But those who proclaim "Mobutu or chaos" should remember "Après moi le déluge." As the cited cases show, dictators cause state collapse, a finding that democrats should find obvious. Finding stability in dictatorship is like the man who jumped off the roof and found the going "so far, so good" at the twenty-ninth floor: the crash at the end is inevitable. To the contrary, the very presence of an egregious ruler in a state that cannot be completely isolated from its neighborhood is prima facie evidence of the need for early attention to provide a transition to more responsible stability. The cases show that the argument that measures to replace the dictator might have made things worse is specious: it is hard to imagine consequences much worse than what happened.

External powers' generic interest in other areas is generally summarized under the headings of *access* and *stability*, elements that are particularly relevant to the United States because of the worldwide scope of its interests. Instability disrupts access, compels great powers' and neighboring states' attention when conditions finally become unavoidably bad, and threatens to explode just at the time when external power least can afford the distraction (as the 2002 Kashmir crisis during the antiterrorist campaign, or the 2001 terrorist crisis during the Middle East peace process, or the 2000 Middle East crisis during the Middle East economic summits illustrate). Undeniably, deadly conflict and state collapse impede commercial and diplomatic access to a country and destroy its stability. Even though this defines a general terrain for interest, it does not provide a finer screen to discriminate between opportunities that justify action and those that do not. Three finer-meshed aspects of interest include *responsibility, subsidiarity,* and *effectiveness.*

Foreign powers bear a special *responsibility* for specific areas of the world, as is often cited in internal debates over whether or not to take action. Responsibility comes from the shadow of past actions and relations. It can derive from historic ties with the target area, such as France had with its former colonies and the United States had with Liberia as a former land of refuge and with Haiti as a former target of intervention. It can also come from previous actions related to the cause of the problem behind the conflict and collapse, such as U.S. responsibility in Zaire for having put Mobutu in power and supported him ever since or Syria's responsibility for stability in Lebanon after its armed interventions. Ability to affect events, whether exercised or not, also affects responsibility, such as the responsibility for inaction and complicity in the Rwandan genocide that became the source of parliamentary inquiry in France and Belgium (and was never pursued beyond the media in the United States, which also had Rwandan blood on its hands).

Where ability is present, both action and inaction create new responsibilities. When Deputy Secretary Eagleburger turned down proposals for evacuating Mobutu and Doe because he did not want the United States to be responsible for the unknown, he was doubtless aware of the U.S. responsibility for putting Mobutu in power in 1965 and certifying Doe's election in 1985 in the first place. But he missed the point that Africa and the world already held the United States responsible for the mess in Zaire and Liberia because it had the ability to do something about the situation and did not. And when President George H. W. Bush allegedly said that he did not want to be responsible for putting an escaped convict in charge of Liberia, referring to Taylor, he was expressing the fear of establishing an even firmer responsibility for Liberian events than already existed. But the responsibility conferred by ability, especially when reinforced by history and past policy, is hard to shake and soon brought the United States back into the fray with financial support for ECOMOG, belying the original judgment.

Responsibilities can of course be ducked or denied. Intervention to evacuate Doe in 1991 was turned down when deputies' meeting chair Robert Gates "refused to recognize any special US responsibility for Liberia's crisis on the basis of our historic ties,"[11] or, as Secretary Baker put it in regard to Yugoslavia, "We don't have a dog in this fight."[12] Although the judgment in both cases was shown by later events to be flawed, they both illustrate the terms of interest involved. U.S. officials were right on noting that evacuation of Doe and Mobutu would entail a U.S. responsibility in the process of rebuilding the Liberian and Zairean states; they were wrong in not recognizing that that responsibility was already engaged, in the many measures deployed over the preceding decade to support Doe and Mobutu in power as they destroyed their respective states. In both cases, the United States was held responsible for events anyhow, and in the opportunities missed, it found it indeed had a beaten dog in the fight.

Subsidiarity prioritizes different levels of responsibility. It indicates that problems should be handled at the lowest effective level, and hence that conflict and collapse should be dealt with first regionally before becoming a global responsibility. Subsidiarity was found to be necessary to the workings of the European Union, and its spirit has permeated UN discussions. "Yugoslavia a European problem" and "African solutions for African conflicts" are two expressions of subsidiary responsibility. Responsibility based on ability alone might well indicate that the United States as the most powerful country should do all or the lion's share of the intervening, an untenable argument that would point to an imperial policeman's role. To overcome the monopoly of intervention that absolute advantage in capabilities might confer, the international community needs to think in terms of comparative advantage. Some conflicts are best handled at the regional level.

Responsibility conferred by geography is often formally expressed in regional organizations' mandates. States have neighborhood responsibilities; collective neighborhood attention, as opposed to single-state intervention, spreads responsibility and tempers narrow interests. Thus the OAS in Haiti, ECOWAS in Liberia, the Southern African Development Community (SADC) in the Democratic Republic of Congo, and IGADD in Somalia (subregional organizations in the absence of an effective OAU[13]), the Arab Summit in Lebanon (in the absence of an effective Arab League), and the EU and OSCE in Yugoslavia bore primary responsibility for activities that fell within their mandate, although it soon became clear that all these neighborhood groups needed help from the outside. It is therefore in the interest of great powers to take measures to build up the material and diplomatic capabilities of regional organizations to deal with neighborhood conflict and collapse, so that external states may be relieved of the responsibility of intervening based on a monopoly of capability.

Subsidiarity, however, is not without its own debate. Within the neighborhood, it has been challenged as an expression of outside neglect and disinterest—or irresponsibility—often in the same breath as outside attention has been decried as external interference. Furthermore, although neighbors know the territory better than foreigners, they also have their own interests that may point to outcomes different from those in the best interest of the conflicted country. The roles of Nigeria in Liberia; of Syria in Lebanon; of Ethiopia in Somalia; of Rwanda, Uganda, Zimbabwe, and Angola in Zaire/Congo; and even of Germany in Slovenia and Croatia raise important questions of neutrality and responsibility. Neighborhood meddling can reverse the ladder of subsidiarity and justify intervention from outside the region, such as that of the Troika in Zaire/Congo or the United States in Liberia and Lebanon or NATO in Yugoslavia, although external meddling of course is not devoid of its own interests or endowed with greater neutrality than the neighbors. As in the matter of responsibility, subsidiarity is not self-interpreting; it only indicates the terrain of debate in defining interest.

Effectiveness is the third element in interest, a point of prudence to restrain the hell-bound best intentions.[14] Two elements are necessary for effectiveness—a sense of need and welcome on the part of the conflicting parties, and the availability of the necessary resources for the intervenor.[15] It is for this reason that ripeness is included in the identification of an opportunity, as discussed in Chapter 1; there is no point in leading the horse to water if it absolutely does not feel thirsty. As already noted, ripeness is not absolute, however, and efforts to ripen are often required as part of the move to forestall conflict and collapse. Effectiveness, too, is a function of effort deployed; one of the most prominent reasons for the ineffectiveness of attempts to use opportunities was unwillingness to commit the necessary resources, especially in time and attention, because of shortsighted satisfaction with superficial results, weariness before sustained effort, and refusal to stay engaged. Arguably, the Constitutional Document of 1976, the Parliamentary Declaration of 1978, and the Geneva-Lausanne initiative of 1984 in Lebanon; the Yamoussoukro IV and Cotonou agreements of 1992 and 1993 in Liberia; the Santiago Declaration of 1991 in Haiti; the Sovereign National Conference in Zaire in 1993–1994; the Cutileiro and Vance-Owen plans of 1992 and 1993 in Yugoslavia; and the Governor's Island agreement of 1993 in Haiti could have provided the basis of effective conflict management and state restoration if they had been supported, pursued, and implemented.

Like the other elements of interest, effectiveness is a criterion for evaluation, not a ready-calibrated yardstick. Nor can it be taken as a counsel of perfection. The notion at the heart of Presidential Decision Directive (PDD) 25 and subsequent U.S. peacekeeping engagements—that there must be an effective cease-fire before monitoring missions can be undertaken—raises the bar of effectiveness unrealistically high.[16] In a world of internal conflict with disorganized rebel groups and ineffective governments, a Chapter VII peace-enforcement mission and robust rules of engagement are necessary components of peacekeeping; to think otherwise is to continue to operate in a bygone world of functioning states making cease-fire with their sovereign authority. Similarly, the often-heard invocation of the (incorrectly attributed) Hippocratic injunction, "First do not harm," is another counsel of perfection that inhibits peacemaking operations by opening them to inappropriate criticisms.[17] It is a wise reminder, but like any purported absolute it is relative to human conditions. Any intervention has its risks and damages and has to be weighed against the harm already taking place; otherwise "no harm" becomes a counsel for inaction.

The debate on the advisability of seizing the proposed opportunities takes place over the identified components of interest. Positions in that debate are a matter of judgment, and it is that judgment that is questioned here. In many cases, the soundness of the judgment was denied by events themselves and by subsequent reruns of the debates that ended in attempts to seize the opportunity anew, after it had passed. Thus the weight of history in the middle run frequently overrides the authority of history in the short run, when it tries to assert that the judgments of the time were sound appreciations of the only way to proceed. Opportunities were missed according to the very criteria by which they were turned down, as history shows; on the basis of their own criteria, the parties showed bad judgment. Then they acted, justified by the very criteria on which their inaction had been based. They found that they did have a dog in the fight after all. It was in the interest of the external parties to do earlier what they eventually did under less favorable circumstances with greater effort and less effect, in Yugoslavia, Haiti, Liberia, Lebanon, and Somalia, as well as what they could no longer do later in Zaire.

Interventions

The actions to be taken to take advantage of opportunities include the normal range of diplomatic interventions and, in a few instances, a peacekeeping/enforcing adjunct as well. They cover a spectrum of involvement, from *mediation* through *convocation* and *deposition* to *consolidation*, and also *enforcement*. The following discussion identifies characteristics of each as they have been practiced when opportunities were properly used, in contrast to the missed moments.

Intervention to Repair: Mediation

Mediation is appropriate when there are a limited number of clear sides and when the interests of all need to be incorporated in ending violence and remaking a functioning political system.[18] Mediated negotiations require authorized spokespersons for the various sides and a small number of parties. Since rebellion is often a broad composite antigovernment activity, mediation may necessitate finding a single negotiating partner capable of making and holding agreements, a selection process that legitimizes one spokesperson over others and may marginalize or exclude the rest. The mediator must take care not to exclude factions that are capable of upsetting the resulting agreement, but also not to include factions that will make agreement impossible. The road between these two conditions is sinuous and narrow and can often only be navigated by a sequential, cumulative process, making an agreement among major factions under a strong spokesperson or coalition, and then adding other factions, piece by piece. The decade-long peace process in Burundi since 1994 has provided a successful example; the Arusha process in Rwanda in 1992–1993 did not. The key move of great skill in preparing for the Dayton talks was the prior negotiation of the Croat-Bosnian Federation in Washington in March 1994, reducing the parties to two composites; the United States then arranged for Serb president Slobodan Milosevic to speak for the Bosnian Serbs and Croat president Franjo Tudjman to speak for the Bosnian Croats, further simplifying the complex party and spokesman array.[19]

Mediation is a standard activity in interstate relations but is more difficult to practice when the conflict is internal. Mediation in an internal conflict is resisted by governments, since it implies that a government cannot handle its own problems; it also inevitably works to strengthen the weaker party, the rebellion, by giving it recognition and equal standing before the mediator. Indeed, the need for mediation indicates that the conflict can no longer be handled hierarchically as "normal politics" and that the only resolving outcome will be a new political system that accords the rebellion a place in legitimate politics.[20] It also assumes that the rebellion is capable of laying down its arms and entering political competition as a normal political party.[21] This condition made the Mozambique mediation possible but long barred successful mediation in Sierra Leone.[22]

Mediation, like any negotiation, also carries with it the implication of the parties' legitimacy and equality in standing (even if not in power), the legitimacy of their interests to be protected, a mutual sense of stalemate in unilateral attempts to win the conflict, and recognition that none of the parties is seeking suicide. It also means that no party is in charge and therefore none is able to convene a hierarchical negotiation between government and aggrieved petitioner. These were the assumptions under which Sant' Egidio (with the United States, Russia, Portugal, Italy, Zimbabwe, Kenya, and Zambia sitting by) mediated in Rome in 1990–1992 on Mozambique between the Mozambique National Resistance (Renamo) and the Mozambique Liberation Front (Frelimo) (rather than with the government of Mozambique),[23] the United States and the UN mediated in Lusaka in 1994 on Angola—and before that Portugal mediated in Estoril in 1992—between UNITA and the Peoples Movement for the Liberation of Angola (MPLA) (not the government of Angola),[24] and the United States and the Intergovernmental Authority on Development (IGAD) mediated in Kenya in 2002–2005 on Sudan between the National Islamic Front (NIF) and the Sudan Peoples Liberation Movement (SPLM). Contests over standing and legitimacy between the government and the rebel movement delayed negotiations for years (as they did in the Middle East, South Africa, Algeria, Sri Lanka, Colombia, and many other conflict scenes).

A special form of mediation is dialogue, informal talks between parties on national issues rather than on the search for a specific conclusion to the conflict. Dialogue is prenegotiation,[25] seeking to unhorn the demons in each side's perception of the other and create a positive atmosphere where substantive issues can be addressed. Sometime it is directly associated with negotiation, a part of the diagnosis phase, as in the early sessions of the 1993 Oslo discussions on the Palestine-Israel conflict.[26] At other times, it is independent of specific negotiations, as practiced by the Kettering Foundation in the U.S.-Soviet Dartmouth talks and the intra-Tajik dialogue or by the United Nations Development Programme (UNDP) in Zimbabwe or by the Carter Center and The Johns Hopkins University in the 1992 Liberian National Reconciliation Workshop, and as proposed as an opportunity in Haiti in the mid-1990s.[27] Dialogue is necessarily informal, low-key, unpublicized, and yet crucial to setting the stage for more focused mediation and negotiation. By its nature, it requires a third party's attention, since it is designed to overcome the barriers to communication that keep the parties themselves from addressing their conflict directly.

A very different situation obtains when the rebellion is asked to surrender or the government is asked to depart; these purposes must be clearly specified from the beginning when applicable because they indicate a special type of intervention not to be confused with mediation in its assumptions. Diplomatic intervention in this situation is not to repair but to replace, related to deposition as discussed below. Its purpose is to assure a smooth transition or succession, a loss of job without a loss of life. Thus, until U.S. Ambassador Bill Richardson clarified U.S. aims as the replacement of Mobutu at the end of April 1997, efforts to produce mediated negotiations in South Africa between the ailing dictator and rebel leader Laurent Kabila hung on the assumption that both parties were legitimate players with a legitimate interest in staying in the game and that a cease-fire would lead to cooperation between two territorial regimes; consequently, neither party had any interest in the mediation since it would serve to legitimize the other. The only mediation that would have made sense in the situation was one to declare Kinshasa an open city, much as the mediation of Assistant Secretary of State Cohen in May 1991 had secured the departure of Mengistu Haile Mariam and then the recognition of Addis Ababa as an open city.[28] The Syrian mediations in 1976 and 1985–1988 were predicated on the replacement of the Franjieh and Gemayel presidencies, respectively, confusing the two types of mediation and making it hard to negotiate with the president as a party. After initial attempts to remove the illegitimate coup in 1991, U.S. and OAS efforts in Haiti wavered between mediation and deposition, treating the junta as a legitimate opposition movement rather than a usurper, confusing the process and hobbling the results.

Intervention to Restore: Convocation

Convocation is the strategy practiced when there is a need to provide new leadership and fill the vacuum by convening a conference of the remaining pluralistic forces in the country. Although it might be thought that an outside state would have little legitimacy in calling a national conference of political forces, this device is frequently used. Examples come from Damascus in 1976, Geneva in 1983, Lausanne in 1984, Damascus in 1985, and Taif in 1989 on Lebanon; from Freetown in 1990, Yamoussoukro in 1991, Cotonou in 1993, Geneva and Akosombo in 1994, and Abuja in 1995 and 1996 on Liberia; from Djibouti in 1991 and Addis Ababa in 1992 on Somalia; from The Hague in 1991 and London in 1992 on Yugoslavia, Dayton in 1995 on

Bosnia, and Rambouillet in 1999 on Kosovo; from New York in 1993 on Haiti; from Libreville in 1993 and 1997 on the Republic of Congo, among many others. Other proposed conferences could have made their impact on the Yugoslav conflict in 1990 and 1991 and on Kosovo in 1998; on Lebanon in 1976, 1978, and 1982; and on Somalia in 1988, 1990, 1991, and 1992, among others. In addition, many of the conferences already convoked provided an opportunity for state restoration that the conveners let slip through their fingers by not pursuing the negotiations to their ultimate details and then further, to implementation.

Like negotiation, convocation depends on the parties' sense of a mutually hurting stalemate or on the conveners' efforts to bring out that perception out of the weariness of a soft stalemate, if it does not occur naturally. The latter situation explains why the conveners must maintain pressure on the participants to keep to the task of negotiating agreements to their conclusion and why the conflicting parties often seek a minimal agreement such as a cease-fire to lift the discomfort of the stalemate and allow a return to their conflict for their own aims. Hence, it is of crucial importance for conveners not to encourage or allow the parties to think that they can do better outside the convocation agreement.

It is not calling the conference that is unusual but its successful conclusion. Each of the cases of conflict and collapse studied here was marked by a number of international conferences to which the various parties were convoked, but most of the conferences broke up with incomplete results. The conveners had already done the hard part, by calling the conference and having the parties attend, but in the joy of their success and then in wearying of their own initiative, they neglected four elements that are needed to bring about a successful outcome.

First, conveners need to include the parties to the conflict as parties to its solution and not negotiate merely among their friends or the moderates. This includes the leaders with guns as well as the leaders with prestige; exclusive reliance on one or the other ignores the elements necessary for an end to conflict and the reconstruction of the state. Excluding ULIMO in mid-1992 condemned the Yamoussoukro attempts to resolve the Liberian civil war; ending the October 1998 mediation in Kosovo short of inclusion of the KLA undid the effort; ignoring one group leader or another bedeviled the efforts at Lausanne on Lebanon in 1984, at Cotonou on Liberia in 1993, and at Djibouti on Somalia in 1991. Criticism against including the warlords because that could be seen as a "reward for their violence" somehow misses the point that it was they who were causing the conflict and their agreement was needed to end it.[29] They either had to be beaten, or effectively isolated, or part of the negotiations: there is no other choice.

But including warlords does not mean excluding political and civic leaders. When the warlords dominate because the political leadership has lost its ability to handle the problems of governance that are its domain, political leadership needs to be included in the convocation because it needs to be part of the solution and to be relegitimized by the process. Thus the need to include nonmilitary leaders often also involves the need to protect and encourage them to act independently and not be cowed by the militias;[30] although the details will vary according to the conflict, special attention is needed to this aspect of the problem. The important implication, again, is that attempts to bring collapse and conflict under control should begin as early as possible, when the politicians still have the upper hand.

Second, conveners need to keep the parties in the room until an agreement on implementing details is reached and not to let them leave when deadlock, superficial agreement, or conference fatigue sets in. Because conflict control is a matter of urgency, it is often thought that it can be handled in a short meeting, so busy people can get back to their business; this is a particularly strong feeling among conveners—especially Western conveners—whose business includes other things than the conflict. Yet in many cultures—notably among Somalis and Lebanese, but also Haitians, Yugoslavs, and other cases discussed here—talking is a lengthy process, schmoozing is a necessary ingredient to serious discussions, and a quick and efficient meeting means either superficiality or a diktat.[31] Conveners have often used unusually firm measures to keep the parties in the room, such as employed by President Carter at Camp David in 1978, or Holbrooke in Dayton in 1995, among others.[32]

Many of the abortive conferences provided for cease-fires, and then the participants went home, leaving the state-rebuilding efforts unattended. These involve specifying the steps of the transition from conflict to peace; handling the military forces through disarmament, demobilization, repatriation, resettlement, and reintegration (DDRRR); creating new institutions of governance; providing for reconciliation and relationships to bridge the conflict divide; and establishing the conditions of justice to deal with the past violence of the conflict, among others.[33] Often, as seen in the Lebanese and Liberian cases, the allocation of seats and offices is a small detail of such huge importance that it needs to be subject to firm agreement from the parties before they break. In internal conflicts, it is unlikely that external powers can be expected to guarantee the details of power allocation and sharing; the guarantees need to be placed within the agreement, so that the parties will not break a part of the agreement because they would then lose the total benefits it grants them.

Third, the conveners need to assure the parties of a worse outcome if they do not move toward an agreement. The ability to control alternatives is crucial to keeping the parties in the room until the work is done, and it is equally crucial to the creation of a new outcome among the parties. Alternatives may be as crass as the threat of sanction or military action, or they may simply be the ability to prevent the parties from turning to their favorite ally for support if the negotiations fail. Thus bringing Russia into the Kosovo negotiations was as important as threatening NATO bombing, and efforts to cut the Libyan-Burkinabe-Ivorian arms pipeline to Taylor or the Liberian pipeline to the RUF were needed to hold the parties' attention to the negotiations.

Fourth, the conveners need to provide and monitor confidence-building measures during and after the negotiations to create trust and allow the parties to verify progress from conflict to reconstruction. Step-by-step agreements and periodic verifications have received a bad name since the Mideast Camp David and Oslo agreements, but the lesson is the reverse: periodic accountability points allow parties to build trust if the steps are accomplished but create distrust if they are not. Proposals were aired in Liberia and Somalia for the creation of zones of security where demobilization and restoration could be implemented, gradually isolating the conflict zones. Implementation of elements of the Constitutional Document or the Parliamentary Declaration in Lebanon would have given the parties something to focus on and absorb, creating the basis for subsequent implementations. Despite all the criticism of an imperfect peace plan, the Dayton agreement on Bosnia created a number of mechanisms—elections, constitutional court, arraignments before the international tribunal—that moved the initial agreement ahead and allowed that progress to be verified.

Nonstate diplomacy advocates argue the need for reconciliation sessions over an extended period of time to turn conflicting parties away from their fixation on each other as enemies and toward a common attention to the task of rebuilding the country together,[34] and one might be tempted to suggest that the series of failed conferences serves this purpose, preparing for a finally successful one: the Yamoussoukros in 1991–1992, Cotonou in 1993, and Akosombo in 1994 prepared for a final Liberia peace agreement at Abuja I and II in 1995 and 1996; the Damascus talks in 1976, the Geneva-Lausanne talks in 1983–1984, and the Damascus talks of 1985 prepared the way for the Riyadh conference of 1989; Washington in 1994 and New York in 1995 (not to speak of the earlier UN/EC series) prepared for the Dayton accords on Bosnia in 1995; and a series of attempts under the OAS from the very beginning of the Cedras coup, followed by Governor's Island in 1993, prepared for the Carter talks in Port-au-Prince in 1994. Were not these series of attempts necessary before the final ones could be put into place, or put otherwise, can one say that any opportunity at all was missed since the maturing process of agreement had first to take its course?

It is hard to use flawed attempts to make a convocation agreement to justify an inherent necessity for many tries. The earlier convocations could have worked if the conveners had spent more time in getting it right the first time (as discussed above) and had implemented their results (as will be discussed further below). Repeated failures were not instructive in finally achieving a success. Convocation was not a necessary learning process, not even for the conveners. "Success," however debatable the term, was possible in Bosnia at Dayton, in Haiti at Port-au-Prince, and in Lebanon at Riyadh because the intervenor finally got across the idea that it meant business. Success was not possible in Mogadishu (or wherever Somalia was being discussed) or Kinshasa because that idea was not conveyed. (It was possible in Liberia at Abuja because of a deal between Taylor and Abacha, former enemies.) If the convener learned at all through the repeated failures, it was to be serious and committed about its effort. Earlier attempts fell short either by being incomplete or by being unapplied, not because the parties were afraid of being ambushed in the application or uncertain of the other parties' intentions,[35] but because they felt they could do better in continued conflict, either on their own or through a new deal offered by one of the conveners.

Failed conferences do not prepare for later successes. They leave relations more hostile and suspicious and further away from a move toward a common goal. Nor do they clarify relations and options, as is sometimes claimed. The substantive formulas for an agreement in Lebanon, Liberia, Haiti, and even Bosnia changed little throughout the series of convocations, leaving only tinkering with the details. When they finally took hold, it was because a firm convener convinced the parties that they faced the only option this time and that either the convener would be on hand to implement it (Haiti, Lebanon, Bosnia, Kosovo) or the agreement was better for all relevant parties (potential spoilers) than no agreement. It takes an authoritative mediator to call this type of negotiation, one who can issue an invitation that cannot be refused at a moment when it is welcome, who has mediating skills and can keep the conference in session until its purpose is achieved, and who will be around afterward to keep the new creation alive until it can run on its own.

Intervention to Replace: Deposition

Deposition is necessary when the presence of an egregious ruler is the problem and no solution to the conflict and collapse is possible as long as he is in control. In some cases, such as Somalia, Liberia, Zaire, and Haiti, state collapse can be clearly and unambiguously laid to the long rule of a debilitating dictator operating on a narrow power base, destroying the opposition, and creating a vacuum around himself. The chances of reforming the individual are beyond hope; power sharing puts the fox in charge of the chicken coop. Left to its devices, the final stage of state collapse will remove the ruler in its own way and complete the vacuum. The purpose of preventive diplomacy is to effectuate that removal earlier and without creating a vacuum. In Liberia, this would have been the aim of decertifying the election results in 1985 in order to bring in Jackson Doe of the LAP and of providing Samuel Doe with a retirement home in 1990 in order to hold new elections and bring in Charles Taylor. In Somalia, it was the aim of proposed diplomatic intervention in 1988 and 1991, where safe conduct for Siad Barre would be exchanged for his retirement, as the Somali sovereign national conference chose his successor. In Zaire, it was the goal of proposed moves in 1991, 1993, and 1994—providing attractive conditions of retirement either under the pressure of disorder, in the first two cases, or in fulfillment of past agreements, in the third—in order to bring in Etienne Tshisekedi or Monsignor Monsengwo, the leaders chosen by the Zairean CNS. In Haiti, where the ruler did not have the long record of tenure as in the other three cases, a Carter type of diplomatic persuasion, associated with some form of military operation, was the policy proposed in all three instances, in 1991, 1993, and earlier in 1994 than it was finally used, in order to allow Jean-Bertrand Aristide to serve his elected term; a decade later, the same policy was practiced on Aristide himself, after his corruption and repression had alienated much of his population.

Intervention of this type is not new or inconceivable, even though it constitutes an extreme measure of interference in internal affairs. Jacobo Arbenz (Guatemala, 1954), Jean Bedel Bokassa (Central African Republic, 1979), Idi Amin Dada (Uganda, 1979), Bernard Coard (Grenada, 1983), Ferdinand Marcos (Philippines, 1986), Manuel Noriega (Panama, 1989), Hajj Omar (Afghanistan, 2002), Saddam Hussein (Iraq, 2003), and Jean-Claude Duvalier, Raoul Cedras, and eventually Jean-Bertrand Aristide himself (Haiti, 1986, 1994, and 2004, respectively) were all the subjects of removal. Most instances of the action proposed here differ from all but the Philippine and Haitian precedents by not involving the military in a major role. It is above all diplomatic intervention that is envisioned, and its means is negotiation, through persuasion and through negative and positive inducements, discussed below. Most of the previous interventions were effectuated by a single state, mainly the United States but one by France in Central Africa (and partially in Haiti) and one by Tanzania; in a few cases, however, a regional organization was associated with the action to enhance its legitimacy. There is little else besides the absence of military action that distinguishes these successful cases from the proposed instances. Indeed, in the case of Haiti the proposals were merely for an earlier intervention, and in Zaire and Liberia, an offer of early retirement to the incumbents was actually considered as U.S. policy and then vetoed at the highest level.

None of the proposed instances of removal of an egregious head of state required any greater use of force than was already or soon to be in the country. Where force was to be involved, it was to be used to keep order, not to remove the leader. Careful diplomacy and delicate persuasion, as eventually practiced by former president Carter in 1994 and by Colin Powell in 2004 in Haiti but as also shown in dealing with Marcos and Duvalier in 1986, were the primary means, backed by the threat or presence rather than the actual use of force. Even where present and used, in some real and all proposed instances, military force had a more active role in filling the ensuing vacuum and holding law and order during the transition than in removing the ruler. As shown ultimately in Haiti, among others, a light military presence, as brief as possible, is needed to set up local forces of order, so as to have someone to whom to hand over an order to be maintained.

There are three nonmilitary ways of deposing an egregious ruler—vote him out, talk him out, or buy him out—used alone or in combination; the alternative is to take him out. Replacement by election has the strong advantage of providing a successor and thereby limiting the dangers of a political vacuum, but it sometimes needs active intervention by external patrons to take effect. If elections are to be regarded as a valued means of stability and succession, there should be no hesitation over intervention to enforce them when necessary. Indeed, a few crucial enforcements work to reduce the need for similar actions in subsequent instances.

Even when voting provides the opportunity, talking (aided by a little buying) may be necessary to consummate it. Like hostage negotiations,[36] early retirement negotiations become possible when the subject shifts from holding out for the original demands to seeking conditions for asylum. The key to proposals for removing Doe between 1985 and 1990, Mobutu between 1990 and 1993, Siad between 1988 and January 1991, and Cedras and company between 1991 and 1994 was diplomatic action that would provide a secure if reduced future instead of an insecure but "important" future, where the attractiveness of the trade-off depends on the intervenors' ability to portray the insecurity inherent in the current course. Cornered, Doe in 1990, Siad Barre in January 1991, and Cedras in 1993 turned down offers of early and secure retirement, doubtless feeling that the chances of holding on were still favorable. Reportedly, the basis of that feeling was mystical in Doe's case, desperate in Said Barre's, and credible in the context of U.S. dithering in the case of the Haitian junta. More and better efforts were needed by the intervenor to convey the idea that "the game is up" and a clear message that was not contradicted by other external parties involved in the problem.

Curious as it may seem to observers, tyrants do feel that they are in office for the good of their country, a perception that intervenors have to work around in their efforts to get them to leave. Only when the egregious ruler becomes convinced that his position on the throne is untenable will he consider other options. Doe, Mobutu, Cedras, Milosevic, Siad Barre, and later Taylor were willing to give up anything, tactically, in order to keep power; they thought they could tough it out and—incredibly, perhaps—that they should do so for the good of the country as they conceived it. Convincing them otherwise required a combination of stiff arm and soft talk and side payments, such as Carter was able to practice in Port-au-Prince and Cohen was poised to try in Monrovia.[37]

But even more is needed. All cases of removed rulers show that an immediately available replacement candidate is necessary, preferably legitimized by a recent fraudulently lost election. Such candidates were available in Liberia, in Haiti, and in 1991, 1993, and 1994 in Zaire, and the absence of such a process in Somalia explains in part why removal never worked. Officials in the Africa Bureau of the State Department have also pointed out that Liberia was not the Philippines—not merely in its strategic value (which, they agree, is debatable) but in the fact that there was no galvanizing, determined opponent to take the egregious ruler's place—"no Aquino, no Cardinal Sin."[38] But neither was there in Haiti in the same year, when Baby Doc was ushered on to a waiting plane by the American ambassador. Furthermore, Liberia and Somalia in 1990 were not nice places for civil society groups to operate; it is not surprising that there was so little civilian response when such attempts had been so thoroughly repressed in the recent past. Yet despite the repression, there was a dedicated civil society mediation by the Inter-Faith Mediation Council in 1991 and there were active political parties operating in Liberia up to the 1985 election and again two decades later as Taylor's regime fell apart. They were not given a chance in the interim. A little effort by mediators to make contacts within

the Liberian political class, or to work with the extremely active community of Liberians in the United States, would have gone a long way to encourage the necessary domestic bed of support for deposition, replacement,
and state reconstruction. The State Department was pressured by Liberian
Americans, but it did not use them.

Another angle that was overlooked in much of the diplomacy, and is
particularly important in the matter of deposition, is the use of personal
and cultural avenues. Appealing to foreign rulers in Western "rational"
terms is not always the most effective medium for the message. Special individual relationships, social institutions, and local belief systems need to
be absorbed and employed. Examples appear on both sides of the instances studied, in a broad range. It took a bully such as Holbrooke to
bully bullies such as Karadzic and Mladic in preparation for Dayton, but
Holbrooke was unable to get beyond the global conspiracy theories of
Mrs. Milosevic in preparation for Rambouillet. It took a careful understanding of the personal situation of Cedras by President Carter, on sug-
gestion by Marc Bazin, to realize that the key to his decision was held by
his wife, and more broadly, to understand the need for a high-ranking military figure, on the occasion General Colin Powell, to talk to the Haitian
generals and to Mrs. Cedras, descendant of army commanders in chief.[39]
On the other side of success, the UN mission to Somalia after the departure of Sahnoun could have used some advisers who understood Somali
culture and the mentality of an Aideed. A major reason why Laurent Kabila refused to meet Mobutu on a South African warship off Kinshasa was
his fear of the power of Mobutu's evil eye. In breaking the final resistance
of Doe to invitations to retirement in 1990, the enlistment of a similar
powerful spirit to counter the magician furnished to Doe by Togolese president Eyadema would have been useful, perhaps even necessary. Western
diplomacy at its best recognizes and deals with the influence of bullies and
family members but recoils before shamans and conspiracy theorists as
not using Western-type logic, when recalcitrant parties need to be engaged
on their own terrain.

Negotiations for early retirement of a rapacious head of state require a
powerful mediator, above all one that can exert the moral pressure in local
terms that is necessary to reevaluate the present and provide the future security that is the basis of the bargain. In addition, it takes a mediator who
is able to apply credible and painful sanctions in the event of refusal, sanctions that may include specific embargoes but also more general ostracism
and a break in an important relationship. Finally, the mediator must not be
susceptible to counterpressure from the target ruler and especially must not
suffer more from the rupture of the relationship than does the target.

Intervention to Rebuild: Consolidation

Consolidation is needed when previous measures of mediation, convocation, and/or deposition have been successful in creating a new situation and beginning the process of managing conflict; external efforts have then to turn to state rebuilding. Although this is an open-ended subject that extends far beyond the present discussion,[40] the point of relevance here is the necessity to connect efforts to end deadly conflicts with efforts to rebuild collapsed states. The one is simply incomplete and doomed without the other. The sad story of the various initiatives ends in each case with a tale of worthy, but incomplete, plans littering the floor and never let out the door to be applied to the challenge of state rebuilding. Ending conflict and leaving a vacuum is an invitation to renewed conflict.

Unimplemented, the Damascus, Riyadh, and Cairo agreements of 1976 left the Lebanese situation open to revived violence when new opportunities for conflict arose. The Cotonou agreement of 1993 was left to the parties to implement, so instead they jockeyed for better positions through increased violence. The intervenors were disorganized and unsure of their missions in 1991, 1992, and 1993 in Somalia, so partial agreements gave way to escalating violence and finally the evacuation of the intervenors. The OAS measures of 1991 and 1992 and the Governor's Island agreement of 1993 in Haiti were weakly applied by the intervenors and so were ineffective. Later the restoration of Aristide and a few accompanying measures in Haiti marked the end of the international process, and Haiti was left on its own to run toward full state restoration, which it never attained because the implementing steps were not established, monitored, and controlled. The Cutileiro and Vance-Owen mediations of 1992–1993 became lost in the negotiations and were never allowed by the sponsors to turn to the task of implementation. The excellent plans for a new Zairean state drawn up by the CNS, beginning with a sound, balanced constitution, were blocked at the door by Mobutu, with pandering by the Troika of interested Western states, and so never met the challenge of application.

As the examples show, implementation depended on a united stance by conveners creative in balancing incentives, committed to maintaining their engagement, and willing to exert a spectrum of pressures on the parties to comply. The pressures need not have been enormous: the instances show that the parties did not comply because they sensed that there were better alternatives available through the conveners themselves. Notably, Nigeria in ECOMOG cooperated with ULIMO and AFL to get around the Liberian agreements; the United States gave Izetbegovic the impression that there were better possibilities for Bosnia than through the UN/EC mediations

and then had trouble bringing him to an agreement at Dayton; and the
United States lifted the sanctions on Haiti before the Governor's Island
agreement was implemented, giving the impression of leakiness and un-
concern. Instead of providing holes to their own agreements, the conveners
needed to make sure they were implemented.

Once a fuller agreement was finally achieved, the conveners tended to
feel the job was done and the problem solved. It was not that they developed an exit strategy: exit was their strategy. The international community
was willing to leave Lebanon to the Syrians, Zaire to the Rwandans,
Liberia to Taylor, Haiti to Aristide, and Somalia to its fate, rather than following through with measures of accountability and assistance to keep the
state-rebuilding process on track. Winners of conflict and elections, or
even the beneficiaries of compromise agreements, were left with the notion that they were now in charge, without any responsibility either to their
populations or to the representatives of the international community who
ended the conflict and restored authority.

Yet continued commitment and engagement were needed. Specifically, funds and a rehabilitation plan are required to remove unemployed
youth and children from militias and reinsert them into the education and
economic systems (which, themselves, need rebuilding). A sustained program of dialogue among sectors of society is necessary to deal with causes
of the conflict and collapse and reestablish notions of legitimacy and relationship that make up the tissue of society. New incumbents need to be
provided with a phased program of responsibilities about which to develop a policy platform and a plan for setting up and setting into motion
the other institutions of governance—legislative, judiciary, local councils.
Codes need to be established, with international assistance, to establish
standards of accountability for government and to ensure that the causes
and excesses of the conflict are not repeated and that perpetrators of excesses in its course are held responsible.

The list is long and heavy, but it should not be equated with a new
colonialism or UN trusteeship.[41] The convenor itself is not directly responsible for the accomplishment of these tasks, and even a formal international institutional responsibility is difficult to envision (if only in memory of the problems of UN operation in a case such as Somalia). The UN
Secretariat or agencies are not organized to function as a trustee, but requiring reports from the state trustee and the entrusted state to an invigor-
ated Trusteeship Council would be useful. The impression must be
avoided that the newly installed authority is in unaccountable, sovereign
control, without any responsibility not to repeat the practices of the previous egregious ruler or, on the other side of the coin, without any commit-

ment from external agencies for assistance. For a limited amount of time, with decreasing interference, the new successors need to be held to a program of restoration in partnership with members of the international community. The best time to establish such a contract is in the early period after the conflict is brought under control and the new authority is coming in. As it is, the international financial institutions (IFIs) are often eager to return with economic programs and assistance, without any similar programs and assistance being required for political and social reconstruction. The result is that Mobutu was succeeded by the Kabilas, Doe by Taylor, and the Duvaliers and the generals by Aristide, all without any obligation to accompany their accession to power with a reinstitutionalization of the state around them.

Intervention to Restrain: Enforcement

Enforcement was required in a few instances, generally involving decisiveness with military forces on hand rather than the introduction of larger forces. The instances were an earlier introduction of a Syrian-led Arab contingent in Lebanon in 1976, financial support for a sustained Nigerian-led ECOMOG campaign in Sierra Leone in 1998, an energetic response to the assassination of U.S. soldiers in Somalia in 1993, reinforcement and landing of troops aboard the *Harlan County* in Haiti in 1993, use of French-led Troika troops to restore order and authority in Zaire in 1991 and 1993, and potential introduction of Chapter VII forces in connection with some of the opportunities in Yugoslavia. All of the enforcement measures involved the use of forces already or soon to be in action, often in lesser number than eventually occurred; at issue were the timing and the rules of engagement.[42] By extension, in a few of these instances and in other cases, different troop numbers and armaments would also be required for an enforcement mission.

The lesson of the missed opportunities was that unheeded threats to use force needed to be implemented to maintain their credibility and to render future threats more effective and less costly, lest their nonimplementation teach the reverse lesson: we don't mean it. That was the pervasive impression given in Haiti, Somalia, and Yugoslavia and so to watching parties in Liberia and Zaire as well. And there should be no doubt: leaders in all these conflicts watched carefully how threats were used in other conflicts and drew their own conclusion. A firm and committed policy of enforcement turns the use of force from a threat to a warning, as discussed below, and leaving no doubt, reduces the need to use it in the future.

The other lesson is that in internal conflicts there are no Chapter VI missions. Already Chapter VI has been extended to "Chapter VI 1/2," to cover peacekeeping missions where cease-fires are already in place, and has slid into "Chapter VI 3/4," where some provision for self-defense is required in rules of engagement. What is required is a clear Chapter VII mandate, with appropriate forces and rules of engagement to cover the accomplishment of necessary tasks—cease-fire enforcement, restoration of order, disarmament, and demobilization, among others. In internal conflicts, where the sides are loose and often out of control of their own forces, full engagement by enforcement forces should be possible without a lengthy and restrictive referral all the way up the chain of command. Sending soldiers into action may be dangerous, but sending diplomats into action without military backing is folly.

Carrots and Sticks

Actions of preventive diplomacy are based on diplomatic persuasion, sometimes combined with forceful entry. As such, diplomatic initiatives must carry an absolute and relative incentive for acceptance by each of the parties involved. The initiative must be attractive in itself, carrying the prospect of a better future if implemented, but it must also carry the assurance of a worse future if it is not implemented. Obduracy on the part of the incumbents produces intractability on the part of the rebels, as seen in Somalia, Lebanon, Kosovo, and outside of the present cases, in the Israel-Palestine and Sri Lankan conflicts. If the rebels have no hope of having their grievances addressed, they have no incentive to lay down their arms in exchange for a role in politics. Warnings have no effect in such cases, since nothing can be worse than the present situation and all that is left are distant predictions—"We will win, in the end," "We shall overcome, some-day." Thus, not surprisingly, the weapons of power need to be chosen to fit the target: grievants need credible gratifications in order to change their behavior, and incumbents respond to deprivations. Although it must be beneficial to the parties, an initiative is no stronger than the alternative that lies behind it in case of rejection, so intervenors need to think of carrots and sticks at the same time. Carrots come in the form of *promises* and *predictions*, or voluntary and involuntary gratifications, and sticks come as *threats* and *warnings*, or voluntary and involuntary deprivations.[43]

As usual in most preventive diplomacy, the instances examined were predicated on the prediction that the intervention itself would improve the lot of the parties by ending conflict and restoring the state, plus few additional promises or voluntary offers by the mediator to add on benefits if the parties accepted the initiative. In addition to the warnings of worse conditions for the parties if the initiative were not taken up, there were also a number of threats or voluntary efforts by the mediator to add to the pain if the parties rejected the initiative. Because preventive diplomacy is interference in a sovereign state's internal affairs, threats tend to be less often used than promises, warnings (involuntary effects pointed out by the mediator that add to the pain of the parties in case of rejection), or predictions (involuntary effects noted by the mediator that add to the benefits for the parties in case of acceptance).

Predictions of benefits from implementation come with any policy démarche and are supposed to carry their own powerful incentive for compliance. The politics of state collapse are variously marked by egregious authoritarianism, narrow power base, surrounding power vacuum, illegitimate power formula, and violent conflict, and preventive initiatives are predicted to overcome these ills. These predictions generally pointed to a better outcome for the country as a whole. But an effective intervention needs incentives also to be directed at the targeted party, who is removed from office and is thereby prima facie worse, not better, off. To ask Siad, Mobutu, Cedras, or Doe to leave office for the good of their country, to prevent their state from collapsing completely, may appeal to their sense of civic duty but not to much else. To work for a new national pact in Lebanon, Yugoslavia, Haiti, Zaire, or Somalia may be attractive to the general population and some of the political leaders but is scarcely an incentive to those who benefit from the old order. In the latter type of instance, an attempt to salvage the state can be made attractive to incumbents by maintaining a place for them in the new political system if they also make room for others, and so would work in Lebanon or Yugoslavia. But that is probably too much to promise to experienced egregious rulers, who will continue to feed on the system if given a chance—the fox-in-the-chicken-coop problem. It is an inherent weakness of preventive diplomacy that its predicted benefits are designed to accrue to the powerless and its costs to the incumbents, scarcely an incentive to change. This means that, for the most part, incentives for change must come from the other expressions of power—promises, warnings, and threats.

Promises come from a rather standard list relating to developing countries: aid, reconstruction assistance, and recognition of the new government.[44] In some cases, the carrots are merely buried sticks: resumption of aid and revival of recognition, or lifting of sanctions. But again these promises are incentives to the outs, rather than to the ins. Special incentive plans need to be devised for early retirees from power, running from

retirement homes to amnesties. Doe, Siad, Mobutu, and (for a while) Cedras resisted such blandishments, which the alternative policies under discussion would make more compelling. But there are real limits to executive buy-out, in terms of both resources and justice, and this reinforces the
dilemma of the intervenor.

The other side of this dilemma is the amnesty that often goes with early
retirement of egregious rulers. Human rights activists chafe at promises of
impunity for causing the collapse and conflict that were given to Cedras in
Haiti and Foday Sankoh in Sierra Leone and implied to Milosevic, point-
ing out that accountability in itself is crucial and the precedent it sets acts
as a deterrent to potential violators in the future. On the other hand, deposition is often possible only at the cost of amnesty, and the culture of retri-
bution that is an element in keeping dictators in office needs to be broken
by the democratic culture of safe retirement from office. The classical attempt to cut the dilemma lies in the granting of domestic impunity and in
the use of truth and reconciliation commissions but leaving accountability—as in the international tribunals for Yugoslavia and Rwanda or the tribunal for Sierra Leone—to the international community.[45] The basic point
is that promises to the parties that cause conflict and collapse may be necessary, even if they may not be enough to remove the problem.

Warnings, like predictions, are inherent in every preventive diplomacy
démarche: the unbearable situation will continue and even worsen if the
initiative is rejected. Indeed, the soul of diplomacy is a mixture of predictions and warnings. Such warnings are most powerful when the moment is
ripe and the stalemate hurts all sides, but this may be an ideal situation (although its absence may explain why the proposed démarches were not
adopted at the time). Internal stalemates tend to be soft and pain is un-
equally distributed, often absent on some sides or outweighed by benefits
from the status quo. To the judgment, "It can't go one like this," those in
power retort, "It will go on like this because the alternatives you offer me
are worse." Beleaguered rulers and warring factions tend to believe that
they can still escalate their way out of any temporary difficulties, in part because of the weakness of the opposition (which often believes the same
thing on its side). As prospect theory emphasizes, people are generally
more concerned about protecting against losses than about achieving
gains;[46] rulers want to preserve their accomplishments (however con-
testable), and rebels want to protect their positions (however contested).

That leaves the matter of *threats*. Every démarche should carry a
threat for nonacceptance. The threat may be clearly stated, so as to pose a
choice, or it may be implied or ambiguous, for tactical reasons. Threats
most frequently come as economic pressures, from aid cutoff to sanctions,

or coercive diplomacy, from embargo to direct military intervention. Sanctions involve a gamut of measures and were involved in reality in all six cases, whether through unilateral trade and travel restrictions or through consolidated international measures. Haiti provides a good example, for sanctions were used from 1991 to 1994.[47] In the proposed policies, they would have been tightened and targeted and loopholes monitored, as early as November 1991 when the first Colombian tanker ran the OAS embargo or as late as the Governor's Island agreement of July 1993 when sanctions were lifted before implementation occurred. The Haitian situation is a sound indication that sanctions can work, when backed by internal resistance and by a higher threat to escalate to direct intervention; they worked in a relatively short time, but they could well have worked faster if the holes had been plugged and if they had been better targeted and graduated. No less important, the Haitian situation is also a clear indication that blunt, late, and prolonged sanctions can cause greatest damage to the innocent bystanders one is trying to help. The economic sanctions on Yugoslavia provided an effective motivation for Milosevic to cooperate over Bosnia at Dayton, but the military sanctions were so often threatened that they lost their credibility on a perceived vital interest such as Kosovo.[48] The argument here is not for sanctions per se, however; it is for the necessity of backing preventive diplomacy with credible threats, in the absence of credible warnings, promises, and predictions.

In addition, threats are needed to make promises look good. Executive buy-out is much more attractive if the alternative is made even worse than the status quo by additional deprivations—isolation, frozen assets, travel and visa restrictions, and others. Measures presented as a means to protect gains and prevent losses rather than as punishment have a better chance of being heard. Furthermore, as noted, promises are merely the obverse of threats, indicating the removal of threatened or activated deprivations. Of course, as is known, threats are usually better when presented as warnings ("congressional legislation obliges me to . . . ," "the international community will not countenance . . . ," "rebel forces are poised to . . ."), making the presenter look less nasty and enabling him to help the target find a way to avoid the warnings by activating the promises. These devices were applicable in Haiti, Somalia, and Liberia, respectively.

Threateners should not make threats that they are not willing to carry out, and policymakers should not make démarches that they are not ready to follow up. The issue of credibility is enormously important. Initiatives in Haiti, Yugoslavia, Lebanon, Somalia, Liberia, and Zaire failed because the United States and Europe trained the potential targets not to believe their threats, particularly in regard to military action and more broadly in regard to their goals in the conflict. The training was given not only in the case itself but also through action in other cases that the targeted governments and rebel movements were watching carefully. A few threats carried to their implementation would have made other threats credible and even unnecessary. So much of the policy attention in many of the instances cited was posturing and bluster that taking real action later so much more difficult.

Such judgments can be turned around, however, and used as excuses for inaction. Indeed, they can justify total inaction anywhere anytime, since they indicate that no policy should be undertaken that would not be carried through to its extreme. "In for a penny, in for a pound" is not a useful guideline, particularly when it suggests "in for a ton" as well.[49] Credible threats along with adequate initial engagement avoid the danger of mission creep from the start, and empty threats pose greater danger of policy quicksand than does a clearly posed consequence for rejecting proposals and a commitment to carry it out. Threats must be credible, but the best threats are never implemented.[50] The challenge therefore is to find threats that are credible enough backups to policy actions that they need not be implemented. Alternatively, credibility can be established by finding targeted, graduated threats that can establish their credibility by small increments.

But there are some important limitations on threats. Intervenors should not make threats that they fear more than the target, a seemingly banal observation but one that applies repeatedly to Yugoslavia, Somalia, and Haiti, although the classic case is the threat of sanctions against South Africa in 1979.[51] Mediators have to be careful in wielding threats to withdraw their good offices, since some of the parties may welcome their ministrations more than others; the EC threat in July 1991 to end its mediation if the Brioni agreement was not observed struck no fear in the hearts of the Serb leaders. Parties should not make threats that are congenial to one side and therefore reinforce the conflict; the European threat to recognize Croatia and Slovenia in 1991 may have sought to restrain Serbia but it certainly encouraged Slovenia and Croatia, and it worked against any attempt to preserve a modicum of Yugoslav federation. Parties should also not make threats that can be turned against them by their targets; the November 1991 NATO threat to recognize Slovenia and Croatia "only" if there were an overall Yugoslav settlement invited Serbs to block such a settlement and so block recognition of the two republics.

In sum, even a good policy démarche needs to contain incentives for its acceptance and disincentives for its rejection. Reliance on the incentive inherent in forestalling state collapse (predictions) or the disincentive inherent in maintaining the current situation (warnings) is not enough and is especially unappealing to the incumbents. Extra inducements (promises) are necessary and above all extra measures (threats) to discourage rejection. Yet none of the proposed measures has any tricks to produce results.

Notes

1. This is notwithstanding Evans and Sahnoun, *The Responsibility to Protect*, 21–22. For good reviews of the literature, see Verstegen, *Conflict Prognostication;* van Walraven, *Early Warning and Conflict Prevention.* An earlier version of parts of this chapter was delivered as the Schwartz Lecture on Dispute Resolution at the Ohio State University Moritz College of Law on 2 April 2002; I. William Zartman, "Cowardly Lions: Missed Opportunities for Dispute Settlement," *Ohio State Journal on Dispute Resolution* 18, no. 1 (2002): 1–21.

2. Brown and Rosecrance, *The Costs of Conflict.*

3. Republic of Lebanon, *Estimation des pertes en revenues en raison des aggressions israéliennes contre le Liban* (Beirut: Government of Lebanon, 2000); Elizabeth Picard, "Trafficking, Rents and Diaspora in the Lebanese War," in Arnson and Zartman, *Rethinking the Economics of War.*

4. Zartman, *Collapsed States.*

5. Herz, *The Nation-State and the Crisis of World Politics;* Lyons and Mastanduno, *Beyond Westphalia;* Maryann Cusimano, *Beyond Sovereignty* (New York: St Martin's Press, 2000).

6. Collier et al., *Breaking the Conflict Trap.*

7. Cusimano, *Operation Restore Hope.*

8. Both Nye and Cook were cited in Lawyers Committee for Human Rights, *In the National Interest,* 3–4.

9. Andrea Jackson, *Paramilitary and Other Violent Organized Groups Operating in Kosovo* (Fayetteville, NC: Eighteenth Airborne Corps, U.S. Army, 2001).

10. Hassan Makhlouf, *Culture et commerce du drogue au Liban* (Paris: L'Harmattan, 1994); Elizabeth Picard, "Trafficking, Rents and Diaspora in the Lebanese War," in Arnson and Zartman, *Rethinking the Economics of War.*

11. Cohen, *Intervening in Africa.*

12. Referred to in Mark Dannen, "Endgame in Kosovo," *New York Review of Books* 46, no. 8, 6 May 1999, 9. The phrase came from a frequent saying of Senator Howard Baker.

13. Zaire had no effective regional organization membership, and its successor, the Democratic Republic of Congo, during the War of the Zairean Succession actually became the subject of a contest between the East Africa Cooperation and the Southern African Development Community, of which it became a member in 1997; it was also a member of a third regional group, the Economic Community of Central African States, which does not function either. IGADD is now the Inter-Governmental Authority on Development (IGAD) and the OAU the African Union (AU), but both still need help from the outside.

14. Evans and Sahnoun, *The Responsibility to Protect,* especially at 37.

15. Saadia Touval and I. William Zartman, "Mediation in the Post-Cold War Era," in Crocker, Hampson, and Aall, *Turbulent Peace;* Maundi et al., *Getting In.*

16. Zartman, "An Apology Needs a Pledge."

17. Christine Ruggere, "Quoting the Hippocratic Oath," *Science* 286 (29 October 1999), 901; I. William Zartman, "Conference Summary," Ditchley Conference on Preventive Diplomacy and Conflict Resolution, in Hamburg, *Preventive Diplomacy, Preventive Defense and Conflict Resolution,* 48; Evans and Sahnoun, *The Responsibility to Protect,* 31.

18. See Stenelo, *Mediation in International Negotiations;* Touval and Zartman, *International Mediation in Theory and Practice;* Rubin, *The Dynamics of Third Party Intervention;* Mitchell and Webb, *New Approaches to International Mediation;* Kressel and Pruitt, *Mediation Research;* Bercovitch and Rubin, *Mediation in International Relations;* Bercovitch, *Resolving International Conflicts;* Kleiboer, *Multiple Realities of International Mediation;* Bercovitch, *Studies in International Mediation;* Jacob Bercovitch, "Mediation," in Zartman, *Peacemaking in International Conflict.*

19. Holbrooke, *To End a War;* James O'Brien, "The Dayton Talks: Ceasefire and Settlement," in Zartman and Kremenyuk, *Peace vs Justice.*

20. Zartman, *Elusive Peace,* especially chap. 13.

21. On such problems, see Walter and Snyder, *Civil Wars, Insecurity, and Intervention.*

22. Mediation is also difficult in internal conflict where cultural clashes are paramount and where the rebellion takes on a terrorist form as well as a broader form of more passive alienation. For example, it has been hard to find an appropriate mediator in the Algerian or the Sri Lankan conflict. Some French and Algerian officials called for mediation in the war that pits state terror against Islamicist terror in Algeria, but there has been little to mediate between these two extremes, and there are few mediators (and certainly not France or the United States) who would be acceptable to both sides. The diligent efforts of the Sant' Egidio community in 1994–1995 brought together dispersed opposition parties to form a political middle where none had previously existed, but those efforts were unable to overcome Algerian nationalistic resistance in order to bring these parties (including the Islamic Salvation Front [FIS]) together with the government. Similarly, in Sri Lanka, India was able to mediate an agreement between the government and the Tamil Tigers in 1987, but soon found itself under attack from the very Tigers that it had brought into the agreement. In such cases, it is only when the terrorists are worn out and have become fully isolated from a population alienated by their tactics that they become amenable to a return to civil politics, and the conflict becomes susceptible to mediation.

23. Hume, *Ending Mozambique's War;* Andrea Bartoli, "Mediating Peace in Mozambique," in Crocker, Hampson, and Aall, *Herding Cats.*

24. Hare, *Angola's Last Best Chance for Peace.*

25. It is called "circum-negotiation" in the word of Saunders, *A Public Peace Process.*

26. Corbin, *The Norway Channel.*

27. Vorhees, *Dialogue Sustained;* Saunders, *A Public Peace Process.*

28. Cohen, *Intervening in Africa,* 37–59.

29. Clarke and Herbst, *Learning from Somalia;* Boutros-Ghali, *Unvanquished;* see also David Laitin, "Somalia: Civil War and International Interven-

tion," in Walter and Snyder, *Civil Wars, Insecurity, and Intervention,* 161–162, and Hirsch and Oakley, *Somalia and Operation Restore Hope,* 56–64, 70–71, 78, 191.

30. That need for protection and encouragement was a problem that occurred in Somalia even when elders were included; see Ken Menkhaus, "Traditional Conflict Management in Contemporary Somalia," in Zartman, *Traditional Cures for Modern Conflicts.*

31. The literature on this topic is enormous and often ignored by practitioners. See Graham and Sano, *Smart Bargaining.* In imposing the 1985 Tripartite agreement, Syrian foreign minister Khaddam foresaw "one brief session, perhaps an hour or more," whereas Lebanese foreign minister Salem "expected the conference to last a week or so"; Salem, *Violence and Diplomacy in Lebanon,* 202.

32. Quandt, *Camp David;* Holbrooke, *To End a War.*

33. Barbara Walter, "Designing Transitions from Civil War," in Walter and Snyder, *Civil Wars, Insecurity, and Intervention* discusses some of this.

34. Saunders, *A Public Peace Process;* Ronald Fisher, "Interactive Conflict Resolution," in Zartman, *Peacemaking in International Conflict,* 269–272.

35. This explanation is argued for in Walter and Snyder, *Civil Wars, Insecurity, and Intervention.* Exceptions might be found at times in Liberia, when Taylor refused to stack arms because he did not trust ECOMOG and in Somalia, particularly in Kismayo in 1991–1992, although in both cases the parties simply were not done trying to take more territory.

36. Richard Hayes, "Negotiating with Terrorists," in Kremenyuk, *International Negotiations;* T. Sandler and J. L. Scott, "Terrorist Success in Hostage-Taking Incidents," *Journal of Conflict Resolution* 31, no. 1 (1987): 35–53; Zartman, "Negotiating with Terrorists."

37. Some claim that the clincher for Cedras was the U.S. agreement with Mrs. Cedras to rent their house; it is not clear which of Doe's many requests would have constituted the clinching buyout.

38. Confidential interview by author.

39. Robert Pastor, "More or Less than It Seemed," in Crocker, Hampson, and Aall, *Herding Cats,* 517.

40. See, however, Rotberg, *When States Fail.*

41. Helman and Ratner, "Saving Failed States," 3–20.

42. Allard, *Somalia Operations.*

43. Schelling, *Strategy of Conflict,* 177; James Tedeschi, "Threats and Promises," in Swingle, *The Structure of Conflict,* 162–180; Baldwin, "The Power of Positive Sanctions," 19–38; Zartman, "The Political Analysis of Negotiations," 385–399; I. William Zartman and Jeffrey Z. Rubin, eds., *Power and Negotiation* (Ann Arbor: University of Michigan Press, 2000).

44. Cortright, *The Price of Peace.*

45. Priscilla Hayner, "Past Truths, Present Dangers: The Role of Official Truth Seeking in Conflict Resolution and Prevention," in Paul Stern and Daniel Druckman, eds., *International Conflict Resolution After the Cold War* (Washington, DC: National Academy Press, 2000).

46. Stein and Pauly, *Choosing to Cooperate;* Farnham, *Avoiding Losses/Taking Risks.*

47. Maguire et al., *Haiti Held Hostage,* 97–100; Perusse, *Haitian Democracy Restored,* 128–130.

48. Daalder, *Getting to Dayton,* passim; Daalder and O'Hanlon, *Winning Ugly,* passim.

49. Paul Meerts, "Escalation and Entrapment," in Zartman and Faure, *Escalation and Negotiation;* Joel Brockner and Jeffrey Z. Rubin, *Entrapment in Escalating Conflicts* (New York: Springer, 1985).

50. High-level U.S. diplomats meeting with an African head of state in 1991 were unable to learn the whereabouts of Charles Taylor to finalize a cease-fire. On leaving, one said to the other, "Go back, ask for a private session, and tell him to produce Taylor or else." "Or else what?" the other asked. "I don't know, but neither does he," was the answer. On leaving the private session, the diplomats received a call from Taylor agreeing to the cease-fire. Confidential interview by author.

51. See Zartman, *Ripe for Resolution,* chap. 5; on the Yugoslav instances, see Libal, *Limits of Persuasion,* 20, 51–52, 71–72.

9

Foreign Policy and International Relations

AN EXAMINATION OF THIRTY ARGUABLE ENTRY POINTS INTO THE DEADLY CON-
flicts in six states on the way to collapse in the last quarter of the twentieth century has shown that there were a number of opportunities for preventive action and that the necessary interventions were no different in
nature than other similar actions taken by the same governments later or
elsewhere. Indeed, more than half of the proposed interventions involved
merely the earlier execution of actions ultimately taken later on, the pursuit of decisions already made but not carried to fruition, or the effectua-
tion of decisions taken at a lower level but vetoed by higher authority. The
measures were already in the system, proposed at the time by people already involved or by knowledgeable observers, not some far-fetched idea
or "academic" proposal.

The year 2000 did not mark the end of such opportunities, seized or
missed, but offered a convenient date at which to stop and take stock with
some perspective, instead of running the analysis up to an elusive last
minute. In addition, in many of the cases analyzed, as noted at the beginning, the time of opportunity has passed, at least for the moment, leaving
a period when the results of inaction or incomplete action needed to be di-
gested before new opportunities to affect events could mature; frequently,
once a moment or period of ripeness has been let pass, a conflict must go
back to its process of ripening all over again before another moment of opportunity can later appear. Exceptionally, Haiti might be seen to offer
missed moments of opportunity at the turn of the century and again in
2004, and the eastern Democratic Republic of the Congo in the 2000s has
continued to present unexploited opportunities for domestic mediation
and international peacekeeping. In other cases, different policies were de-

bated and could have been adopted over time, but sharp opportunities for preventive action simply did not appear.

This is not to say that opportunities were a function only of the immediate post–Cold War era of world politics. Opportunities appear within the course of the individual countries' conflicts; reasons for inaction, valid or no, can come from the context in which the conflicts occur, but the dynamics of the conflict and the opportunities it provides are its own creation. Nor does the twenty-first century, with its signal date of 11 September 2001, mark a new era where opportunities no longer appear or where their nature has changed. As noted, the situation in Iraq vividly illustrates the difficulties of discerning and justifying the need for prevention, and other situations could be examined for missed opportunities in the same terms as used in the analysis here. Arguably, the Palestine-Israel conflict contained such moments, beginning with the return of the negotiators from Oslo in 1993 but posed again in the events of 2000 leading up to and at Camp David;[1] Sri Lanka could have benefited from more vigorous and sustained mediation under the Norwegian initiative in the early 2000s; and crucial opportunities for a robust reconstruction were allowed to slip away during the immediate postinvasion period in Iraq. The same search for ripe moments and entry points, for early awareness and enlightened responsibility, for goal-oriented policy and contingency planning, and for decisive action and sustained mediation needs to guide attention in situations of conflict and collapse in the new millennium as in the old.

As its first lesson, this study has shown that the three principal strategies for dealing with state collapse and deadly conflict—mediation when there was still a government to face the rebellion, convocation when there was a need to refill the political vacuum, and early retirement of the egregious ruler when reform was no longer possible—constitute standard, conceivable measures practiced by external intervenors and that opportune moments are available to put them into practice. Furthermore, as a second lesson, these measures usually constitute their own entry point within a situation of mutually hurting or soft stalemate, rather than requiring specific justification by event or context. In other words, these strategies do not need a particular signal but are simply appropriate responses to gradually worsening situations.

The third lesson is that the success of measures to prevent conflict and collapse depends to a large extent on diplomatic elements, including the provision of positive and negative trade-offs and authoritative persuasion to hold the parties' attention to the completion of the reconstruction agree-

ment. Constructive interventions cannot be sold to the leaders of the conflicted state as a value in and of themselves, when in fact it is the opposition or the country at large, and not the incumbents, that benefits. But
diplomatic inducements are appropriate and usually sufficient for the purpose, not costly military involvement.

The fourth lesson is that the United States has a unique position in regard to preventive diplomacy, although other external powers and regional
groups of states also have their roles to play, often operating under the le-
gitimizing authority of a regional organization or the global United Nations
(Security Council). Private agencies and NGOs can also have a role where
a nonstate facilitator is needed in the negotiations themselves and also
where training is needed to raise diplomats to the level of their challenges.[2]

The most important lesson of this study is that conflict management
requires state building.[3] Thinking of one without the other is condemning
the prevention of deadly conflict to futility and discrediting the effort in
general. It is impossible to call a truce to deadly disorder and expect it to
hold without engaging in the process of restoring order. The destructive
effects of conflict and the ruins of collapsed states need focused and sustained attention to be overcome, or else the conflict will burst forth again,
building on the bitterness, blood, and penury that its earlier round created.[4] Internal war cease-fires are not the same as interstate truces: they
are not made between ongoing, functioning agencies that can apply the
agreements' provisions while running their own affairs, but between
weak, exhausted, wounded parties without the power or authority to monitor their own implementations.[5] The parties emerging from conflict and
collapse do not take over functioning structures, reliable institutions,
working bureaucracies, or recognized authorities. The very purpose of the
civil conflict is to destroy the authority of the state; when the conflict ends,
by mediation, convocation, or deposition, that authority needs to be restored, confidence rebuilt, output revived, and the causes and effects of
conflict erased. For conflict prevention and management to work, the
states must be restored.

A persistent misunderstanding that stands in the way of the task is the
aversion to "nation building." The problem is so badly misconceived that
its authors do not even know what their term means: nation building is a
long-standing concept referring to the creation of a single object of identification and allegiance out of component social groups, or turning traditional societies into modern nations.[6] Although foreign mediators and intervenors can undertake actions that contribute to building national
identity as a final goal, they have neither the charge nor the capacity to

take on directly the essentially domestic work of building a nation. What outsiders can—and must—help do is to build the state, the institutions, functions, and authorities on which local efforts can then focus a sense of belonging and ownership as they rebuild their nation.

Once reborn, states can grow into their functions, a growth that has no determined end state or fixed limit. But their start, or re-start, needs to be assisted. Specifically, this means that the cease-fire must be monitored, with muscle, and remediated when infractions and interpretations reappear. Disarmament and demobilization of combatants need to be organized and conducted, the individuals rehabilitated and the economy reconstructed; a national army has to be recruited out of the various combatant groups, retained, and given reliable command structures. Local councils have to be established under appropriate rules of selection, involving civil society and traditional leaders as well as the local combatants' leaders; from these, national representative institutions need to be built and filled, and national executive leadership chosen. A police system needs to be installed. The education system needs quick restoration, with local consumer participation, its staff replenished, parent-teacher associations created, security assured, materials and buildings located.

There is more. All this needs to be done at once, with no one charged and/or having the capacity to do it. Certainly the new political forces within the conflict area are the primary participants in this process and may even be nominally in charge. But their capacities are lame and limited by the preceding struggle, and they need assistance from an external party to hold the rules, provide technical capacity, ensure security, supervise reconciliation and justice, jump-start functions, give training, and provide resources, among others. Leaving all this to the unassisted parties is asking the sick and wounded person to cure himself.

The great U.S. tendency to wait until the mess in a foreign arena is beyond local capacities, roll up our sleeves and set it straight in short order, and then go back home is shortsighted and outmoded. The United States showed that it learned this lesson *en gros* in its shift of attitude from the League of Nations after World War I to the United Nations after World War II, but it has not learned the lesson in detail, in specific applications, and even its attitude toward the UN is one of suspicion and underutilization. If deadly conflict and state collapse are going to compel U.S. attention in extremis, they need also to compel preventive attention before the extreme moment and regenerative attention after the immediate intervention. That means attention to the reinstatement of a state apparatus, functioning well enough to keep the conflict managed, move to its resolution, and prevent its reemergence.

Excuses and Misperceptions

In all thirty instances in the six collapsing states, early warnings were more than adequate, the proposed measures had a good chance of succeeding, and their cost in lives and money was foreseeably much less than the final cost of the unarrested collapse and conflict in reality. It is not that the tools were unavailable at the time or that their manuals had not yet been invented; it is that current ways of thinking blocked their use. Excuses generally came in common but flawed perceptions of international politics.

1. "It is hard to see a conflict coming so as to take action in time." Yet early warning abounds, as already discussed. Even if the future date of a crisis may not be able to be identified beforehand, plenty of information is publicly available about impending conflict situations and even about likely crisis points (except in the UN Secretariat, which continues to be woefully bereft of intelligence and early awareness facilities). The real problem is rather one of sorting out likely crises from simply dangerous situations. We do not abandon hurricane warnings simply because they do not always produce hurricanes. Instead of hiding behind the problem, it is important to work at it, to improve techniques for identifying turning points and opportunities for positive intervention, and to devise appropriate responses to uncertainty, such as contingency planning and positioning. Military preparedness emphasizes contingency plans; diplomatic readiness can equally benefit from forward-looking scenarios.[7] Any plans that there may have been for dealing with a post-Mobutu, post-Siad, post-Doe, or indeed post-Yugoslav situation before the triggering event were not evident in the response. If moments of opportunity are not immediately available in impending conflicts, third parties can position themselves—indicate availability, identify goals and values, open communications—in preparation for later action.

2. "Intervention conflicts with past policy, in the area or elsewhere." Beyond the shield of interest, already discussed, the most specific reason for inaction is that the measures were contrary to policy, which supported the status quo even when the status quo was falling apart. It is rather hard to paint a very positive picture of Doe, Mobutu, Milosevic, Siad Barre, Duvalier, or Cedras, but support for them was supposed to avoid "adventurism" or "a leap into the unknown" or a reputedly unsavory alternative; Western supporters, in varying degrees, clung to a blind faith in friends who turned out to be the problem. Mobutu and Doe were long viewed as bulwarks against communism, and their support and assistance for U.S.

African policy was viewed with gratitude. In dealing with Zaire, the United States was often in the lead in trying to combine transition with continuity; it long held to the policy of "Mobutu or chaos," and the whole Troika worked hard to make that mantra come true.[8] U.S. policy was committed to the continued independence of Lebanon under its 1943 National Pact, in part because of the radicalism of the opponents, and it held to that policy to the point of ignoring neighboring states' interests and Lebanese demographics. Thus, in many cases, the safe status quo was preferred to risky change, and the state kept sliding down the slippery slope of conflict toward collapse. A careful evaluation of the dangers of deepening the vacuum inherent in continuing support for "the devil we know" would show the need to support measures—elections, convocations, depositions—that make a clear break with the old order and ease in the new.

3. "More important things are going on, and the United States can only do one crisis at a time." The idea of a one-crisis superpower is simply not true in the absolute. Furthermore, given the fact that the proposed preventive diplomacy démarches were not of crisis magnitude, many should have been possible, even during the time of pressing events elsewhere. Since the needed preventions were not of global proportions, they could have been the subject of a delegation of authority and handled, with support from higher level, at the assistant secretary and regional bureau level. The license given to Assistant Secretary Crocker to handle the Namibian-Angolan issue in the 1980s and the concentration of the Africa Bureau of the State Department on Sudan during the Afghani and Iraqi crises in the early 2000s are good examples.[9]

Nonetheless, a crisis such as the Gulf War, which dominated U.S. and UN attention from late 1990 through 1991, blocking attention to a number of promising démarches, especially in Somalia and Yugoslavia, does point to one limitation—the difficulty of securing support and cooperation from allies on several projects at the same time. Such needs overrode the possibilities of building alliances and coalitions for preventive actions in 1991, when the United States was already too deeply in political debt to its allies on the Gulf front to be able to contract additional debts on other issues.[10] The experience shows how dangerous it is to allow one crisis to monopolize attentions and energies so thoroughly. Nikita Khrushchev knew this, in springing the Hungarian crisis during the Suez crisis in 1956.

Other contextual distractions involved Cold War considerations in the late 1980s in cases such as Lebanon, Liberia, Haiti, and Somalia. But Cold War inhibitions on the U.S. side were usually the result of a bogus calculation. Support and participation in the Damascus and Lausanne negotiations on Lebanon would have left the United States in a stronger position in the Middle East, particularly in regard to Syria, the ally claimed by the Soviet Union, but also with Saudi Arabia and of course with Muslims as well as Christians in Lebanon. The idea that Doe and Siad Barre were bulwarks against communism in Africa, which was invoked to inhibit preventive diplomacy in 1985 and 1988, respectively, is as far-fetched as they come, and even more so since their oppositions were Communist in neither case. Using the Cold War as the reason for inaction was based on faulty perceptions of danger and calculations of benefit.

Another policy distraction where one policy got in the way of another related to the handling of the post-Soviet evolution. Although policymakers felt that keeping Yugoslavia together might impinge unfavorably on efforts to help the Soviet Union fall apart peacefully, such reasoning was not beyond challenge. A loose federation or confederation of Yugoslav states would be similar to the Confederation of Independent States (CIS), a mechanism that helped smooth over the post-Soviet evolution. Even more pertinently, disintegration of the Soviet Union stopped short of the disintegration of the Russian Federation, whose continuity was a pertinent model for maintaining the Yugoslav Federation, since Yugoslavia was much more similar to the multiethnic Russian Federation before and after the USSR than to the imperial Soviet Union. Even more curious was the German reasoning that the self-determination that brought East and West Germany together should be invoked to tear Yugoslavia apart. A more straightforward logic would indicate that the unity that was favorable to German security and welfare should be so for Yugoslavia as well. Policy arguments transposed from one place to another can account for missed opportunities, but they need not, if correct logic is used.

4. "Resolution by third parties is not feasible in internal conflicts, since only the parties themselves can manage their own conflicts, and they are historic enemies always at conflict anyhow." Such thinking inhibited timely intervention into conflict and collapse in Yugoslavia, Somalia, Zaire, and Liberia, where ethnic enmity, segmentary politics, secessionist tendencies, and tribal hatreds, respectively, were cited by policymakers knowledgeable enough to know about the country's characteristics but not to know how they operated. Yet in none of these cases had conflict been a permanent condition. Although it is understood that third parties cannot remove the underlying causes and perceptions of conflict, they can undertake and encourage measures to set the conflicting parties' relations onto a new course. Parties in conflict need help; they tend to be too absorbed in their conflict to be able to see and adopt positive-sum exit measures. The historic record shows that discovering and navigating the path between conflict and resolution usually requires the services of a third-party

pilot. On the way, specific measures can be taken to reduce the chances of escalation and crisis; if conflict is the work of political entrepreneurs working a dangerous context, measures can be envisaged to reduce combustible situations and isolate the pyromaniacs.

5. "There is no political will for taking casualties and getting involved in other peoples' conflicts in the post–Cold-War world." Much policy inaction is grounded in the fervent hope that the crisis will go away. There never is any absolutely convincing evidence that it will not, or that things will turn out as badly as they seem. In the absence of irrefutable confirmatory intelligence about impending conflicts, there is always the danger of appearing to be crying "Wolf!" and of evoking the response from superiors, "Go away with your stories of smoke; can't you see I'm busy putting out fires!"[11] The uncertainties of prevention tend to work against early action and favor last-minute responses when it is almost too late. The 2003 invasion of Iraq is an eloquent example of all the risks involved in meeting a clear and future danger, and its controversial nature will throw a long shadow over preventive initiatives in the future. As a preventive—not "preemptive"—measure, the need and wisdom of the invasion will be forever debated, despite a danger that appeared convincing enough to policymakers at the time of decision.

Fear of casualties plays on will as well. The basis for official fear of military deaths, laid by the Bush administration as early as 1991 by the way the casualtyless Gulf War was touted, was heightened in June 1993 by the slaying of the UN Pakistani soldiers and then U.S. rangers, and was played to the hilt by the Clinton administration. The attitude has been consistently instilled and propagated, not just by the military, but by the political leaders who have bought into the idea of protecting U.S. soldiers rather than U.S. interests. The lesson of Somalia in the United States was one of nonengagement, but the lesson of Somalia abroad was that the U.S. military can be defeated and a few casualties will make it withdraw; it has taken ten years to overcome both lessons. Instead of developing such themes as leadership, post–Cold War order, UN usefulness to U.S. objectives, regional security regimes, protection of human rights, and values as interest, the United States, joined by other Western countries, hid behind its own rhetoric about casualties even when the danger of deaths was minimal. As a result, it allowed forces of disorder and spirals of violence to prove its point. A little exemplary firmness in Liberia, Somalia, and Yugoslavia in 1990 or in Liberia, Somalia, Zaire, Yugoslavia, and Haiti in 1991 would have involved no troops in most instances and few troops (mostly non-U.S.) in the rest and would have forestalled much larger troop use and danger later. The absence of such a response showed the forces of disorder in these countries that they could get away with it. Thus, a firm response not only inhibits specific disorder in the short run; it also inhibits its escalation in the long run.

What then makes statesmen willing to take risks for prevention? No doubt a mixture of calculations—a certainty of impending danger and an interest in reducing it, a sense of moral obligation and international legitimacy, an awareness of future opportunity costs, and a belief in an ability to do the job. The decision to act is captured in a number of commonplace phrases: "it can't go on like this," "handle it now, or it will come back to haunt us," "this time they've gone too far," "we can't let this happen," "act before it's too late," or "while we still have a chance." Although the strategic pressure for engagement in conflict management that operated under the Cold War has been removed, other justifications are compelling in the post–Cold War period, as seen in regard to diplomatic and military interventions in Sudan, Afghanistan, Colombia, and Israel in the 2000s. U.S. polls show that the public will support conflict management intervention abroad if the government articulates a clear strategy and defines its aims. The cost of late action and lost opportunities, the pressure of public opinion, the vigilance of a responsible press, and above all vigorous leadership can redefine the terms of political will. Thus, the decision rests on feelings of future versus present certainties—the certainty of impending disaster and the certainty of present effectiveness—tied together by a moral and interest-based responsibility to act. Lack of will is a state of mind, but it is also a calculation. Press and public need to work on the first, analysts and activists on the second.

Most broadly, the major reasons for missed opportunities lie at the feet of some of the leading tenets of the study of international relations, which in turn influence policymakers' thinking on what is possible and desirable. International relations theory is torn between the realist tenets of state supremacy and the liberal and constructivist assumptions that the state is increasingly bypassed by a multitude of other actors. To the first, perhaps paradoxically, what is not already a state does not matter, and to some, what is not a great power does not matter at all.[12] The need to construct and support legitimate authority in the softer areas of the globe where it does not exist is not considered and is not deemed important to the interest of the major states. To the liberals and constructivists, the rise of other actors than the state draws attention away from the need for a state to perform essential functions for domestic society.

The school of scholarship that urged "bringing the state back in" in the 1970s and 1980s has paled, as attention swings elsewhere.[13] Yet the classic functions of the state are necessary to modern society, even as other agencies take on other functions that cut across state boundaries. States provide an overarching sense of identity and allegiance that empowers their institutions to function in the name of the population. They regulate transactions and ensure efficiencies that need continual renegotiation in their absence. They provide standardized means of conflict management, problem solving, law enforcement, and the dispensing of justice as well as standards of economic exchange, justice, education, and social interaction that no other agency can offer. They assure external defense and international cooperation. Absent an agency to perform these functions, conflict over them has found its cause, and the management of that conflict is inoperable.

In its focus on relative gains, international relations theory in its dominant realist expression lends credence to the notion that state collapse and deadly conflict are of interest only to the extent that they affect the competitive standing of the major states vis-à-vis each other.[14] From this point of view, support for the debilitating regimes of Doe, Siad Barre, and Mobutu was important for the United States as long as it kept them out of Soviet (and Libyan) influence, and Yugoslavia mattered as long as it could be kept out of the Soviet orbit. A State Department official justified support for Doe in the 1985 elections by saying, "We gained five years of support in the Cold War."[15] When the Cold War passed, this justification of interest passed with it. The end of the Cold War is history, but the legacy it leaves of relative gains deprives conflict control and state restoration of an argument for policymakers' attention.

Relative gains thinking exists, but it makes conflict management more difficult. The Fashoda complex that inhibited French and American cooperation in Zaire and Rwanda, the rivalry between Nigeria and Francophile states over Liberia, the competition for influence between Ethiopia and Egypt over Somalia, the rivalry among the EC members over their relative positions within the European Community and vis-à-vis successor republics of Yugoslavia,[16] the strident confrontation between India and Pakistan, and the Arab cold war[17] and the Arab-Israeli hot wars over Lebanon were all the products of relative gains thinking that blocked the resolution of conflict and the restoration of the target states. Yet that resolution and restoration was in the interest of the blocking states, who were prevented from moving forward in constructive, collective, and evenhanded involvement by the habit of looking over their shoulder at their rivals. The alternative conceptualization, of absolute gains, relates to the achievement of a state's interests without regard to other states' positions.

In teaching relative gains as the sole criterion of interest, international relations theory gives bad advice in taking poor practice for the norm.

Current international relations theory not only clouds an appreciation of agents but also distorts an understanding of means. Power is taught as essentially military, and the power of states is judged by their military capabilities. Politics is expected to follow the military, obediently. It was this type of thinking that led a top U.S. diplomat to remind the Lebanese that they "did lose the war" and to forget the politics of a durable peace, that made mediators see warlords as the agents of peace in Liberia and Somalia and forget the importance of civil society leaders, that let intervenors treat the junta and its goons as the government in power in Haiti rather than as a usurper, and, later, that let the preventive intervention in Iraq in 2003 focus on a rapid military victory in the expectation that indigenous political support would rapidly fall in line. *Power,* correctly understood, means merely "to be able" to effectuate policy (in French the noun and the verb are the same), in which force is only one element. The need to remind the public that "soft" power is useful too is only testimony to dominance of "hard" power thinking.[18] The underplaying—and underfunding—of diplomacy is a natural result of this conceptual misunderstanding, and yet, as noted, seizing opportunity is primarily a diplomatic action.

Indeed, most broadly, the most serious source of error in international relations theory lies in its weak database. By assuming that what states did is what they do, it mistakes human choice for givens, individual errors for scientific determinations, and good or bad decisions for the only decisions possible. In this view, there are no missed opportunities, because state behavior is determined by data-based laws. But the vote of the League of Nations compared with the vote on the UN, the sides in the debate over NATO enlargement, the very different outcomes of the 1978 and 2000 Camp David mediations between Israelis and Arabs, and the repeated failures compared to the ultimate but tardy success of attempts to end the Liberian, Lebanese, Haitian, Mozambican, or Bosnian civil wars can neither be explained nor prescriptively analyzed by this approach. The results are then presented as regularities derived from the observation of scientific data, with the recommendations that the military is the only source of power, relative gains are the only motivation, states are impelled by a drive for power, norms and institutions have no impact on state actions, and values have no role in determining vital interests. Armed with such notions, decisionmakers feel justified in pursuing narrow understandings of their own possibilities and responsibilities. To understand and improve the behavior of statesmen, acting in the name of their states, it is necessary to separate what states do badly from what they do well and to study their decision moments, in order to learn from their missed opportunities.

Clear and Future Dangers

Beyond clear lessons and flawed perceptions relevant across the millennia concerning preventive action in times of deadly conflict and state collapse lies a broader and deeper change in the philosophical basis of such action.[19] Until recently, states were protected from intervention by the Westphalian doctrine of sovereignty as protection.[20] Sovereignty was seen as an indivisible attribute that prevented interference in internal affairs, protected smaller states from larger state impingement, and provided impunity for a government's actions toward its citizenry. Abuses on the third count, in the context of a shrinking world of permeable states, led in the 1990s to intervention by the UN into internal affairs, for both security and humanitarian reasons, in northern Iraq and in Somalia, respectively. Despite the clear prohibition of interference in sovereign states' internal affairs in the UN Charter (articles 2.1 and 2.7), UN Secretary-General Boutros-Ghali, in his *Agenda for Peace* in 1992, declared that "the time of absolute and exclusive sovereignty, however, has passed; its theory was never matched by reality. It is the task of leaders of States today to understand this and to find a balance between the needs of good internal governance and the requirements of an ever more interdependent world."[21] His successor, Kofi Annan, has reiterated the same notion that "sovereignty implies responsibility, not just power."[22] Sovereignty as responsibility means that states are responsible for the individual security and welfare of their people, that other states have a responsibility to help them in accomplishing this task, and that when the original state defaults on its responsibility, other states have the responsibility to exercise it in its absence.[23]

Sovereignty as responsibility is as significant but also as dangerous a doctrine as its predecessor. The difference is that the old doctrine was dangerous for the people of the repressive state, whereas the new doctrine is dangerous for its government. Once the idea has been launched, the international community faces the delicate task of defining the conditions of its operation, so that it not mean just a return to a pre-Westphalian acceptance of interference by the large in the affairs of the small. The important statement by the International Commission on Intervention and State Sovereignty (ICISS) urges the UN General Assembly to "affirm . . . the idea of sovereignty as responsibility" and seeks to set out threshold and precautionary criteria for its exercise.[24] Two sides of the criteria are important and need further sharpening beyond the initial statement.

One side of the coin is the responsibility to act, the subject of emphasis in this study. Missed opportunities in the last quarter of the twentieth century emerged from a weak sense of the need for action by those who had an interest-as-responsibility to do so. Alerted by clear warnings of impending conflict and collapse, they decided not to act, or to act too little, claiming they had no dog in the fight and ignoring the fact that it was the fight itself that was the dog: the interest of the intervenor was not in backing one side over another but in preventing the dogfight and its destructive violence. Responsible states and NGOs had an interest in involvement, when irresponsible states created the conditions of their own conflict and collapse. This responsibility was exercised on occasion in the 1990s, in Mozambique, in the initial operations in Somalia, laggardly in Haiti, in Cambodia, in Burundi, in Norway (the Oslo talks on Israel-Palestine), among others; it was exercised again in the 2000s, in Sudan, limitedly in Côte d'Ivoire, in Afghanistan, in Iraq (where it would have been better justified in humanitarian terms rather than against weapons of mass destruction), among others. The needs and mechanisms of responsibility are the same in one decade as in another, as laid out in this study. In the twenty-first as in the twentieth century, states and NGOs have a responsibility to act to prevent egregious infringements of security and welfare.

The other side of the coin contains the limitations on and definitions of that responsibility to act. The Iraq invasion has shifted the debate from early action to its governing limitations and raised important questions about the authority of a coalition of the willing, the responsibility of the international community to live up to its own Security Council resolutions, the degree of evidence required for prevention, the conditions of deposition, and the estimations of effectiveness; many of these are questions raised for further discussion in the ICISS statement.[25] With or without Iraq, however, it is natural in the enunciation of a new doctrine that the debate turn to the conditions of its operation and particularly the limitations to prevent its abuse.

But one side of the coin should not cover the other. The responsibility to act in the twenty-first century is not suspended until the conditions of action are fully worked out, any more than the debate over criteria is suspended until international politics is over. Intellectual debate is important to clarifying these conditions, but it remains abstract without policy initiatives to test and apply it. As with any hypothesis, logical or internal verification is important in establishing the idea, but empirical or external verification is the second, crucial test of its validity. As the invasion of Iraq has tested the ICISS attempt to lay out conditions for intervention, so other actions will help sharpen the norms for the exercise of responsibility in preventing conflict and collapse. The debate focuses primarily on deposition as a policy; mediation, convocation, consolidation, and enforcement all remain available tools with much less controversial conditions for their operation (above all because they involve the consent of the parties in one way or another). While the debate on standards goes on, as it must, states and NGOs need to act in pursuit of their responsibility to prevent conflict and state collapse, with its costly effects on populations and relations.

Notes

1. Enderlin, *Le rêve brisé*.
2. Ward, "Training for Peacemaking," in Zartman, *Peacemaking in International Conflict*.
3. Lyons, *Demilitarizing Politics*.
4. Collier et al., *Breaking the Conflict Trap;* Arnson and Zartman, *Rethinking the Economics of War*.
5. On the need for external guarantors, see Walter, *Committing to Peace*.
6. See Deutsch and Foltz, *Nation-Building;* Riggs, "The Theory of Political Development."
7. "The bureaucracy abhors contingency plans," Quandt, *Peace Process* (1993), 149.
8. Forbes Pachter, "Our Man in Kinshasa"; Schatzberg, *Mobutu or Chaos?*
9. Crocker, *High Noon in Southern Africa*.
10. Another conclusion is that preventive diplomacy lost its opportunity throughout 1990, when careful attention and appropriate responses to signals from Baghdad might well have prevented the crisis and left the United States and other states and organizations free to deal with other problems of state collapse. See Jentleson, *With Friends Like These;* Karsh and Rautsi, "Why Saddam Invaded Kuwait"; Cooley, "Pre-War Gulf Diplomacy"; Mike Blakeley, "The Persian Gulf," in Brown and Rosecrance, *The Costs of Conflict,* 109–130.
11. The problem is graphically captured by a discussion of UN Secretariat procedure in regard to a crucial memo from the field from UN force commander General Romeo Dallaire just before the Rwandan genocide: "[Secretary-General] Boutros-Ghali's aide told me that he was certain 'Boutros didn't see the actual document,' but that it was likely he had 'heard the essence of it, in summary.' [Deputy Under Secretary-General Iqbal] Riza said, 'That's credible.' During that period, daily cable traffic was 'a stack about a foot high,' Riza explained, and Dallaire's fax 'was not a report on a serious incident where there were casualties, or something like that,' but 'something that was forecast.' If the forecast had come true 'a week later or something,' Riza said, then 'I think they would have said, "Yes, there is this fax, and this is what happened."' Philip Gourevitch, "The Genocide Fax," *New Yorker,* 11 May 1998, 44.

12. Waltz, *Theory of International Politics,* 72.

13. Evans, Rueschmayer, and Skocpol, *Bringing the State Back In.*

14. Powell, "Absolute and Relative Gains in IR Theory."

15. Confidential interview by author.

16. Libal, *Limits of Persuasion;* Wynaendts, *L'Engrenage.*

17. Malcolm Kerr, *The Arab Cold War* (New York: Oxford University Press, 1967); Patrick Seale, *The Struggle for Syria* (New York: Oxford University Press, 1965).

18. Nye, "Soft Power."

19. Deng et al., *Sovereignty as Responsibility.* For a review of the recent evolution of the idea and its relation to the methods of prevention, see Zartman, "Early and 'Early Late' Prevention."

20. Stephen Krasner, *Sovereignty: Organized Hypocrisy* (Princeton, NJ: Princeton University Press, 1999).

21. Boutros-Ghali, *Agenda for Peace*, 44.

22. Kofi Annan, "Intervention," 35, Ditchley Park, UK, Ditchley Foundation Lecture, 28 June 1998, 2.

23. Deng et al., *Sovereignty as Responsibility;* a slightly different version is found in Evans and Sahnoun, *The Responsibility to Protect*, 13.

24. Evans and Sahnoun, *The Responsibility to Protect,* 74 (without acknowledging the source of the term) and chaps. 4, 6, and 7.

25. Other efforts to engage the debate include Jentleson, *Opportunities Missed, Opportunities Seized;* Zartman, *Preventive Negotiation;* Hamburg, *No More Killing Fields;* Rubin, *Blood on the Doorstep;* Rotberg, *When States Fail;* Steiner, *Collective Preventive Diplomacy;* Chesterman, Ignatieff, and Thakur, *Making States Work;* and the *Report of the High-Level Panel on UN Reform.*

Acronyms

ACTORD   NATO action order
ACTWARN   NATO activation warning
ADF   Arab Deterrent Force
AFDL   Alliance of Democratic Forces for the Liberation of
     Congo
AFL   Liberian Armed Forces
AID   Agency for International Development
AU   African Union
CDG   chicken dilemma game
CIA   Central Intelligence Agency
CIS   Confederation of Independent States
CNN   Cable News Network
CNS   sovereign national conference
CSCE   Conference on Security and Cooperation in Europe
DDRR   disarmament, demobilization, resettlement, and
     reintegration
DDRRR   disarmament, demobilization, repatriation, resettlement,
     and reintegration
DPKO   UN Department of Peace-Keeping Operations
DSP   Special Presidential Division (Zaire)
EC   European Community
ECOMOG   Economic Community of West African States Monitoring
     Group
ECOWAS   Economic Community of West African States
ECU   European Currency Unit
EU   European Union
FAd'H   Armed Forces of Haiti

FAR	Rwandan Armed Forces
FAZ	Zairean Armed Forces
FIS	Islamic Salvation Front (Algeria)
FRAPH	Front for the Advancement and Progress of Haiti
Frelimo	Mozambique Liberation Front
FRY	Federal Republic of Yugoslavia
GDP	gross domestic product
HCR	High Council of the Republic (Zaire)
ICFY	International Conference on the Former Yugoslavia
ICISS	International Commission on Intervention and State Sovereignty
IDF	Israeli Defense Force
IDP	internally displaced person
IFI	international financial institutions
IFMC	Inter-Faith Mediation Council (Liberia)
IGAD	Inter-Governmental Authority on Development
IGADD	Inter-Governmental Agency on Drought and Development
IGNU	Interim Government of National Unity (Liberia)
IMF	International Monetary Fund
IMTD	Institute for Multi-Track Diplomacy
INN	International Negotiation Network (of Carter Center)
INPFL	Independent National Patriotic Front (Liberia)
IRI	International Republican Institute
JCS	joint security committee
JNA	Yugoslav National Army
KFOR	NATO military force to Kosovo
KLA	Kosovo Liberation Army
KVM	Kosovo Verification Mission
LAP	Liberian Action Party
LAS	Arab League
LCC	Liberian Council of Churches
LDF	Lofa Defense Force (Liberia)
LDK	Democratic League of Kosovo
LF	Lebanese Front
LNM	Lebanese National Movement
LNTG	Liberian National Transition Government
LPC	Liberian Peace Council
LPP	Liberian Peoples Party
LURD	Liberians United for Revolution and Democracy
MARG	Marine Amphibious Readiness Group
MNF	multinational force

MPLA	Peoples Movement for the Liberation of Angola
NAMFREL	National Movement for Free Elections
NATO	North Atlantic Treaty Organization
NDI	National Democratic Institute
NED	National Endowment for Democracy
NIF	National Islamic Front (Sudan)
NGO	nongovernmental organization
NMCL	National Muslim Council of Liberia
NPFL	National Patriotic Front of Liberia
NSC	National Security Council
OAS	Organization of American States
OAU	Organization of African Unity
ODA	Official Development Assistance
OFDA	USAID Office of Foreign Disaster Assistance
OIC	Organization of the Islamic Conference
OPIC	Overseas Private Investment Corporation
OSCE	Organization for Security and Cooperation in Europe
PA&E	Pacific Architects and Engineers
PDD	Presidential Decision Directive
PLA	Palestine Liberation Army
PLO	Palestine Liberation Organization
PSP	Progressive Socialist Party
PT	transitional parliament (Zaire)
Renamo	Mozambique National Resistance
RUF	Revolutionary United Front (Sierra Leone)
SADC	Southern African Development Community
SDA	Gadabursi Dir (Somalia)
SDS	Serbian Democratic Party
SMC	Standing Mediation Committee (of ECOWAS)
SNA	Somali National Alliance
SNF	Somali National Front
SNM	Somali National Movement
SPLM	Sudan Peoples Liberation Movement
SPM	Somali Patriotic Movement
SRSG	special representative of the UN Secretary-General
SSDF	Mijertein Darod (Somalia)
TNC	Transitional National Council (Somalia)
UDPS	Democratic Union for Social Progress (Zaire)
ULIMO	United Liberation Movement for Democracy (Liberia)
UNAMSIL	UN Armed Mission in Sierra Leone
UNDP	United Nations Development Programme

UNIFIL	UN Interim Force in Lebanon
UNITA	National Union for the Total Independence of Angola
UNITAF	Unified Task Force (UN)
UNOMIL	UN military observers
UNOSOM	UN Operation in Somalia
UNSC	UN Security Council
UP	Unity Party (Liberia)
UPP	United Peoples Party (Liberia)
USAID	U.S. Agency for International Development
USC	United Somali Congress
USF	Issa Dir (Somalia)
USIA	U.S. Information Agency
WEU	Western European Union

Selected Bibliography

Abdullah, Ibrahim. "Bush Path to Destruction: The Origin and Character of the Revolutionary United Front/Sierra Leone." *Journal of Modern African Studies* 36, no. 2 (1998): 203–236.

Abul-Husn, Latif. *The Lebanese Conflict: Looking Inward.* Boulder, CO: Lynne Rienner, 1998.

Ahrens, Geert. *Negotiating Ethnic Conflict in Former Yugoslavia.* Washington, DC: Woodrow Wilson Center Press, 2005.

Alao, Abiodun. *The Burden of Collective Goodwill.* Brookfield, VT: Ashgate, 1998.

Alie, Joe. "Background to the Conflict." In Anatole Ayissi and Robin-Edward Poulton, eds., *Bound to Cooperate: Conflict, Peace and People in Sierra Leone,* 15–36. Geneva: UNIDIR, 2000.

Allard, Kenneth. *Somalia Operations: Lessons Learned.* Washington, DC: National Defense University Press, 1995.

Almond, Mark. *Europe's Backyard War: The War in the Balkans.* London: Mandarin, 1995.

Aristide, Jean-Bertrand. *Aristide: An Autobiography.* Maryknoll, NY: Orbis Books, 1993.

Arlinghaus, Bruce. *African Security Issues.* Boulder, CO: Westview Press, 1984.

Armon, Jeremy, and Andy Carl, eds. "The Liberian Peace Process 1990–1996." *Accord: An International Review of Peace Initiatives,* no. 1. London: Conciliation Resources, 1998.

Arnson, Cynthia, and I. William Zartman, eds. *Rethinking the Economics of War: The Intersection of Need, Creed and Greed.* Baltimore: Johns Hopkins University Press; Washington, DC: Woodrow Wilson Center, 2005.

Assefa, Hizkias. *Mediation of Civil Wars.* Boulder, CO: Westview Press, 1987.

Avi-Ran, Reuven. *Involvement in Lebanon Since 1975.* Boulder, CO: Westview Press, 1991.

Baker, James A., III. *The Politics of Diplomacy: Revolution, War and Peace, 1989–1992.* New York: Putnam, 1995.

Baker, Pauline, and Angeli Weller. *An Analytical Model of Internal Conflict and State Collapse.* Washington, DC: Fund for Peace, 1998.

Baldwin, David. "The Power of Positive Sanctions." *World Politics* 24 (1971): 19–38.

Bayart, Jean-François. *La politique africaine de François Mitterrand*. Paris: Karthala, 1984.

Beloff, Nora. *An Avoidable War*. London: New European Publications, 1997.

Bercovitch, Jacob, ed. *Resolving International Conflicts*. Boulder, CO: Lynne Rienner, 1996.

———. *Studies in International Mediation: Essays in Honor of Jeffrey Z. Rubin*. New York: Palgrave Macmillan, 2003.

Bercovitch, Jacob, and Jeffrey Z. Rubin, eds. *Mediation in International Relations*. New York: St. Martin's Press, 1992.

Bernard, Jessie, et al. *The Nature of Conflict*. Paris: UNESCO, 1957.

Bert, Wayne. *The Reluctant Superpower: United States' Policy in Bosnia 1991–95*. New York: St. Martin's Press, 1997.

Beydoun, Ahmed. *Le Liban: Itinéraires d'une guerre civile*. Paris: Karthala-CERMOC, 1993.

Blakeley, Mike. "Haiti." In Michael Brown and Richard Rosecrance, eds., *Costs of Conflict*, 91–108. Lanham, MD: Rowman and Littlefield, 1999.

———. "The Persian Gulf." In Michael Brown and Richard Rosecrance, eds., *Costs of Conflict*, 109–130. Lanham, MD: Rowman and Littlefield, 1999.

Bongartz, Maria. *The Civil War in Somalia: Its Genesis and Dynamics*. Current African Issues 11. Uppsala: Scandinavian Institute of African Studies, 1991.

Bonner, Michael, Negan Reif, and Mark Tessler, eds. "Islam, Democracy and the State in Algeria." Special issue, *The Journal of Modern North African Studies* 9, no. 2 (Summer 2004).

Botes, Jannie. *An Exit Interview with "Hank" Cohen*. CSIS Africa Notes 147. Washington, DC: Center for Strategic and International Studies, 1993.

Boutros-Ghali, Boutros. *Agenda for Peace*. UN Report no. S/23500 (31 January 1992). New York: United Nations, 1995.

———. *Unvanquished*. New York: Random House, 1999.

Brams, Steven J. *Negotiation Games: Applying Game Theory to Bargaining and Arbitration*. New York: Routledge, 1990.

Brown, Kenneth. "Mediation by Influence: American Policy Toward the Liberian War." Ph.D. diss., University of Cape Coast, 1995.

Brown, Michael, ed. *Ethnic Conflict and International Security*. Princeton, NJ: Princeton University Press, 1993.

———. *The International Dimensions of Internal Conflict*. Cambridge, MA: MIT Press, 1996.

Brown, Michael, and Richard Rosecrance, eds. *The Costs of Conflict: Prevention and Cure in the Global Arena*. Lanham, MD: Rowman and Littlefield, 1999.

Carter, Jimmy, et al. *The 1990 General Elections in Haiti*. Washington, DC: National Democratic Institute, 1991.

Chesterman, Simon, Michael Ignatieff, and Ramesh Thakur, eds. *Making States Work*. New York: UNU Press, 2005.

Chipman, John. *French Power in Africa*. Cambridge, UK: Blackwell, 1989.

Clarke, Walter, and Jeffrey Herbst, eds. *Learning from Somalia*. Boulder, CO: Westview Press, 1997.

Clement, Caty. *Common Patterns of State Collapse: A Comparative Study of Former Yugoslavia, Lebanon, and Somalia.* Louvain, Belgium: Catholic University of Louvain, 2003.

Cohen, Herman J. *Intervening in Africa: Superpower Peacemaking in a Troubled Continent.* New York: St. Martin's Press, 2000.

Cohen, Leonard. *Broken Bonds: Yugoslavia's Disintegration and Balkan Politics in Transition.* Boulder, CO: Westview Press, 1995.

Coll, Alberto. *Operation Restore Hope.* Pew Case Study 518. Washington, DC: Institute for the Study of Diplomacy, Georgetown University, 1997.

Collier, Paul, et al. *Breaking the Conflict Trap: Civil War and Development Policy.* Washington, DC: World Bank; New York: Oxford University Press, 2003.

Cooley, John. "Pre-War Gulf Diplomacy." *Survival* 33 (1991): 125–139.

Corbin, Jane. *The Norway Channel.* New York: Atlantic Monthly Press, 1994.

Cortright, David, ed. *The Price of Peace: Incentive and International Conflict Prevention.* Lanham, MD: Rowman and Littlefield, 1997.

Coser, Lewis. *Continuities in the Study of Social Conflict.* New York: Free Press, 1967.

———. *The Functions of Social Conflict.* Glencoe, IL: Free Press, 1956.

Cousens, Elizabeth, and Chetan Kumar, eds. *Peacebuilding as Politics.* Boulder, CO: Lynne Rienner, 2001.

Crocker, Chester A. *High Noon in Southern Africa.* New York: Norton, 1992.

Crocker, Chester A., Fen Osler Hampson, and Pamela Aall, eds. *Grasping the Nettle.* Washington, DC: United States Institute of Peace Press, 2004.

———. *Herding Cats: Multiparty Mediation in a Complex World.* Washington, DC: United States Institute of Peace Press, 1999.

———. *Turbulent Peace.* Washington, DC: United States Institute of Peace Press, 2001.

Curtius, Mary. "US Defends Actions on Uprising." *The Boston Globe,* 2 August 1990.

Cusimano, Maryann. *Operation Restore Hope: The Bush Administration's Decision to Intervene in Somalia.* Pew Case Study 463. Washington, DC: Institute for the Study of Diplomacy, Georgetown University, 1995.

Daalder, Ivo. *Getting to Dayton: The Making of America's Bosnia Policy.* Washington, DC: Brookings Institution Press, 2000.

Daalder, Ivo, and Michael O'Hanlon. *Winning Ugly: NATO's War to Save Kosovo.* Washington, DC: Brookings Institution Press, 2000.

Dawisha, Adeed. *Syria and the Lebanese Crisis.* New York: St. Martin's Press, 1980.

Deng, Francis, et al. *Sovereignty as Responsibility.* Washington, DC: Brookings Institution Press, 1996.

Deutsch, Karl, and William Foltz, eds. *Nation-Building.* New York: Atherton, 1963.

Drysdale, Alasdair, and Raymond Hinnebusch. *Syria and the Middle East Peace Process.* New York: Council on Foreign Relations, 1991.

Dumoulin, André, ed. *La France et la sécurité en Afrique subsaharienne.* Dossier 825. Paris: Documentation française, 1999.

Dunn, D. Elwood, and S. Byron Tarr. *Liberia: A National Polity in Transition.* Metuchen, NJ: Scarecrow Press, 1988.

Enderlin, Charles. *Le rêve brisé: Histoire de l'échec du processus de paix au Proche-Orient (1995–2002)*. Paris: Fayard, 2002.

Esty, Daniel, et al. *State Failure Task Force Reports I, II, III*. McLean, VA: CIA, 1996, 1998, 2000.

Evans, Gareth, and Mohamed Sahnoun. *The Responsibility to Protect: Report of the International Commission on Intervention and State Sovereignty*. Ottawa, Canada: International Development Research Center, 2001.

Evans, Peter, Dietrich Rueschmayer, and Theda Skocpol, eds. *Bringing the State Back In*. New York: Cambridge University Press, 1985.

Eyal, Jonathan. *Europe and Yugoslavia: Lessons from a Failure*. London: Royal United Services Institute for Defence Studies, 1993.

Farnham, Barbara, ed. *Avoiding Losses/Taking Risks: Prospect Theory and International Conflict*. Ann Arbor: University of Michigan Press, 1994.

Fauriol, Georges, ed. *The Haitian Challenge*. Washington, DC: Center for Strategic and International Studies, 1993.

Feil, Scott. *Preventing Genocide*. New York: Carnegie Commission for the Prevention of Deadly Conflict, 1998.

Forbes Pachter, Elise. "Our Man in Kinshasa." Ph.D. diss., Johns Hopkins University, 1987.

Furley, Oliver, ed. *Conflict in Africa*. London: I. B. Tauris, 1995.

George, Alexander, and Jane Holl. *The Warning-Response Problem and Missed Opportunities in Preventive Diplomacy*. New York: Carnegie Commission for the Prevention of Deadly Conflict, 1997.

George, Alexander, and William Simons, eds. *The Limits of Coercive Diplomacy*. 2nd ed. Boulder, CO: Westview Press, 1994.

George, Kevin, et al. *Liberia: Opportunities and Obstacles for Peace*. Washington, DC: Friends of Liberia, 1996.

German, Tracy. *Russia's Chechen War*. New York: Taylor and Francis, 2003.

Gerson, Allan. *The Kirkpatrick Mission: Diplomacy Without Apology*. New York: Free Press, 1991.

Gersony, Robert. *Why Somalis Flee: Synthesis of Accounts of Conflict Experience in Northern Somalia by Somali Refugees, Displaced Persons and Others*. Washington, DC: Bureau of Refugee Programs, 1989.

Gordon, David. *Lebanon: The Fragmented Nation*. London: Croom Helm, 1980.

Gow, James. *Triumph of the Lack of Will: International Diplomacy and the Yugoslav War*. New York: Columbia University Press, 1997.

Gow, James, and James D. D. Smith. *Peace-Making, Peace-Keeping: European Security and the Yugoslav Wars*. London Defence Studies 11. London: Brassey's for the Centre for Defence Studies, 1992.

Graham, John L., and Yoshihiro Sano. *Smart Bargaining: Doing Business with the Japanese*. New York: Harper and Row, 1989.

Haddad, Walid. *Lebanon: The Politics of Revolving Doors*. New York: Praeger, 1985.

Hagman, Lotta. *Lessons Learned: Peacebuilding in Haiti*. New York: International Peace Academy, 2002.

Haley, P. Edward, and Lewis W. Snider, eds. *Lebanon in Crisis*. Syracuse, NY: Syracuse University Press, 1979.

Hamburg, David. *No More Killing Fields: Preventing Deadly Conflict*. Lanham, MD: Rowman and Littlefield, 2002.

Hamburg, David, ed. *Preventive Diplomacy, Preventive Defense and Conflict Resolution.* New York: Carnegie Commission for the Prevention of Deadly Conflict, 1999.

Hampson, Fen Osler. *Nurturing Peace: Why Peace Settlements Succeed or Fail.* Washington, DC: United States Institute of Peace Press, 1996.

Hanf, Theodor. *Coexistence in Wartime Lebanon.* London: I. B. Tauris, 1993.

Hansen, Peter Viggo. *Haiti: A Textbook Case.* Institut for Statskundskab Working Paper 1997/6. Copenhagen: Københavns Universitetet Institut for Statskundskab, 1997.

Hare, Paul. *Angola's Last Best Chance for Peace: An Insider's Account of the Peace Process.* Washington, DC: United States Institute of Peace Press, 1998.

Harris, William W. *Faces of Lebanon: Sects, Wars, and Global Extensions.* Princeton, NJ: Markus Wiener, 1997.

Helman, Gerald B., and Steven R. Ratner. "Saving Failed States." *Foreign Policy* 89 (Winter 1992–1993): 3–20.

Henkin, Alice H., ed. *Honoring Human Rights.* Boston: Kluwer Law International, 2000.

Herz, John. *The Nation-State and the Crisis of World Politics.* New York: McKay, 1976.

Hirsch, John. *Sierra Leone.* Boulder, CO: Lynne Rienner, 2001.

Hirsch, John, and Robert Oakley. *Somalia and Operation Restore Hope.* Washington, DC: United States Institute of Peace Press, 1995.

Holbrooke, Richard. *To End a War.* New York: Modern Library, 1999.

Hudson, Michael. "Domestic Content and Perspectives." In Milton Esman and Shibley Telhami, eds., *International Organization and Ethnic Conflict,* 126–147. Ithaca, NY: Cornell University Press, 1995.

Hume, Cameron. *Ending Mozambique's War: The Role of Mediation and Good Offices.* Washington, DC: United States Institute of Peace Press, 1994.

Issa-Salwe, Abdisalam. *The Collapse of the Somali State.* London: Issa-Salwe and HAAN Associates, 1994.

Ivanov, Andrey. *The Balkans Divided: Nationalism, Minorities and Security.* Euro-Atlantic Security Studies, NATO Defense College. Frankfurt am Main: Peter Lang, 1996.

Jentleson, Bruce. *With Friends like These: Reagan, Bush and Saddam.* New York: W. W. Norton, 1994.

Jentleson, Bruce, ed. *Opportunities Missed, Opportunities Seized: Preventive Diplomacy in the Post–Cold War World.* Lanham, MD: Rowman and Littlefield, 2000.

Johnson, Michael. *Class and Client in Beirut: The Sunni Muslim Community and the Lebanese State, 1840–1985.* London: Ithaca Press, 1986.

Karsh, Efraim, and Inari Rautsi. "Why Saddam Invaded Kuwait." *Survival* 33 (1991): 18–39.

Kass, Ilana. *The Lebanon Civil War 1975–76: A Case of Crisis Mismanagement.* Jerusalem: Hebrew University of Jerusalem, Leonard David Institute for International Relations, 1979.

Kellerman, Barbara, and Jeffrey Z. Rubin, eds. *Leadership and Negotiation in the Middle East.* New York: Praeger, 1988.

el-Khazen, Farid. *The Breakdown of the State in Lebanon, 1967–1976.* London: I. B. Tauris, 2000.

Kissinger, Henry A. *Years of Renewal.* New York: Simon and Schuster, 1999.

Kleiboer, Marieke. *Multiple Realities of International Mediation.* Boulder, CO: Lynne Rienner, 1998.

Kliot, N. *The Territorial Disintegration of a State: The Case of Lebanon.* Durham, NC: Center for Middle Eastern and Islamic Studies, 1986.

Kosovo Dialogue: Too Little, Too Late. USIP Special Report 33. Washington, DC: United States Institute of Peace Press, 1998.

Kramer, Reed. *Liberia: A Casualty of the Cold War's End?* CSIS Africa Notes 174. Washington, DC: Center for Strategic and International Studies, 1995.

Kremenyuk, Victor, ed. *International Negotiations.* San Francisco: Jossey-Bass, 2002.

Kremenyuk, Victor, and I. William Zartman, eds. *Peace vs. Justice: Negotiating Forward- and Backward-Looking Outcomes.* Lanham, MD: Rowman and Littlefield, 2005.

Kressel, Kenneth, and Dean G. Pruitt, eds. *Mediation Research.* San Francisco: Jossey-Bass, 1989.

Kumar, Chetan. *Building Peace in Haiti.* Boulder, CO: Lynne Rienner, for the International Peace Academy, 1998.

———. *Interim Report on the Project on Policy Advocacy and Facilitation in Haiti.* New York: International Peace Academy, 1998.

Kumar, Chetan, and Elizabeth M. Cousens. *Peacebuilding in Haiti.* International Peace Academy Policy Briefing Series. New York: International Peace Academy, 1996.

Kumar, Chetan, and Marlye Gélin-Adams. *Project on Policy Advocacy and Facilitation in Haiti.* IPA Facilitation Report. New York: International Peace Academy, 1999.

Kuperman, Alan. *The Limits of Humanitarian Intervention: Genocide in Rwanda.* Washington, DC: Brookings Institution Press, 2001.

Lahneman, William, ed. *Military Intervention.* Lanham, MD: Rowman and Littlefield, 2004.

Laitin, David, and Said Samatar. *Somalia: Nation in Search of a State.* Boulder, CO: Westview Press, 1987.

Lake, David, and Donald Rothchild, eds. *The International Spread of Ethnic Conflict.* Princeton, NJ: Princeton University Press, 1999.

Lampe, John R. *Yugoslavia as History: Twice There Was a Country.* New York: Cambridge University Press, 1996.

Larrabee, Stephen, ed. *The Volatile Powder Keg: Balkan Security After the Cold War.* A RAND study. Washington, DC: American University Press, 1994.

Lawyers Committee for Human Rights. *In the National Interest 2001.* Washington: Lawyers Committee for Human Rights, 2001.

———. *Liberia: A Promise Betrayed.* New York: Lawyers Committee for Human Rights, 1986.

Levitin, Oleg. "Inside Moscow's Kosovo Muddle." *Survival* 42 (Spring 2000): 130–140.

Lewis, Flora. "How to Stop a Civil War." *New York Times,* 31 May 1991.

Lewis, I. M. *A Pastoral Democracy.* London: Oxford University Press, 1961.

Libal, Michael. *Limits of Persuasion: Germany and the Yugoslav Crisis 1991–1992*. Westport, CT: Praeger, 1997.

Liebenow, J. Gus. *Liberia: The Quest for Democracy*. Bloomington: Indiana University Press, 1987.

Lute, Jane Holl, ed. *Preventing Deadly Conflict*. New York: Carnegie Commission for the Prevention of Deadly Conflict, 1997.

Lyons, Gene M., and Michael Mastanduno, eds. *Beyond Westphalia: National Sovereignty and International Intervention*. Baltimore: Johns Hopkins University Press, 1995.

Lyons, Terrence. *Demilitarizing Politics: Transforming the Institutions of War*. Boulder, CO: Lynne Rienner, 2005.

Lyons, Terrence, and Ahmed Samatar. *Somalia: State Collapse, Multilateral Intervention, and Strategies for Postwar Political Reconstruction*. Washington, DC: Brookings Institution Press, 1995.

Maguire, Robert, et al. *Haiti Held Hostage*. Occasional Paper 23. Providence, RI: Watson Institute for International Studies, 1996.

Magyar, Karl P., and Earl Conteh-Morgan, eds. *Peacekeeping in Africa: ECOMOG in Liberia*. New York: St. Martin's Press, 1998.

Malone, David. *Decision-Making in the UN Security Council: The Case of Haiti 1990–1997*. Oxford: Oxford University Press, 1998.

Maresca, John. "Lost Opportunities in Negotiating the Conflict over Nagorno Karabakh." *International Negotiation* 1, no. 3 (1996): 471–499.

Martin, Ian. "Haiti: Mangled Multilateralism." *Foreign Policy* 95 (Summer 1994): 72–89.

Masland, Thomas, et al. "How Did We Get Here." *Newsweek* 124, no. 13 (26 September 1994), 19.

Maundi, Mohammed, et al. *Getting In: Mediators' Entry into the Settlement of African Conflicts*. Washington, DC: United States Institute of Peace Press, 2005.

McCormick, Shawn, and Bruce Whitehouse. "Zaire at the Crossroads." CSIS Africa Notes 166. Washington, DC: Center for Strategic and International Studies, 1994.

McFadyen, Deidre, et al. *Haiti: Dangerous Crossroads*. Boston: South End Press, 1995.

McKinley, James C. "Stoked by Rwandans, Tribal Violence." *New York Times*, 16 June 1996, 3.

McNamara, Francis Terry. *France in Black Africa*. Washington, DC: National Defense University Press, 1989.

Menkhaus, Ken. *Somalia: State Collapse and the Threat of Terrorism*. Adelphi Paper 364. Oxford: International Institute of Strategic Studies and Oxford University Press, 2004.

Messarra, Antoine N. *The Challenge of Coexistence*. Oxford: Center for Lebanese Studies, 1988.

Misser, François. "Two Governments." *New African*, May 1993, 32.

Mitchell, C. R., and Keith Webb, eds. *New Approaches to International Mediation*. New York: Greenwood, 1988.

Mitchell, Christopher, and Michael Banks. *Handbook of Conflict Resolution: The Analytical Problem-Solving Approach*. New York: Pinter, 1996.

Mutambo Jondwe, Joseph. *Les Banyamulenge*. Kinshasa: St Paul, 1997.

Nasr, Salim, George Irani, and James Sams. *Working Paper: Conference on Lebanon.* Washington, DC: Task Force on Lebanon, 1991.

Ngangoue, Nana Rosine. "Refugees Pawns in Mobutu's Gamesmanship," Inter-Press Service, 27 August 1995.

Noble, Kenneth B. "U.S. and Allies Discuss Sanctions to Force Mobutu to Yield Power." *New York Times*, 19 February 1993.

Nye, Joseph S., Jr. "Soft Power." *Foreign Policy* 80, no. 3 (Fall 1990): 153–171.

———. *Soft Power: The Means to Success in World Politics.* New York: Public Affairs, 2004.

O'Balance, Edgar. *Civil War in Lebanon, 1975–92.* New York: St. Martin's Press, 1998.

Owen, David. *Balkan Odyssey.* New York: Harcourt Brace, 1995.

Parker, Richard B. *The Politics of Miscalculation in the Middle East.* Bloomington: Indiana University Press, 1993.

Pastor, Robert A. "A Short History of Haiti." *Foreign Service Journal* 72, no. 11 (November 1995): 20–25.

———. "With Carter in Haiti." *Worldview* 8, no. 2 (Spring 1995): 5–7.

Perusse, Roland. *Haitian Democracy Restored 1991–1995.* Lanham, MD: University Press of America, 1995.

Picard, Elizabeth. "The Political Economy of Civil War in Lebanon." In Steven Heydemann, ed., *War, Institutions, and Social Change in the Middle East,* 292–322. Berkeley: University of California Press, 2000.

Pillar, Paul. *Negotiating Peace.* Princeton, NJ: Princeton University Press, 1983.

Powell, Robert. "Absolute and Relative Gains in IR Theory." *American Political Science Review* 85 (1991): 1303–1320.

Pruitt, Dean G. *Negotiation Behavior.* New York: Academic, 1980.

Pruitt, Dean G., and Sung Hee Kim. *Social Conflict: Escalation, Stalemate, and Settlement.* 3rd ed. New York: McGraw-Hill, 2004.

Quandt, William. *Camp David.* Washington, DC: Brookings Institution Press, 1986.

———. *Peace Process.* Washington, DC: Brookings Institution Press, 1993.

———. *Peace Process.* 2nd ed. Washington, DC: Brookings Institution Press, 2001.

Rabinovich, Itamar. *The War for Lebanon, 1970–1985.* Ithaca, NY: Cornell University Press, 1985.

Rake, Alan. "Mobutu Fights for His Life." *New African,* March 1993, 42.

Ramet, Sabrina P. *Balkan Babel: The Disintegration of Yugoslavia from the Death of Tito to Ethnic War.* 2nd ed. Boulder, CO: Westview Press, 1996.

———. *Nationalism and Federalism in Yugoslavia 1963-1992.* Bloomington: Indiana University Press, 1993.

Reno, William. *Corruption and State Politics in Sierra Leone.* New York: Cambridge University Press, 1995.

République du Zaire. *Commission Nationale des Élections, Budget estimatif des élections au Zaire 1997.* Kinshasa: République du Zaire, 1996.

Reyntjens, Filip. *La Guerre des Grands Lacs.* Paris: L'Harmattan, 1999.

Riding, Alan. "Mobutu Visits France." *New York Times,* 23 February 1993, 16.

———. "Mobutu Visits France for Medical Treatment." *New York Times*, 21 February 1993.

Riggs, Fred. "The Theory of Political Development." In James Charlesworth, ed., *Contemporary Political Analysis*. New York: Free Press, 1967.

Roberts, Les, et al. *Mortality in the Democratic Republic of Congo: Results from a Nation-wide Survey*. New York: International Rescue Committee, 2003.

Rosegrant, Susan, with Michael Watkins. *A "Seamless" Transition: United States and United Nations Operations in Somalia, 1992–1993*. Case Studies in Public Policy and Management. Cambridge, MA: John F. Kennedy School of Government, 1996.

Rosenau, James. "The State in an Era of Cascading Politics." In James Caporaso, ed., *The Elusive State: International and Comparative Perspectives*, 17–48. Newbury Park, CA: Sage Publications, 1989.

Rosenau, James, et al. "Intervention." Special issue, *Journal of International Affairs* 22, no. 2 (1968): 165–176.

Rotberg, Robert, ed. *Creating Peace in Sri Lanka*. Washington, DC: Brookings Institution Press, 1999.

———. *State Failure and State Weakness in a Time of Terror*. Washington, DC: Brookings Institution Press, 2003.

———. *When States Fail: Causes and Consequences*. Princeton, NJ: Princeton University Press, 2004.

Rouvez, Alain. *Disconsolate Empires*. Lanham, MD: University Press of America, 1994.

Rubin, Barnett. *Blood on the Doorstep: The Politics of Preventive Action*. Washington, DC: Brookings Institution Press, 2003.

———. *The Search for Peace in Afghanistan: From Buffer State to Failed State*. New Haven, CT: Yale University Press, 1995.

Rubin, Barry, and Laura Blum. *The May 1983 Agreement over Lebanon*. Case study 7. Washington, DC: Foreign Policy Institute, School of Advanced International Studies, Johns Hopkins University, 1987.

Rubin, Jeffrey Z., ed. *The Dynamics of Third Party Intervention*. New York: Praeger, 1981.

Rudman, George. "Negotiations in Yugoslavia." Manuscript, The Johns Hopkins University, 1998.

"Rwanda Calls for Immediate Response." *UN Africa News*, 24 May 1996.

Sahnoun, Mohamed. *Somalia: The Missed Opportunities*. Washington, DC: United States Institute of Peace, 1994.

Salem, Elie A. *Violence and Diplomacy in Lebanon: The Troubled Years, 1982–1988*. London: I. B. Tauris, 1995.

Salibi, Kamal S. *Crossroads to Civil War: Lebanon, 1958–1976*. Delmar, NY: Caravan Books, 1976.

———. *East Side Story, West Side Story: Contrasting Lebanese Views of the Civil War*. Washington, DC: Center for Contemporary Arab Studies, Georgetown University, 1985.

Samatar, Ahmed I., ed. *The Somali Challenge: From Catastrophe to Renewal?* Boulder, CO: Lynne Rienner, 1994.

Samatar, Said S. *Somalia: A Nation in Turmoil*. London: Minority Rights Group, 1991.

Sambanis, Nicholas. "Using Case Studies to Expand Economic Models of Civil War." *Perspectives on Politics* 2, no. 2 (June 2004): 2549–2579.

Saunders, Harold. *A Public Peace Process*. New York: St. Martin's Press, 1999.

Sawyer, Amos. *The Emergence of Autocracy in Liberia*. San Francisco: Institute for Contemporary Studies, l992.

————. *The Dynamics of Conflict Management in Liberia*. Accra, Ghana: Institute of Economic Affairs, 1997.

Schatzberg, Michael G. *Mobutu or Chaos? The US and Zaire 1960-1990*. Philadelphia: Foreign Policy Research Institute; Lanham, MD: University Press of America, 1991.

Schelling, Thomas. *Strategy of Conflict*. Cambridge, MA: Harvard University Press, 1960.

Schraeder, Peter. *United States Foreign Policy Toward Africa*. Cambridge: Cambridge University Press, 1994.

Schulz, Donald, and Marcella Gabriel. *Reconciling the Irreconcilable: The Troubled Outlook for US Policy Toward Haiti*. Carlisle Barracks, PA: Strategic Studies Institute, U.S. Army War College, 1994.

Scott, Colin, with Larry Minear and Thomas Weiss. *Humanitarian Action and Security in Liberia 1989–94*. Occasional Paper 20. Providence, RI: Watson Institute for International Studies, 1995.

Shields, Frederick. *Preventable Disasters: Why Governments Fail*. Lanham, MD: Rowman and Littlefield, 1991.

Sremac, Danielle S. *War of Words: Washington Tackles the Yugoslav Conflict*. Westport, CT: Praeger, 1999.

Staravoitova, Galina. *National Self-Determination: Approaches and Case Studies*. Occasional Paper 27. Providence, RI: Watson Institute for International Studies, Brown University, 1997.

Stein, Janice, and Louis Pauly, eds. *Choosing to Cooperate*. Baltimore: Johns Hopkins University Press, 1992.

Steiner, Barry. *Collective Preventive Diplomacy: A Study in International Conflict Management*. Albany: State University of New York Press, 2004.

Stenelo, Lars-Göran. *Mediation in International Negotiations*. Malmö, Sweden: Nordens Boktryckeri, 1972.

Swingle, Paul, ed. *The Structure of Conflict*. New York: Academic Press, 1970.

Tarrow, Sidney. *Power in Movement*. New York: Cambridge University Press, 1998.

Tetlock, Philip, and Aaron Belkin. *Counterfactual Thought Experiments in World Politics*. Princeton, NJ: Princeton University Press, 1996.

Thomas, Lynn, and Steve Spataro. *Peacekeeping and Policing in Somalia*. Washington, DC: Institute for National Strategic Studies, n.d.

Toure, Augustine. *The Role of Civil Society in National Reconciliation and Peacebuilding in Liberia*. New York: International Peace Academy, 2002.

Touval, Saadia. *Mediation in the Yugoslav Wars: The Critical Years 1990–95*. New York: Palgrave, 2002.

Touval, Saadia, and I. William Zartman, eds. *International Mediation in Theory and Practice*. Boulder, CO: Westview Press, 1985.

Tuchman, Barbara. *The March of Folly*. New York: Knopf, 1984.

Valasova, Maria. "Facing the Dilemma of Re-Integration Versus Independence in the Transitional Period: Basic Models of CIS Negotiations." *International Negotiation* 1, no. 3 (1996): 423–443.

van Walraven, Klaas. *Containing Conflict in the Economic Community of West African States*. The Hague, Netherlands: Clingendael, 1999.

van Walraven, Klaas, ed. *Early Warning and Conflict Prevention: Limitations and Possibilities*. The Hague, Netherlands: Kluwer Law International, 1998.

Verstegen, Suzanne. *Conflict Prognostication: Toward a Tentative Framework for Conflict Assessment*. The Hague, Netherlands: Clingendael, 1999.

Vocke, Harald. *The Lebanese War: Its Origins and Political Dimensions*. Translated from German by A.K.H. Weinrich and Ilse Fisher. New York: St. Martin's Press, 1978.

Vogt, Margaret, ed. *The Liberian Crisis and ECOMOG*. Lagos, Nigeria: Gabumo, 1992.

Vorhees, James. *Dialogue Sustained: The Multilevel Peace Process and the Dartmouth Conference*. Washington, DC: United States Institute of Peace Press, 2002.

Walter, Barbara. *Committing to Peace: The Successful Settlement of Civil Wars*. Princeton, NJ: Princeton University Press, 2002.

Walter, Barbara, and Jack Snyder, eds. *Civil Wars, Insecurity, and Intervention*. New York: Columbia University Press, 1999.

Waltz, Kenneth. *Theory of International Politics*. New York: Random House, 1979.

Weinberger, Naomi. "How Peace Keeping Becomes Intervention: Lessons from the Lebanese Experience." In Milton Esman and Shibley Telhami, eds., *International Organization and Ethnic Conflict*, 148–175. Ithaca, NY: Cornell University Press, 1995.

———. *Syrian Intervention in Lebanon: The 1975–76 Civil War*. New York: Oxford University Press, 1986.

Weiss, Herbert, and Titania Carayannis. "The Enduring Idea of the Congo." In Ricardo René Laremont, ed., *Borders, Nationalism, and the African State*, 137–177. Boulder, CO: Lynne Rienner, 2005.

Weller, Marc. "The Rambouillet Conference on Kosovo." *International Affairs* 65 (1999): 211–251.

"West Raises Pressure." *The Independent*, 18 February 1993, 12.

Willame, Jean-Claude. *Banyarwanda et Banyamulenge: Violences ethniques et gestion de l'identitaire au Kivu*. Cahiers Africains 25. Paris: L'Harmattan, 1996.

Woodward, Susan L. *Balkan Tragedy: Chaos and Dissolution After the Cold War*. Washington DC: Brookings Institution Press, 1995.

Wynaendts, Henry. *L'Engrenage: Chroniques yougoslaves, juillet 1991–aout 1992*. Paris: Denoel, 1996.

Yaniv, Avner. *Dilemmas of Security*. New York: Oxford University Press, 1987.

Yett, Shelden. *Masisi, Down the Road from Goma*. Washington, DC: U.S. Committee for Refugees, 1996.

Youboty, James. *Liberian Civil War*. Philadelphia: Parkside, 1993.

Young, Ronald J. *Missed Opportunities for Peace*. Philadelphia: American Friends Service Committee, 1987.

"Zaire: Mobutu's Monetary Mutiny." *Africa Confidential* 34, no. 3 (5 February 1993): 4–5.

"Zaire: Whose Man in Kinshasa?" *Africa Confidential* 35, no. 25 (16 December 1994): 1–4.

Zartman, I. William. "An Apology Needs a Pledge." *New York Times*, 2 April 1998.

———. "Early and 'Early Late' Prevention." In Simon Chesterman, Michael Ignatieff, and Ramesh Thakur, eds., *Making States Work*. New York: UNU
Press, 2005.

———. "Explaining Oslo." *International Negotiation* 2, no. 2 (1997): 195–215.

———. "Negotiating Effectively with Terrorists." In Barry Rubin, ed., *The Politics of Counter-Terrorism*. Washington, DC: University Press of America for
The Johns Hopkins Foreign Policy Institute, 1990.

———. "The Political Analysis of Negotiations." *World Politics* 26 (1974):
385–399.

———. *Ripe for Resolution*. New York: Oxford University Press, 1989.

———. "Ripeness: The Hurting Stalemate and Beyond." In Paul Stern and Daniel
Druckman, eds., *International Conflict Resolution After the Cold War*,
225–250. Washington, DC: National Academics Press, 2000.

———. "Ripening Conflict, Ripe Moment, Formula and Mediation." In Diane
BenDahmane and John McDonald, eds., *Perspectives on Negotiation*,
205–228. Washington, DC: Government Printing Office, 1986.

———. "The Strategy of Preventive Diplomacy in Third World Conflicts." In
Alexander George, ed., *Managing US-Soviet Rivalry*. Boulder, CO: Westview
Press, 1983.

Zartman, I. William, ed. *Collapsed States: The Disintegration and Restoration of
Legitimate Authority*. Boulder, CO: Lynne Rienner, 1995.

———. *Elusive Peace: Negotiating an End to Civil Wars*. Washington, DC:
Brookings Institution Press, 1995.

———. *Governance as Conflict Management: Politics and Violence in West
Africa*. Washington, DC: Brookings Institution Press, 1996.

———. "Negotiating with Terrorists." Special issue, *International Negotiation* 83
(2003).

———. *Peacemaking in International Conflict*. 2nd ed. Washington, DC: United
States Institute of Peace Press, 2005.

———. *Preventive Negotiation: Avoiding Conflict Escalation*. Lanham, MD:
Rowman and Littlefield, 2001.

———. *Traditional Cures for Modern Conflicts: Traditional African Conflict
"Medicine."* Boulder, CO: Lynne Rienner, 2000.

Zartman, I. William, and Guy Olivier Faure, eds. *Escalation and Negotiation*.
Cambridge: Cambridge University Press, 2005.

Zartman, I. William, and Victor Kremenyuk, eds. *Peace vs Justice: Negotiating
Forward- and Backward-Looking Outcomes*. Lanham, MD: Rowman and
Littlefield, 2005.

Zimmermann, Warren. *The Origins of a Catastrophe: Yugoslavia and Its Destroyers*. New York: Random House, 1996.

Index

About the Book

What would have happened had the "road not taken" been the chosen action in past conflict interventions? What can we learn from a close look at alternatives that were not selected? Drawing on six detailed case studies (the Balkans, Haiti, Lebanon, Liberia, Somalia, and Zaire/Congo), I. William Zartman identifies a series of missed opportunities—options that arguably would have provided feasible and better outcomes for the reduction of violent conflict and the prevention of state collapse.

Zartman specifies potential solutions within the entire trajectory of each conflict, considering in each instance why the indicated decisions were not taken. The principles and mechanisms that he develops in the course of his analysis have profound implications for the actions of the international community in preventing conflicts from escalating to violence and for managing violent situations when they do occur.

I. William Zartman is Jacob Blaustein Professor of International Organization and Conflict Resolution at the School of Advanced International Studies, Johns Hopkins University. His many publications in the field of conflict negotiation and management include *Ripe for Resolution, Preventive Negotiation: Avoiding Conflict Escalation, Negotiating an End to Civil War*, and *The 50% Solution*. He is recipient of the Lifetime Achievement Award of the International Association for Conflict Management and was awarded an honorary doctorate by the Catholic University of Louvain.